D1012598

"Warren's book . . . is exceptionally well-researched, thorough, and very well written. Warren has done a masterful job of looking at the topic from every angle. . . . It is one thing to read a book to get information. It is another thing to read a book to find comfort and hope. This book does both. The much needed facts are there, but so is the power and encouragement of God's love and grace."

Charles M. Lee, Ph.D.
Director, Life Resources Center of Miami

"Mr. Kniskern has done extensive research of the scriptures and other facts, and thus the information he gives is not only credible but trustworthy. . . . This is such a valuable asset, as lay persons are given helpful advice to take them through the complicated legal process which usually results from a divorce."

Karlene Punancy, attorney

WHEN THE VOW BREAKS

A DIVORCE *Care* Resource

Foreword by Steve Grissom, Founder and President of DivorceCare®

WHEN THE VOW BREAKS

A Survival and Recovery Guide for Christians Facing Divorce

Joseph Warren Kniskern

PRACTICAL ADVICE ON CARING FOR CHILDREN, MANAGING FINANCES, RESOLVING
LEGAL ISSUES, AND COPING WITH ANGER, DEPRESSION, AND LONELINESS

When the Vow Breaks: A Survival and Recovery Guide for
Christians Facing Divorce

Copyright © 1993 by Joseph Warren Kniskern
Revised and Updated, 2008
All Rights Reserved

ISBN: 978-0-8054-4653-1
B&H Publishing Group
Nashville, Tennessee
BHPublishingGroup.com

Dewey Decimal Classification: 306.89
Subject Heading: Divorce / Marriage

Printed in the USA

8 9 10 11 12 13   20 19 18 17 16

Table of Contents

Table of Contents

This book is lovingly dedicated to:
The Bride of My Youth

with special inscription
to my good friend and brother in Christ,
Dr. Kieth A. Mitchell

This book would not have been possible without the unselfish service and encouragement of these good people who are among my dearest family and friends: Chris Anderson, Kathy Barnes, Chuck Bryant, Elise S. Kniskern, Wayne F. Kniskern, Diane Mitchell, Dr. Rex Moorer, Marjorie Owen-Baillie, Sylva Neubauer, Karlene Punancy, Hugh M. Turner, Esq., and Peggy Wilson.

Special recognition and gratitude also go to Dr. Charles M. Lee, Juan D. Milian, Janis Whipple, and Lawrence Kimbrough.

Foreword

Steve Grissom

Dianne didn't want to come to our DivorceCare group. She didn't want to be identified with divorce in any way, even though she was a single mother, and yes, she was divorced.

I coaxed. I encouraged her to come, explaining how much the group would help her. After months of trying, Dianne reluctantly agreed to try the group. The next words out of her mouth were poignant and representative of so many hurting people who find themselves in the process of divorcing. "I'll be easy to spot," said Dianne. "I'll be the one with a brown paper bag over my head!"

Are you like Dianne? Are you embarrassed that your marriage has unraveled? Do you feel like an outcast, believing that no one could possibly understand what you are going through?

If you are a Christian, you may feel that you have let God down, or that you are guilty of a something that will forever put a barrier between you and Him.

When the Vow Breaks is one of the most helpful books we recommend to people who participate in DivorceCare groups. It is packed with practical advice on what to expect as you (or someone you know) goes through the divorce process. It contains great information about God's perspective on divorce as found in the Bible.

Best of all, it is written from the perspective of a man who lived through and survived divorce himself. But added to that personal experience, Warren Kniskern brings a unique additional dimension to *When the Vow Breaks*. His career as an attorney helps him guide you through the legal labyrinth that inevitably accompanies separation and divorce. He does so in a way that helps a Christian construct a godly, biblical response to the adversarial nature of "family law," (a misnomer of grand proportions). There is no other book out there that better equips Christians to understand, navigate and survive the legal process in a God-honoring way.

We like this book so much that we invited Warren Kniskern to join the roster of experts that appear within the DivorceCare videos shown as part of each DivorceCare group. Warren is genuine, knowledgeable, and cares deeply for people going through the divorce experience. His compassion is clear as he appears on the videos. Thousands of DivorceCare groups are meeting around the world and enjoying his advice. The problem is, of course, that the video format limits the amount of time we can devote to the topics Warren covers. You need to read *When the Vow Breaks* to benefit from the depth and breadth of his counsel.

As you go through divorce, you wrestle with a numbing, jumbled mix of emotions. Part of what make this book special is that it addresses so many divorce issues.

Maybe you are not at all like Dianne, who I mentioned above. Maybe you are like Don, who was hungry for help when he showed up at the support group. "I was ripped apart. I felt like my whole life was gone. I came running to the support group," he said. If you are feeling like Don, you'll find comfort in *When the Vow Breaks*.

Perhaps you are like Joanne, who was filled with rage. "I wanted to hurt him as badly as he hurt me," she admitted to her support group quite candidly. I'm sure you know that anger and unforgiveness can destroy you. *When the Vow Breaks* will show you how to resolve these destructive emotions.

The list of topics goes on, including issues related to your children as well as practical advice on how to deal with your finances during and post-divorce. You'll find actionable, nuts-and-bolts help within these pages. Whether your marriage is restored or you find yourself divorced, your life going forward will be healthier and more joyful by following the advice in *When the Vow Breaks*.

Through the years, in the process of working with him, Warren has become a dear personal friend. I believe you'll count him as your friend as well when you get to know him through this book and are helped by his wise and encouraging words.

Steve Grissom, Founder
DivorceCare (divorce recovery support groups)
www.divorcecare.org

For more information on DivorceCare, please see page 438.

Foreword

Kieth A. Mitchell

It is my privilege and pleasure to introduce this Christian attorney, to endorse his central position on marriage and divorce, and to emphasize the spiritual and practical benefits that can come from reading this major resource volume. As a mental health professional, I especially appreciate Warren's attention to the details of coping with separation and divorce, an element often missing from other divorce resources.

My wife and I count Warren among our closest and dearest Christian friends. For six years I have met weekly with him to share lunch, prayer, and spiritual fellowship. I also knew Warren's ex-wife during much of their marriage.

My wife suggests these adjectives to describe Warren: faithful, committed, dependable, courageous, and tenacious. To me five attributes stand out: his *intelligence* as a Christian layman which leads to his being a careful and scholarly student of the Scriptures; his *commitment* to the Lord Jesus Christ and not to a particular sectarian position; his *integrity* as consistent as any other disciple I have seen in all my years in Christ; his *spirituality* rooted in his deep desire to be the Lord's man in every role, relationship, and situation of his life; and his *motivation* with this written divorce survival guide to benefit others out of the pain of his divorce.

Warren has shown himself very open to the counseling process. Many principles of this book were forged out of his own struggle. Warren believes a child of God can discover the Father's will through the insights of spiritual counselors. One suggestion made to him was that he not commit to anyone else for at least two years after the divorce. He accepted this suggestion and communicated his decision to his wife prior to the divorce's finality, with his stated reasons of giving maximum time and opportunity for any possible reconciliation, avoiding the emotional trap of a rebound relationship, and protecting any possible remarriage from the social and spiritual stigma of being ill-advised and without proper preparation.

Some may see a divorce survival guide as scripturally inappropriate for Christians. I assure you that Warren believes in the lifelong sanctity of marriage; he feels the passion of Malachi's statement of how the Lord hates divorce. He does not recommend or endorse divorce. Warren believes a faithful Christian should not initiate divorce action unless, reluctantly, it is in accordance with scriptural guidelines. However, he is realistic in knowing that those divorcing for any reason still need to avoid making a most unfortunate situation even worse.

As a close friend, I know how difficult it was for Warren to accept the reality and finality of his own divorce, realizing even a Christian marriage cannot continue without two consenting partners. While you may or may not subscribe to every position Warren concludes from his study of the Scripture, I believe you will clearly see his fairness in accurately presenting different interpretations on controversial points where equally honest persons may differ without compromising their faith.

Pastors and other Christian counselors who want to help men and women discover the Lord's will and walk in His ways will find this book an invaluable resource. Every section and chapter has a plausible balance between spiritual sensitivity and practical guidance. It can be a comfort and source of hope for others who, like Warren, may be coping with their own unwanted divorces and who earnestly desire to minimize the damage to one's life and relationships in a loving and spiritual manner.

Dr. Kieth A. Mitchell
Florida State Licensed Mental Health Counselor
Academy Certified Clinical Mental Health Counselor
New York State Certified Pastoral Counselor
Counselor to United Nations Delegate Families
Urban Pastor in New York City

Foreword

I am pleased to recommend *When the Vow Breaks* to anyone confronting separation or divorce. Like Warren, I experienced a divorce that I did not initiate. Unlike Warren, I was not a Christian at that time.

I believe divorce, in fact, is worse than death because we must face not only our ex-mates but our own responsibility in the death of the marriage.

Following my divorce, I returned to law school. In doing so, I made a decision to become a lawyer in family law. Through my own experience, I know that the court system does not work for families. While my own divorce was not contested in the legal proceedings, it brought out the worst in me—anger and behavior that could only be released through forgiveness from God and others. Only my relationship with Jesus Christ as Lord provided the wisdom and forgiveness I needed to help others.

I sincerely wish I'd had Warren's book at the time of my divorce. I can also think of hundreds of clients over the years who could have benefited greatly from this book. Like Warren, I am convinced that mediation is the best process for folks to resolve family disputes. Though I am a Florida board-certified marital and family lawyer, with the highest rating given to attorneys in the Martindale-Hubbell Law Directory, I could not give my clients what they truly needed through the court system.

Fortunately, God has blessed me and shown mercy. I am remarried to a wonderful man and now I have a family that includes "yours," "mine," "ours," and "theirs." We are blended and blessed, but only through God's grace and our commitment to His Word.

I pray that this book will touch you as it did me, and that through the witness of your life you will tell others about the practical wisdom it provides, the mediation process, and God's love.

Nancy S. Palmer, Attorney/Mediator
1993-94 Chairperson, Marital and Family Law Section,
Florida Bar Member, Executive Committee of the
American Bar Association Custody and Adoption Committees

Preface

How to Use This Book Wisely

The information in these pages is for your personal comfort and to stimulate creative thinking in the difficult circumstances of divorce. This book will help you understand the divorce process and save you time in researching many options and decisions at a time of personal stress.

This book does not promote divorce; it only deals with the harsh realities of it. You can use it wisely by asking yourself two questions, both of which are answered in these pages:

- "Is there any way to avoid divorce?"
- "If divorce is unavoidable, how can I limit the damage to myself and those I love in each stage of the process?"

The material in this book is obviously not intended as a substitute for wise legal counsel or the advice of a competent mental health professional. If you have any questions at all about matters in this book, you are urged to consult immediately with your minister, attorney, doctor, or mental health professional. Be sure that the specifics of your particular situation are carefully and professionally analyzed *before* taking any action. If you receive advice contrary to what is offered in this book, good reasons known only to you and your advisors may require you to consider alternative approaches. Your personal advisors will have the experience and information that will make the difference in your case. Accordingly, neither the author nor the publisher can provide you with any independent legal advice in this book.

Introduction

"I feel so sorry for them, but thank God it hasn't happened to me!" How many times have you heard those very words expressed about another couple facing a divorce? Maybe you have even said this to yourself; I know I have. But it did happen to me, and it probably has to you as well if you are reading this book. You are hurting and need some answers.

If you are like many others facing divorce, you seek out friends for advice. You may be buying all the books you can read on the subject in order to cope. But too often the advice you receive comes from those who are either happily married or never married. This book provides practical counsel from one who has been through the pain of the entire divorce process. Like you, I know the hollow sadness of feeling the inside of a ring finger for the wedding band that is no longer there.

Before we get started, let me introduce myself. I am a Christian lawyer who specializes in real estate law. When first penning this introduction in 1993, I was a senior partner in a large international law firm headquartered on Park Avenue in New York City. (See the epilogue on page 434 for a current update.) After committing my life to Christ in August of 1976, I graduated from the University of Florida Law School. In 1984, I courted and married a beautiful Christian woman.

My wife and I first met and worked together in an active, evangelistic Christian ministry. We married in July 1984 among many of our beloved Christian friends and family. It was a candlelight wedding ceremony with music and singing that was almost like a fairy tale. We did everything right. We spent time trying to get to know each other. We received counseling from ministers in our congregation. Everything was going our way. It was a marriage I thought would never end. This was the bride of my life.

We had the usual ups and downs of marriage and communication problems, but we always seemed to move ahead with no real disasters. My wife is an actress, and a very good one at that. When she became more involved in the theater, I was pleased to support her work because I trusted her 100 percent.

Then, at 2:00 one morning in late July 1989, she came home to shock me with this news: "Warren, I'm just not happy. I love someone else more than you. I want an immediate divorce. You draw up the papers and I'll sign." I was completely floored with this announcement. She was through with me.

That dreadful night began a two-year period of dealing with just about every divorce issue imaginable. It did not end until July 1991. We tried separation, considered church mediation, and engaged in months of counseling—all to no avail. We explored every option for reconciliation until it became apparent that all was lost. *Really* finished in every sense of the word! But the Lord used this time to teach me more about graciousness, love, and forgiveness than I would have learned otherwise. You will learn these lessons too, if you keep your spiritual focus with the help of Christ and use the practical suggestions in this book.

I do not pretend to be an expert in the field. I am only a divorce survivor who has learned by experience. Steve Brown, former pastor of Key Biscayne Presbyterian Church and host of the popular "Key Life" Christian radio program, frequently is introduced as a "normal, struggling, and sometimes victorious Christian." I like that. Aren't we all? I'm just a normal Christian who unfortunately has been through a divorce. I do not have all the answers. But God does.

Are you feeling wounded about your situation now? Do you dread your spouse forcing you into divorce? Are your friends slowly drawing away from you as if you were a wounded animal to whom they can give no comfort? Are you writing letters pleading, bargaining, and expressing your anger toward your spouse, only to tear them up? Do you dread those long nights alone when sleep is a luxury? I can appreciate these feelings and emotions. They welled up in my heart during the crisis in my own life. Although only the Lord can be totally one with you in spirit right now, I can imagine how much you must hurt inside. These are the times when you deeply desire comfort from anyone who can relate in any way with what you are suffering.

Take courage. This book will give you many solid, practical solutions to many pressing problems that you may not know how to handle now. It will encourage you and give you hope. Brighter days are ahead. But your greatest source of comfort and strength will be Jesus Christ Himself. He gives us that special peace that transcends all understanding and knowledge. Jesus is worthy of your personal faith and trust when others have failed you. He is One who sticks closer than a brother.

Divorce is one of the most intensely personal and painful experiences anyone faces in a lifetime. But it can also be one of the most spiritual journeys of your life! Like childbirth, many good blessings come from painful endeavors. The key is allowing your pain and grief to lead you into dependence upon God. Use this time to grow. Do not deny your difficulties and escape by taking the easy way out.

If you're curious about the title of this book, think of the nursery rhyme that has the line, "When the bough breaks, the cradle will fall . . ." If your spouse has not honored vows to "love, honor, and obey . . . for richer or poorer, in sickness and in health until death do you part," God will not let you down. When marriage vows break and you feel despair, you will see it through as if God Himself is cradling you.

Do you know how it feels sinking into bed after being totally worn out from a long day? You hit those cool sheets on that soft comfortable mattress, and "Ah-h-h . . ." is all you can say, You really know the meaning of *rest!* Having that same peace in dealing with divorce trauma can come only when you allow God to sustain you. He holds you up when you are too weary to go on. His unfailing love whispers throughout eternity, "Never will I leave you. Never will I forsake you." That's good news! Unlike the nursery rhyme, God's cradle will not fall from under you.

If you ever go to Israel, as my wife and I did on our honeymoon, you will be fascinated by two beautiful bodies of water—the Sea of Galilee and the Dead Sea. There they are in a dry, hot desert region of God's earth. The Jordan River winds its way down through the hills and flows into the cool, turquoise waters of the Sea of Galilee. You can immediately see why Jesus spent so much of His time around this very beautiful and alluring lake. Its pure refreshing waters are alive with fish and other sea life. Emerald green marshes and grassy hills rim its shore. Birds flock to this resting place and feast on minnows in the shallows. It is one of God's masterpieces you will never forget.

After using the life-giving flow of the Jordan River to the fullest, the Sea of Galilee gently and generously sends a beautiful stream southward along the river to the Dead Sea—a watery enigma if ever there was one! It is also beautiful to see—from a distance. With bright, shining waters and the most intriguing blue colors that change with the light, it beckons to you as if it were a Galilean twin. But the Dead Sea is so salty that absolutely nothing lives in it. After receiving fresh waters from the Jordan River, the Dead Sea lives up to its name. It does not produce or sustain life. Nothing benefits the land around its tepid waters. It soaks up everything good into its camouflaged brine and gives nothing back.

People can be like that too. Some will receive good news and it will uplift them. It will cause them to thrive and be full of life. They receive blessings and share it with others closest to them. Unfortunately, others are like the Dead Sea. They continually take from others. What they take does nothing for them. Even worse, whatever good they receive does not flow through them so that others might enjoy it. These people are often bitter and selfish souls who will always feel the emptiness inside. They desperately need the Lord to turn their death into life and their darkness into light.

My prayer is that you will receive whatever you find to be good in this book like the wonderful, living Sea of Galilee. Share whatever you find useful with others around you. Let it speak to your heart and inspire you with hope!

Part One

Examining the Thoughts and Attitudes of Your Heart

Do not conform any longer to the pattern of this world,
but be transformed by the renewing of your mind.
Then you will be able to test and approve what
God's will is—His good, pleasing and perfect will.
Romans 12:2

Above all else, guard your heart,
for it is the wellspring of life.
Proverbs 4:23

For the Word of God is living and active.
Sharper than any double-edged sword,
it penetrates even to dividing soul and spirit,
joints and marrow; it judges the thoughts
and attitudes of the heart.
Hebrews 4:12

One of the first lessons law school students learn is, "Don't lose sight of the big picture." In focusing on the details, don't miss the most important issues.

Your life in marriage has had joy and sorrow, victories and defeats, companionship and loneliness. Right now you may be feeling about as sorrowful, defeated, and lonely as you have ever felt in your life. Take heart and be patient! You will move on to times of greater joy. You will taste sweet victories once again. Don't lose sight of how you feel about yourself and others. Your thoughts and attitudes are a key to whether you will lovingly rise above your difficulties or will sink into a depression fueled by bitterness, resentment, and self-pity.

In Part One, we will look at ways of coping with the initial shock of a terminal marriage. Family, friends, and others may immediately rush to give you counsel, but it may not be the best for you. Still, you can learn how to keep your spiritual focus. This section will alert you to many of the thoughts and emotions that will tempt you to abandon a Christ-like attitude. Finally, and most importantly, Jesus' parable of the prodigal son will amaze you with its wisdom about having a loving attitude toward those who are most unloving toward you!

CHAPTER 1

Terminal Marriage Shock

Why do our marriages break down and end up in divorce?
Quite often answers come by looking at the different mindsets
of a couple heading for divorce. Perception factors and mar-
riage stressors also contribute to the conflict. Almost certainly,
each spouse has a role in dealing a deathblow to a marriage.
It is important to understand why this conflict exists so that
appropriate solutions are applied to the problems.

Divorce is as close as you can get to death without actually dying. Only those who have experienced it can truly understand its dark power to test emotions and intellect to the ultimate degree. The only social trauma greater than divorce is the physical death of a loved one.

In his popular book, *Mere Christianity*, the late British author and Christian apologist C. S. Lewis accurately described the divorce dilemma this way:

> They [the Christian church community] all regard divorce as something like cutting up a living body, as a kind of surgical operation. Some of them think the operation is so violent that it cannot be done at all; others admit it is a desperate remedy in extreme cases. They are all agreed that it is more like having both of your legs cut off than it is like dissolving a business partnership or even deserting a regiment.[1]

Saying that divorce is an ugly nightmare is an understatement. Divorce is fullscale devastation! It cuts into hearts and souls deeper than most any other tragedy imaginable. It shatters precious memories as it strips us of family, roles, and identity. It saps our strength and breaks down the core of our spirits until emotional numbness and fog set in. It reduces one of the most intimately personal relationships we can ever share with another human being to sharp shards of broken dreams. Divorce, quite simply, is the most brutal, bloodless crime of passion known to man. Even that description diminishes the destruction if physical violence and abuse are also present.

Realizing that a marriage cannot be salvaged and that the death of the relationship is imminent can hit you suddenly or settle in over time. But it almost always first comes as a total shock, at least to one of the spouses, when the other says, *"It's over."* The pain, anxiety, bitterness, and grief of the divorce process, especially one that is unexpected, can overwhelm us. It does not matter whether the divorce is amicable and uncontested or hostile, or who filed the legal papers. Divorce is an immediate, radical, and painful change in our lives, welcome or not, with highly charged emotional consequences.

How does it happen? What forces work in our relationships to lead us to divorce? Before we provide the remedies, we must understand the problems. Look at the people caught up in this human drama and see how competing forces meld together in a final conflict.

The Warriors

We may not think our spouses are going to war against us, but plans for divorce, and the completion of it, are often warlike. The spoils of this conflict are everything we treasure and worked hard for all our lives. The battlefield is in the most private and intimate recesses of our lives. It is a contest of wills and a battle of hearts and minds—all on our home turf. When love falls prey to hatred or apathy and the personal stakes are high, there are no dispassionate foot soldiers.

Who are the people involved? Is one spouse the "divorcer" and the other the "divorcee"? Is one the "dumper" or "rejector" while the other is the "dumpee" or "rejectee"? Does the "aggressor" divorce the "victim"? One views the other partner as the "mate from hell," while the other sees his or her spouse as "The Terminator." But all these terms assign blame or fault that can cloud our judgment in seeing beyond descriptions to the real underlying issues. This is why thoughtful psychologists and counselors neutrally describe the one desiring the divorce as the "initiator," and the one resisting the divorce as the "non-initiator."

Our use of "initiator" and "non-initiator" does not imply that one spouse is more to blame for a divorce than the other. You may well have good reason to be the initiator in your situation if your spouse has destroyed your marriage already.

Calling the spouses "warriors" does not mean the combatants are evil or mean. After all, they are people who love others, work hard, and try to live decent lives. But the entire divorce process can force the best of people—husbands and wives, mothers and fathers—into positions of aggression and defense, depending upon the matters at stake (finances, children, social status, etc.). Also, referring to the "initiator" as "she," or the "non-initiator" as "he," does not imply that the wife is always the initiator or that the husband is the non-initiator. These descriptions are words of convenience only. In the past the husband was often the initiator since he usually controlled most of the economic power. However, as women have become more self-reliant and divorce carries less of a social stigma than it once did, the wife can force the issue of divorce in many relationships. Each marriage is unique.

There are a few common characteristics of both initiators and non-initiators. The initiator spouse who first decides to get out of the marriage usually wants personal freedom and happiness more than what is best for the other partner. There may be a third party love interest involved. Unless a divorce occurs by mutual consent, the non-initiator usually is the unwilling party to the severance of the marriage, for any number of good or bad reasons.

Children also have an important role in the breakdown of a marriage relationship. (Because of their special needs over a wide range of subjects, we will discuss children's issues in chapter 15).

Preparing for Battle

Divorce usually begins with a seed of doubt or lack of faith. Some small fear surfaces that a mistake was made in choosing the non-initiator as a mate.

At first, the initiator marries with all sorts of expectations that often only begin to take shape after the marriage vows are made. The biblical concept of "two become one flesh" is initially embraced. The initiator is content to be spiritually, financially, physically and emotionally intertwined with a loving mate. Joys and sorrows ebb and flow as the couple changes and adapts to each other.

Initially both spouses are in the "honeymoon stage" of the marriage. The basic needs of security, love, and acceptance are satisfied. Then, slowly but surely, the initiator's focus begins to change—for better or for worse.

Why does this happen?

Various "perception factors" affect the initiator (and non-initiator) and prompt these doubts:

The Romance Myth

The media constantly masquerades romance as love. But the two can be very different. On television, it takes thirty minutes to resolve a conflict. Many of us grew up watching the "Father Knows Best" family, where clothes did not become soiled and everyone smiled at every meal. Romance creates the illusion that our spouse is that beautiful princess or the knight in shining armor. We look to our marriage partners to give us a lifetime of pure bliss as they meet all our needs and strengthen our weaknesses. But this is *not* reality!

If we let our emotions run over us, we marry someone with the potential for fulfilling our mental fantasies. We cannot accept them for who they are. Instead we dream of making them what we want them to be.

Then there is the intoxication of sexual attraction. We may not know how to separate love from sex. We think sex substitutes for emotional intimacy. Instead of reminding ourselves that beauty is fleeting, we somehow think that this good-looking person will compensate for everything else that may be lacking.

Romance, disguised as love, will appreciate the lovely qualities in life. It falls at the feet of the vivacious personality, the alluring appearance, the sense of humor, and all the other trappings of a "good catch." But romance will not get its own feet dirty when these qualities fade. This type of "love" lasts only as long as the initial attraction.

Every marriage is tested. That is where real love begins and romance starts heading for the exit. Love digs in deep and accepts the person while dealing firmly with the circumstances. It is grounded in an irrevocable commitment. Love says, "I am with you to the end." Romance falters when flexibility or endurance is required. The cruel barb of accepting the romance lie is that we cannot accept our spouses for who they are, but quickly reject them when they fail to meet our flawed expectations.

The Urge to Give Our Mates a Makeover

All humankind is created in the image of God. But sometimes we are not content with His creation. We seek to put the finishing touch on our mate. We try, in a wide variety of ways, to make him or her over in *our* own image. In doing so we fall into the greatest temptation of all—the desire to be like God.

We encroach upon the personal freedom and identity of our mates and try to control them at will. If they do not, we want to bail out of the marriage.

These makeovers are doomed. We are not qualified for the makeover game. Why? Because the way we view our mates is often flawed. Our personal histories and value judgments distort our perception. Many of us grew up unfulfilled in love. Early experiences with parents and siblings determine whom we love and how we love.

Dysfunctional families with histories of violence, sexual abuse, or alcoholism leave scars on each family member. If our parents treated each other with disrespect and unkindness, we inherit a negative role model for adult love relationships. As we move on in life, peers reject us, superiors judge us inferior in school and work, and seasonal changes in our lives affect us.

As we are all changed during our life journey, any deprivations influence us and skew our vision of reality. That is why any makeovers are best left to the Lord. He speaks to the hearts of individuals who seek Him, and He ministers best to their personal needs.

Gender Role Confusion and Parental Fulfillment

Husbands traditionally were seen to be caretakers, providers—the spouse who is more "business oriented." Wives were nurturers, keepers of the home—the ones more communicative and emotional. Children watch parents in these roles. Then as married adults, they try to emulate what they saw.

We could make a good start in our marriages if the example of our parents was constructive and well adjusted. But if our parental role models were flawed, or missing entirely through death or divorce, then we can only learn from our own bad experiences.

Changing roles in society for men and women work against traditional family relationships and bonding. More women are leaving children in day care and joining the working world. Business pressures force workers to put in long hours. By necessity children often must look to television characters or other adults as role models.

We also may unfairly look to our mates to be parent figures for fulfillment of personal needs unmet in childhood. Instead of reaching out to friends, our church, or counselors for help, we put an enormous burden on our mates. Rather than companions, we want our mates to be surrogate parents. We expect them to right the wrongs that scarred us when we were children. When our spouses refuse to act out our parental fantasies, we become disappointed and angry. No wonder! We cannot selfishly depend upon our mates to complete us as persons.

Very few people can survive this suffocation in a relationship. The marriage is doomed unless the partners consciously break the mold of past experience and build a healthy marriage.

Alienation of Relationships Outside of Marriage

Meaningful relationships outside the marriage today are hard to find. Neighbors and friends used to enjoy relationships that lasted over decades. Husbands would hunt, fish, or golf together; wives would share coffee with each other in the mornings. Folks on our block even planned joint vacations.

But today, jobs uproot families and move them in an instant. People lose touch with each other. Visits with extended families thousands of miles away are expensive and impractical. These facts of life can push spouses toward making increasing demands on each other.

Boredom flattens out the joy of marriage. "Why won't you talk to me? I don't have any friends!" is the cry. It rings in the ears of the spouse who is too drained to listen. Frustration and depression well up within us. Our spouses have enough responsibility in being our marriage partners. Are they now expected to fulfill all our friendship needs? This is too much to ask.

Low Self-Esteem

Most of us struggle at times with low self-esteem, but some handle it better than others. There is an emptiness inside, and the world beckons us to fill this vacuum with the pursuit of money, sex, power, and freedom.

Anything keeping us from becoming a whole person is externalized. We feel an urge to jump from job to job, person to person, and place to place on a personal quest for happiness and fulfillment. Excuses run rampant. We fall into "if onlys"—"If only I inherited a million dollars . . . ," or "If only I had married my high school sweetheart . . . ," or "If only I could be head of that company . . . ,"—*then* we would truly be happy.

There is also the discontent of advancing age. We feel less desirable when we see those dreaded bulges, sags, and creases. "Would someone else still find me attractive?" becomes a nagging question. We suddenly need compliments from members of the opposite sex to feel good about ourselves.

The real trap of low self-esteem is that our compelling objective in life focuses on reorganizing the outside world, including our marriage. Everybody else has the problem—not us. We try to fix others rather than take an honest look at our own lives.

At first we were concerned about meeting the "right one" to marry. Now we are learning how important it is to *be* the "right one" for someone else. Zig Ziglar said it well:

> If you treat the wrong person like the right person, you could well end up having married the right person after all. On the other hand, if you marry the right person, and treat that person wrong, you certainly will have ended up marrying the wrong person. I also know that it is far more important to be the right kind of person than it is to marry the right person. In short, whether you married the right or wrong person is primarily up to you.[2]

These are only some of the "perception factors" that work on our minds. They distort the way we view people and events and often become the initial catalysts for dissolving relationships. The marriage does not fall to a quick kill but a slow death. Our perception of reality creates doubt and feeds a hunger within for something better. The battle is ready to begin.

The Mind of the Initiator

Subconsciously the initiator begins reacting negatively to any patterns of rigidity, alienation of affection, changing priorities, competition for time and events, and similar stresses in a marriage. Eventually these displeasures build until they are impossible to ignore any longer.

This process can take months, but most often it evolves over a period of years. There is vacillation and indecision. One struggles with the morality of these thoughts, but a desire to escape is always there feeding on itself and growing. Eventually the ethics of divorce are worked out in the mind, which may take three to five years to settle in fully.

The initiator thinks, *This marriage is not really working out.* There are fantasies about freedom. The non-initiator's weaknesses become more noticeable and irritating. The marriage may have many positive qualities and satisfactions, but the initiator focuses on the negatives.

As the initiator looks for more shortcomings and weaknesses in his or her mate, the non-initiator may make this task easy. It is difficult to tolerate an unshaven face, excessive weight gain, incessant nagging, wearing unattractive clothes, or failings in personal hygiene for long—especially if one is looking for shortcomings. The initiator makes mental notes of every checkbook imbalance, improper positioning of the toilet seat, or uncapped toothpaste tube. Clothes dumped on the floor, curlers worn at the breakfast table, or stockings hung over the sink infuriate the initiator as he or she builds a case for divorce.

With criticism of these shortcomings, the initiator and non-initiator punish each other with the infamous "silent treatment" or take other deliberately punitive measures. If the non-initiator reacts with defensiveness and self-justification, this perceived lack of repentance leads the initiator to further criticism. The non-initiator feels nagged. The initiator believes the non-initiator "just won't listen to me." Both spouses drive the problems deep inside their hearts and minds to fester for another day. Rather than discussing and resolving problems, each mate secretly stockpiles evidence. These weapons are used to justify, and rationalize away, the guilt of thinking about divorce.

If the initiator finds divorce scripturally indefensible, he or she may lay the Bible aside and keep Christian friends at a distance. Situational ethics impress the initiator; biblical literacy declines; vows made and the initial joy of the marriage fade from memory. Self-sacrifice, honesty, purity, justice, humility, and servanthood inevitably yield to selfish pursuits without consideration of one's marriage partner. As personal offenses combine with compromised religious beliefs, the initiator's Christian faith may wither and die long before the marriage does. There is isolation and hopelessness. The initiator thinks, *Maybe God doesn't care about me or what I do.* Alternative living relationships become more plausible—even reasonable. In numbing the pain and loneliness, God is put on the shelf, and a shady side of the initiator's life may begin. After all, with duplicity in one's life, the choice is to cover up the deceit with lie upon lie, or slowly to lose one's mind.

Worldly acclaim and financial and emotional control may be prized and pursued with vigor by the initiator. Happiness comes from dreams of exotic vacations, moving to a mansion in a new city, or gaining a powerful business position to call the shots. Fantasies shift the focus away from the dying marriage.

While the initiator is satisfied at first with the release provided by mental escapes and avoidance, an overwhelming, forbidden desire grows to shed the marriage in pursuit of something perceived to be better. Another love interest or potential mate usually appears during these vulnerable times. There is a lusting for *total* independence. Anything to escape the reality of what is happening. Impatience grows to take a shortcut to freedom regardless of morality and potentially enormous risks. "After all," the initiator rationalizes, "it's my partner's fault that I feel this way."

The gathering storm in the marriage darkens hope. Intimacy is gone. Conversations seem flat and boring. The couple's sexual relationship wanes into non-existence. The initiator suggests separate vacations. More time is spent with single or divorced friends. More arguments arise over trivial matters. There is a battle for control. Tension builds, bit by bit.

But the initiator also feels a certain degree of exhilaration. These thoughts coursing through the mind are heady stuff. Pride swells in the heart as the initiator takes great satisfaction in being in control of his or her own destiny. The certainty of the impending death of the marriage may be a secret known only to the initiator, but the knowledge is ready to be used when the unsuspecting partner is most off guard. Many of the emotions arising from a divorce are worked through at the initiator's leisure until the "right time" is chosen to act. Any negotiation of issues between spouses at this point is virtually fruitless. They are not in the same place emotionally.

Resentments, a deeper impatience to act, and anger make demands on the initiator. Marriage is now less a relationship to be enjoyed than a journey to be endured and survived. The initiator decides that it is time to divorce and prepares an escape plan. He or she quietly tests fantasy scenarios for confronting the non-initiator, with the initiator in different roles, and mentally evaluates the results. How can the subject of divorce first be introduced to the non-initiator? What reactions can be expected? Where should each one go after the dilemma is put on the table? How soon can this marriage end? What will it cost in time, money, and mental anguish? When can dating other, more exciting people begin? Battle plans are made, but the non-initiator is told nothing.

The Unsuspecting Accomplice
The Denial Mind-Set of the Non-Initiator

While the initiator prepares for a showdown, the non-initiator may be blissfully ignorant of all that is happening. He or she usually is a naive accomplice in everything planned. The initiator's signals of trouble may be obvious to others detached from the relationship. Witnesses to a dying marriage sometimes marvel that the non-initiator missed the handwriting on the wall. But it happens.

Why do so many problems pass by completely unnoticed by the non-initiator? Perception factors affecting non-initiators are part of the reason, but there are some other significant differences. Non-initiators, for example, may settle into marriage roles that are more comfortable and secure, regardless of how their mates feel. The non-initiator may be the weaker marriage partner in communication and intimacy. He or she may view the marriage more as an institution to be preserved than a dynamic relationship. Confrontations can be deflected by interruptions or distractions. The non-initiator may externalize and depersonalize matters more to avoid any introspection about serious difficulties.

A typical non-initiator might be the working husband, self-satisfied in being the successful businessman and family provider, coming home to a clean house and wonderful meal. He wants to read the paper or watch the news without being disturbed. His wife may desperately need to talk to him, but he is emotionally spent after putting out fires at the office all day. He believes that he is loyal and faithful to the marriage, even if this may not be true. But his wife's needs are being ignored. She is receiving the scraps after he takes care of himself.

Meanwhile his wife is so stifled and bottled up emotionally that she is ready to scream and self-detonate! She is crying out, as best she can, for communication, emotional support, and intimacy. But her husband will not hear or understand. If she pushes her way into his peace and quiet, he becomes irritated and dumps pent-up frustrations from the office on her. Physical comforts of home are no consolation for her unfulfilled emotional needs. If this husband was less concerned about himself and more sensitive to what is going on around him in the home, he would have surely seen the problems festering.

Apathy is the most damaging flaw of the non-initiator. He or she just does not care enough to act. In a healthy marriage, partners try to keep themselves physically attractive, work hard to foster good, clear communication and emotional intimacy, develop similar interests, and seek mutual friends. But not in this marriage. More often than not, the initiator and non-initiator are like two ships passing in the night to and from the same port. Husband and wife live in the same home and share the same bed but have less and less in common. Gone are the romance and shared dreams. The relationship has slipped into a comfortable but very bland, boring existence. The non-initiator's spouse may almost want an argument, some conflict, or even hatred rather than to feel ignored and unappreciated. At least it shows some emotional involvement. The isolation and discontent will reach a breaking point for the initiator if the marriage does not crumble from sheer neglect.

If the initiator confronts the non-initiator with problems, denial is quite often immediate. "You can't be right. We love each other." If a problem is acknowledged, the non-initiator is convinced that everything can be resolved easily. The non-initiator may be more skilled in bargaining away any difficulties and more willing to accept intolerable circumstances than the initiator. Any complaints by the non-initiator's spouse are frequently trivialized as just "clearing the air" and summarily dismissed as nothing serious. The non-initiator believes and sees only what he or she wants; the rest is simply ignored.

The non-initiator may have no sense of timing, so vital to a marriage. One partner may try to revitalize a dying relationship, but the non-initiator ignores these efforts. He or she is an ideal candidate for being blindsided by the initiator and absolutely shocked to the core whenever the divorce announcement is made. Long after the initiator has abandoned all salvage efforts, the non-initiator then wants to spring into action, a classic example of one trying to do too little too late. The bell has tolled for this marriage; it is dead and ready for burial.

Why Do We War Against Each Other?

How did all this happen? It begins with a total failure to communicate, coupled with competition for control. Instead of committing themselves to conflict resolution to save the relationship, the initiator is secretly scheming to escape while the non-initiator does not care enough to hear about it! A selfishness running rampant among both partners destroys the day-to-day rhythms of a healthy marriage. The marriage breakdown is a living example of what the Bible says in James 1:13–15:

> When tempted, no one should say, "God is tempting me." For God cannot be tempted by evil, nor does he tempt anyone; but each one is tempted when, *by his own evil desire,* he is dragged away and enticed. Then, after desire has conceived, it gives birth to sin; and sin, when it is full-grown, gives birth to death. [Emphasis added.]

Unhappiness and loneliness reign in the marriage. There may be spouse or child abuse, illicit affairs, anorexia or bulimia, alcoholism, workaholism, and other problems. But these are all symptoms of deeper problems: pride and selfishness rooted in the hearts of the marriage partners. A showdown is coming. The pre-divorce process reaches a breaking point where a divorce war is inevitable. The joy of "you and me against the world," is quickly becoming just you against me.

Other marriage stressors also work against the spouses at this point, making any truce and reconciliation even more difficult:

Work and Financial Pressures

If businesses relocate a spouse, it uproots a family and pushes extended families farther away. Demands to spend more time at the office force compliance to keep a job. If both spouses work, schedules do not always mesh. This limits the couple's time alone. If finances are tight, the temptation grows to work even harder. Naturally these fires burn white hot if either spouse is laid off or fired. Is it any wonder that divorces often occur when a marriage partner is in serious trouble at work?

On the other hand, the breadwinner spouse may be very successful at work. He or she may receive accolades and monetary rewards while the homemaker spouse is stuck with unrewarding housework. If the spouse at home is not fully appreciated for years on end, he or she will feel isolated and trapped. If the homemaker tries to break out of the home for other projects, the other spouse may strongly object. For the spouse who is bored at home watching soap operas or reading romance novels, the working spouse is expected to come home with the same adoration as the fantasy characters. That is tough for the working spouse!

Advancing Age

Our bodies change over the years. Who still looks the same ten years after the wedding? Hair turns gray, or falls out entirely; sports prove that we have lost the youthful spring in our step; clothes do not fit the way they used to. We spend fortunes on health clubs and exercise equipment, yet the battle is never won. Women may look to cosmetics, breast implants, facelifts, liposuction, or other improvements to look younger. Men may find that, despite all efforts, their bellies hang over their belts. For spouses falling out of love, these are just more reasons to look at each other and think, "Blech!"

Age reminds us of our own mortality. Are we missing something by being tied down in our marriages? Will we later regret not bailing out on a stifling marriage to enjoy the "high life" while we are young? These powerful forces of nature can drive us to a divorce decision.

Life Achievements

We ask ourselves, "What have I really achieved in my life? What do I have to show for my life's work?" Both spouses will step back, question the meaning of life, and evaluate their performance. An unfulfilling marriage and boring family routines will suffer low marks.

Social Relationships

Who can we count on if we're in deep trouble? Who are our real friends? If we feel isolated from everyone else, and our marriage is not fulfilling, the temptation grows to bail out.

Some review all their social relationships with the question, "Is my marriage holding me back from enjoying an exciting new person?" New love interests promise excitement and quick thrills, which make affairs attractive and marriage commitments feel like an anchor.

Basic Compatibility

Some people are not compatible at the time they married. Other couples become incompatible over time as goals and interests change. Perhaps at first both spouses want children, then one spouse becomes deadset against it. One spouse may want frequent time alone to read a book or watch television quietly at home; the other spouse wants constant companionship and needs to be "on the go." A good marriage often hinges on whether both partners travel on the same track in life. Poor adjustments derail them.

The Showdown

As Amos asks, "Do two walk together unless they have agreed to do so?" (Amos 3:3). The initiator and non-initiator are now far from honoring their marriage vow to walk together. All the forces at work in and around them hit a crescendo, and a final confrontation occurs. When "divorce" is spoken seriously for the first time, a marriage may never be the same. The marriage is terminal. Saying the word acknowledges the effort already underway to bury it as quickly as possible.

The confrontation may occur at home very late at night. It may happen after one spouse works up the courage with the help of confidants or even after using stimulants. An event may become the "last straw." Whenever the showdown occurs, it shocks both parties. Telling a spouse, "I want a divorce! I want out now!" is an unforgettable event, much like Kennedy's assassination or the *Challenger* explosion.

There is no way for the naive non-initiator to ignore the deteriorating marriage now. Everything goes into slow motion; it seems unreal. All kinds of thoughts flash through the mind. The non-initiator usually asks the first question: "Is there someone else?" More often than not the answer is yes, whether the initiator will admit it or not.

The initiator may justify the decision with familiar rationalizations: *We are really so different. We're not right for each other. The marriage was a mistake in the first place. We fight and argue constantly. You don't need me. Our sex life is nonexistent. We don't do anything together or spend time with each other. You don't appreciate me. You'll see, we'll be better off apart from each other.*

Suddenly the naive non-initiator is hit with an unbelievable load of problems. The initiator may have privately sorted out everything for months, and perhaps even years, while preparing for this moment. For the non-initiator, however, it is almost always chaos. There is shock and hurt. The non-initiator receives the immediate responsibility of managing an unwanted divorce, but then, the initiator may have been slowly suffering with the same emotions and pain for years. In any case, it does not matter now what else is going on in the non-initiator's life. The initiator looks the non-initiator in the eyes, hands over an enormous plate of emotional and business issues, and says, "Deal with it!"

The non-initiator may spend the first of many sleepless nights reviewing the few words exchanged. In virtual unbelief, he or she may think: *Of all the people I have ever known, this person was the love of my life. This was the one I had gone through so many other relationships to find. He [or she] was everything that I wanted or needed. He loved God. And he loved me too. What more could I ask for? Marriage was so very right and natural—just like everyone said it should be. I was ready to sail gently through the years with my mate. I committed myself fully to my marriage partner. We had years to share with each other. Years to make plans, to go places and do things. Time without end to live our lives to the fullest. But now, almost in an instant, a decision was quietly made and an announcement given that would shatter the dream. Could it really be over? Really over? Just like that? Action so swift and sudden that shock is an afterthought? Does this happen almost without a second thought? It's just unthinkable! It's totally unbelievable!*

The non-initiator quickly retreats into denial for self-protection against overwhelming emotions. Humiliation, desperation, disbelief, anxiety, and guilt flood the heart and mind. For self-protection against an emotional breakdown, denial is probably the most important reaction until time allows everything to be sorted out. In an instant, the marriage partner is now an adversary. There is a feeling of betrayal and breach of trust. Now the entire relationship must change.

A new struggle begins with each spouse striving for independent economic survival and emotional identity. What will people say? Relatives and friends make judgments as to which spouse is more at fault; others will look on helplessly and quietly withdraw. Deep sorrow and loss set in.

The non-initiator faces the loss of family, friends, memories of the past, and dreams for the future. Identity as a couple is shattered. He or she may feel guilt, remorse, unworthiness, and self-doubt in seeing the marriage fail. The non-initiator suddenly may realize that the death of the marriage started long ago and may feel very responsible for the entire collapse. On the other hand, the initiator may feel some exhilaration in finally speaking the truth kept hidden for so long. He or she feels relief that, after months of rationalization and self-justification, the gauntlet finally has been cast down. To cope with personal guilt, the initiator may want the non-initiator to feel 100 percent to blame for the coming divorce.

Regardless of what role you play in a divorce showdown, odd thoughts come to mind because of the confusion and rush of emotions. As the naive non-initiator in my own marriage, I thought back to a brief scene in an old documentary on the life of Elvis Presley. His wife, Priscilla, had left him for some good reasons. The film shows Elvis, wearing dark glasses and obviously in deep emotional pain, sitting in his Graceland home recording a song for his next album. I remember being deeply touched as he sang the words, "Maybe I didn't love you, just as much as I could have. Maybe I didn't want you, just as much as I should have. But you were always on my mind. You were always on my mind."[3] I really felt that way about my wife then.

A sense of longing wells up in your heart that the marriage could somehow be saved. *What did I do wrong? I should have found a way to keep my marriage together. My life will never be the same.* However, it may be too late for that.

Remember that life will not always be the horror show we have just run through. Brighter days are ahead for everyone who goes through a divorce. Many suggestions in this book will help you make the divorce process more bearable, loving, and fair. If you and your spouse are poles apart in your devotion to Christ, your values, and your moral standards, perhaps only God can keep your marriage together. But even if divorce is inevitable, you can still act lovingly and responsibly. You can grow in your own relationship with the Lord and set a good example for others. Let it be so.

Questions for Personal Reflection

1) Am I the initiator or non-initiator in my marriage? What characteristics of each can I see in my spouse and myself?
2) What perception factors have contributed to the struggles in my marriage? Which have affected my spouse? Which have affected me?
3) Am I facing the truth of what is happening in my marriage? Am I denying any unpleasant realities?
4) What factors have created or added to the stress my spouse and I are experiencing now? What can I do to address these problems?
5) Am I ready, willing, and able to understand my situation honestly? Am I willing to consider ways to limit the damage of divorce and to take some action—even if it works against my best interests?

CHAPTER 2

The Stages of Grief

*What happens to us as we try to cope with the trauma
of separation and divorce? Crucial stages of working
through our grief promote healing and acceptance of
sorrow with each phase.*

My mother loves roses. She laboriously built a beautiful rose garden in our backyard just outside my parents' bedroom window. The planting, spraying, and weeding in the hot sun took countless hours, but the pleasure of seeing those lovely multicolored roses made it all worthwhile. She enjoyed cutting the best buds and sharing them with elderly shut-ins and friends.

One year, while I was home from college, my parents hit a very rough stretch in their marriage. Anger and resentment had put a wedge between Mom and Dad. After almost twenty-five years of being together, their relationship hit the rocks. I knew my mother was in pain, but walking through the backyard and seeing her little rose garden really brought it home to me. The bushes were ragged and barren; grass and weeds had grown up and choked out the beautiful blooms. It was obvious that the garden had suffered from many months of neglect.

This scene deeply moved me—what a melancholy picture of how the weeds of neglect and weight of marriage problems had choked out my mother's joy. Her heart was not in it anymore. Sadly, the flowers could not give my mother pleasure when she needed it the most because the garden needed her caring, loving touch before it could give back to her.

Fortunately, my parents resolved their differences those many years ago. With reconciliation, busy hands cleaned up the garden and it sprang back to life! Everything was joyful and beautiful again.

How does your garden grow? During marriage crises, our private gardens of happiness are going to suffer. Grief and turmoil will divert our time and attention. But there are ways to keep our gardens growing for personal comfort while bearing up under a separation or divorce!

Being the most personal form of rejection, the loss of a marriage relationship strikes at the core of our self-esteem. Our "significant other" is moving out of the picture. The break-up of a marriage breeds self-doubt and feelings of inadequacy. The non-initiator thinks, *I'm not lovable. There's something very wrong with me. I'm damaged goods.*

The best way to survive this crisis is to let go of the emotional attachments invested in the relationship. If saving the marriage is beyond your ability, it is time to detach so you can get on with your life. This is done by going through a grieving process, similar to mourning a death. How do people grieve? Although each of us reacts differently, research has shown that certain stages are common to us all. These stages are:

1) *Denial*—the psychological defense of not accepting the obvious by telling ourselves, "It's not true. He didn't really mean it. This isn't happening to me. He'll come back to our marriage."

2) *Anger*—directed at the source of our pain, often expressed in demanding, "How could you do this to me after all I've done for you?"

3) *Guilt*—turning our anger inward and berating ourselves by thinking, "It's all my fault—I wasn't good enough to keep this from happening."

4) *Bargaining*—believing the unrealistic beliefs that circumstances will change if *we* change or by our making concessions such as saying, "If she comes back, I'll do whatever she wants."

5) *Depression*—experienced as we face the reality that matters are beyond our control, acknowledging, "It's really true. Our marriage is over."

6) *Acceptance*—recognizing the finality involved and the freedom to leave the past behind for a new life.

There is no right or wrong way to go through this grieving process. One can experience any stage at any time and in any order when coping with a loss. We may go through the entire cycle several times before we really come to a peaceful acceptance of our circumstances.

Often, the initiator goes through this grieving process before seeking a divorce, while the non-initiator completes the process later. Regardless of how or when the process occurs, we must come to a point of peace within ourselves. The end of the crisis and turmoil is in accepting reality, coming to terms with where we are in life, and deciding how best to move forward from there.

Denial
Exchanging Truth for a Lie,
Or a Means of Slow Healing?

Denial is the use of an unconscious mental defense mechanism by which we refuse to see and understand the obvious. We shield ourselves against painful or unacceptable realities of life. If our ego feels threatened by a perception or memory, it is automatically taken away from our conscious thought as if it did not exist. We think, *There must be some mistake.*

Some time ago I remember seeing a cartoon showing General Custer riding with his troops through the valley as, along the rims of the hills in all directions, Indians on horses were peering down at him. The caption had Custer saying, "Oh, they'll NEVER find us!" That's denial.

Denial does help reduce our anxiety by keeping unwanted thoughts and feelings out of our conscious mind. We can deny or "stuff" our feelings about a matter (repression) or refuse to admit the truth of what happens to us, but with the same result—we escape reality. How is it that family and friends may be acutely aware of how our marriages are falling apart, or how one spouse is cheating on the other, while we are blissfully ignorant? Quite simply, we may not want to face the truth.

There are many ways we can deny the truth. Here are a few examples:

Projection: "You have the problem—not me!" We refuse to acknowledge our faults and instead see these same faults in others. When we feel annoyed, we may think that everyone else is excessively annoying while we are calm and reasonable.

Rationalization: "It's wrong, but I had to do it." This is the art of making excuses and justifying ourselves. "I had no choice but to get a divorce. You were 100 percent of the reason we couldn't live together." "I know that having an affair was wrong, but you weren't satisfying me sexually." "I couldn't help myself. Most people in my situation would have bailed out too."

Intellectualization: "I've analyzed the problem and applied logical, text-book solutions." We can avoid dealing with feelings and emotions by substituting knowledge and wisdom. We read up on quick fixes for problems and study self-help books, but avoid looking inside ourselves and working through personal grief. We control our lives by shutting down our feelings. But what is churning in our hearts underneath all the outward calm?

Withdrawal and isolation: "I can't handle it, so just leave me alone." We avoid painful circumstances by separating ourselves to more "safe" environments—no confrontations. But if we become silent and uncommunicative people, we also inhibit expression of our feelings. Our homes are quiet, but our unconscious minds start to scream.

Reversal through apologies: "Look, I said I was sorry, so can't we just drop it?" Somehow we believe this will cancel the harm of every wrong we did beforehand. By trying to escape unavoidable consequences of our actions, we lose touch with ourselves.

Substitution: "It's better for me to be at work to provide for you and the kids." We consciously form ideas and beliefs that are socially acceptable and exchange these thoughts for destructive motivations. In doing so, we bury the real truth into our unconscious mind. To deal with lust or to avoid having an affair, we may focus on problems from work or church. But we just ignore the real problem; it simply falls to a momentarily full agenda.

Avoiding commitment: "Yeah, it's a good idea, but what if . . ." If someone offers a solution for dealing with our problems, we think of "a thousand reasons why not." Psychologists call this *ambivalence*. We summarily reject the benefits of change and adjustment by going to extremes, proving to ourselves and others why it will not work.

Redirecting reactions: "Sure, I had a tough day, but don't think I'm taking it out on you!" Often called *displacement*, this reaction transfers feeling away from the source of discomfort to someone or something else. If times are tough at work, anger and abuse flares up at home. If our marriage is falling apart, we may become unbearable with friends or at work. To avoid painful circumstances and distract ourselves, we become "workaholics" or exercise fanatics. We fill up our time with activities rather than quietly reflecting upon our situations. We ignore the inner misery.

During a separation or divorce, some become excessively attentive to children or pets. After moving into her apartment, my wife faithfully put out dishes of food for stray cats in her complex even while she was on a limited budget. Her kindness to these helpless critters touched my heart, but I also knew she was showing stray animals more attention than her own husband. Perhaps she felt the need to show this kindness since she did not feel comfortable expressing this emotion to me at that time.

Identification: "Okay, we'll do it your way. Will that get me out of the doghouse?" To compensate for our own lack of self-worth or powerlessness, sometimes we try to identify with those hurting us. We secretly hope they will like us and become less abusive. We become compliant with our spouses and do their bidding. We can even adopt their tone of voice, gestures, opinions, and personality characteristics to please them. But in the process we can lose our own identity through appeasement.

Saving face: "It wasn't a mistake—I meant to do that." Our pride and ego will not allow us to show weakness. Like schoolboys trading punches after lunch, we cannot allow others see how they have hurt us. After a while, we begin to believe we are not hurt, even with all the pain. We also avoid fighting in front of our children. So instead of learning that no one is perfect and that marriage, like life, has times of conflict and friction, our children follow our example. They learn to suppress feelings and cultivate their own forms of denial that will carry into adult life.

As we shall see, denial shields us from overwhelmingly stressful events in our lives. But denial and repression that is too frequent, too intense, or too continuous becomes unhealthy. It keeps us from correcting the real problems. The key is to gradually sensitize ourselves throughout our grieving process. We need to alert ourselves to denial that can unreasonably disrupt our relationships and our ability to work.

Allowing Time for Healing

Denial can serve a useful purpose in allowing us time to face reality. Without denial, it would be difficult to live normal lives in a hectic and dangerous world. After all, if we did not believe we were perfectly safe from muggings and death on the highways, we might never leave home.

The stress of separation or divorce wears down our bodily immune systems. This can lead to dependency and addictions to alcohol or drugs (or both) and cause physical and mental illness—even premature death. We can become emotionally overloaded unless we protect ourselves to some degree. It is then that denial can serve as a gracious anesthetic. Our bodies automatically move into denial whenever we receive excessive psychological shock so that overwhelming pain, sorrow, and anxiety will not drive us insane. Our feelings are frozen for a time until we are fully ready to experience them. Given this fact, how can we manage our denial in a healthy and spiritual way?

Use denial for constructive healing. There is no universal prescription for how to grieve because the timing for healthy denial varies from person to person. Do not let others tell you that your time is up. If you are not yet ready to receive the full measure of pain from your situation, let it come naturally. But do not delay the process.

Do not be afraid to cry. Do not believe those who tell you, "Don't cry; you'll be all right." Crying is a natural emotional and spiritual cleansing that releases some of those pent-up feelings inside. It is a release given to us by God for our comfort and healing. When you are alone, shout or scream if you feel like it. This will help purge some of the tension and emotion locked up inside. The Bible tells us that Jesus often offered up prayers and petitions with loud cries and tears to the Father (Heb. 5:7). Certainly, if the Son of God felt the need to do this, we can too!

Use the power of prayer. What does the Bible say about dealing with anxiety and stress? "Cast your cares on the Lord and he will sustain you; he will never let the righteous fall" (Ps. 55:22). "Do not be anxious about anything, but in everything, by prayer and petition, with thanksgiving, present your requests to God. And the peace of God, which transcends all understanding, will guard your hearts and your minds in Christ Jesus" (Phil. 4:6–7).

The first verse in the old hymn "What a Friend We Have in Jesus" also says it well: "What a friend we have in Jesus, all our sins and griefs to bear! What a privilege to carry everything to God in prayer! Oh, what peace we often forfeit; Oh, what needless pain we bear, all because we do not carry everything to God in prayer."[1] That lonely pain of going to an empty bed or eating dinner alone packs less of a punch as we feel the presence of the One who always stands with us. Prayer is vital at every stage throughout the grieving process.

Recognize that sorrow and sadness are okay. If you feel distress and sorrow, don't keep it bottled up; let it come out. Certain events may bring back memories of when your spouse was at your side. You may hear your mate's favorite song. Dinnertime may remind you of preparing special meals for your spouse. Even lighter laundry loads remind you that someone is missing. And perhaps the saddest of all, you may try to hug your missing companion in bed during the night. The pain will slip away in time, but now it is natural and healthy to feel sadness. If possible, talk it out with someone you trust.

Seek trustworthy friends. We must find others who will help us accept the truth. If we can confess to our closest friends that we are not coping well, then we are moving through the denial stage of grieving. Having concerned friends who are willing to listen to you, rather than give advice you have not asked for, is a blessing. We do not need those who say, "You'll get over this," or "Don't question God's purpose," or "I know how you feel." No one except the Lord can truly know how we feel. True friends express caring concern by simply asking, "Would you like to talk?" or "It must be hard to live without Wally; how are you adjusting?" Having someone there to talk to and hug means so much. A comforting touch disarms pain.

Acknowledge pain rather than avoid it. The best antidote for denial is facing the truth. Recognize the difference between fantasy and reality. Because of inward yearnings, we may "see" our spouses in crowds or hear their voices. A car coming into the driveway may cause us to think our mates are coming home. After each of these fantasies, it is healthy to say, "I must accept that my mate is gone." Moving back and forth between fantasy and reality brings frustration and confusion. Learning to live with memories—birthdays, anniversaries, or holidays, going to church for the first time without your mate—is a long-term task. Face each event one at a time.

Try to adjust your lifestyle gradually. As soon as possible, adjust daily routines to meet the needs of yourself, your children, and loved ones. Keeping schedules that revolve around a missing mate is an unnecessarily painful reminder which just prolongs acceptance of the loss. If your world is upside down, start a new life using little details. Put fresh flowers in the kitchen. Straighten up the bedroom. Watch a favorite television show or go to a movie with a friend. Invite church members to lunch after services. There are so many ways you can make your life happy once again.

Anger
Power and Revenge Unleashed,
Or a Controlled, Focused Response?

Feeling anger is a step in the right direction because it is the beginning of acceptance of a loss. We now recognize that a problem exists, but we refuse to accept the consequences. Through anger we try to control others and shift the balance in our favor because we do not like the results.

What is anger? It is an emotion of control and manipulation to undo actions we perceive to be unjust, unfair, foolish, or negligent. We have experienced an unwanted and (as we may perceive it) undeserved and unfair loss. We want others to live up to our expectations, which can often be unrealistic or unreasonable.

Do we feel significant only if we are in charge? Do we threaten others with dire consequences if they are not compliant with our wishes? Are we easily hurt by what others say or do? Do we somehow feel we have the right to hurt them as well? Do we want our spouses to suffer? Have we fantasized about harming ourselves or others to make our spouses feel guilty? The answers highlight ways we may have allowed inner desires for power or revenge to control us.

Causes of Anger

Some believe that anger instinctively arises within an individual rather than from surrounding circumstances in life. Emotions build until our restraints rupture. Others contend that the heart of anger comes from frustration in not achieving one's goals. As achievements fall short of expectations, our self-esteem takes a nose dive and frustration builds into an eruption of anger. Still others believe anger is an emotion we learn through experience, by seeing how other people achieve success through aggressive behavior.

We fuel anger's fire by holding grudges spawned from the pain of losing face in front of others, assuming the worst motives in others who have hurt us, overreacting against harsh criticism, and even basic personality conflicts. Stoked-up anger then erupts in different ways. There is the explosive, loud outburst, where we lash out whenever the world shortchanges us. Then there are those who become cool—icy cool—by turning hostility into a cold, suppressed silence. "Cool anger" is a slow burn leading to depression, cynicism, or sarcasm.

In separation or divorce, anger comes quickly through unfulfilled expectations in resolving property distribution, money, and child visitation rights. The most trivial of incidents can spark a firestorm of protests. Parents may use children as informers against each other. But power, control, and hurting others in revenge for personal pain are self-defeating reactions.

Using Anger Constructively

In a separation or divorce, how can we deal with anger in a healthy and constructive way? Here are some suggestions on how to turn anger into a controlled, focused response:

Realize that not all anger is sin. God is spoken of as being angry in Psalm 2:5–9 and Nehemiah 1:2–8. Jesus also showed anger in Mark 3:4–5, John 2:13–17 and Matthew 23:1–36. The apostle Paul makes a distinction between anger and sin: "'In your anger do not sin': Do not let the sun go down while you are still angry, and do not give the devil a foothold" (Eph. 4:26–27).

The account of Jesus clearing the temple of the moneychangers with a whip of small cords in Mark 11:15–19 and John 2:15–17 is an excellent example of the difference between sinful anger and being angry without sinning. Notice that:

1) Jesus had *altruistic anger* for the benefit of those wronged (exploitation of worshipers and desecration of God's temple), rather than for some personal offense.

2) He *focused His anger* on the behavior deserving of rebuke rather than venting anger at innocent people.

3) He *controlled His expression of anger* and used it in a socially constructive way (by letting everyone know of God's moral position on the matter).

4) He *did not nurse a grudge in bitterness* that eats away at the soul with a seething vengeance.

Sinful anger cultivates a retaliatory spirit (see Luke 9:54). It is intolerant of the failings of others, as Jonah exemplified in not wanting to preach to Nineveh (Jonah 1:1–3; 4:1–3). It makes no distinction between the sinner and the sin involved.

How can we use anger constructively? James 1:19–20 tells us: "My dear brothers, take note of this: Everyone should be quick to listen, slow to speak and slow to become angry, for man's anger does not bring about the righteous life that God desires." Proverbs 29:11 also says, "A fool gives full vent to his anger, but a wise man keeps himself under control." Self-control is a fruit of the Holy Spirit (Gal. 5:22–24). We can use our anger positively by having a vigilant love for others, regardless of what they may have done to us.

Use a cooling-off period. Take time to stop and think rather than to stop thinking. Losing control of ourselves is a humiliating experience. We lose credibility, loyalty, and respect, while earning a reputation for intimidation. We gain nothing if others respond to us out of fear. "A patient man has great understanding, but a quick-tempered man displays folly" (Prov. 14:29). This may mean breaking off a confrontation to take a long walk, talk to a friend, or pray for a peaceful spirit. Keeping a journal of events prompting anger can help us understand what triggers it and also allow us to prepare against future overreactions.

Honestly express feelings to others. This means calmly describing what we see, how we feel about it, and what we believe needs to be done. We address the issues and problems while not attacking the person who is making us angry. Why not follow the steps in Matthew 18:15–17? Meet face-to-face with the person to discuss the problem. Use a neutral third-party mediator for unresolved matters. It is often a good idea to write a letter to the person first, describing our irritation in detail, then to throw it away. This helps purge us of feelings of bitterness and revenge before meeting the person and encourages us to focus on the most important issues.

Negotiate rather than self-detonate. Avoiding a conflict does not make it go away—that is a "lose-lose" proposition. It resolves nothing. Domination and intimidating others into submission makes victims resentful and eager to seek revenge, while acquiescing to the expectations of others makes us a doormat for further abuse. Don't confuse compromise with being compromised. The best way to negotiate peacefully with a warring spouse is through collaboration on creative "win-win" solutions.

Admit that some expectations are unreasonable or unimportant. We must recognize when our need for love, freedom, and control is out of balance. If you sit in rush hour traffic for an hour or more each day or see others trying to sneak a cartload of groceries into the ten-item express line, then you know how anger arises from unfulfilled personal expectations. But we have to let some matters go without confrontation—especially if we have no control over the situation or if what we want is really not all that important. Proverbs 19:11 tells us: "A man's wisdom gives him patience; it is to his glory to overlook an offense." Forgiveness is critical. Patiently allow the actions of others to result in natural and logical consequences. This is the concept of using tough love that we discuss in detail in chapter 9.

Guilt
Feeling Like a Loser,
Or Accepting Accountability for Errors?

Frequently, the initiator feels guilt for ending a relationship with a spouse. The non-initiator often feels rejection and guilt for being an inadequate marriage partner. Feeling guilty about our circumstances and our role in bringing everything about is natural. But there is a positive and constructive way to experience guilt, just as there is a negative and destructive guilt that can affect us adversely for years to come. Guilt is where many people get stuck in the grieving process.

Feeling guilt comes from the imbalance we perceive between ideals and realities. The key is in understanding what standard we are using in evaluating ourselves.

Unhealthy guilt condemns us with responsibility for our spouse's errors in judgment. We berate ourselves for not doing enough sooner to change matters. Mistakes flash through our minds. We condemn and torture ourselves with "I should haves," "Maybe ifs," and "If onlys" as we withdraw into our own private world of suffering. *Maybe we should have had more family times of prayer and Bible reading,* we reason. The list never ends.

The more we remember, the more we blame ourselves for the downfall of the marriage. We dwell on all that went wrong, while overlooking all that went right. Even well-meaning family members and friends may innocently make matters worse through uninformed judgments or implied blame. Statements such as, "You must have done something to bring this on," or "I knew this would happen the way your marriage was going," or "If I was your spouse, I'd have left a long time ago," spear us with guilt and increased pain at a very vulnerable time.

There is a cycle to feeling guilt. We search our souls and find faults, mistakes, and inadequacies. This creates guilt as we see how far we fall short and miss the mark. We make an effort to change. This brings mixed results, but we fear that we can never completely change, and doubt we have the power to overcome our weaknesses. This leads to more self-searching and fault-finding. More reasons to feel guilty. So we spiral downward into self-pity. Certainly guilt can be a punitive measure—we punish ourselves or allow others to punish us with it. But healthy guilt feelings are not neurotic and destructive.

Objective Guilt vs. Subjective Guilt

Guilt can be objective, arising from violation of an objective standard, such as when we disobey God's Word or a civil law. Guilt can also be subjective, arising from violation of personal, internal standards of conduct.

Certain standards, whether God's law or the civil law of nations, exist as reasonable codes of conduct to benefit the greatest number of people. When we violate these external standards of conduct, quite often the guilt we feel motivates us to change in healthy ways. That is *objective guilt*. It helps us to see our relationship to others and the world around us. *Subjective guilt*, however, cuts from a flawed perspective. It relies upon internal standards coming from often inconsistent rules and expectations given to us by our parents, peers, and life as we alone perceive it. Unlike objective standards of conduct that can be reviewed and changed from time to time, we do not always evaluate or challenge the truth of our internal standards. Consequently, internal subjective standards of conduct can be riddled with inconsistencies and distortions, leading to self-punishment, self-rejection, and low self-esteem.

Self-centered subjective guilt roots itself in selfish anger. It focuses on past failures and condemnation rather than on the problems at hand. It refuses to learn from mistakes and fails to forgive. Those who feel guilt in this way often become martyrs full of self-pity. But objective guilt is forward-looking. It leads us to consider damage done to others and fosters a desire to see justice done. We confess our wrongs, seek forgiveness, and change with hope for a better future.[2]

Relief from objective guilt comes through penance and restitution (civil law) or repentance and forgiveness through Christ (God's law). Condemnation is finite, if it exists at all. (See Rom. 8:1.) Subjective guilt, however, can punish without end. Any legalistic self-atonement fails to satisfy a conscience with impossibly high expectations. Subjective guilt turns inward with introspective, excessive self-examination to see what fault within us causes others to reject us. Objective guilt can help us to see ourselves more clearly and discover ways to change how we relate to others.

Using Guilt Constructively

In the grieving process, objective guilt—when used in a healthy way—keeps us from rebellion. It is the shortest route toward a positive, more fulfilling life in harmony with God and others. We can use guilt in a positive way for accountability and change.

Readjust thinking processes. We need to isolate the causes of the guilt we feel. We can think of matters we did not handle very well in our marriages. But what can we do about them? We try to understand our errors and change course for the future. If we find ourselves trapped by unreasonable, internal standards of conduct creating subjective guilt, we need to readjust our thinking. This means ridding ourselves of self-destructive mental images and replacing them with personal, positive, and true statements about ourselves. One way to do this is by writing out lists of positive and negative qualities. Then we rely upon God's forgiveness to forgive ourselves. This frees us to work to resolve the problems and focus our minds on constructive solutions.

Get rid of perfectionism. We do some tasks well and others not as well. But within our abilities and limitations, we can still live, love, and laugh with others. We can aim for balance in all areas of life. We can learn from the past and let it go. We do not have to worry about "could have beens" or "should have beens."

Form realistic expectations. The story is told that the late actress Helen Hayes was not a very good cook. After many years of eating out, she asked her family to have one Thanksgiving dinner at home. She told her husband and son, "Now, I've cooked turkey for the first time and I'm gonna bring it to the table. And if it's not good, I don't want anybody to say a word. We'll just quietly get up from the table, and without any negative comments, we'll go to a restaurant and have a Thanksgiving meal." She went into the kitchen to retrieve the turkey, and returned to find her husband and son both sitting at the table with their hat and coat on. Now that's a family with realistic expectations on all sides!

There is great truth in Reinhold Niehbur's famous Serenity Prayer: "God grant me the serenity to accept the things I cannot change; the courage to change the things I can; and the wisdom to know the difference." We *cannot* change others, rewrite history, always get our own way, or make people do what we want them to do. We *can* change ourselves, our present and future, how we feel when we do not get our own way, and how we act when people will not do what we want them to do.

Seek freedom through forgiveness and letting go. The best relief from guilt is forgiveness. Confessing our wrongs and seeking forgiveness from God and those we have sinned against—and forgiving ourselves in the process—frees us to move on in life with the wisdom of experience. First John 1:9 reassures us: "If we confess our sins, He is faithful and just and will forgive us our sins and purify us from all unrighteousness."

Bargaining
Bribing Our Way to Happiness, Or Exploring Options?

Now we come to the stage of grieving when we want to recover what we are losing in a separation or divorce. We bargain for a "second chance." We agree to everything we failed, neglected, or refused to do before. Some,

35

on the other hand, play "hardball." They bargain by using power plays, many times with the children as chips. They threaten their spouses with, "Do it my way or you'll lose in court!"

Bargaining may mark the beginning of the end of a marriage. It is a last-ditch effort to postpone an inevitable separation or divorce, or to keep as much of whatever the couple owns to oneself. Husbands promise to spend more time at home, share in the housework, exercise to lose weight, and buy gifts and flowers to shower wives with belated affection. Wives will be more permissive in letting husbands come and go as they please, dress differently, and become servants around the house. Appeasement is the name, and anything that works is the game.

Why is bargaining often such a futile process? Because it is too little too late. If welcome change comes, it is often temporary and the couple is right back at the door of divorce. Trust—the glue of any marriage—disappears before the reforms begin. In the process, we also bargain away our feelings and perhaps even sacrifice our identity in the hope that our spouses will accept us.

The Dangers of Compliance and Codependency

Codependency arises when love for our spouses causes us to neglect our own needs or the needs of our children or others for whom we are responsible. Are we tempted to submerge our identity into our relationships with our spouses? Is our love for them more of a compulsion than a choice? Are we becoming compliant or offering too much because we feel we cannot live without them?

Healthy boundaries blur and break down if we become too enmeshed with spouses on the way out of our lives. We feel the pain of emotional or physical abandonment. In childlike fashion, we become needy and clingy. This is humiliating since our spouses will surely lose all respect for us. If we lose our identities in our pursuit of any human relationship, we also forfeit direction and control over our personal lives. Instead we should do everything possible to become interdependent with our spouses—at least until we become truly independent through divorce.

Using Bargaining Constructively

Bargaining can interfere with letting our spouses go and moving on with our lives. But this stage of the grieving process can still work for the mutual advantage of everyone. Here are some constructive suggestions:

Make every reasonable effort to save the marriage. We can try to negotiate reconciliation with our spouses on neutral ground and from neutral positions. This is a time to avoid anger and maintain self-control so as not to make bad judgments. Creative thinking and compromise are critical. The key is to explore the situation and satisfy ourselves that we have done everything possible either to reverse the separation and divorce or to limit the damage. After that is done, we need to let the relationship go.

Negotiate inevitable issues of separation or divorce. Bargaining can serve a useful purpose in helping us work out legal matters such as property division, child custody and visitation rights, and financial support. But throughout the entire process, we should be true to our convictions and treat others evenhandedly. We begin by doing our homework on the important issues. Then we present proposals to our spouses (or their representatives) in a positive manner, showing them proper respect.

Since negotiations of any type can be an emotional experience, we need to have clear sight of our goals and objectives. Healthy bargaining means listening more and talking less. Talking too much may cause us to use the wrong words or press the wrong point; it also prevents others from responding. Regardless of what happens, we must keep any commitments made. We should not give our word to do something lightly, but once we do we should stick to it. We must model integrity and character in everything. Since trust is an issue between spouses, this will be important and encouraging.

Sadness and Depression
The End of Life, Or Facing Reality
Before Experiencing Freedom?

If uncontrolled anger marries excessive guilt, often the child born of that union is depression. Many psychologists believe that depression is anger turned inward. It occurs when we avoid expressing our anger for fear of reprisals or further abandonment. As we do, we become easy targets for our own anger. Inward anger springs forth in self-criticism, and eventually this feeling of worthlessness lowers our self-esteem.

The Difference Between Sadness and Depression
Sadness and "feeling blue," a relatively temporary unhappiness, is different from depression, a chronic and more painful, deep sorrow that can

cripple daily life. Who would not feel sad over the loss of a spouse? Sadness can lead to a temporary period of withdrawal from family and friends; after all, a brief period of isolation and tears is healthy and appropriate. Then adjustment and recovery helps us to recover from the grief of loss.

Sadness may make us think we are getting worse, when in fact we are getting better. Sadness, crying, and releasing one's feelings are God-given, healthy events. They free us to face reality and accept our circumstances. If we do not release our bottled-up feelings, however, we can fall into depression, and that depression lasts considerably longer than short-lived sadness. It can destroy us emotionally.[3]

Depression can lead to a cyclical, downward spiral. It brings indecision, which leads to self-blame and feeling like a failure. This destroys self-esteem, which leads to further depression, and on and on the hopeless cycle goes. It is a trapped feeling: "I can't get out of this. . . . It's hopeless. . . . Things will never change. . . . I'm powerless to do anything. . . . I'm drained and empty. . . . I can't sleep. . . . There's no way out." Unless dealt with aggressively, depression can put you into a psychological cage of isolation and despair until you just give up on life.

Ten times as many people suffer from depression today as fifty years ago. If you are between twenty-five and forty-four years old, many researchers believe that your age group has the greatest vulnerability for depression. Women are more prone to depression than men by a factor of two to one. Those in higher socio-economic groups experience it three times more often than other groups.

Few of us are immune to depression. Winston Churchill was beset by what he called the "black dog" of depression. Abraham Lincoln had frequent depressive moods. King David experienced some depression through self-punishment over his adultery with Bathsheba. He described himself as experiencing physical weakness, mourning, feeling spent and crushed, having tumult in his heart, longing, sighing, alienation from others, and apathy (Ps. 6; 32; 51). Moses, Job, Elijah, Jeremiah, Jonah, and many others in the Bible went through periods of deep depression as well—even to the point of wanting to die (1 Kings 19:4; Jonah 4:9). God personally diagnosed Cain: "Why are you angry? And why is your face downcast?" (Gen. 4:6). Judas, the betrayer of Jesus, became so distressed that he sought relief through self-destruction instead of forgiveness from the Lord (Matt. 27:3–5).

Using Sadness or Depression Constructively

How can we deal with sadness and depression in a healthy way so these feelings can help us face reality and prepare for acceptance?

We can realize that we are not alone in our suffering. "No temptation has seized you except what is common to man. And God is faithful; he will not let you be tempted beyond what you can bear. But when you are tempted, he will also provide a way out so that you can stand up under it" (1 Cor. 10:13).

Everyone goes through tough times and circumstances in life. Can you think of a person who does not have scars of some sort? We do not feel better because others suffer, of course, and misery loves company. But it does give us hope that, like others before us, we can survive whatever comes our way. There is hope! Our lives do not have to end; we can endure and persevere. Many times in working through my own sadness, I reassured myself by saying aloud: "You and me forever, Lord." I found Romans 8:35–39 to be of particular personal comfort: "Who shall separate us from the love of Christ? . . . We are more than conquerors through him who loved us!

Like a child feeling the security of snuggling up in a parent's arms during a stormy night, we find comfort in knowing that God is near. Even if family and friends fail us and we walk through the valley of the shadow of death, God is always with us (Ps. 23). We *are* more than conquerors!

We can live as victors rather than victims. Since sadness and depression thrive on inactivity, the more inert we are, the less we want to do. It is time to be accountable for ourselves and to take action. By scheduling small, doable tasks from day to day, we can rejoice in making progress. We must decide to become victors rather than victims, taking reasonable steps to feel better—to move away from a rigid lifestyle toward being flexible and adjusting fully to changing circumstances.

We can focus on positive thoughts and optimism. Let's face it. Pessimism is *in* as a routine comment on the state of the world today with the breakdown of families. We can laugh with our children at the morose donkey Eeyore in the *Winnie the Pooh* stories, but his outlook on life can mirror our own pessimism. Within an environment of pessimism, sad or depressed individuals can become preoccupied with the pain of past or present experiences. They selectively recall negative thoughts and memories, while ignoring positive or neutral events. They expect more negative results.

But there is reason to have hope. We can reverse the process through training ourselves to focus on the positive qualities of ourselves, others, and life in general. "Finally, brothers, whatever is true, whatever is noble, whatever is right, whatever is pure, whatever is lovely, whatever is admirable—if anything is excellent or praiseworthy—think about such things. . . . And the God of peace will be with you" (Phil. 4:8, 9b). Pleasant words and thoughts are "sweet to the soul and healing to the bones" (Prov. 16:24). We can concentrate on what we do well rather than upon whatever is beyond our abilities. Whenever questions arise, we can assume the best of others rather than the worst.

An optimist is happier, healthier, and a better problem-solver. Optimists consider options and new possibilities. Pessimists summarily dismiss options; they see failure as a very personal, permanent, and pervasive problem. Optimists see reversals of fortune as impersonal, short-term, and specific setbacks that can be overcome in time. It is so true that as a man thinks within his heart, so is he (Prov. 23:7 KJV; also, Mark 7:21–23). It is vital that we keep these matters in perspective, for we know that "weeping may remain for a night, but rejoicing comes in the morning" (Ps. 30:5). Time does heal all wounds.

We can develop a servant's heart. Serving others can reinforce our value and self-worth. Community service, volunteer work, and becoming more active in church activities counteract the temptation to withdraw from the world. Touching other people and their hearts is a healing process all the way around. We also need to let others give to us.

We can develop a support network of family and friends. The best defense against sadness and depression is to not face them alone. A strong, personal relationship with God makes a difference. Family and friends can offer advice and encouragement when we need it most.

We can take care of our bodies. Take time for healing. Proper diet and vigorous exercise—followed by a nice shower—deeply soothe a weary soul. Getting out of the house into the sunlight brightens the day. Activity can dramatically reduce tension and anxiety and provide an important release of bottled-up feelings. If falling asleep is difficult, adjust your sleeping habits. If sleep does not come within fifteen minutes, read the Bible or a pleasant book or watch some television until you feel tired.

Acceptance
The Truth Will Set Us Free

These suggestions for working through each stage of grief focus on facing up to existing circumstances. Acceptance comes from realizing that happiness does not depend upon needing people to please us, nor does it require a change of circumstances. Happiness comes from seeing our situations honestly, without exaggeration or understatement, and dealing with the issues responsibly. We tell ourselves, *This is how matters are. I'll accept the situation as it is. I can handle it.* This frees us to have vision for ourselves and to make and act upon our own choices in life as we believe best.

Isaiah prophesied that Jesus would be a man of sorrows, familiar with suffering and grief (Isa. 53:3). The Lord knew the depth of grief over loss of a loved one as he wept over the death of His friend Lazarus (John 11:35). After hearing of the beheading of his cousin John the Baptist, He withdrew to a lonely place to deal with His sorrow and grief (Matt. 14:13). Not being able to gather Jerusalem to Himself just before His crucifixion grieved Him (Matt. 23:37). In the Garden of Gethsemane, His anguished prayers brought sweat like drops of blood falling to the ground (Luke 22:44). The agony of the cross, in comparison, is almost beyond comprehension. Yet Jesus always faced reality unselfishly. He relied upon the Father for strength and perseverance. In every way, He epitomized the freedom that comes through acceptance of His mission in life and never giving up.

Acceptance of our circumstances is a time for stabilization and reconstruction. We have moved beyond merely allowing our suffering to make us vindictive, resentful, and bitter. We find renewed trust in ourselves and others. Although we feel deep loss over our spouses, we invest no further time and energy than is reasonably necessary to save our marriages. We do not enslave ourselves into chasing after an unwilling partner. Instead, we learn from our mistakes and shift our focus from the past to the future.

In our valleys of defeat, hope returns. We can still praise God whether our spouse is unfaithful or our children are rebellious. Life is not as we expected, but we begin to see new possibilities for ourselves. Laughter comes into our lives once again. We embrace church fellowship, not to numb our pain but to rejoice with God's people and praise Him who is the source of life and hope. Loving the brethren helps us to pass from death to life

(1 John 3:14). We are back into the joy of living—able to celebrate good memories without obsession. Life is good again.

Shakespeare once wrote, "Everyone can master a grief but he that has it."[4] But with God's help, anyone can master grief. More than that, we can become "wounded healers" in encouraging others through their own grief. In my sorrow of divorce, I have become a brother to others who suffer. Turn your own loss into victory as well by helping others to bear their heavy burden.

Questions for Personal Reflection

1) Am I trapped in denial about any of the issues surrounding my separation or divorce?
2) Am I angry with my spouse to get power, control, or revenge? If not, do I use restraint in a controlled, focused response for his or her best interests or the needs of others?
3) Do I feel guilty about wronging others in a way that will lead me to make constructive changes in my life, or am I simply condemning myself for who I am?
4) Am I using my sadness over separation or divorce as a personal time of cleansing and healing, or do I find myself sinking into self-pity and misery?
5) Am I ready to accept the truth that my marriage may be over and face the reality of having to move on in life without my partner?

CHAPTER 3

The Message of the Prodigal Son

Nurturing qualities of unconditional love and having an attitude of forgiveness toward our spouses are the best defenses against divorce. There must be a time of letting go and release, much as it hurts. Hindrances such as pride and selfishness keep us enslaved to anger and resentment. If we fail to forgive, dealing with an unwanted divorce is much more difficult.

This first part of this book is entitled, "Examining the Thoughts and Attitudes of Your Heart." We need a continual self-evaluation to keep our spiritual focus. If we truly want to follow the example of Christ, we must deal with problems as they come up in a loving and gracious way rather than with a vindictive spirit. Easy to say but difficult to do, right? How is this done when anger and resentment have gripped our hearts?

I want to begin this chapter by being open and honest with you about my own divorce struggle. I know if you are struggling with a troublesome divorce, advice from the sidelines can seem rather empty. But I hope the personal challenges I faced will encourage you to have the right attitude so that your situation will be less of a burden. The following is a journal entry I wrote a year and a half after initial separation from my wife:[1]

> I had a very rough time last night. I tossed and turned all night long, staring into the darkness at the ceiling. Thoughts churned in my mind as I asked God for guidance and considered options as to what is best. On and on this went throughout the night until I fell asleep from sheer exhaustion in brief periods between 4 and 5 a.m.
>
> It was agony to think about everything and to consider divorce from my wife. What did God want me to do? How would He deal with my wife for taking steps contrary to His Word? I thought about our marriage relationship. I thought about her salvation.

I thought and prayed about many of these matters through Monday night and through the day today. What could I say? There was really nothing I could do to change her mind if she really has decided what she's going to do! That much is clear! So the Lord impressed upon my heart that I must continue to be faithful to Him and to my wife. I need to love her with grace, mercy, and forgiveness *without expecting anything in return*. I must trust Him that everything will work together for good in my life (Rom. 8:28).

I thought back to our marriage counselor's question to my wife and me yesterday, "What would Jesus say to you right now?" My wife thought that He might use a parable. Then I asked myself what parable God would share with me. The parable I have constantly come back to throughout this whole time has been the parable of the prodigal son. Wow! There's just so much in that parable. It shows us how we think, and how God deals with us in meeting our needs! If I really want to be God's man in this situation, I must reflect the nature of God to my wife and to everyone else involved in a powerful way. I must strive to see issues as God would in this situation regardless of how others act or feel!

The parable is a classic picture of unhappiness at home. The young son was fed up. He checked out (after taking a portion of an estate that was rightfully not even his yet) to live the good life. What he did was not right. After a while, he paid the price by losing everything. Then he came to his senses. The prodigal son realized that what he had at home was not as bad as he had thought after all. So he came back home. The father did not go out and rescue the son when he hit rock bottom. However, the father (unlike many of us who probably would have told him to hit the road again) was ready and eager to welcome the repentant son home. Now that's a picture of God's love that is so contrary to how I would have handled the situation! That's the type of love I want to show to my wife now because of my love for God and for her personally.

Now you may be asking yourself, "What does the parable of the prodigal son have to do with me and my marriage? My spouse is not my child." But do not miss the point here: Keep your focus on how the father deals with his family as they selfishly ignore him to seek their own happiness. All of the attitudes shown by the father are just as valid, and more than applicable, to divorce situations. This beloved parable capsulizes the essence of what we need in dealing with our anger and resentment toward our spouses. We need a release from the pressure cooker of these pent-up emotions. That release can come only through forgiveness and letting go of our spouses. Consider your own divorce situation as we look into this beautiful story from Jesus.

The Parable of the Prodigal Son
Forgiveness and Unconditional Love in Action

As we try to understand how this parable applies to our marriages, we must resist the temptation to see our spouse as the louse. Remember, our goal is not to compare him or her to the prodigal son but for us to emulate the loving attitudes of the father. Why? Because we cannot control what our spouses do. Thinking of how our spouses may have let us down only tempts us to have a martyr complex and to justify our own actions. This leads to pride and selfishness—certainly not attitudes that heal. Therefore, forget about your spouse's actions for now. At the same time, consider how much like the younger (and older) son we are. Then we can appreciate the attitudes and actions of the father in this parable as a picture of how God relates to each of us as His own rebellious children.

This parable, appearing in Luke 15, is a lesson in dealing with broken relationships. But some readers will have great trouble with this parable; it will disturb them. Why? Because Jesus talks of doing something they absolutely do not want to do—forgive their spouses. If you feel this way, please try to remain open and let God speak to your heart. Forgiveness may seem an impossible task, but with God all things are possible (Mark 10:27).

Now, please take a moment to read the parable of the prodigal son in Luke 15:11–32. Jesus was talking with religious leaders, lawyers, and tax collectors (Luke 15:1–2). Note that He shared this parable (and the preceding stories of the lost sheep and coin) to emphasize the great worth, in God's eyes, of relationships and of each individual. What are some principles we can use from this parable?

45

Relationship Busters: Pride and Selfishness

First, try to understand the analogy of the son's request to our divorce situations. The son in this story is really divorcing himself from his father. What do you think the initial talk between the father and son was like? What did the son really want? Why did the son decide to leave the secure comforts and love of home to go out into an uncertain world? Did he want freedom from the values and judgments of his father? Could he have bailed out simply because he felt unappreciated at home? Did a challenging rush of adventure or a need to control his own life without the father's interference tempt him out the door? Perhaps. But I suspect that the real fuel for this fire in the son's heart was a deep pride in wanting to be independent and in being selfish. Any of us can fall to these same temptations in a failing marriage. When a relationship breaks down, it is easy to think about ourselves first.

Obviously there was deep dissatisfaction and rebellion in the son's heart. The parable doesn't tell us what the talk between the father and son was like. As I thought about this, I remembered the 1967 movie *Guess Who's Coming to Dinner*. Remember the scene where Sidney Portier, playing a young black doctor wanting to marry a white woman, argued with his father about his marriage plans? In the movie, the father was arguing with the son against the marriage. He tried to shame his son by labeling his interracial wedding plans as criminal. Then he went to great lengths to say how hard he worked to provide for his son, and how he and his wife had denied themselves a better life to do it. After quietly listening to his father for awhile, the son finally burst forth with a magnificent defense of his independence from his father. He defiantly stated that he did not owe his father anything just because his father brought him into the world. Rather, his father owed him everything that could be done, just like the son will owe his own children. It was a powerful scene!

When this film first came out, I sat in the theater eating my popcorn and saying to myself, "That's it! Yeah! That's how it is! That's exactly how I feel!" I saw this as the root of my own conflict at that time with my father. So I memorized the dialogue, trotted home to my father, and blurted out all the son's script in the first person. You will know enough about his reaction if I tell you that forty years later, he has never forgotten that conversation!

The attitudes of both men in the movie are so typical of relationships in general. Father wants to control son. Son wants father to butt out. This same tension is found in many marriages. Like so many other tempting lies, it sounds good for someone to cry out that he has to be in control of his own life and move his own way. But too often the dark underbelly of it all is a hotbed of manipulation and control, rebellion and selfish independence. If any relationship fails to satisfy these needs, it must either be the way we want it to be or it gets axed! Is this not how many marriages end up on the chopping block as well?

I recall a very dear friend's account of how, as a young child, she once dealt with her mother. When told to do a chore, this little bundle of joy thrust her hands on her hips, puffed out her little chest, cocked her head, and said, "You're not the boss of me, Mommy!" How often we do the same things with our spouses—and with God! To the contrary, God, through Solomon, tells us, "Pride goes before destruction, a haughty spirit before a fall" (Prov. 16:18).

The son acted selfishly and severed his relationship with his father. Like the rich fool in Luke 12, the son may have said to himself, "You have plenty of good things laid up for many years. Take life easy; eat, drink and be merry" (Luke 12:19).

The result? The son diligently and slavishly chased after wild living and pleasures of this world. But in pursuing selfish gain and resisting his father's authority, he sold out his relationship with one who loved him more than anyone else.

The Bitter Fruit of Terminal Relationships

The son wanted "his share" of what the father owned. He did not care about anyone or anything else. In doing so, he lost his perspective about the important treasures in life. Think about it. When selfishness like this creeps into any partnership and is left unchecked, how long can the relationship survive? What are the consequences?

Losing one relationship usually means losing more. Notice that the son did not take off for a distant country right away. He waited around for a time (v. 13). Staying at home probably worked for a while, but it was not enough; the son eventually had to get away. He decided he would be happier elsewhere. After all, if we're going to hurt the ones who love us the most, we do not feel comfortable staying around them for very long. This is also why the hearts of some Christians grow so cold that they cannot face church fellowship. It is why spouses leave good, salvageable marriages. They must avoid the constant reminder that what they are doing may be wrong.

It is a fallacy to blame outward circumstances for inward problems. The son talked himself into believing that everyone and everything around him was the source of his own unhappiness. It was only logical that a change of scenery would naturally bring joy to his heart, right? Wrong.

Have you ever known folks who believe that where they live makes them miserable? They convince themselves that they have to get away to be happy. Sure enough, they move on and what happens? After the move, they're even more unhappy in a new city. Why? Because the source of true happiness is not in the externals of life—it's in the heart. This is why God encourages us to be content in most any situation (Phil. 4:11–12; 1 Tim. 6:8; Heb. 13:5). It is a *heart* problem—not a hearth problem!

Many marriage counselors, with the best of intentions, counsel spouses to "follow your heart." But Jeremiah 17:9 says that the heart is deceitful above all things to the point that no one can understand it. We can quickly rationalize and convince ourselves that everyone else has the problem. Our own unhappiness is always tied to our spouse, other people, and outward circumstances. We really believe that we know our hearts. God, of course, knows better. This fallacy can lead us down some dangerous roads.

We may convince ourselves that we are really in control of our lives. But we can be just like the housefly that lands on sticky flypaper. He struggles this way and that for a long while. But then, curiously, he hunkers down, looks slyly around as if to ward off others, and seems to shout, "*My* flypaper!" Do we really control our circumstances as much as we would like to think?

How God must wonder about our feeble lives and the deceptions we believe about ourselves—and yet He still loves us. That is good news!

We reap what we sow. This parable shows us what inevitably happens when a drunken, selfish spree melts into the sober light of reality (v. 14). There is famine and degeneration. It may not come quickly in every instance, but a time of reckoning comes for the decisions we make. Many choices have unavoidable consequences; the piper will be paid.

When famine came, the son began to be in need. In Hebrews 12, Paul reminds us that God disciplines those He loves. That discipline is not pleasant but painful. In the end, however, it produces a harvest of righteousness for those trained by it. Our sin follows through to its logical conclusion if repentance does not turn our hearts toward God first. Selfishness usually ends up wearing us out.

I learned this lesson as a young boy the summer I went to Athens YMCA Camp in the Georgia hills. For weeks, all new campers heard glorious stories about the famous ice cream factory on top of the mountain near the camp. "Boy, won't it be great to go up to the ice cream factory at the end of the camp?" one camp veteran would say with the greatest anticipation. Another would chime in, "Boy howdy, I can taste that cherry chocolate chip ice cream now!" Everyone got excited about the ice cream factory. "Ice cream factory! Ice cream factory!" we would all yell after dinner in the mess hall after a few weeks of this talk. It was going to be *the* event of the summer.

But there was a catch: the factory owners would dish out a camper's favorite flavor of ice cream in a weight equal to the rocks he brought up the mountain. The factory had *plenty* of ice cream for the little boys, and the owners received enough rocks to build an addition to the factory without paying hauling fees. Great bargain, right? Well, no one wanted to come up short at the ice cream factory. So, when the big day came, kids lined up everywhere with the biggest boulders you ever saw in your life!

Up the mountain we went. Then something strange happened. The weight of those rocks, light enough when we started, grew heavier and heavier. We felt like we were carrying the entire state of Georgia in our arms. Soon the pleasure of ice cream faded away. The stark reality was that we were hauling the Rock of Gibraltar up a steep mountain! We stopped laughing and singing our favorite hiking song, "Ice cream! Ice cream! We all scream for ice cream!" Now, more sullenly, we sang the Volga boatman song with the most tortuous "Yo-Heave-Ho!" chorus you ever heard. We began making calculations of how to pitch some rocks while keeping enough to exchange for at least *some* ice cream.

Something else was peculiar. All the camp veterans and counselors walking with us did not carry any rocks at all. How come? "Well," they told us, "the factory owners give us a break because we've helped them out in years past." Sounded reasonable so far. "By the way," they warned, "you have to carry all the rocks you started with all the way to the top or you don't get any ice cream at all!" *What was this?!?* We tried to bribe the counselors into allowing us to throw off some of the heavier rocks, but to no avail. So we tortuously dragged ourselves to the top of the hill and carried our rocks all the way. We didn't care about the ice cream factory anymore.

Even ice cream was losing its appeal. We just wanted to ditch those rocks!

In the end, as we looked around the hilltop, we did not see any ice cream factory. In fact, we didn't see anything at all except . . . a big pile of rocks. The counselors told us to throw our rocks on the pile, and they quietly taught us a lesson I will never forget.

In our selfish drive for personal pleasure, we can compromise and carry a load of sin that will burden us down just like that load of rocks. Ultimately, it is all worthless from a material standpoint while still costing us great personal pain. Those rocks, which probably still grow in number with each new summer camp session, are a picture of our own greed and self-indulgence. Then one of the counselors read Hebrews 12:1–3:

> Therefore, since we are surrounded by such a great cloud of witnesses, let us throw off everything that hinders and the sin that so easily entangles, and let us run with perseverance the race marked out for us. Let us fix our eyes on Jesus, the author and perfecter of our faith, who for the joy set before him endured the cross, scorning its shame, and sat down at the right hand of the throne of God. Consider him who endured such opposition from sinful men, so that you will not grow weary and lose heart.

What a lesson! There is more to life than filling ourselves up with personal pleasure. Too many of us pursue foolish pleasures like that. We cash in marriages for the chance to hike up that mountain. We think the grass is greener on top of the hill. But what do we find on the hilltop? Just a pile of rocks. Maybe then we will think back to the price we paid for the chance. We may remember how much we hurt those who loved us. Or maybe we will just forget everything, nurse our wounds, and move on to another hill. In the end, however, we always reap what we sow.

False friends bail out when the party is over. Notice the son's predicament while away from home (v. 15–16). If you want to know what real slavery is, try indenturing yourself to the world. It will love you as its own as long as you are attractive, smart, wealthy, or move in the right social circles. But if you lose those assets, loneliness comes in a flash. How quickly friends disappear when times get tough and you are on your own!

Unnatural Acts
Unconditional Love and Letting Go

How did the father in the parable react to the son's leaving home? Was it wise for the father to give his son the inheritance early when he knew his son would probably blow it? The father—who is a picture of how God relates to us—gave the son what he asked for even though he neither earned it nor deserved it. This mirrors so much of the beautifully gracious nature of God, yet we stop short of using this same spirit of grace with our spouses. "God can be gracious, but don't ask me to do that with my mate after all I've been through!" we murmur. Somehow we can applaud God's mercy and forgiveness, but we want those who have hurt *us* to pay.

Did you also notice what the father did after his son left and then lost everything? Nothing! If the father knew where the son was, do you think he should have gone out to rescue him? It is difficult to say no to this question. After all, if your loved one ran away but was starving and suffering, would you ignore it? Yet that is just what the father did! He might have received reports about his son from merchants traveling through, but he stayed at home—no wire of emergency money, no rushing to his son's side with credit cards in hand. He let the son stew in his own soup! This was not cruel; it is part of God's grace. It was just what the son needed to come to his senses. He was given the freedom to make his own choices—and to face the consequences of those choices with or without the father.

When our spouses leave to go their own way, times of need may arise. If we love them, we really have to fight against rushing to their aid. They chose to leave. We cannot shield them from their own decisions; codependency strangles relationships. Protecting others from themselves does no one any good. Like the father in the parable, we have to love them from a distance for their own good.

Letting go while still loving those who leave a relationship—that is radical love. The father's actions do not come naturally to us; they cut against the grain. But this parable illustrates how the essence of unconditional love is in still loving the sinner while hating the sin. It is not natural for us to do this. But it is a very godly action.

If we want to do what ought not to be done, God will give us over to our sinful desires (Rom. 1:21–32). He will let us go! Although it breaks His heart, God loves us enough to allow us to ignore Him and follow our own desires. But we must bear the consequences of our actions, and those can be costly indeed! Letting go is tough to do when you know that those you love the most are going to hurt themselves as they hurt you, but that is a scriptural response. If God does this with all humankind, we should not treat our spouses any differently.

Release
The Healing Power of Repentance and Forgiveness

Why is forgiveness so difficult? Because it is so unnatural for us to do. We live in a world founded on the principle of rewards and punishments. If we perform well, we are rewarded. If we fail, we are punished. Restoration requires a "payback." After all, restitution is what the law requires. But God doesn't always require the scales of legal justice to balance.[2] As Dr. James Dobson so succinctly states many times on his national radio program, "Forgiveness is giving up my right to hurt you for hurting me." That isn't natural for us—it actually bothers us—but it is the gracious way of God.

What does it really mean to forgive someone? It means to "remember no more." It does not mean to "forgive and forget." There is a difference. If we really could forget life events, then we would never learn from our mistakes. We would lose some precious memories as well.

The essence of responsible biblical forgiveness is threefold:

1) *To release bitterness and resentment* that is self-destructive.

2) *To focus our anger* toward motivating repentance in those who have wronged us for their benefit.

3) *To offer to restore and reconcile* broken relationships whenever possible, even if others will not repent and accept it. If the person we forgive repents and desires reconciliation, then we should restore the relationship promptly if reasonably possible (Luke 17:3b–4).

Biblical forgiveness encourages repentance from sin by offering the best incentives to restore fractured relationships. And we should desire to forgive our former spouses because God has forgiven us. That is what the parable of the unmerciful servant is all about (Matt. 18:21–35). Forgiveness is not sacrificed even though the scales are still imbalanced. Forgiveness accepts a score that may never come out even.

Forgiveness blesses others through our personal pain. A little boy defined forgiveness this way: "It is like the odor that flowers give off when you step all over 'em." I like that. Consider Jesus hanging in agony on the cross saying, "Father, forgive them for they do not know what they are doing!" (Luke 23:34). He thought of those spitting and cursing accusers at the foot of the cross more than His own pain and anguish. To me, that's incredible! If I hung on that cross, between moaning and complaining about all the pain I was in, I would find a moment to look at that crowd and yell, "Father, pulverize them for they know exactly what they're doing!" But that is not God's way. We should strive to see life His way, not ours.

Since forgiveness is not natural for us, some time may be needed to let it well up within us. Divorce can be very hurtful. Some describe the experience as if their spouses had murdered one of their children. So let it come from your heart when you are able to feel good about it, but let it come without delay. Do not use time as an excuse not to forgive.

Forgiveness of our spouses is for our benefit. Isn't this a bit presumptuous, especially if a spouse who has left for good never returns? It is true that our spouses may never come back home like the prodigal son, but the attitude in our hearts is critical. Forgiveness frees us from the spiritual bondage of hatred, resentment, and a desire for revenge. We need this release to move on with our lives.

We may think forgiveness is our gracious act toward those who hurt us. We may think it is for their benefit. Not so! Forgiveness is primarily for our good. It allows us to lay down a relationship gently and move on. Otherwise we chain ourselves into living in the past. Experiencing release of our resentments through forgiveness allows us to pick up the pieces of our lives and start over without requiring that others suffer for our satisfaction. After all, Christ already paid that price.

Our spouses also need forgiveness. Forgiveness is a two-way street. The son needed forgiveness as much as the father needed to give forgiveness (vv. 18–20). Both needed to experience release. There is no way to deal with that guilt and live joyfully without it.

There is a story in Spain of a son who ran away from his estranged father. The father searched him out for months without success. In desperation, the father placed an advertisement in a Madrid newspaper. The ad read: "Dear Paco, meet me in front of this newspaper office at noon on Saturday. All is forgiven. I love you, your father." That Saturday, eight hundred Pacos showed up yearning for forgiveness from their fathers.[3]

Compassion and mercy smooth out the rough road leading home. Forgiveness is an invitation, not a threat. It is a sweet aroma beckoning those who fracture a relationship to be peacefully restored.

Forgiveness accepts repentance without judging reasons. Before returning home, the son came to his senses after hitting rock bottom (v. 17). Maybe it was homesickness. He may have felt guilty about what he had done. Certainly he felt sorry for himself; maybe he also felt sorry for his father. Did he realize that he had made a stupid mistake? Was it because all his friends had abandoned him? What role did his empty wallet play in his decision? Could it have been the humiliation of being enslaved? All of these could be true. But the real reason highlighted by the story is that a very hungry young Jewish boy was fed up with fighting pigs for food! If you had been the father in this parable, would this reason be good enough for you to welcome the son home?

What was the father's attitude and reaction when the son did return (vv. 20–24)? He could have told the son to hit the road again. He could have said, "Come in, after you've wiped off your dirty feet, but you're grounded for eternity!" He could have laid a guilt trip on the son about how much he had disgraced the family, but he didn't. In every way the father's attitude was, "Welcome home, son. I've missed you so much!" Even more than that, the father ran down the road to greet the son as if he had been looking for him to come back! The father was *eager*, not reluctant, to forgive. It poured over into his actions. He didn't wait for his son to explain his repentance. He just loved him unconditionally.

The point here is this: Sometimes we expect our spouses to come to repentance for rational reasons. We demand that they fully realize their part in killing our marriages. We want to hear our spouses admit that we are the saints and they are the skunks. But genuine forgiveness does not work that way. Jesus tells us, "If your brother sins, rebuke him, and if he repents, forgive him. If he sins against you seven times in a day, and seven times comes back to you and says, 'I repent,' forgive him" (Luke 17:3b–4). Now that's tough to do! Even the apostles thought so as they said to Jesus, "Increase our faith!" (Luke 17:5). And that's exactly what it takes—great faith!

As we let our spouses go, we also must leave room for repentance. But God's way is *active*, not passive forgiveness toward those who have wronged us. If those who have done us wrong truly come to their senses, we should be glad they are home. After all, it is not easy coming back to say, "I'm sorry." Checking out all the details of repentance can come later.

Let their hearts speak and their actions show us the fruit of their repentance. Unconditional love accepts this response. It does not insist upon its own way. We must be ready to love them when they stand in our doorway, even if it is too late to save the marriage.

Forgiveness leads to restoration of a broken relationship. Was it wise for the father to kill the fatted calf and celebrate when his son came home? How about the ring, robe, and sandals (which symbolize restoration to sonship, honor, authority in the house, and freedom)? When the father saw the son's repentant attitude, he made no conditions. He just gave and gave! The son who was lost and dead to the father was now found and alive—that was all that mattered to the father. The son could have died in that foreign land, separated from his father and out of relationship with him. But the son repented and came back home. The father was ready to restore the relationship because forgiveness reigned in his heart.

If your spouse comes home and wants to start over, what will you do? What conditions will you set down?[4] Having the father's attitude of unconditional love and forgiveness guides us toward making right decisions.

Failure to forgive distorts our vision and burns our bridges. There is more to this parable in showing us how to deal with cold hearts (vv. 25–32). Notice that *both* sons were away from home—in heart if not physically. Both sons had broken relationships with their father. Some have even described the older son as the *real* prodigal son. Ironically, the older son's relationship with his father broke down as his brother was being restored.

The father left the house to go out to the older son. He beckoned him to come inside for the celebration of his brother's return. There was reason for joy, but the older son wanted his brother to pay. In pride and jealousy, the older son isolated himself from the reunion so he could remain bitter and angry at feeling shortchanged. The father pleaded, "Everything is yours!" But that was not good enough for the older son. "This is totally unfair," the older son might have replied. "It just proves that working hard and doing the right thing instead of leaving home isn't worth it. This son of yours has gone off and blown his inheritance. Don't expect me to forgive him for what he has done!"

How the father must have ached inside as he heard the older son bellow about his brother! Without forgiveness, bitterness was eating away at the older son's heart. It kept him away from home.

"For if you forgive men when they sin against you, your heavenly Father will also forgive you. But if you do not forgive men their sins, your

Father will not forgive your sins" (Matt. 6:14–15). The older son was losing what his younger brother was gaining by having an unforgiving attitude. As Christian apologist Josh McDowell has so cogently remarked, "The failure to forgive burns the bridge over which you must someday travel!" How true that really is!

What is the message of this parable? How does it relate to how we treat our spouses in a divorce situation? It reminds us that we need a constant attitude of forgiveness. We need to let our spouses go, if that is what they really want. As they go, we need to release our anger, bitterness, and resentment by soothing our hearts with forgiveness. This brings closure to a failed relationship and helps us to move on to new relationships. The bottom line is this: failure is not fatal unless we fail to forgive.

A Personal Quest For a Forgiving Heart

As I wrote the journal entry excerpted at the beginning of this chapter, I wondered how I could specifically apply the love of the father in the parable to my situation. How could I practically convey this type of love to my wife as she was leaving me?

First, I let her go. That is what she wanted. If I had tried to stop her against her will, it would have been wrong. She would have been like a caged bird looking for the next opportunity to escape. It was her choice to leave. As much as it grieved me to see her go, I respected her freedom.

Next, I tried to show her that our relationship still meant something to me. I asked myself, "Should I wait on her to return for years to come?" After all, the Bible does have something to say about remarriage if a Christian spouse leaves. How can I let my wife know that I have forgiven her and am ready to accept her, but that I need to move on with my life too? What is reasonable?

I believe it is unhealthy to remain alone and wait forever on the return of a departed spouse. This is especially true if there are scriptural reasons for divorce. God calls us to live in peace. But in love, I wanted to make a personal commitment to my wife in addition to our marriage vows. I verbally pledged to her that I would not become romantically involved with anyone else for two years, even if the Lord allowed me to remarry. This would assure her that she had time to see if she made the right decision in leaving the marriage. In my situation, this outwardly confirmed my renewed commitment to our marriage before God for a reasonable period of time. Some would view this commitment as an unwarranted personal cost. Why give up two years of one's life to a spouse who has broken the original marriage vows? But I believe this was one way to express unconditional love and concern to my wife without making any demands upon her to love me back. This is not a rigid rule for others to follow. It is simply one way I wanted to express love to my wife. When the time came to share this matter directly with my wife during a counseling session, my heart was racing. I felt anxious. I took a quick moment for some deep breaths and silently asked for God's help to speak lovingly. This is what I shared:

> Honey, you know I love you with all my heart. I love you more than any other person on the face of this earth. I would marry you again if I had the opportunity. That's how much I love you.
>
> I believe we need more time before any decisions are made about our marriage. But this is not to take away from your decision and your feelings that you want to seek a divorce now. If that is what you want, then I will accept it.
>
> I have spent a lot of time reading Scripture on this matter and asking God for guidance. It is clear to me that seeking a divorce is wrong and not approved by God. I feel that you are breaking faith with me in our marriage. When God says, "I hate divorce," as He does in Malachi 2, I believe that you are also breaking faith with God. I am really wrestling with all this because it is so serious. I don't say this to make you feel guilty. I say it only because I sincerely believe it to be true. But you can read the Bible for yourself and make your own decision.
>
> I know that you will do what you want to do. I cannot control your decisions or your life, nor do I want to. Forcing you to do anything against your will would not be good for you or me. I can only try to control my own life and seek God as best I can.
>
> Having said all that, I want you to know that I am not in denial about our situation or your wanting a divorce. I have heard you clearly. But I want to make an additional commitment to you here and now. I want to commit to

you that for two years, and regardless of whatever actions you take, I will not make a personal commitment to any other woman. Should you find that you have made a mistake or regret this decision and decide that you want to come home, the door will be open to you for this two-year period. I know that you may never come back. God only knows what will happen. But I'm willing to make this pledge to you because of my love for you and for the Lord. The only caveat to this covenant is if waiting any longer would clearly be fruitless due to the circumstances. I'm making this commitment to you now without expecting anything in return from you.

That is a day in the life of two people going through a divorce. You may disagree with what I did or said on that day. But it was my effort to try and follow the example of the father from the parable of the prodigal son. It was an attempt to put unconditional love to work in my difficult situation. You may handle your circumstances differently. But the message sent to our spouses should be that our love is complete and not conditional upon their actions—or reactions—to whatever we do.

Think about your own situation. Have you shared the same love of the father with your spouse—even if your situation is hopeless? If so, even if nothing else happens, you will find a comforting peace from God flowing into you that will really bless your life. This humility and vulnerability will open your heart to God. It will reinforce your decisions in many other areas as you deal with the problems of separation or divorce. It will allow God to speak to you about areas in your life that need to change.

Questions for Personal Reflection

1) How do I feel about my spouse right now? How do I feel about myself?
2) Am I experiencing freedom from anger and resentment?
3) Have I let go of my spouse?
4) Do I have an attitude of forgiveness which does not depend on whatever my spouse does?
5) What are some practical ways I can show unconditional love and forgiveness to my spouse?

Part Two

What Does the Bible Really Say about Divorce?

"Haven't you read," he replied, "that at the beginning
the Creator 'made them male and female,' and said, 'For
this reason a man will leave his father and mother and be
united to his wife, and the two will become one flesh'?
So they are no longer two, but one. Therefore, what
God has joined together, let man not separate."
Matthew 19:4–6

"I hate divorce," says the Lord God of Israel, . . . So guard
yourself in your spirit, and do not break faith.
Malachi 2:16

During the reign of King Josiah, the Lord said to me,
"Have you seen what faithless Israel has done? She has
gone up on every high hill and under every spreading
tree and has committed adultery there. I thought that
after she had done all this she would return to me but
she did not, and her unfaithful sister Judah saw it.
I gave faithless Israel her certificate of divorce and
sent her away because of all her adulteries."
Jeremiah 3:6–8

God has called us to live in peace. . . . For God is not a
God of disorder but of peace.
1 Corinthians 7:15; 14:33

If you are facing divorce, you may want to know what God has to say about it. You may also want to know your spiritual options during and after the divorce.

I read a book on divorce and remarriage recently with an attractive title about God's renewing grace. It spoke beautifully of honoring grace above the letter of the law, redemption above condemnation, and renewal above prohibitions and restrictions on our freedom in Christ. But then the authors suggested we should de-emphasize what the Bible says, and instead apply our own concept of God's grace to our own circumstances. It sounds good to a point, but do we not run the risk of leaving God on the sidelines? We should not be legalistic about Scripture. But why disobey God's clear commands?

We know how society today feels about divorce. If you want out of a marriage, no problem! But look at the fruit of this poisonous tree: shattered families, economic chaos, ruptured personal lives, and children scarred for life. There has to be a better way.

What does God say? Is divorce absolutely prohibited? Was man made for marriage, or was marriage made for man? What is meant by a husband and wife becoming "one flesh"? How does adultery affect a divorce decision? Who is free to remarry after a divorce? In this part of the book, we will learn how God views marriage and divorce—even from His view as One rejected by His people. Next, we will review what Jesus taught about the subject, including His exceptions permitting divorce and remarriage. Then we will consider the apostle Paul's comments on the teachings of Jesus. Finally, since biblical interpretations differ as to divorce and remarriage, we will examine some alternative viewpoints to which reasonable men and women might disagree. I will also share some personal conclusions drawn from everything reviewed in this section.

If you are tempted to skip over this part because you think you know what God says, let me urge you to reconsider. This material may surprise you. You will learn something you did not know about divorce and remarriage. Be wise. Have your Bible in hand and take the time to read through these chapters before moving on to Part Three. The issues discussed could be a matter of spiritual life or death for you and your spouse. It will help you put everything else in this book into a godly perspective.

CHAPTER 4

God's Marriage Foundation

*Many of us have ignored God's plan for marriage from the
beginning of time. We need to go back to the basics. What
does the Old Testament tell us about God's original design
for marriage as part of creation? Does it provide for divorce?*

As a young law student in 1976 who had rejected organized religion
for many years, I decided to give church attendance one more chance.
Quite frankly, many issues disturbed me—hypocrisy, boring services,
church cliques, and the constant plea for money.

But I really felt a need to be in church. I had just enough of a religious
upbringing to know I should be there. Even so, I was not ready to be a
regular churchgoer. My plan was to visit a local congregation during my
last year of law school. My goals were (in this order) to find a nice Christian
girl to date and marry, and to get closer to God. Many of the men in
the congregation I visited just quietly smiled when I confessed my mission.
"Better seek a relationship with God first, Warren," they told me. "The
women here deeply commit themselves to Christ. They wouldn't think of
dating someone who did not share their same love for God."

It struck a nerve. Looking back, I now see how foolishly out of kilter
my priorities were. Fortunately, loving men and women of God dealt gently
with me. They encouraged me to read the Bible for the first time and
really focus on what it said to me personally.

In any event, as I attended services over the coming months I distinctly
recall the preacher making a stunning claim. "There's nothing more
beautiful than a Christian wedding, when a brother and sister in Christ
unite in the presence of God and their Christian family. But the key is marrying
God's way. I've had the privilege of counseling and presiding over
marriages of hundreds of couples through the years, *and not one has ended
in divorce!* Let God's record stand against that of the world."

Some might think that this preacher had a special pipeline to God.
But the real power of this preacher's claim was in the message—not in the
messenger. How did God do this wonderful work of love in the marriages
of common people when so many others failed? What motivated these

Christians to stay together when problems inevitably plagued their marriages? Why did they struggle on if it was easier to bail out?

God makes the key difference in a Christian marriage. So before we explore how God feels about divorce, we need to appreciate His unique concept of the marriage relationship.

What Is Marriage Anyway?

Why even ask this question when divorce is stalking our marriages? But whenever problems arise, it is always healthy to ask, "Where did I go wrong?" Did we ever really understand God's view of marriage? Too often we learn through trial and error. We bring such romantic ideas and preconceptions into the relationship that it is difficult to keep a proper focus.

Keeping God's marriage plan in perspective is critical to understanding the Scriptures. Remember this key point from Part One? "Never lose sight of the big picture." That's good advice. We get bogged down with minutia. We chase off on tangents and reach too many wrong conclusions. We forget our primary goals.

What is the true foundation of any marriage relationship? Dictionaries blandly define marriage as the social institution under which a man and a woman show their decision to live as husband and wife by legal commitments and religious ceremonies. But God's definition roots itself in the creation and the original union of Adam and Eve. If we do not understand the foundational aspects of marriage, we distort our view of divorce and remarriage and make it unrealistic. So let's begin by looking at God's original blueprint for the relationship between man and woman.

> Then God said, "Let us make man in our image, in our likeness, and let them rule over the fish of the sea and the birds of the air, over the livestock, over all the earth, and over all the creatures that move along the ground." So God created man in his own image, in the image of God he created him; male and female he created them (Gen. 1:26–27).
>
> The Lord God took the man and put him in the Garden of Eden to work it and take care of it. And the Lord God commanded the man, "You are free to eat from any tree in the garden; but you must not eat from the tree of

the knowledge of good and evil, for when you eat of it you will surely die." The Lord God said, 'It is not good for the man to be alone. I will make a helper suitable for him ...'"

So the Lord God caused the man to fall into a deep sleep; and while he was sleeping, He took one of the man's ribs and closed up the place with flesh. Then the Lord God made a woman from the rib He had taken out of the man, and He brought her to the man. The man said, "This is now bone of my bones and flesh of my flesh; she shall be called 'woman,' for she was taken out of man." For this reason a man will leave his father and mother and be united to his wife, and they will become one flesh (Gen. 2:15–18, 21–24).

Jesus Christ commented on these verses this way:

> "Haven't you read," he replied, "that at the beginning the Creator 'made them male and female,' and said, 'For this reason a man will leave his father and mother and be united to his wife, and the two will become one flesh'? So they are no longer two, but one. Therefore what God has joined together, let man not separate" (Matt. 19:4–6).

God created man and woman as complementary and necessary beings for each other—equally yoked partners. In the beginning Adam and Eve were God's total creation of mankind, one husband for one wife. Jesus reminds us that God's plan from the beginning was that the "two become one." If two become one, how can that be split apart? Can we split our physical bodies in half and survive? Splitting a single unit of anything destroys the whole. This union is God's creation plan for marriage.

What does it mean to "become one"? From God's perspective, a marriage means "leaving" parents and family, and "cleaving" to a spouse in starting a new home. They become "one flesh," not only physically through consummation of the marriage but with a total commitment to each other. God is not only a witness but actually a participant in joining the two together into one—the ultimate interdependent relationship. This original plan of God, first expressed in Genesis 2:24, is what Jesus refers to.

"To leave" (Hebrew, azab) means to forsake, leave behind, and depart

63

from, in the sense of letting go or setting loose. It describes a change in one's devotion and loyalty from one person to another. It does not mean abandonment of parents; sons and daughters are to always honor them (Ex. 20:12; Mark 7:6–13; 1 Tim. 5:3–4). It simply means that one's role as a child in the parent's home changes to that of being a husband or wife in his or her own home.

"To cleave" (Hebrew, *dabaq*) means to cling onto, keep close by, or to stick to someone as if glued together. Husband and wife join in the closest union spiritually and physically possible between two human beings. More than a physical sexual relationship, more than love among close friends, wholehearted commitment and sacrificial submission to each other transcends changes in emotions and feelings. It is a covenant for the lifetime of the man and woman so joined.

After leaving and cleaving, God did not say that the two become "one team" or "one mind" or "one goal," but "one flesh." It is the most intimate of relationships on earth, far greater than with father, mother, and others. The Hebrew word for "one flesh" is almost inadequate to express God's meaning fully. God supplies the glue and cements husband and wife together. There is nothing else on earth that quite matches this special union.

Is Marriage a Sacrament?

There is absolutely nothing in the Bible about God-ordained marriage ceremonies with ministers officiating. People through the ages have felt the need to express the importance of the marriage relationship in a visual way with ceremonies and rings, but God's Word doesn't require it.

Ceremonial aspects of marriage have led to much confusion and misunderstanding of God's plan. Some religious leaders have viewed marriage as a "sacrament,"[1] or a holy union. God seals His grace in salvation with those receiving such a sacrament by outwardly visible signs (like marriage ceremonies). It assumes that marriage is indissoluble and that only God can make or break it. But is this biblical?[2]

Problems arose over the years with the sacramental view of marriage. To protect what some perceived to be a sacred, indissoluble relationship, the church became more involved in decisions to marry. This tragically led some church leaders throughout history to forbid others to marry at all, despite the warnings in 1 Timothy 4:1–3.

Contrary to the sacramental view of marriage, as we shall see, God made marriage to serve, not enslave partners. God looks on the hearts of husbands and wives. The covenant-love vows of fidelity, unity, and trust they make to each other mean more than outward ceremonial circumstance.

Is Marriage Part of God's Plan for Men and Women?

Why did God create humans after His own likeness in male and female forms? Why did He make men and women different? Did God intend that marriage be a vital part of human life, or was it merely an afterthought to fill a basic need? Let's look again at God's creation plan.

Humans are different from other male and female creations. While all experience hunger, sexual desires, and the need for self-preservation, God created humans unique—in His image. Unlike animals, humans have minds to receive knowledge and to reason from it. Men and women can create, think, make plans, and exercise judgment to make free choices, carry out decisions, and use self-discipline. Humans can receive revelation about God's nature and comprehend spiritual knowledge. He created us to glorify Him.

Men and women need companionship. In surveying His creation, God graciously considered Adam's personal welfare. He saw it was not good for him to be alone. He created Adam with a need for fellowship with another being like himself. All of us have an inward, God-given motivation for self-expression, self-development, and self-fulfillment that revolves around marriage and family. Therefore God made Eve, a helper suitable for Adam, to finish His creation.

Men and women are creative beings. God gave us the ultimate joy and self-fulfillment of creating other creatures like ourselves. He began by giving Adam and Eve a sexual urge and compatible body parts. He commanded them to "be fruitful and multiply" (Gen. 1:28, NASB). Male and female bodies are visual examples of their need for interdependence. Unlike some lower forms of creation, we are not asexual reproducers. By our very nature, only a man and woman can come together to produce another human. God has authorized this sexual union and reproduction only within marriage. This type of procreation is good and honorable; in fact, it is even commanded (1 Cor. 7:3–5; Heb. 13:4).

God's plan for men and women is to form a permanent "one flesh" family relationship. For those choosing to marry, God's will is for them to leave their parents and join themselves to another of the opposite sex in a new, unified family unit. This special relationship is not just an evolutionary process as the marriage partners grow and mature in their love for each other. It is a change of state; two become one. Marriage is a unity of body, mind, and spirit! A covenant arises between husband and wife before God (Prov. 2:17; Mal. 2:14). Each makes a vow or promise to the other in the presence of God. God intends for spouses to honor their vows—even when it hurts (Num. 30:2; Eccles. 5:4–6; Ps. 15:4). He clearly wants husband and wife to remain in the "one flesh" relationship. His will is that the marriage last until the death of one spouse.

Why is this "one flesh" relationship commitment so important to God? One reason is to care for our children. While marriages do not need children, children do need marriages. God created most animals to procreate indiscriminately. Their offspring are born with instinct to know how to live without marriage or any teaching. God's plan for mankind is different. Newborn humans do not instinctively walk to food and shelter; husband and wife must guide and direct them. Children also need the nurture and admonition of the Lord (Eph. 6:4). They need a stable home environment with a mother and father actively parenting them to grow up and mature with a minimum of complications. This family bond then continues in later years as children take care of their elderly parents.

God's plan for marriage is heterosexual monogamy. One man for one woman for life is God's plan. He did not make two Eves for Adam, or vice versa. He did not clone Adam or Eve—all human life begins with this couple. God gives each of us the right to choose a spouse (1 Cor. 7:2). He had the power to do otherwise, but His plan for marriage was monogamy. How can a man be of "one flesh" in a marriage relationship with many wives? Even so, polygamy arose. Genesis 4:19 tells us that Lamech took two wives. Samuel's father, Elkanah, had two wives also (1 Sam. 1:2). Deuteronomy 17:17 forbade the king from taking "many wives," warning that if he did, his heart could grow cold. Nevertheless, David and Solomon took many wives and concubines (1 Sam. 27:3; 1 Kings 11:1–3).

Did God change His mind about monogamous marriages? No, in His graciousness God allowed man free moral choice to do what ought not to be done—with the inevitable consequences (Rom. 1:18–32). God overlooked hard-hearted ignorance of His commands for a time before calling everyone to repentance (Acts 17:30; Matt. 19:8). Monogamy was God's original plan for marriage. As Jesus restored this plan, the Christian church no longer condoned polygamy. (See for example, 1 Tim. 3:2, 12, 5:9–10; Titus 1:6.)

Marriage was made for humankind, not humankind for marriage. Throughout history, God provides for our welfare with compassion. Redemptive grace bridges the gap in our inevitable failings to fulfill God's ideal. God designed marriage to meet the needs of husbands and wives and to protect His creation; He knew they needed to help each other in raising a family. The purpose of marriage is God's merciful provision for our weaknesses—not to perpetuate marriage as an independent institution.

Marriage is for those who choose to be married. God does not require marriage for everyone. After all, it is an awesome responsibility. He lovingly gives us free moral choice to decide. He warns against any other person forbidding you to marry if you are scripturally free to do so (1 Tim. 4:1–5). But to make marriage appealing, God also created us with a desire for an intimate, personal relationship with others. As a marriage blessing, He made it pleasurable for husbands and wives to enjoy a sexual union and to reproduce. The only condition is that if we marry, we must obey His will.

How God's Plan for Marriage Was Frustrated

From the account of Genesis 3, problems arose in paradise. Everything that was right started to go wrong with Adam and Eve. The serpent deceived Eve into violating God's command against eating the forbidden fruit of the tree of knowledge of good and evil. Adam also ignored God's command and took the fruit from Eve. Believing the serpent's lies, husband and wife were not content with what God had provided them. They wanted more—a bigger thrill, perhaps a mountaintop experience. So they tripped into the serpent's trap by falling for the oldest, most difficult temptation known to humankind—they wanted equality with God. And so this sinful rebellion began a sad journey of tears and heartbreak for all of us, who likewise sinned against God in the centuries that followed.

After knowing no shame, Adam and Eve opened their eyes to guilt and shame without limit through their disobedience. They hid from God. Adam even blamed God for giving him the woman in the first place. Then he blamed Eve for giving him the fruit. Eve blamed the serpent for deceiving her, though she completely understood God's command. Each was desperately looking to throw the guilt onto someone else. Adam and Eve's relationship with God and with each other fell apart.

When Adam and Eve disobeyed, death came into the world as God had promised. This spiritual death reigned from generation to generation until Christ paid the penalty for sin in full with His own death on the cross in our place (Rom. 5:12–21). Banished from the beautiful garden, Adam and Eve faced pain and hard labor for the rest of their lives.

After this fall of man in the garden, pride and selfishness gripped people's hearts. Crime, injustice, and war escalated our inhumanity toward each other. Men and women quickly rebelled against God by marrying and divorcing indiscriminately. God's beautiful plan for a man and a woman intimately uniting in marriage quickly became a distorted horror for many people. Seeing that the hard-heartedness of humankind was destroying them, in grace God permitted—not commanded—divorce to occur for a time.

Understanding God's Grace in the Old Testament

To understand God's graciousness throughout the Old Testament, there are a few principles we need to keep in proper perspective:

First, we must let God tell us through His Word how He sees our situation and what He asks of us. We cannot stress rules and laws if it nullifies God's grace. But we must not emphasize God's compassion and mercy to such an extent that "anything goes" with conclusions that contradict Scripture.

Second, we must understand how Scripture confirms God's grace. Scripture and God's grace complement each other much like our skeletal frame supports our flesh body. We use Scripture as a uniform framework to give our lives substance, shape, and form as He intended. God's grace then builds on this framework in uniquely beautiful ways for each one of us as He guides us into *His* way of life. With God's help, we use Scripture to make choices and decisions in Christ. Then we mature spiritually and reflect the glory of God in different ways, making it attractive to others. But every part of Scripture immerses itself in God's redemptive grace, and every part of God's grace supports the truth of His Word.

Third, we must appreciate how God responds to our needs. Although His principles of life do not change, God deals with each of us differently over time as we learn more about Him and ourselves. We do not treat children like adults, nor do we treat adults like children. God lovingly deals with us the same way. God meets us where we are, when we are there!

Fourth, we must understand the limited purpose of the law of Moses.

The law of Moses is rooted in the covenant that God first made with Israel in the form of the Ten Commandments (Ex. 20:1–17; Deut. 5:1–22). This covenant was made through Moses as the mediator at Horeb after God delivered the Israelites from Egypt (Deut. 5:2; 1 Kings 8:9). But centuries before Christ, God decreed that He would make a "new covenant" with all those who believe in Jesus. As mediator of this new covenant, Christ fulfilled the purpose of the first covenant given through Moses.

God gave the "old covenant," which embraces the law of Moses, to make people aware of sin and to tell them that sin's penalty is death. It prepared us to receive the good news by leading us to Christ (Gal. 3:1–4:7). The "letter" of the old covenant "kills" by cutting us off from God as we fail to keep the whole law (Gal. 3:10). We desperately need forgiveness. The good news is that God did not leave us powerless. Christ nailed to the cross the old covenant that condemned us (Col. 2:13–15). The new covenant of grace and forgiveness, written by the Spirit, frees us from the law of sin and death arising from the old covenant (Rom. 8:2).

Fifth, we serve an awesome and incredibly powerful God. Our disobedience does not limit God in any way. He has more than enough power to make us do whatever He desires. But He does not. His plan graciously allows us to make our own choices. Incredibly, God gives us the opportunity to tell Him "no" and to face the inevitable consequences of our decisions.

Finally, God absolutely rejects heartless legalism. Legalism involves coldly going through the motions of outward obedience to God's commands. It is having a form of godliness but denying its power. Since the law of Moses consisted of rules and regulations, it invited legalistic compliance. But God's purpose is to continually lead us to Christ (Gal. 3:24; Heb. 8–10). He earnestly searches for those who devote their *hearts* to Him (2 Chron. 16:9; Matt. 22:34–40).

God's Word is not a dead letter—it is living and active! (Heb. 4:12). We should obey God's Word, not legalistically because we have to, but because in every way we love God and want to please Him. Our lives and hearts are in step with the Spirit through the guidance of Scripture (Gal. 5:25). When we ignore His Word and run ahead on our own without keeping in step with the Spirit, we may leave God behind—a tragic consequence indeed (2 John 4–11). The Old Testament law of Moses is consistent with God's grace because it always points us to Jesus, the epitome of grace and truth. In this chapter, and in the ones to follow in this part of the book, we will see how consistent God's grace is in marriage and divorce.

What the Old Testament Says About Divorce

We have seen how God's original plan for marriage was for one husband to leave his parents and cleave to one wife in a one-flesh relationship for life. Nevertheless, men and women quickly ignored God's desires.

Divorce and remarriage to others became routine and frequent. God permitted this to occur because people had hardened their hearts. As He acted through Jesus to call all people to repentance about marriage and divorce, God still extended His grace and mercy to all transgressors.

With these principles in mind, this is what the Old Testament tells us about divorce:

Permission to Divorce under the Law of Moses

Not many years after the fall of man in the garden, "quickie divorces" became common. A husband simply told his wife, "You are no longer my wife," and gave her a certificate of divorce.[3] The divorced wife had to leave home without entitlement to her husband's property.

Moses acted to regulate the aftermath of divorce among the Israelites by including Deuteronomy 24:1–4 in the law. Some believe this Scripture shows God's implicit approval of divorce. In context, however, it appears to address only remarriage after a divorce and intervening marriage. Verses 1–3 assume, but may not endorse, various conditions that have occurred. If so, the only command from God is in verse 4. In that verse only, God prohibits any remarriage of a man to his former wife after the wife remarries someone else.

Many disagree about the meaning of "something indecent" in Deuteronomy 24:1. The Hebrew words *erwat dabar* literally mean "nakedness of a thing" or a "naked matter." Some believe it means infertility or other physical deficiency. Others argue that it refers to a shameful or repulsive act (like that referred to in Deuteronomy 23:13). Whatever the meaning, it probably does not refer to adultery because the law commanded death, not divorce, for an adulterer (Lev. 20:10; Deut. 22:22–24).

God does prohibit remarriage to the former spouse; the second marriage rendered the wife "defiled"[4] (v. 4). Any such remarriage was "detestable in the eyes of the Lord." We can only guess at the reasons why this was true. The law of Moses does not tell us. We only know that any remarriage by a wife to her former husband after an intervening marriage is detestable to God. The larger question is whether this circumstance continues to be detestable to God under the new covenant instituted by Christ.[5]

As we shall see in the next chapter, Jesus Christ and the Pharisees indirectly address this Scripture in Matthew 19:1–12. Jesus acknowledged that God permitted divorce to occur under Mosaic law because of hardened hearts. It was futile to ask for obedience from those whose hearts were cold, hateful, stubborn, rebellious, and without spiritual perception. But Jesus quickly added that God never abandoned His original plan for marriage of one husband for one wife in a one-flesh relationship for life.

God Hates Divorce That Leads to Marriage outside the Faith

God sent His prophet Malachi to give a stern message to the people of Judah. They had fallen into hypocrisy and curtailed their giving (Mal. 2:17; 3:7–9). They had divorced their older Jewish wives in order to marry younger, more attractive, but unbelieving Gentile women. The law of Moses prohibited such marriages with unbelievers to protect God's people from idolatry (Ex. 34:14–16; Deut. 7:1–4). Nevertheless, some Jews ignored their heritage and relationship with God to race selfishly after "daughters of a foreign god."

In Malachi 2:10–16, Malachi addressed two problems: mixed marriages (vv. 10–12) and divorce (vv. 13–16). First, he called the people to honor the covenant of faithfulness and fidelity by marrying within the Jewish nation. Marrying outside the faith profaned this covenant and put Israel's unique faith and national purity at risk. In verse 12, he called for divine judgment upon those who broke marriage covenants. To be "cut off" meant instant death (Ex. 31:14). This was a serious matter.[6] Malachi revealed one reason: God wanted marriages within the faith so "godly offspring" would result.

Second, Malachi said that breaking their covenant against mixed marriages would hinder their prayers (vv. 13–14). Carelessly casting aside faithful wives in a one-flesh marriage covenant deeply offended God (vv. 14–15), for God hates divorce—the "putting away" of a marriage partner (v. 16). In this instance God viewed the divorcing husband as one who treacherously covered himself with violence.

The context of verse 11 shows that God hates divorce; however, this may not include *all* divorce. In this instance it may be just divorce for the purpose of marrying *outside the faith*. But note that He does *not* say He hates divorced people. He is against those who selfishly divorce to pursue their own pleasures, but He lovingly defends the Jewish wives who are victims of abandonment through the treachery of their husbands.

Contrast that passage from Malachi with the following actions of Ezra. God, despite His hatred for divorce, approved of Israelites putting away their existing pagan wives—even with children involved.

God Wants to Promote Marriages within the Faith

God's servant, Ezra, led a group of Jewish exiles back into Jerusalem about twenty-five years before Malachi's challenge. Ezra was a highly regarded and godly leader, priest, and scribe whose goal was to restore Israel to God and teach them the Scriptures (Ezra 7:10, 25).

During their years of Babylonian captivity, the Israelites intermarried with Gentile women living in the land of Judah. When the Jerusalem city officials brought this problem to Ezra, he was overcome with grief. The unfaithfulness of God's people in this way appalled him (Ezra 9:1-4).

Ezra feared that idolatry would rear its ugly head once again among the Israelites as it had in the past (Judg. 3:5-6; 1 Kings 11:1-6; 16:31-33). Nehemiah 13:23-31 tells us of the sins committed by Israel in marrying pagan women. Something had to be done about this serious problem. God did not approve of mixed marriages, but He also hated divorce.

Not knowing what to do, Ezra prayed about the entire situation (Ezra 9:5-15). As he did so, everyone who had married a foreign woman had a convicting change of heart. The offending Israelites publicly confessed the sin of mixed marriages. Their repentance also brought a solution. One of the men of Israel, Shecaniah, recommended that the offenders covenant with God to "put away" their pagan wives and children. They would terminate their existing marriages because the pollution of the faith was too important to let those relationships stand. Ezra accepted this proposal with God's implicit approval (Ezra 10:1-5). To fulfill the covenant, Ezra required all of the returned exiles to meet in Jerusalem. Those who had intermarried separated from their pagan wives. Since God prohibited mixed marriages, godly men saw that putting away their pagan wives was absolutely necessary for repentance.

In the accounts of Malachi and Ezra, see how strongly God deals with mixed marriages. In Malachi, husbands put away faithful wives to marry pagan women. In Ezra, husbands put away pagan wives (and children), presumably to remarry within the faith. Curiously, however, we shall see that God commands Christians today not to divorce unbelieving spouses.[7]

God's Plan for Marriage

Let's review what we have learned to this point. God's plan for marriage is for a man and a woman to leave their parents and cleave to each other. He joins them together in a permanent one-flesh relationship. However, because mankind (beginning with Adam and Eve) disobeyed God, what was perfect and good became polluted and tragic. Death entered the world as God had promised. Guilt, shame, and heartbreak plagued humankind from that time forward.

As people ignored God through the ages, the ideal marriage became a distant memory. Polygamy arose. Mixed marriages threatened to pull God's people away from Him. Divorce was as easy to get as the husband telling his wife, "I divorce you!" Marriage breakups and family splits were rampant.

How God's heart must have ached to see this happen! However, God showed His compassion and mercy by permitting divorce for a time to avoid further misery among His hard-hearted people. He forgave this sin and rebellion in Christ's sacrifice on the cross. He desired reconciliation with His people. He asked for faithful obedience. But there were limits to His patience. That is why, much as God hated divorce (as we saw in Malachi and Ezra), He did not approve of any marriage or divorce that led His people away from Him into idolatry. The ultimate disaster was for God's people to completely abandon Him.

We have reviewed God's marriage ideal and seen how His people rejected His plan through divorce and other misconduct. But how did God deal with King David, who committed adultery with another man's wife, had the man killed, and then took the man's wife as his own? There is probably no better example of God's graciousness toward disobedience than that of David and Bathsheba. Here we see a striking portrait of how a *repentant heart* transcends violation of the law in God's eyes.

David and Bathsheba: God's Mercy in a Bad Situation

As we learn in 2 Samuel 11, David, king of Israel, took a leave of absence from his armies at war in the field and returned to his Jerusalem palace for rest and relaxation. As he looked out his window one day, his eyes fell upon Bathsheba, the beautiful wife of Uriah, a member of David's army. As she bathed, David lusted for her. This led him to commit adultery with her. Bathsheba soon discovered she was pregnant.

To escape the inevitable public embarrassment of this situation, David tried to cover his tracks. He arranged to have Uriah come home from the wars, hoping that Uriah would sleep with his wife and think that her child was his rather than David's. Uriah did come home, but he refused to sleep with Bathsheba in deference to fellow warriors denied the pleasures of home.

Foiled in his first plan, David quickly devised another. He sent Uriah back to the wars with orders to go to the front lines, which meant certain death. The plan worked and Uriah died in the fighting.

After a period of mourning, David did not forget about the lovely Bathsheba. In 2 Samuel 11:27 we learn, "David had her brought to his house, and she became his wife and bore him a son. But the thing David had done displeased the Lord." God knew what was in David's heart. He was aware of the entire story of violence in killing Uriah. David had committed adultery, followed by murder. These sins resulted in his taking Uriah's wife as his own. He violated the sixth, seventh, and tenth Commandments (Ex. 20:13–14, 17). The penalty was death.[8] But how did God handle David's accountability for these sins?

In 2 Samuel 12 we read how God sent the prophet Nathan to David to let him know that his sin had not escaped God's notice. When David realized the full weight of his sin, he fell into great remorse and repented. Psalm 51 is an account of David's reaction to his sin.

Though David repented of his sin and was forgiven by God, there were consequences. Since David used violence in having Uriah killed, violence would plague his own house (2 Sam. 12:10–11). Also, David's wives would be given to his neighbors to lie with them in broad daylight (2 Sam. 12:11). Finally, the son conceived by his adulterous union with Bathsheba would die (2 Sam. 12:14). But God, knowing David's heart and that he truly repented, graciously spared his life.

What about Bathsheba? She was taken into David's home as his wife. God did not require David to put her away because, legally, Uriah's death freed Bathsheba from her marriage covenant to her deceased husband. From a practical standpoint, she could have been destitute without a husband to provide for her. Would it have been better if God had required David to abandon Bathsheba after taking her as his wife? For whatever the reason (or reasons), God did not ask David to end this relationship. In fact, Solomon was later born from their marriage (Matt. 1:16).

This story understandably troubles many people. Consider, for example, the logical extension of Bathsheba being free to remarry after Uriah's death. Who caused Uriah to die? David did not stop at adultery—he had Uriah killed! Does this mean that a spouse caught in adultery should kill his or her partner's mate so the murderer is free to remarry? Certainly not! God poured out His mercy on David's repentant heart—not on merit, but as an act of His marvelous grace.

We may ask whether it was for David and Bathsheba alone to profit, in essence, from their own sin by continuing their relationship after committing such crimes. We may wonder whether God showed favoritism by sparing David and Bathsheba from death for their actions, when others in the same situation might not have escaped penalty. God did allow David and Bathsheba to continue their relationship while escaping capital punishment. But have we not also benefitted from Christ's sacrificial death on the cross for our sins and escaped our own death penalty? To deny this would empty the cross of its power. Even so, no one should sin so that grace would abound—and the Bible speaks against this strongly.[9]

Why did God spare David and Bathsheba from the full consequences of their sin? No one can know for sure. Perhaps God spared David from the death penalty because He knew David truly had repented from his heart, as David expressed in Psalm 51. The essence of God's mercy and grace is to withhold sanctions in instances when our sinful deeds deserve punishment. In His wisdom, God determined it best that David and Bathsheba continue their relationship. We must not second guess His judgments. Instead we rejoice that God, as Creator and sovereign Lord, showed grace to His servant David. His grace transcended the punishments for violations of the law of Moses.

These same mercies extend to us today, as we shall see in the next chapter. Like David, adulterers today escape a physical death penalty. But let's not take the case of David and Bathsheba beyond its legitimate bounds. This sort of conduct by others will not always bring the same result. God knows more about this situation than we do. We should not tempt Him by sinning in the same fashion.

The Heartbreak of Hosea: God Knows How Divorce Feels

We have learned about God's plan for marriage and how He hates divorce. We have seen His graciousness in dealing with those who violate His commands. But does He really know the pain of parties to a broken marriage? Does He truly understand our sorrows? Does He empathize with those facing divorce at all? In closing this chapter, God's sorrow and heartache over a broken marriage and adultery is seen in the tragic story of Hosea. Some describe it as the greatest love story of the Bible, second only to the gospel accounts. God shares our pain. He knows our grief as we cope with our own divorces.

By virtue of a covenant of faithfulness made with the nations of Israel and Judah, the Lord viewed His relationship with His people as a marriage. Faithfulness in worshiping God alone and obeying His commandments were part of this covenant.

God kept His covenant. He loved His people deeply, as a husband loves a wife. But by the eighth century before Christ, the Israelites had fallen into idolatry. In God's eyes, this was adultery. The prophet Hosea's mission was to expose the breach of the covenant and warn of the consequences.

As a visual aid to His people of His suffering with their unfaithfulness, God commanded Hosea to marry an adulterous woman. Hosea did so in taking Gomer as his wife. Three children were born. The first child was a son named Jezreel, meaning "The Lord sows or scatters." The next child was a daughter named Lo-Ruhamah, meaning "Not loved or pitied." The last child was another son named Lo-Ammi, meaning "Not my people." Each of these names expressed the Lord's feelings toward Israel's unfaithfulness. He could tolerate her adulteries through idolatry no longer. Hosea felt His pain.

In metaphoric fashion, Gomer left Hosea for a life as a prostitute. In Hosea 2, Gomer's children pled for her to give up her adulteries. They begged her to return to her husband before she suffered the full consequences of her sin, but Gomer was oblivious to her husband's provision. She foolishly believed that her lovers would provide her with a better life. But she was cut off from her lovers (Hos. 2:7). When Gomer was alone on the slave auction block and unwanted by others, Hosea purchased her as his own (Hos. 3).

Hosea's unwavering love for Gomer in the face of such unfaithfulness is an example of God's love for His people, even as they reveled in idolatry. Just like Gomer, Israel left the Lord to pursue pagan gods of the Midianites and Moabites. At the time of the Exodus, Israel loved God and followed Him through the wilderness. But her faithfulness waned. There were times of complaint and rebellion against God. She forgot about God's miraculous deliverance of her from Egyptian bondage, the manna from heaven, and many other blessings. Her priests, leaders, and prophets ignored God. Like one abandoning a spring of living water for broken pottery jugs, Israel had forsaken God and replaced Him with false idols in an act of spiritual prostitution. Like a wayward wife, Israel separated from the Lord and gave herself to many other lovers. She had abandoned her marriage to the Lord to marry another—the idols of the nations.

But God pursued His spiritual wife. He used "tough love" to cut off many of the blessings Israel enjoyed. This was necessary because she thought these blessings were the result of idolatrous worship. The Lord hoped that Israel would realize that her other lovers were false and empty objects of worship, and that she would then appreciate who her real Provider was.

Hosea, in expressing God's own pain, described the nation of Israel as a dying man, a flaming fire, a half-baked cake, a silly dove, a deceitful bow, a pleasureless vessel, and a forgetful servant. Even so, God yearned for her to return for healing and redemption. She arrogantly refused. God cried out for Israel to return to Him as her spiritual husband; but Israel, hardened by sin, rejected God's final gracious appeal. She stood guilty and defenseless.

Finally, God's forbearance ended. He gave the Northern Kingdom of Israel a certificate of divorce, as Jeremiah 3:6–10 describes. As a consequence, pagans (Assyria) destroyed her cities in 722 B.C. In the years that followed, the Southern Kingdom—Judah—was even worse than the Northern Kingdom had been. She refused to learn from Israel's loss and continued in idolatry while merely appearing to return to the Lord. So the Babylonians captured Judah in the sixth century B.C. Nevertheless, God showed a continuing love for His people. He fulfilled His promise of ultimate restoration in the most personal way. His only Son, Jesus, came to seek their return to Him.

Yes, God knows our pain in seeing a marriage partner leave for other lovers. He knows our heartbreak and grief. Some say the book of Hosea is a story of God crying. Yet He models for us an unfailing love despite the unfaithfulness of His spiritual wife, Israel. Only after bearing with adulteries for years on end did God finally divorce His people, much as He hated divorce.[10] His strong statements against divorce in Malachi were more than disappointment. God had personal empathy and compassion for those faithful wives cast aside by husbands chasing after younger pagan women.

How Does God Really Feel About Divorce?

God's view of marriage, divorce, and remarriage in the Old Testament is clear. A man and a woman desiring to marry are to leave their parents to cleave to each other, joined by God into a one-flesh relationship. This is not a temporary matter—it lasts as long as humankind exists in the flesh. The law of Moses did not change this, and Jesus reinforced its truth for eternity.

When a marriage leads one or both partners to forsake God, in the past He has allowed that relationship to end. Malachi condemned mixed marriages, as did Ezra and Shecaniah—even if it affected children born of those marriages—because it is worse to preserve a marriage at the expense of forsaking God. On the other hand, if a marriage is initially wrong and one or both partners seek God with all their heart, mind, soul, and strength, it would be worse for that marriage to end. More than anything else, this may be why God allowed David to keep Bathsheba. God's grace sweetly oils the abrasions caused when sin rubs against sin and there is no loving way out of a difficult situation.

In the next chapter we will review Jesus' teachings about marriage, divorce, and remarriage. We will see that He fully shares the heartache God has suffered as One divorced from His people.

Questions for Personal Reflection

1) Do I really understand God's original plan for marriage?
2) How did men and women ignore God's marriage plan?
3) Is there a circumstance when divorce is necessary?
4) How do I feel about God's graciousness toward David and Bathsheba?
5) Do I really believe that God understands my personal pain in going through a divorce?

CHAPTER 5

Jesus Tells the Truth about Divorce

What did Jesus say about marriage, divorce, and
remarriage? Can He help us see the consistency of God's
plan for marriage in the Old and New Testaments?
Does Jesus deal with divorce issues not addressed in the
Old Testament? What constitutes adultery?
What are its consequences?

As we shall see, some of Jesus' teachings on marriage and divorce are difficult to accept. But it is critical to keep in mind who Jesus is and why He came to earth. His gracious, forgiving nature is the foundation of everything He told us. We can trust Him to tell us the truth.

We look to Jesus from His perspective as the true Messiah and Son of God (John 1:1–3; 5:18). Although He told us of God's judgment toward disobedience and sin (John 9:39), Jesus came primarily to redeem, not to condemn (John 3:16–17). He also preached the good news of deliverance from sin. In love, He moved among people to set captives free. He healed those broken in heart and proclaimed the time of the Lord's favor (Luke 4:18).

What Jesus says is credible, not just because He is God's Son, but also because He lives to serve others without manipulation or expecting anything in return. He came to teach people in their own language, in their own territory, and at the point of their most personal need. No wonder He was such a refreshing change from the legalistic righteousness of the Pharisees!

Jesus covered His life with mercy and compassion and taught us to do likewise (Matt. 5:7; 6:14–15; Eph. 4:32; James 2:13). He knew condemnation and hypocrisy would spring to life in the absence of redemptive mercy. But Jesus did not take sin lightly. His mere presence made others aware of their sin (Luke 5:8). Jesus acknowledged the sin of humankind but called all sinners to repentance (John 5:14; 8:11).

How could we improve upon what God inspired the apostle John to say about Jesus Christ?

> In the beginning was the Word, and the Word was
> with God, and the Word was God. He was with God in
> the beginning. . . . The Word became flesh and lived for
> a while among us. We have seen his glory, the glory of
> the one and only Son, who came from the Father, full of
> grace and truth. . . . From the fullness of his grace we have
> all received one blessing after another. For the law was
> given through Moses; grace and truth came through Jesus
> Christ (John 1:1–2, 14, 16–17).

In short, Jesus Christ represents God and humanity at their very best. Jesus is the one who proclaims the truth and God's favor.

Many times during His ministry on earth Jesus would begin teaching by saying, "I tell you the truth" (Matt. 5:18, 10:15, 17:20). Just before the crucifixion, Pilate asked Jesus, "What is truth?" (John 18:38). God's Word is truth (John 17:17). Jesus *is* the Word of God (John 1:1). The irony is that in asking Jesus this question, Pilate was staring Truth in the face! Jesus is the Way, the Truth, and the Life (John 14:6).

God's truth will set us free, not enslave us (John 8:31–32, 34–36). It always draws us to Christ; it is not a law unto itself. As Jesus told the Pharisees, "You diligently study the Scriptures because you think that by them you possess eternal life. These are the Scriptures which testify about Me, yet you refuse to come to Me to have life" (John 5:39–40). We use Scripture to understand Jesus and receive His guidance in our divorce situations more than to lay down a law.

We can faithfully interpret what Jesus tells us only by carefully considering each passage in context. We first look at the historical background, noting who is speaking to whom, and under what circumstances. We must *want* to understand His teachings.[1]

We also must guard against being overcome with sympathy for hurting individuals if it means compromising Scripture in the process.[2] Leave those circumstances to God and His mercy, resisting the temptation to take His rightful place as Judge. On the other hand, we do not live our lives in a spiritual vacuum that ignores the wisdom and compassion of biblical principles. God intends for us to use Scripture to make spiritual decisions. He did not give us scriptural guidelines for use as rigid rules of oppression. Therefore, we strive for balance in knowing God's truth, leaving room for His grace, compassion, and forgiveness.

The best foundation for understanding the truth today comes from what God has revealed to us in Scripture. This is the standard of truth we try to use in this book.

Jesus: Fulfillment of the Law of Moses

In chapter 4 we reviewed the purposes of the law of Moses. Now, at the time of Jesus and the dawn of the Christian age, the focus shifts to fulfillment of the law.

In Matthew 5:17–19, what did Jesus mean when He said He had come to *fulfill* the law of Moses? Through the law, God gave us a code of righteousness, but it did not make us righteous. If the law could have done this, Christ's sacrifice was unnecessary (Rom. 7:10–11; Gal. 3:1–5, 10–14, 21–25). Instead, the law made us aware of our sin. Its purpose was to lead us to Christ (Gal. 3:23–25). Forgiveness and life come to those having faith in Jesus Christ, the promise of God. Jesus revealed the true intent and foundation of the Law. In this sense, Jesus fulfilled the law so we are no longer under its supervision (Gal. 3:21–25). He completed the work of the law (John 6:28–29). He nailed it to the cross (Col. 2:13–15).

Understanding how the old covenant law of Moses and the new covenant of God's grace and mercy work together is no easy challenge.[3] Rubel Shelly gives us this excellent perspective: "Law makes grace desirable, and grace makes law bearable. . . . Law demands what it cannot give, and grace gives us all that law demands."[4] But grace is not always neat and tidy.

The law of Moses set the scene for showcasing the beauty of God's grace and mercy. Our difficulties are not so much with God's laws, because we can understand rules and regulations even though we may not always like them. The truth is that we are not always comfortable with God's grace and mercy. This same tension occurs under our civil laws today. If we break the civil law, we get punished. We expect everyone else to receive the same penalties. When ticketed for breaking the speed limit, we expect a fine. When others do the same, we want them to taste the whip the same way. But even the civil laws allow for graciousness under principles of equity and justice.[5]

Another problem arises from our penchant to look at outward appearances of law-keeping and make worldly judgments on that basis alone. But God looks into our hearts (1 Sam. 16:7; Matt. 12:33–37; Luke 16:15; Heb. 4:12–13). He deals with us according to our needs. We tend to blindly and

81

rigidly apply legal principles without considering the hearts of people and their circumstances, without attempting to apply healthy doses of grace and forgiveness. If it were up to us, the great fish might have digested Jonah, Nathan might have stoned David to death, and Peter's ministry might have stopped abruptly as he warmed himself by the fire and denied Christ. But even under the law of Moses, God could redeem those who fell short of total obedience and missed the mark. He can always enforce, change, or withhold penalties in Scripture as He searches our hearts in the context of our lives. This is what makes the redemption of the thief on the cross so amazing and beautiful (Luke 23:39–43).

No, the scales of justice do not always level out as we expect. To this day, I do not pretend to come anywhere close to understanding God's grace and His mercy epitomized in Jesus Christ. The truth part of Jesus I can accept and follow; it is His gracious nature that is extremely difficult to grasp.[6]

What does this all mean? Simply this. God tells us what He desires, as He did in the law of Moses. We fail, neglect, or refuse to fulfill His desires. This disobedience has consequences. As Judge, God can enforce penalties for our transgressions as His law provides, but He also can show mercy by not enforcing the penalty that we do deserve. He can show grace by giving us a pardon that we don't deserve. We deserve the penalty; we expect the sentence; but God has always reserved the right to pardon us and commute our sentence. He searches the hearts of men and women to find those truly devoted to Him. When He finds His people, He loves to lavish His mercy and grace upon them.

Grace Touches Law:
The Woman Caught in Adultery

We begin with an event toward the end of Jesus' ministry recorded in John 8:1–11. Like the story of David and Bathsheba, it highlights how God's graciousness fulfills the law and rejects legalistic self-righteousness.

The setting is Jerusalem. Jesus appears in the temple courts and teaches the people during the last days of the Feast of Tabernacles. He immediately impresses everyone hearing Him (John 7:14–15), but some are out to kill Him. Nevertheless, Jesus fearlessly attacks their hypocrisy as contrary to the law of Moses they supposedly revered (John 7:19). The Pharisees, jealous of protecting Jewish traditions, know that a fresh wind is blowing that could jeopardize their religious positions. Something must be done to stop

Jesus and His popularity (John 7:32, 45–52).

The religious leaders become aware of a woman and unknown man caught in the act of adultery.[7] The Pharisees plot to use this incident to trap Jesus. They want to embarrass Him publicly into violating the law of Moses. This would infuriate the Jews and aggravate the civil authorities.

This is the trap: If Jesus condemns the woman under the law of Moses, He will reinforce the Pharisees' position as religious leaders. If He does not, His admirers will think He condones adultery. The scribes and Pharisees bring the woman (What happened to the man?) to stand before Jesus and the crowd.[8] But Jesus turns the challenge against the accusers. First, He stoops down to write on the ground with His finger. What is Jesus thinking as He ponders this scene? No one knows for sure.[9] As He waits and writes on the ground, He hears the Pharisees pressing Him to respond.

What a dramatic scene now unfolds! Jesus deals first with the unrepentant, cold, critical hearts of the accusers. He simply says: "Let those who are without sin cast the first stone." The only person present without sin is Jesus Himself (Heb. 4:15; 1 Pet. 2:22). Those demanding enforcement of the Law against this woman violate the Law through hypocrisy (Rom. 2:1–3, 17–23). Under the law, only witnesses to the adultery can legally cast the first stone (Deut. 17:6–7), but they hide in the shadows. Everyone is silent as Jesus stoops again to write in the dirt. They know that no one is righteous—not even one (Rom. 3:9–12). Without a word the accusers retreat one by one, from the oldest to the youngest, leaving the woman and Jesus alone.

Now for the finale. Jesus stands with a woman who violated the Law. The Law commanded a death penalty. He knows the critical need for fidelity in marriage. He has taught that adultery is a sin serious enough to permit a spouse to divorce another (Matt. 19:3–12). Even the *thought* of adultery was serious (Matt. 5:27–32). Here is one who has violated these principles. She is guilty; she deserves death by stoning under the law. As the sinless Son of God, will Jesus condemn her? Judgment beckons. The woman has absolutely no defense. But with compassion, Jesus asks her if anyone (including Himself) has condemned her. She realizes that no one has done so, and she is given a second chance.

In keeping with His teachings on forgiveness (Matt. 18:21–22; Luke 17:4), Jesus separates the person from the sin.[10] He reaffirms His acceptance of this woman while admonishing her to stop her adultery. He is her advocate before the Father in withholding the penalty for her sin (1 John

2:1–2; Rom. 8:34). Mercy triumphs over judgment. But her repentance is critical to receiving this forgiveness (John 5:14).

Did Jesus Break the Law of Moses?

Did Jesus contradict the law by sparing the woman? Jesus did not say the woman was guiltless; she clearly broke the law. But Jesus endorsed withholding enforcement of the *penalty*. Knowing her heart, he knew that she was repentant. Christ showed grace and mercy. In essence He pardoned her from the penalty by the authority of God as she left her life of sin.[11]

If we complain about God's withholding sanctions for sins today, we are no different from the scribes and Pharisees in John 8. We should rejoice that God spares sinners for a second chance to glorify and please Him. His love and mercy are a creative force in an ugly world. The story of the adulterous woman gives us a better understanding of why God dealt graciously with David and Bathsheba. Sin is not pleasing to God, but as we fall into sin, we see His grace at work. He is not blind or uncompassionate to the hearts and circumstances of sinners. He uses justice mercifully. This mercy is consistent with, not contrary to, the law of Moses. The heart is the key.

The story of this woman brings up another question. The law of Moses required a physical death penalty for committing adultery. Why? Also, what is the penalty for this sin under the new covenant of God's grace?

Adultery, Death, and God's Grace

There are two aspects to adultery in the Bible. First, when one breaks faith with God and turns away from Him, he or she commits spiritual adultery. We are given a sad picture of how people prostituted themselves by leaving God to pursue other lovers in Ezekiel 16. The Bible describes Israel, God's spiritual wife, as adulterous for turning from Him to live in idolatry with divided hearts and disloyalty (Jer. 3:8; Ezek. 23:45). Forsaking God to live in worldly ways is spiritual adultery (Jas. 4:4).

Second, in a marriage context, Jesus tells us that an unscriptural divorce followed by remarriage is adultery.[12] A spouse is breaking faith and sexual intimacy with a mate established by marriage.

The seventh commandment says it plainly: "You shall not commit adultery." Leviticus 20:10 passes the sentence of death on both the man and the woman who commit adultery. The practical effect of this death penalty certainly made people aware of their sin. It also kept adulterers from defiling their marriages again. But did it change their hearts? Did it deter other adulterers? Did it vindicate violation of God's laws? What about enforcement of the penalty? Was Israel able to judge accurately, consistently carrying out the death sentence for all adulterers? What if they executed an innocent person?[13] If an adulterer had already repented, were they killing a potential "prodigal son" who might faithfully return to his spouse? Why did God command capital punishment for adultery? It certainly gave Him no satisfaction. "'As surely as I live,' declares the Sovereign Lord, 'I take no pleasure in the death of the wicked, but rather that they turn from their ways and live'" (Ezek. 33:11). God desires reconciliation and restoration. He wants His people to live. If so, why kill adulterers under the law of Moses?

There could be many answers to this last question. One possibility, I believe, goes back to Adam and Eve's relationship in the garden of Eden. This one-flesh bond between one man and one woman for life is a picture of God's plan for marriage. It is the most personal and uniquely intimate relationship that humans can share with each other. Anything that destroys this sexual fidelity and trust, as adultery does, may have prompted God to act strongly to prevent it and to protect those hurt by it.

Perhaps the law of Moses commanded physical death to remind adulterers and others of what was happening spiritually. Perhaps, by allowing the *physical* death of adulterers for a time under the law of Moses, God gave us a picture of what happens to us *spiritually* when we sin today. Like the prodigal son was to his father, without repentance we are truly "dead" and "lost" to our Father (Luke 15:24, 32).

Here is the point: Under the Old Testament, if you committed adultery, you could lose your life. With the new covenant, God states that (through Jesus Christ) adultery is still a sin. But the required physical death penalty ceased when the law of Moses was nailed to the cross of Christ and God's new covenant of grace began (Col. 2:14–17). Perhaps if God spares the physical lives of adulterers today by His grace, His hope is that His graciousness will move them to repent of this sin and be faithful to Him. Adulterers receive a second chance for repentance, but eternal, spiritual death awaits at judgment if no repentance occurs (1 Cor. 5:1–13; Gal. 5:19–21).

A powerful synergy exists between the one-flesh nature of marriage, defilement of that exclusive bond by adultery with death as a consequence, and God's mercy and grace in dealing with this sin.

Jesus on Marriage and Divorce

In Matthew 19:1–12—one of the most controversial passages in the Bible—Jesus reveals more of God's intent about marriage, divorce, and adultery.

Back to the Plan of Creation

Divorce was commonplace in Jesus' day. Men and women had ignored God's ideal plan for marriage for a long time. Even so, some realized that divorce was not morally right; consequently, there was continuous debate within religious circles on when divorce was acceptable. The controversy centered on "something indecent" in Deuteronomy 24:1.[14]

Is it lawful to divorce for any reason? The Pharisees questioned Jesus, "Is it lawful for a man to divorce his wife for *any and every reason?*" It was a loaded question. It guaranteed that almost any answer would offend someone and stir up controversy. Jesus responded to this question throughout the entire passage.

By asking "Is it lawful . . ." in Matthew 19:3 (in context with verse 7), the Pharisees were referring to the law of Moses. They believed that greater obedience to the law would raise one up another rung in the spiritual hierarchy. But was this the right question? Instead, purer hearts might have asked, "Is it lawful for a man to remain married to his wife when there are good reasons to divorce?" The Pharisees wanted reasons to break up a marriage; Jesus responded by emphasizing what keeps a marriage together—God's way.

Jesus reminded the Pharisees of God's original purpose and design for marriage from creation. He went back to the original blueprint of the Master Architect rather than argue with some of the contractors over how they built the house. People may fail in the construction of their marriages, but God's original design for husband and wife is flawless.

"Haven't you read," Jesus asked the Pharisees, knowing they knew well the Creation account in Scripture, "that at the beginning the Creator 'made them male and female?'" God (actually, Jesus Himself—Col. 1:17; Heb. 1:3; Ps. 33:9) created one man (Adam) for one woman (Eve). God designed and created men and women for each other from the creation of humankind.

In verse 5, Jesus confirmed that this creation ideal is the reason *anyone* (without limiting this to Jews or any other group of people) leaves parents and cleaves to his or her mate in a one-flesh relationship. Anything that destroys the new family structure is contrary to God's will. In verse 6, Jesus concluded by adding, "Therefore what God has joined together, let man not separate." God joins husband and wife together—not civil contracts or a sexual relationship. Spiritually they become like one person. No human being is to separate them. This is a creation law of God given before the law of Moses.

How are two persons "joined together?"[15] Marriage is both a binding and bonding commitment between husband and wife. They make lifelong vows of fidelity, and God is a witness to these vows. He yokes them together, and those in a single yoke cannot separate themselves without removing the collar.

In context, the last part of verse 6 literally says, "and keep on not letting man separate."[16] This is a continuous command throughout a marriage. Can a husband and wife separate? Yes. Should they separate? No.[17] Why? God's will is that husband and wife remain yoked together as "one flesh."

Did Jesus answer the question of the Pharisees? The question was: "Is it lawful for a man to divorce his wife for any and every reason?" The answer: "The Creator made male and female so the two become one flesh. What God has joined together, let man not separate." The Pharisees understood that Jesus had answered "no" to their first question. Man and woman leave parents and cleave to each other in a one-flesh relationship. God joins them together. That's the sum of marriage. No exceptions. Some may seek separation; they may want to end a marriage—but that was not God's plan.

Why did Moses permit divorce? The Pharisees heard Jesus' response and believed they saw a contradiction with Deuteronomy 24:1–4. They immediately asked Jesus, "Why then did Moses command that a man give his wife a certificate of divorce and send her away?"

Jesus answered the Pharisees by giving them the reasoning behind Deuteronomy 24:1–4. First, Moses *permitted* the Israelites to divorce their wives; it was not a command as the Pharisees suggested. Nor did Moses *create* divorce—it was already a common practice among the Israelites. The law of Moses was really a damage control measure as divorces occurred.

Jesus told His questioners that divorce was permitted under Moses "because your hearts were hard."[18] Nevertheless, He quickly pointed out,

87

"It was not this way from the beginning." God never wanted divorce. It was not part of His plan for marriage. And, as Jesus said, this creation law still governs all humankind.[19]

Now we come to the most controversial statement of all. Jesus said in Matthew 19:9, "I tell you that anyone who divorces his wife, except for marital unfaithfulness, and marries another woman commits adultery." Jesus restored God's creation law rather than merely commenting on the law of Moses. He spoke of two classes of persons who commit adultery[20]: explicitly, husbands who divorce their wives without the cause of "marital unfaithfulness" to marry other women; and implicitly, women who marry husbands who have divorced their wives for reasons other than "marital unfaithfulness." Let's review the meaning of the operative words.

The word "divorces" is the same term the Pharisees used in verses 3 and 7.[21] It is the Greek word for "letting go." Also, "marries"[22] refers to the marriage bond between a husband and wife. These words grammatically link together and equally relate to the word "anyone."

What does the exception for "marital unfaithfulness" mean? The only divorce that does not lead to adultery arises from "marital unfaithfulness." Its meaning is critical to understanding Matthew 19:9.

There are differing views on whether this word modifies the word "divorces" preceding it or the word "marries" following it.[23] But clearly Jesus is telling the world that divorce for marital unfaithfulness is the only divorce with God's permission—not approval—that generally applies to all people from that time forward.[24]

"Marital unfaithfulness" in Greek is *porneia,* meaning "fornication and all forms of illicit or unlawful sexual intercourse in general." The proper application of this single term is the most important key to understanding verse 9. Does this term require some sexual involvement on the part of a marriage partner? Can it simply mean breaking faith with one's partner by forsaking the marriage relationship without any sexual involvement with others?[25] According to Greek authorities[26], the word has a broad sexual connotation—including unlawful heterosexual relationships, homosexuality (also sodomy and lesbianism), incest, and bestiality. It appears to require more than mere covenant breaking, marital incompatibility, or disloyalty.

Does the exception Jesus used for "marital unfaithfulness" refer only to adultery? No, Jesus did not use the specific word for "adultery"—the Greek root word *moicheia.* In emphasizing the purity of the marriage bond, Jesus spoke broadly against *any* sexual involvement with others (*porneia*) that breaks the sexually exclusive bond between husband and wife. He did not restrict this sin to adultery only, but rejected both it and all other forms of sexual infidelity. Jesus permits divorce whenever a spouse commits any *porneia*, which is not limited solely to *moicheia*.

How much *porneia* must a spouse commit before the exception applies?[27] Is it a one-time act, or must it be a continual, unrepentant state of marital unfaithfulness? How does one know for sure if and when *porneia* occurs, especially since it is usually a secretive act? The word and context do not tell us. The exception could apply immediately upon any sexual infidelity. The first act could break the exclusive sexual bond between husband and wife. It may also require a continuous and unrepentant lifestyle of sexual infidelity with a hard heart before divorce occurs scripturally.[28] There is no clear consensus on this issue. But if *porneia* is present and active, divorce is permitted.

How does one prove marital unfaithfulness? Under Mosaic law, witnesses must verify adulterous behavior (Lev. 20:10; Deut. 17:2–7; 19:15–21; Num. 35:30). No such biblical requirement exists today.[29] Apart from the Bible, some civil courts struggling with legal proof of adultery in divorce cases have resolved the problem this way:

> Because adultery usually takes place in secret or seclusion, proof thereof in most instances is by circumstantial evidence, through showing *desire*, by evidence of mutual affection or otherwise, coupled with *opportunity* under conditions or circumstances from which a reasonable judge of human nature would be led to conclude that adultery was committed.[30] [Emphasis added.]

We must act wisely to arrive at an honest conclusion on this important matter. If reasonable Christians, aware of the relevant facts, believe that the circumstances (through desire and opportunity) support sexual infidelity (*porneia*), perhaps that is enough to fulfill the intent of verse 9.[31]

Divorce (except for *porneia*) and remarriage are adultery. If there is no marital unfaithfulness (*porneia*), divorce and remarriage to another person while both spouses to the first marriage remain alive cause both parties to the remarriage to "commit adultery." (The Greek root word is *moikaomai*, meaning "to have unlawful intercourse with another's wife; to commit adultery with.") But does this term refer to a one-time act of adultery or a continuing state of adultery?

For example, let's say an unscriptural divorce occurs (without *porneia*). One spouse remarries another person; therefore, both parties to that remarriage commit adultery. But does this adultery continue? Some believe it does not. They argue that once an adulterous marriage occurs, there is no way to undo it.[32] At that instant, the remarriage becomes legitimate.[33]

Alternatively, does *moikaomai* mean such a remarriage is a continuing state of adultery? As opposed to a one-time adulterous act, is it adultery that continues while the relationship exists? This may mean that anyone remarrying after an unscriptural divorce from a living spouse enters into a lifestyle of adultery (Col. 3:5–8).

The debate on this critical point continues. However, if a continuous state of adultery truly exists in the remarriage, who would argue against terminating this relationship? Repentance would clearly require breaking off the adulterous relationship.[34]

Many questions arise. Does the exception Jesus made in verse 9 for marital unfaithfulness permit a divorce but not remarriage? I feel this is a very strict construction. Jesus clearly addresses a situation where divorce *and* remarriage have occurred, not each action as an isolated incident.

May a spouse (the "divorcee") divorced by a mate for reasons other than *porneia* remarry? Verse 9 does not tell us, but Matthew 5:32 indicates that the remarriage may be adulterous. What rights does the divorcing spouse (the "divorcer") have when *porneia* has occurred? When the exception does apply, Jesus does not say whether the divorcer may remarry. However, by implication, if a divorce is permissible for *porneia*, then the marriage is broken. It is as if a death of the unfaithful spouse has occurred.

What about the divorcee who is guilty of *porneia*? Does he or she give up any chance to marry again? Jesus does not say anything about this person. The one engaging in *porneia* commits a grievous sin in breaking the marriage bond. What are the consequences? Jesus does not mention any penalty in verse 9. Many say that the adulterer spiritually dies (as discussed earlier in this chapter). The only redemption is through repentance and forgiveness from God, but this may not allow for any remarriage. Others argue, however, that if the marriage ends in God's judgment, why would both parties not be free to remarry another as if the marriage had never occurred?

What happens to the divorcer who remarries after an unscriptural divorce? Jesus says in verse 9 that the divorcer commits adultery. If the remarriage is a continuing state of adultery, are the parties now required to end their new marriage as part of repentance? If they divorce, can the spouses ever marry again? Must they return to their mates from their first marriages?[35]

As you can see, many remarriage issues remain unanswered by Jesus. He does not tell us much about how a scriptural remarriage may occur after either a scriptural or unscriptural divorce. It appears that we are to answer these questions for ourselves, using the Scriptures as God leads us.

What we do know from Matthew 19:9? We know Jesus reaffirmed the marriage bond of one woman for one man in a monogamous marriage for life. *Porneia* is a serious breach of fidelity and trust in a marriage. If it were not, God would not permit divorce even in that exceptional circumstance. By recognizing this exception, Jesus acknowledged that the marriage bond can be broken, but He did not say that a divorce *must* occur after marital unfaithfulness. He only *permits* it. Even so, His focus throughout this conversation is not on divorce or the exception permitting divorce. He honors God's ideal plan for marriage from creation.

The teaching that an unscriptural divorce followed by remarriage is adultery is a very hard principle to receive. It shows how important the purity and longevity of a marriage is to God.

Is it better not to be married at all? Verse 10 tells us that Jesus' statements shocked His disciples. If this was the way God viewed divorce and remarriage, why marry at all? In saying this, did the disciples prefer easy divorces over being obedient to God's plan for marriage? Were they so concerned about sin in marriage that they would turn their back on marriage entirely?

The disciples show how far we all fall short of God's ideal. They missed the point. Jesus did not tell anyone to avoid marriage. His focus was always on loving God with all of one's heart, mind, soul, and strength; that must be the priority in this life. If marriage, money, or anything else keeps one out of the kingdom of God, then it is better to part with it. We have a choice, but it is impossible for people to enter the kingdom of God on worldly resources. Only with God is everything possible.

How did Jesus respond? He did not equivocate or say that He was misunderstood. He only added: "Not everyone can accept this teaching, but only those to whom it has been given. For some are eunuchs because they were born that way; others were made that way by men; and others have renounced marriage because of the kingdom of heaven" (Matt. 19:11–12).

He relied upon God to help them through any situation. This goes beyond the question of marriage and divorce. It is a faith problem. Will the disciples trust in God or themselves?

Who can accept this teaching? In verse 12, Jesus added: "The one who can accept this [teaching] should accept it." Marriage is a matter of free choice; God does not coerce anyone into it. If anyone wants to marry, then he or she should accept the responsibilities of marriage. The couple should glorify God through their union as He intended from creation and honor its permanence and fidelity. Likewise, if anyone remains single, he or she should glorify God as an unmarried individual (1 Cor. 7:32–35).

Further Teachings on Divorce and Remarriage

The circumstances of Jesus' teaching the Pharisees in Mark 10:1–12 are very similar to Matthew 19:1–12. Very likely, they are different accounts of the same meeting—with some differences, however. In Mark's passage, Jesus speaks first of a husband as the divorcer of his wife. If that man marries another woman, he commits adultery against his wife. Then He describes the wife as the divorcer of her husband. If she marries another man, she commits adultery. Important differences from Matthew 19 are these: Mark entirely omits the exception for "marital unfaithfulness" (*porneia*) in Matthew 19:9; and Jesus' teachings apply to both husbands and wives if they are the divorcers.

Since Jesus did not restate the "marital unfaithfulness" exception in Mark's Gospel, some argue that Jesus either did not mean for the exception to apply at all, or He made a public statement to the Pharisees using the exception and another to His disciples privately without any exception, implying that different rules apply to non-believers and believers. But the missing exception in Mark does not nullify Jesus' statement in Matthew's version. Also, since Jesus rooted all His teachings in God's creation plan for marriage, these apply to all people for all time without limitation to any particular group.

The second difference is of particular interest since existing Jewish law did not allow a wife to divorce her husband. The mention by Jesus of women as divorcers affirms God's view that men and women who divorce are equally accountable to Him.

Teachings on Divorce in the
Sermon on the Mount

In Matthew 5:27–28, Jesus warns us: "You have heard that it was said, 'Do not commit adultery.' But I tell you that anyone who looks at a woman lustfully has already committed adultery with her in his heart." In verses 29–30, Jesus then figuratively points up the serious nature of sin. Do not miss the point He is making here, however, He does not advocate physical mutilation. A blind man can lust without sight, and a limbless person can still sin as much as a whole person. He is emphasizing that to rid ourselves of evil motivations and desires, our *hearts* must change.

People violate God's Law not only by outward acts but also by inward motivations of the heart leading to those actions. Murder begins with anger (Matt. 5:21–22). Adultery begins with lust in the heart. Jesus seems to say that the *desire* is as wrong as the actual act.

Matthew 5:31–32 tells us that a husband's unscriptural divorce (without *porneia*) of his wife causes her to become an adulterer. Also, anyone who marries a divorcee not divorced for marital unfaithfulness (*porneia*) commits adultery (*moikaomai*). Does divorce "cause"[36] a divorcee to become an adulterer, even *before* any remarriage? No, because the divorcee may be an innocent and faithful spouse subjected to an unscriptural divorce by the divorcer. The passive nature of the Greek tells us that this divorcee is in a present position of *becoming* an adulterer upon any remarriage while the divorcer is still alive. But Jesus also warns that if a divorcee, unscripturally divorced, remarries an otherwise eligible third person, both commit adultery.[37] This is difficult because both persons could be *innocent* parties.

When divorce occurs, opportunities for adultery spring to life. When adultery occurs, there is spiritual death (as there is for any sin that is not repented of—Rom. 6:23). We can understand that. But why does Jesus take this harsh stand against "innocent" persons? Perhaps it is because the first marriage still exists until it is scripturally broken through *porneia* while both spouses are alive. God wants the first husband and wife to either remain unmarried or reconcile with each other to fulfill His plan for marriage.[38] By warning married persons of adultery, Jesus reinforces the relationship.[39]

Answered and Unanswered Questions

Let's summarize what Jesus has shared with us about marriage, divorce, and remarriage:

- God joins together a male and female, who leave their parents and cleave together in marriage, into a strong, sexually exclusive bond of fidelity and trust.
- Once a marriage has occurred, no human being should separate a married couple.
- Anyone who has never married may, without sin, marry anyone else of the opposite sex as he or she chooses as long as that other person is also eligible to marry in God's view.
- If a spouse commits marital unfaithfulness (*porneia*), the faithful spouse is permitted (not commanded) to divorce and remarry another person.
- Spouses divorced for reasons other than marital unfaithfulness may not remarry anyone else without committing adultery while both spouses are alive.
- Anyone who marries a formerly married person, divorced for reasons other than marital unfaithfulness, commits adultery if the spouses to the former marriage are still living.

In contrast, consider these questions that Jesus did *not* directly address in foregoing passages:

- Why is the death of a spouse (Rom. 7:2–3) not mentioned? Does the death of a spouse after an unscriptural divorce free the surviving spouse to remarry without committing adultery?
- What happens to a divorcer or divorcee who commits marital unfaithfulness (*porneia*)? Is he or she free to remarry despite breaking the bond of marital fidelity?
- How does one determine if his or her spouse has committed *porneia*?
- What happens if a spouse who is not aware of the other spouse's marital unfaithfulness believes that he or she is *not* scripturally free to remarry when, in fact, the opposite is true?

94

- What if a couple divorces for reasons other than *porneia* (an unscriptural divorce), but one or both spouses engage in *porneia* after the divorce? Does this allow one or both spouses to remarry?
- If a spouse from an unscriptural divorce does remarry, thereby committing adultery, is the remarriage a one-time act of adultery that ceases or a continuing adulterous relationship?

Jesus' teachings are tough. These unanswered questions do not make matters any easier for us.

What if we disobey what Jesus told us about divorce and remarriage? Welcome to the realities of life. Everyone has sinned and fallen short of the glory of God. The good news is that God justifies us freely by His grace through the redemption given us in Christ (Rom. 3:23–24). If adultery occurs, repentance brings forgiveness from God. If in obedient faith we return to God like the prodigal son, seeking His forgiveness and guidance to correct our situation, He will shower us with His loving grace and mercy.

Even so, some would ask Jesus, "Why is it so tough to get out of a failing marriage?" But if we really understand how God feels about divorce, the answer to this question becomes clear. God was there when each man and woman loved each other and made the vow, "For better or for worse; for richer or for poorer; in sickness and in health, for as long as we both shall live." Broken vows are serious concerns to Him. He commands everyone who marries to honor the commitment and permanency of marriage.

Divorce hurts everyone involved. God is protective of the helpless children Jesus loves so much, caught in the crossfire of mommies and daddies tearing each other apart. He hates divorce when wives and husbands deal treacherously with each other. He hurts for all of them. Divorce is the worst option.

With the traps and pitfalls in life, we sinners must always come back to the thoughts and attitudes of our own hearts. This is the key to receiving forgiveness and allowing God's grace to become a reality in our lives. We should never sin so that grace will abound (Rom. 6:1–4). But when sin traps us and we earnestly desire God's forgiveness from our hearts, He will not turn us away (2 Tim. 2:11–13; 1 John 1:8–9). Do we have the same heart attitude of David after he was in over his head with sin? When Nathan helped him realize the depth of his disobedience, look at David's words offered to the Lord in Psalm 51:

Have mercy on me, O God, according to your unfailing love; according to your great compassion blot out my transgressions. Wash away all my iniquity and cleanse me from my sin. . . . Create in me a pure heart, O God, and renew a steadfast spirit within me. Restore to me the joy of your salvation and grant me a willing spirit, to sustain me. (vv. 1–2, 10, 12)

How could our loving God resist such heartfelt repentance? Why would God, after searching our hearts and finding contrition, not lovingly save us from our sinful failings (Isa. 57:14–19)? With the temptations of life, we certainly need to heed God. But more than that, we just desperately need Him.

Questions for Personal Reflection

1) Is honoring God's original plan for marriage important to me?
2) How do Jesus' teachings on divorce and remarriage foster reconciliation in my situation?
3) Has there been any marital unfaithfulness (*porneia*) in my marriage?
4) What appeals have I made to God and to my spouse for forgiveness and reconciliation?
5) Am I willing to trust God in my divorce by being obedient to His Word—no matter what?

CHAPTER 6

Paul Builds on Jesus' Teaching

God's commands always build upon His creation plan
for marriage. Jesus emphasized these commitments of
marriage. Paul, too, dealt with those sticky situations
when marriages go wrong.

During his ministry, Paul's chief concern was unity among Christians (1 Cor. 1:10). He was jealous of anything that disrupted this unity. Paul did not wait for others to resolve problems; he worked diligently to keep the peace, confronted wrong, and forged solidarity among all Christians. This could be why God commissioned him to deal with Christians whose marriages were in shambles.

Paul was unmarried, at least during his ministry to the church in Corinth.[1] If so, why should we listen to him? Because he speaks with the authority of God as an apostle of Jesus Christ. Although Paul was not among the first apostles chosen by Jesus, the risen Christ confronted him and commissioned him to preach the good news (Acts 9:1–19). Paul credited Jesus with his teachings (Gal. 1:12). The apostles and disciples closest to Christ during His ministry accepted Paul as an apostle of Christ (Acts 9:26–30).

Paul's competence came not as one qualified under the old covenant law of Moses (2 Cor. 3:4–6) but as a minister of reconciliation under the new covenant of grace. The same Holy Spirit that Jesus promised to send to believers (John 17) also inspired Paul. Every time Paul wrote by the Spirit's inspiration, Jesus was in agreement.

Paul addressed marriage issues that Jesus did not. We find many examples of this in Paul's letters to the Christians in Corinth. But in order to understand how his teaching coincides with that of Jesus, it is critical that we know the background and context of Paul's writings.

The Corinthian Letters
Addressed to Christians in a Worldly City

Corinth was a seaport city, fourth largest of the Roman empire, home to roughly 600,000 people (mostly slaves). It was also a multinational city, much like New York City, Los Angeles, or Miami is today. But Corinth had a very dark side. A high mountain at its southern boundary was the site of the temple of Aphrodite, or Venus, the goddess of love, where as many as a thousand "sacred" temple prostitutes engaged in sexual orgies. Vice ruled everywhere. Corinth had a reputation for being very immoral.[2]

What was the Corinthian church like? Acts 18 gives us some of its early history. We know it had a large, predominantly Gentile membership (Acts 18:8, 10; 1 Cor. 1:14). Many of the Christians used to be idolaters, homo-sexuals, prostitutes, alcoholics, thieves, and swindlers—a rough crowd indeed (1 Cor. 6:9–11). Imagine the religious conflicts between Jew and Gentile as they rubbed shoulders in the same church.

Seeing deep divisions and disunity among the believers, Paul stressed unity as a priority (1 Cor. 1:10–12; 11:17–34). This was a church filled with doctrinal confusion, as many Christians struggled to live in Corinth without compromising their faith (1 Cor. 7:31). There were easy divorces at law, mixed marriages between believers and non-believers, adultery, and incest. No wonder Paul agonized over all the churches (2 Cor. 11:28)!

In 1 Corinthians 1:2, Paul addressed his letter to the "church of God in Corinth, to those sanctified in Christ Jesus and called to be holy, together with all those *everywhere* who call on the name of our Lord Jesus Christ— their Lord and ours."[3]

These letters are to Christians for their instruction on living godly lives in a pagan world. Unlike Jesus' addressing the world at large in Matthew 19, Paul spoke primarily to Christians—directly, in the Corinthian church, and indirectly, throughout the world. He dealt with problems foreign to unbelievers—divisions in the church, Christian marriages, celebration of the Lord's Supper, propriety in Christian worship, and church contributions. Paul distinguished between problems of those outside the church and those inside the church (1 Cor. 5:12–13). This distinction becomes more apparent as we review the passages in this chapter.

The Christian Sexually Involved with His Stepmother

In 1 Corinthians 5:1–13, Paul addressed a shameful situation. A Christian was having an incestuous affair with his own stepmother.[4] The law of Moses (now fulfilled) specifically prohibited this relationship (Lev. 18:8; Deut. 22:22). This matter was scandalous even in immoral Corinth; it also was illegal under Roman law. But the Corinthians, caught up in conceited self-satisfaction and indifference, were doing nothing about it. They enjoyed freedom in Christ (1 Cor. 6:12; 10:23), but this was never meant to be a license for sin. This disgusted Paul. He boiled with righteous anger about this intolerable situation.[5] He called for immediate action against this obvious sin by expulsion of the man from the church assembly.[6]

This church action is an important part of Paul's teachings. It is a disciplinary measure using "tough love."[7] Jesus spoke about it this way in Matthew 18:15–17:

> If your brother sins against you, go and show him his fault, just between the two of you. If he listens to you, you have won your brother over. But if he will not listen, take one or two others along, so that 'every matter may be established by the testimony of two or three witnesses.' If he refuses to listen to them, tell it to the church; and if he refuses to listen even to the church, treat him as you would a pagan or a tax collector.

The secondary goal of this entire process is not to impose punishment for sins committed, but to promote personal accountability through loving but direct confrontations with the person in error. The focus of each step is to foster understanding and repentance toward full reconciliation and restoration of fellowship.[8]

But how does this apply to the situation Paul was addressing? What does repentance from sin of this type require? Could this man's incestuous relationship continue? Implicitly, Paul told him to end the relationship.[9] How else could the sin cease? (We will discuss this issue later in this chapter and in chapter 7.) The manner in which Paul, moved by the Spirit, told Christians how to handle a sinful situation like this will guide us later on in this chapter regarding an adulterous remarriage after an unscriptural divorce.

Sexual Immorality Is Not Part of the Christian Life

In 1 Corinthians 6, Paul exhorted Christians to avoid sexual immorality. The clear warning in verses 9 and 10 is this: immoral people will not inherit the kingdom of God. This includes the "sexually immoral,"[10] who are, interestingly, mentioned separately from "adulterers"[11] in verse 9. In God's eyes, any number of sexual sins (*porneia*), including adultery, shatters a marriage. The Bible warns that all such unrepentant sinners are lost (Rev. 21:8; 22:15).

But verse 11 reaffirms the good news in Jesus Christ. Verses 9 and 10 describe what some of the Corinthians were like before coming to Christ; verse 11 tells us a change occurred. These Christians were "washed," "sanctified," and "justified" by the Spirit of God in the name of Jesus Christ. That truly is good news! The old sinful way of life did not continue; a new life in Christ began (Titus 3:3–7).

Now, if we compare 1 Corinthians 6:11 with Matthew 19:9, a compelling question arises. Some of the Corinthians were adulterers before being washed, sanctified, and justified in Christ. How did these Christians repent of their sin? How did one repent of an adulterous relationship, such as a remarriage after an unscriptural divorce? Was it somehow purified and made acceptable to God upon conversion, or was it dissolved as part of repentance? Unfortunately, there are no clear examples in the New Testament telling us exactly what happened. These Christians may have felt compelled to end their relationships, like the man in 1 Corinthians 5, but no one knows for sure. All we know is that they were forgiven. No adultery continued after conversion since Paul spoke against it.

In 1 Corinthians 6:13–17, Paul focused on an eternal principle: God created our physical bodies both to serve and glorify Him, not to selfishly indulge in sinful pleasures. Illicit sex creates the ultimate interpersonal conflict. Since Christ dwells in Christians as our hope of glory (Eph. 3:17; Col. 1:27), we dishonor Him and our bodies as His temple by abusing ourselves sexually. God's plan is for sexual intimacy to occur exclusively within the "one flesh" marriage relationship described in Genesis 2:24.[12]

Paul's Teaching on Marriage

With 1 Corinthians 5 and 6 in mind, Paul then gave the only major discourse on marriage in the New Testament beyond Christ's teachings. Before we review 1 Corinthians 7, however, let us briefly note some factors that will help our understanding of this Scripture.

First, Paul was answering specific questions of Christians, not unbelievers. In Matthew 19:9, Jesus applied His teachings on marriage to all people. He did this by referring to God's creation ideal for husband and wife. In contrast, Paul was addressing specific needs of Christians struggling to live in an immoral world. Paul mentioned many issues that affect everyone, but he addressed specific problems that are uniquely Christian. Unbelievers would have little interest in much of what Paul wrote to the Corinthians.

Second, Paul addressed Christians under unusual circumstances. His teachings on marriage consider the severe distress affecting the Corinthians then. Therefore, some instructions may apply to that specific time and abnormal circumstance.

The Scriptures do not tell us what the "present crisis" was in 1 Corinthians 7:26.[13] But whatever it was, it obviously affected Paul's teachings on marriage. Notice how Paul went to extreme lengths in emphasizing singleness and discouraging marriage (1 Cor. 7:26–28). Nowhere else in Paul's epistles does he urge this as strongly. Perhaps he anticipated the crisis would tempt married Christians to forsake Christ while protecting their families from hardship.

Third, some of Paul's answers address specific groups of Christians. In 1 Corinthians 7, note the specific instructions Paul gave to different groups of men and women within the Corinthian church. For example, one striking difference are Paul's separate references to the "unmarried"[14] in contrast to "virgins."[15] (Verse 34 clearly distinguishes between the two.) Not all unmarried Christians are virgins, though all virgins have not married (or sexually consummated a marriage if engaged). The "unmarried" probably includes *formerly married* as well as divorced Christians (see for example 1 Cor. 7:11). Paul also gave separate instructions to "widows" in 1 Corinthians 7:8 and 39–40, and to the "married." After addressing these groups, Paul then generally referred to the "rest" in 1 Corinthians 7:12.[16] Verses 12–16 following this reference confirm that this group included Christians married to unbelievers.

Fourth, Paul carefully distinguished between the Lord's commands and his own spiritual judgment. In a manner rarely found in the New Testament, Paul wrote several instructions on issues to which Christ gave no specific command (1 Cor. 7:6, 10, 12, 25 and 40). Therefore, some people question the divine inspiration of these verses. Were they merely Paul's opinion? In context, Paul did not disclaim inspiration from the Holy Spirit. He merely acknowledged that Jesus did not specifically address these matters.

Paul offered three kinds of responses to questions of the Corinthians: answers that follow Jesus' teachings (1 Cor. 7:10); answers not specifically addressed by Jesus but which the Holy Spirit inspired Paul to give as a divine commandment (1 Cor. 7:12); and answers not addressed by Jesus but which Paul used his spiritual judgment as one having the Spirit of God (see, for example, 1 Cor. 7:6–9). In this last instance, the Spirit inspired Paul to advise rather than to command. But Paul's advice was more than just personal preference—it was the advice of a highly qualified apostle of God. It still merits our serious consideration today.

Finally, **Paul's instruction supplements the teachings of Jesus.** Jesus and Paul agree that God's eternal creation laws govern marriage, that marriage is to be monogamous and permanent. They agree that no human being should separate husband and wife, that the married have a divine charge of sexual fidelity. Jesus and Paul also agree that celibacy is good if it encourages devotion to God. No conflict exists between Jesus' words in Matthew 19:1–12 to all people and Paul's writings in 1 Corinthians 7 to Christians.

In Matthew 19:1–12, Jesus addressed the Pharisee's questions about the grounds for divorce. He added warnings about adultery in any remarriage after an unscriptural divorce occurs. Paul applied these teachings to *different* questions from concerned Christians about marriage for virgins, the unmarried, widows, and Christians married to unbelievers.

Paul used Jesus' general teachings to address difficult and uniquely different Christian situations. In Matthew 19:9, Jesus may have been referring to married persons with a different marital status before God than Paul does in 1 Corinthians 7:15.

Now let's review the specific words of Paul.

The Need for Marriage

In 1 Corinthians 7:1–7, Paul responded to these implied questions: First, is marriage acceptable to God? Second, should married persons have sexual intercourse? He answers "yes" to both questions. After speaking against sexual immorality outside marriage in 1 Corinthians 6:13–20, Paul begins 1 Corinthians 7 by saying that sexual abstinence inside marriage is going too far. Marriage avoids sinful temptations for those without the gift of celibacy (Matt. 19:12). Verse 5 shows that any abstention from sexual relations within a marriage should (not *must*) be mutually agreed upon, temporary, and have a spiritual goal. Mandatory celibacy for those not able to handle it may lead them into the sexual immorality that Paul had just spoken against in 1 Corinthians 6.

Instructions to the Unmarried and Widows

Question: Should the unmarried (formerly married) or widowed remarry? The answer comes from 1 Corinthians 7:8–9, that it is good to be single; but if they cannot live a pure life, it is better to marry again.[17] Paul believed that the best option for the unmarried and the widowed was to remain single. There are two reasons: first, because of the "present crisis" (v. 26), and second, so they can give themselves fully to the service of the Lord without distractions (v. 35).

Instructions to the Married

Question: Are divorced Christians allowed to remarry others? Answer: No. If a divorce is not scriptural, husband and wife must reconcile or choose to live separate lives without remarriage to others as long as they both live (1 Cor. 7:10–11).

This instruction is the *Lord's* command. Spouses must not separate.[18] The term "separate" is not merely a temporary physical separation; it means ripping a marriage apart as in a divorce.[19] Though Paul mentioned, "But if she does [separate] . . ." in verse 11, he did not condone a husband and wife terminating normal marital relations. This only introduces God's will that unscripturally divorced spouses "be reconciled" or remain unmarried. As a general principle, no spouse referred to in verses 10 and 11 should remarry another person as long as his or her mate is alive.[20]

Instructions to Christians Married to Unbelievers

In 1 Corinthians 7:12–16, we find the answers to these questions: First, should Christians divorce unbelieving spouses? No. If an unbeliever wishes to stay in a marriage, it should continue. But if the unbeliever wants a divorce, let the unbeliever go. Second, are Christians unacceptable to God through marriage with unbelievers? No, the Lord sanctifies the unbeliever "through" the Christian. Third, are children born into such marriages unacceptable? No, the children also are acceptable to God through Christ. And fourth, do Christians sin if unbelievers leave a marriage? No, they do not.

Who is an "unbeliever"? "Unbelievers" are those who have not received or who have rejected Christ as Savior and Lord. They are the unsaved.

The problems of mixed marriages (those between Christians and unbelievers) arises through the conversion of one but not both spouses in an existing marriage, although some Christians may have married unbelievers. Regardless of how it arises, some fundamental differences exist

103

in a marriage between a believer and an unbeliever: Christians often lose interest in some temporal, worldly matters that used to hold great value. Through self-denial, a Christian's motivation focuses more on love for God and a desire to please Him. Believers see beyond mere daily circumstances toward eternity and one's ultimate purpose in life. In doing so, Christians yearn to share this newfound love, joy, and excitement with their unbelieving mates.

By contrast, the unbeliever, perhaps to please the Christian, may tolerate Christian values for a short while. This task soon becomes tedious, however. Intimacy breaks down. The Christian cannot share the deepest longings in life arising out of a personal relationship with God. Loneliness and lack of fulfillment settle in. Inevitably, "spiritual" competition increases between the Christian and non-Christian mate.

If the spouses in a mixed marriage have children, these young ones may see diminishing family unity. A sense of togetherness where each family member desires to see the others reach their fullest potential may be lacking. The parents inevitably disagree on how to raise the children with discipline. Acceptable attitudes and behaviors as well as learning about God become controversial subjects. Parents argue with each other. The children play one parent against the other for selfish gain. Family life is chaotic and confusing. With constant turmoil, everyone is unhappy.

Paul's primary concern in verses 12–16 was this: Christians in mixed marriages are unable to share fully their love for Jesus with their spouses, while unbelievers frequently yearn for mates who love the world. Who will give in? Does the believer compromise his or her faith to save the marriage, or does he or she continue the Christian life and risk divorce from the unbeliever?

The fact is that God is not pleased with mixed marriages. He strongly discourages any marriage (or other close relationship) that unequally yokes His people to unbelievers.[21] He urged the Israelites not to intermarry with Gentiles, as we saw in Malachi 2:10–16 and Ezra 9 and 10. Solomon's heart grew cold by ignoring God's command about intermarriage with foreign wives (1 Kings 11:1–13). Does the same warning apply to Christians married to unbelievers? How does God, through Paul, deal with this matter?

In 2 Corinthians 6:14–17, Paul warned Christians not to be yoked together with unbelievers. For what does a believer have in common with an unbeliever? Given this fact, what does God really desire? "'Therefore come out from them and be separate,' says the Lord" (v. 17). Any relationship or circumstance that could destroy a Christian's faith is not acceptable to Him.

But would God ask a Christian to break up his or her marriage to an unbeliever (as Ezra and Shecaniah did of the Israelites in Ezra 9 and 10)? Paul does not recommend this action but seeks to preserve the peace of an existing marriage. We know from 1 Corinthians 7:12–13 that despite the many disadvantages of a mixed marriage, the Christian is *not* to divorce an unbeliever who wishes to remain in the marriage. If the unbeliever wants to leave the marriage, the Christian is to let the unbeliever go. The Lord is not quick to salvage a failing mixed marriage because of His greater concern for the faith of His people.

Do not resist an unbeliever who wants a divorce. It is clear from 1 Corinthians 7:15 that if the unbeliever chooses to separate, the Christian is not to resist it.[22] (Compare this instruction to that given to Christian spouses in verse 10. Paul does not command unbelievers to stay in the marriage. He does not address the unbeliever in the same manner as a Christian divorced from another believer.)

If an unbeliever leaves a marriage, a Christian is "not bound."[23] This is a controversial statement in 1 Corinthians 7:15. What does Paul mean by "not bound"? Is he only releasing a Christian from resisting the *divorce*, or does he mean that the marriage bond dissolves with God's permission? Is the Christian allowed to remarry? If so, does Paul contradict Jesus in Matthew 19:9?

Paul's objective in making this statement was to preserve the "peace." Peace in a marriage only comes as each spouse works to preserve the relationship. Peace in a divorce comes through letting each other go. Paul recognized that a Christian spouse cannot force salvation upon an unbelieving mate who stubbornly refuses to accept it. Similarly if the unbeliever decides to divorce and leave a marriage, the Christian clearly has no further responsibility to that person.

But does being "not bound" change a Christian's marital status before God? Is a Christian free to remarry "in such circumstances"? If a Christian remarries after a divorce by the unbeliever for reasons other than *porneia*, is this consistent with Matthew 19:9? Opinions are split.

Paul does not specifically address remarriage in this passage. But notice that he does not specifically tell the Christian in verse 15, as he did in 1 Corinthians 7:11, to remain unmarried or reconcile to his or her spouse (the unbeliever). Also, the words "not bound" seem to antithetically refer back to "not divorce" in verses 12 and 13. How is one "not bound" to an unbeliever but still bound in some way to the marriage and therefore not free to remarry?

In a legal contract, both parties are bound to the agreement or neither is bound. But verse 15 could mean only that Christians are "not bound" to chase after unbelieving mates who leave marriages, since this could lead to compromising one's faith. The Christian and unbeliever remain bound to the marriage, however, unless and until the unbeliever commits *porneia* or dies.

Many believe any remarriage by the Christian contradicts Jesus' statement that any divorce except for marital unfaithfulness (*porneia*) followed by remarriage is adultery. Jesus never made an additional exception anywhere in the Gospels for instances where an unbeliever divorces a believer. Others argue, however, that Paul fulfills God's will for marriage and His desire that His people not yoke themselves with unbelievers.

Jesus would not speak to the Pharisees or unbelievers about special problems concerning only Christians. He knew there would be a time to address Christians about this matter, as Paul did in verse 15. Jesus also may have been referring to those with a different marital status in Matthew 19:9.[24] Therefore, they maintain, there is no conflict between the teachings of Jesus and Paul. Since there are no clear answers from Scripture on this point, we must make our own decision.

Is a Christian who falls away and divorces his or her faithful Christian spouse an "unbeliever" in 1 Corinthians 7:15 based upon Matthew 18:15–17? If so, does this interpretation conflict with the Lord's command to married Christians in 1 Corinthians 7:11? Once again, it is not easy to resolve these controversial issues.

Advice for Widows

From 1 Corinthians 7:39–40 and Romans 7:2–3, this next question is introduced: May a widow remarry? Answer: Yes, but only in the Lord. A marriage ends when one spouse dies or the couple scripturally divorces. The widowed may remarry if they wish.[25]

Paul tells us that a woman is "bound" to her husband as long as he lives, but if he dies, she is released from the marriage. The word "bound" in 1 Corinthians 7:39 and in Romans 7:2 is the same root word in Greek as the one used in 1 Corinthians 7:27. It is *not* the same word used in 1 Corinthians 7:15, speaking of a Christian being "not bound" to an unbeliever, although the meanings are similar. Some believe this technical difference proves that a Christian is "not bound" to chase after a divorcing unbeliever, not that the marriage bond is broken. If Paul had intended otherwise, why did he not use the same term in 1 Corinthians 7:15 as he did in verse 39 and in Romans 7:2—which clearly speak of breaking the marriage bond?

Others contend, however, that the meanings in 1 Corinthians 7:15 and 39 are the same. Use of different words with such similar meanings is a technical distinction without any real difference. In 1 Corinthians 7:29, for example, a wife is bound until her husband "dies." Paul uses a different Greek word for "dies" in Romans 7:2, but both describe the same event— the death of a husband. Similarly if a Christian is "bound" to a marriage, or "not bound," both references speak about the marriage relationship.

If a spouse dies, is the surviving spouse completely free to remarry in the sight of God? In 1 Corinthians 7:39 and Romans 7:3, Paul described the survivor as being "free." Romans 7:2 also says that a widowed person is "released." It is clear that a surviving spouse is absolutely free to remarry.

But in 1 Corinthians 7:39, Paul also commanded the widowed who chose to remarry to do so only "in the Lord." There are two views about what this limitation means: The widowed person must remarry a Christian, meaning that one is *not* free to marry an unbeliever; or he or she may remarry anyone who is scripturally free to marry. To test the difference between these views, consider this example: Ephesians 6:1 commands children to "obey your parents in the Lord." Under the first view, are children only to obey Christian parents? What if the children are Christians and the parents are not, or only one parent is a believer? Therefore, the second view may be more reasonable.

Everyone Should Live in Undivided Devotion to God

Paul reinforced the underlying message consistently given throughout 1 Corinthians 7. Singleminded focus on Christ with a minimum of distracting worldly obligations is the key. Paul wanted to spare unmarried Christians the stress of family responsibilities because of the "present crisis" that existed (vv. 26–28); Christ's return is more important (vv. 29–31); and a single person has a better opportunity for devotion to Christ free of a divided heart (vv. 32–35).

Married Christians must continually concern themselves with family welfare (Luke 10:38–42; 1 Tim. 5:8). Those who are not married (divorced, widowed, or single) are better able to serve God. An unencumbered single life offers more simplicity and a greater opportunity for commitment of time and resources to the Lord's work.

Conclusions from Paul's Message
Marriage, Divorce, and Remarriage

What have we learned about marriage, divorce, and remarriage that applies to Christians today?

- God joins together a male and female, who leave their parents and cleave together in a strong, sexually exclusive bond of fidelity and trust.
- Once a marriage has occurred, no human being should separate a married couple.
- Anyone who has never married may, without sin, marry anyone else of the opposite sex as long as that other person is eligible in God's view.
- If a spouse commits marital unfaithfulness (*porneia*), the faithful spouse is permitted (not commanded) to divorce and remarry another person. Neither Jesus nor Paul tells us whether, or when, the unfaithful spouse may remarry another person while the faithful spouse is still alive.
- Spouses divorced for reasons other than *porneia* may not remarry anyone else without committing adultery while both spouses are alive. However, Paul tells us that in the limited case where an unbeliever leaves or divorces a Christian, the Christian is "not bound" to the unbeliever. This may free the Christian to remarry, but it is not conclusive.
- Anyone who marries a formerly married person who is unscripturally divorced commits adultery if his or her spouse from the former marriage is still living.
- If a marriage involving a Christian is incestuous or adulterous, the church should exercise discipline to disfellowship the unrepentant person(s). It is probable that repentance requires ending a sinful relationship as a condition to restoration into the fellowship once again.

In contrast, Paul did not directly address these questions in the foregoing passages:

- What does Paul precisely mean by saying that a Christian is "not bound" after an unbeliever departs? Does this free the Christian to remarry? Does this conflict with Matthew 19:9?
- What happens to a spouse who commits *porneia* or the unbeliever who divorces a Christian mate? Is he or she free to remarry despite breaking the bond of marital fidelity?
- How much of the teachings in 1 Corinthians 7 are applicable only to the "present crisis" affecting Christians in Corinth? What applications can and should be made to Christians today?
- If a spouse from an unscriptural divorce does remarry, thereby committing adultery, is the remarriage a one-time act of adultery that ceases, or is it a continuing, adulterous relationship?

Questions for Personal Reflection

1) How do Paul's teachings on divorce and remarriage foster reconciliation?
2) Which verses in 1 Corinthians 7 most closely describe my present situation?
3) Will I follow 1 Corinthians 7:10–11? Am I open to reconciliation no matter what it takes?
4) Is my spouse an "unbeliever" within a reasonable interpretation of 1 Corinthians 7:15?
5) Am I content to be a formerly married person if it means I will serve God better?

CHAPTER 7

Which View Do You Choose?

Have you seen the consistency in God's plan for marriage?
But how do we handle the questions for which there are no
easy answers? Let's wrestle a little more with the Scriptures
as we look at questions of divorce, domestic violence, how
one repents of engaging in an adulterous remarriage, and
other issues. I also want to share some personal guidelines
to help you draw your own conclusions about your
separation or divorce.

Years ago I helped my congregation buy an old church building for worship services. It had suffered from years of neglect with dirty white paint peeling off the outside.

Our group diligently worked together on weekends to clean everything up. After giving the building a face-lift, I stepped across the street to take everything in. It was beautiful, except for this dinky little cactus plant stuck in the ground right out front! In every way it was an eyesore.

Seeing that cactus gave me an idea. I had already quietly decided to donate a small black olive tree to the church that would grow over the years with the congregation. Why not get rid of that ugly cactus by planting the tree in the same spot? Brilliant, I thought.

After the planting, the property looked lush and green with the nice tree greeting passersby. Then I received a telephone call. It was a deacon from the church that formerly owned the building. "Warren," he began, "everyone on our end really likes the way your folks have fixed up the building. It's really looking great!" *A nice compliment*, I thought. "There's something you should know about, though. You see, our folks noticed you removed that cactus in front of the building. Now, you couldn't have known this, but that plant was very carefully brought over on a plane as a seedling from Israel years ago."

Well, I didn't hear much of anything else that my deacon friend said after that. I felt terrible and apologized profusely! That episode taught me a valuable lesson about ancient landmarks. Never remove them without knowing their purpose and significance.

Since my legal specialty is real estate law, I am extremely familiar with property surveys. Points of reference and landmarks are critical in legally describing parcels of land accurately. If a surveyor uses the wrong landmark, his or her directions may lead us to land across the street from the parcel we want to find. If we want to find the same parcel surveyed in 1910, we must use the same landmarks.

The Bible is like that too. Proverbs 22:28 tells us, "Do not move an ancient boundary stone set up by your forefathers." Jeremiah 6:16 is even stronger: "This is what the Lord says: 'Stand at the crossroads and look; ask for the ancient paths, ask where the good way is, and walk in it, and you will find rest for your souls.'" In our haste to modernize and renovate, in our hunger for new and exciting ways of achieving our goals, we can easily miss or even destroy precious gifts from the past.

The Good Ways of God

The old ways are often better. How many times have the "experts" come full circle to find that our grandparents had good common sense after all? God made us and knows what is best for us. What He taught us about ourselves in Scripture from the beginning of time is still true today. We may not like what God has shared with us about marriage, divorce, and remarriage—but we must trust Him to guide us into paths that lead to righteousness.

What do we know about marriage and divorce? Let's briefly summarize what God has told us.

God's View of Marriage

God began marriage as one male and one female leaving their parents and cleaving to each other. He joins husbands and wives into monogamous, one-flesh relationships for life. Marriage is not a human creation but one given by God from the beginning of time to serve people.

God came with Eve, undoubtedly pleased like the father of any bride today, to present her to Adam. All three parties to this first marriage "saw that it was good." This joyful marriage relationship in the garden was a picture of the love relationship God shares with His people. From the beginning, Israel is often spoken of as the wife of the Lord (Isa. 54:5; Jer. 3:8; Hos. 2:19–20). The Christian church is the beautiful and radiant "bride of Christ" (Eph. 5:22–32). Just as no one is to snatch God's people from His

111

hand (John 10:28–29), no one is to separate those whom God has joined in marriage. There was no room for divorce in creation.

God's View of Divorce and Adultery

Despite God's will for His people, Israel was unfaithful. She willingly left Him for another suitor—idol worship. Just as sin corrupted and distorted God's relationship with Israel, so too does a marriage often fall prey to it. A divorce is frequently a result of sin.

God does hate divorce—especially when His people divorce faithful partners to chase after unbelievers. Much as He detests it, God did allow divorce for a time under Moses due to the hard hearts and exceedingly sinful nature of people. According to Jesus' teaching, He allows divorce whenever one partner breaks the sexually exclusive bond of marriage. He also permits a divorce of a Christian by an unbeliever to stand. Divorce is a concession to an imperfect and fallen world, but how it all must grieve Him!

There are no truly "innocent" parties to a divorce. Everyone has sinned and fallen short of the glory of God. Every spouse has sinned against his or her mate at one time or another. But there are wrongs that can hurt a relationship and those that can kill it altogether. And *porneia* is one sin that destroys a marriage. One or both spouses allow a stranger to intrude and break the one-flesh bond of sexual fidelity and trust inherent in marriage. It is not a violation of a legal rule but a crime against the persons (and the Lord) in a marriage. *Porneia* breaches the unique and fundamental nature of marriage so severely that a couple will never truly be the same again. Who can fully recover from the death of a marriage that ends in this manner? Many times, divorce merely formalizes what has already occurred.

When divorce occurs, God's intent is that forgiveness and reconciliation of the original marriage partners should always be available. Until it is impossible due to circumstances such as death or scriptural divorce, God desires reconciliation and restoration.[1]

God's View of Remarriage

If a marriage is scripturally broken or the death of a spouse occurs, God permits (not requires) remarriage to others. This is a concession—not a command. It flows from God's gracious nature. He calls all people to lives of peace, not discord and strife. Those faithful to Him have a chance for a new life.

But being eligible to remarry depends upon one's *marital status* before God.[2] The real issue is whether a person at the time of remarriage is married or unmarried. We know that a spouse can scripturally divorce his or her mate for *porneia* and remarry another person without committing adultery. But an unscripturally divorced person may *not* remarry without committing adultery if his or her spouse still lives and if neither spouse commits *porneia* before the remarriage, according to Jesus. We know that *porneia* (which also can occur through remarriage by either spouse) or death can break the first marriage. And by definition, when no marriage exists, there can be no adultery (although the sin of fornication occurs). So the key factor to remember in studying the Scripture is first to determine what your marital status is in God's view before you consider remarriage.

God does not specifically tell us whether those divorced for committing *porneia* may remarry. It is arguable that if God views a marriage as dissolved for one spouse, it ends for both. Both spouses may be free to remarry regardless of who committed *porneia*.[3] But this challenges our sense of justice.[4] One would hope, however, that God's graciousness would minister to those with a repentant heart and unchain them from their past mistakes.

Some Questions to Focus the Issues

Now let's review some troublesome questions about divorce and remarriage. By doing so, hopefully you will have a better understanding of how each question may affect your life and marital situation. But always be sure to test everything before drawing your own conclusions (Prov. 18:17).

Morality of Divorce

Are all divorces wrong? Some believe this is so without qualification. They believe it is a sin for a husband and wife to even separate. Who can imagine a divorce without sin and violation of the most basic laws of God? Others, however, would answer the "morality of divorce" question with a qualified yes. Divorce was not part of God's plan of creation. The prophet Malachi reaffirmed God's statement, "I hate divorce." However, divorces do occur in Scripture—sometimes with God's permission.

In Jeremiah 3:8, God divorced Israel for idolatry (spiritual adultery). In the times of Ezra and Malachi, any marriage with idolatrous spiritual entanglements destructive to one's faith was unacceptable to God. In those instances, God sanctioned divorce. In Mark 6:17–18, John the Baptist told

Herod that it was unlawful for him to have "his brother Philip's wife." (It was unlawful because it involved incest spoken against in Leviticus 18. Adultery also may have occurred).[5] If a relationship remains "unlawful," how could it become lawful? Implicitly, was God (through John the Baptist) commanding Herod to divorce Herodias?

In 1 Corinthians 5:1–5, the Christian man who had his father's wife committed a sin so grievous that even immoral unbelievers did not practice it. Paul commanded the Corinthian church to expel the man from the congregation. How could this man repent and return to fellowship? Did it require divorce (assuming a marriage existed) and breakup of the relationship? The implication is that the marriage was invalid and should end.

In a different context unique to Christians married to unbelievers, Paul advised Christians (in 1 Cor. 7:15) to accept divorce if unbelievers abandon their families and leave their marriages.[6] A Christian is "not bound" to try to save this marriage from divorce.

Are all divorces wrong? Much as God hates divorce, there are instances when He permits it to occur. In those limited, God-sanctioned conditions and circumstances, we cannot say divorce is wrong. However, few would agree that divorce is good. It may be said simply that in some instances, God recognizes sinful human frailties and allows divorce as a divine concession to avoid greater tragedies.

Consequences of an Adulterous Remarriage

In Matthew 19:9, Jesus said that an unscriptural divorce followed by a remarriage to another person is adultery. But is there any penalty for continuing in the remarriage after it occurs? When does this adultery begin and end? How can one repent of this sin once it has occurred? This verse does not specifically tell us. Do other verses in the Bible help us? Romans 6:23 tells us that the penalty for sin is (spiritual) death. That is the penalty for all sin when a person does not repent. Adultery, therefore, has the same penalty as hate and murder—loss of eternal life if one's heart is unrepentant and separated from God. Unrepentant adulterers cannot inherit the kingdom of God (1 Cor. 6:9–10; Rev. 21:6–8). The wages of sin are eternal death, but the gift of God is eternal life in Christ (Eph. 2:8–10).

How can one avoid this penalty? How can one repent of entering into a relationship that was adulterous, at least initially?[7] Jesus said, "Go and sin no more" to the woman caught in adultery (John 8:11). First Corinthians 6:11 says some of those Christians were once adulterers. What changed them? Scripture tells us that they were washed, sanctified, and justified by the blood of Christ. But the Bible says nothing about the details of their repentance. Was one required to divorce a mate if an unscriptural marriage existed? Were vows of the remarriage to be broken? Must remarried spouses abandon families created by the remarriage? God does not tell us. But would God really condone *more* divorce from a remarriage in a questionable effort to restore the former marriage? For the sake of peace and order and to spare further heartbreak to innocents (children), is it not better for the couple to stay as they are and to seek repentance and forgiveness in the existing remarriage?

There are no conclusive solutions to this problem. We know without repentance, adulterers are out of favor with God. However, no Scripture *commands* divorce for any Christian couple in a non-incestuous relationship that may have involved adultery at one time between the parties. Although adultery preceded murder in their case, God permitted David and Bathsheba to continue their marriage. Their example shows that the key to forgiveness for adultery is whether our hearts are truly repentant and devoted to God.

Adultery is a serious sin—but it is a forgivable sin. God always beckons all sinners to come to a heart-piercing repentance and receive the benefits of His forgiveness continually offered to everyone in Jesus Christ (1 John 1:8–10). God also can exercise His grace to withhold any penalty as our righteous Judge. The faithful sincerity of our hearts expressed in submissive repentance to God is a key to receiving His grace and forgiveness. He will guide us into making the necessary decisions in expressing our repentance.

Quite often this means reconciliation with a spouse, if that is still possible. (Restoration of a relationship may be painful or expensive, but that is a consequence of sin and repentance.) Or it may mean accepting divorce and its consequences. But commanding termination of a remarriage may compound sin's destruction rather than alleviate it. It requires careful thought and prayer.

Divorce and Remarriage before Becoming a Christian

If anyone is a party to an unscriptural divorce before becoming a Christian and remarries either before or after becoming a Christian, is the remarriage acceptable to God? Many believe that an unscriptural divorce— or an unscriptural divorce followed by a remarriage that is adulterous—is forgiven upon one's becoming a Christian. All sins are forgiven in Christ. An unscriptural divorce or later remarriage is not an unpardonable sin.

Christians are new creations in Christ. Second Corinthians 5:17 tells us: "Therefore, if anyone is in Christ, he is a new creation; the old has gone, the new has come!" Everything about a Christian is "new," "fresh," and "cleansed of sin"—completely forgiven. That's why Christianity is such good news—God does not hold our sins against us. He removes our sins from us as far as the east is from the west (Ps. 103:10–12).

Remember how Paul addressed adulterers in 1 Corinthians 6:9–11? Christians are forgiven, set apart as belonging to God, and *justified*—"just as if I'd" never sinned. If so, why would an unscriptural divorce and remarriage (that is not inherently sinful due to incest, homosexuality, etc.) be the only sin not covered by the blood of Christ? Why shouldn't new converts receive a "fresh start" with Christ as new creations without breaking up families who want to stay together?

But let's also consider the alternate view. Are unbelievers exempt from obeying Scripture?[8] Receiving forgiveness requires repentance (Acts 2:38; 3:19; 17:30; 26:20). What were those referred to in 1 Corinthians 6:9–11 implicitly required to do? Thieves must no longer steal. Drunkards must stop their drinking. Idolaters must no longer worship idols but must serve the true, living God. Homosexuals must stop their perversion. Likewise, adulterers must no longer commit adultery. In all cases, the Corinthians *were* engaging in these sinful practices; repentance occurred as part of their conversion. Stopping all sinful practices to the best of one's ability and ending sinful relationships is part of repentance (Rom. 6:2; 1 John 3:6–10; 1 Cor. 6:9–11; Acts 19:18–19).[9]

This brings us back once again to the critical issues of one's marital status before God and the nature of a remarriage relationship after an unscriptural divorce. Is remarriage a continuing state of adultery? Is it so because one remains married to a former spouse? Or is the remarriage the result of a single adulterous act that immediately breaks the former marriage such that the adultery does not continue? If it is the latter, and if the persons involved sincerely repent from their hearts against repeating this act, then few would deny that God forgives them upon coming to Christ. If, however, the relationship continues as an adulterous relationship in God's eyes, then few dispute that the remarriage must end as part of repentance. In all events, the sin of adultery cannot continue if one truly desires forgiveness.

Domestic Violence

Does the possibility of an adulterous remarriage after an unscriptural divorce force a divorced husband and wife to reconcile? What if domestic violence or sexual abuse threatens a spouse or children? Does Scripture require an abused spouse to return to the abuser?

After separation or an unscriptural divorce, a Christian couple has the option to remain separate (and therefore celibate) or to reconcile with each other, according to 1 Corinthians 7:11. God seems to encourage reconciliation in every way by removing tempting distractions of third parties. But if this is impossible, a separated or divorced Christian must remain unremarried. Since this is a tough choice for spouses who really desire a marriage relationship, it can tempt a spouse to return to a dangerous marriage.

Mutual submission is important in a marriage, as Paul stresses in Ephesians 5. He tells wives, "Submit to your husbands as to the Lord. . . . As the church submits to Christ, so also wives should submit to their husbands in everything" (Eph. 5:22, 24). To husbands he says, "Love your wives, just as Christ loved the church and gave Himself up for her. . . . In this same way, husbands ought to love their wives as their own bodies" (Eph. 5:25, 28). It is easy for a wife to submit to a husband who loves her the way Christ loved the church. But what happens to the many women who do not have husbands like this? Must a spouse submit to a mate who threatens him or her physically or emotionally?

Too often, insensitive outsiders will blame the victims of domestic violence or sexual abuse for somehow bringing this abuse upon themselves. They feel those abused need to work harder in the marriage to please their mates. Some even believe that an abused spouse receives some sort of masochistic pleasure from the abuse. Many well-meaning people counsel the abused spouse to suffer silently and endure the abuse. Perhaps the abused will win the abusers over through continued submissiveness (as suggested in 1 Pet. 3:1–2)—but this is bad advice in this situation and a misapplication of Scripture![10] No Scripture approves of a spouse being violent or of family members enduring it.

What is a spouse to do in these circumstances? Do not think that God overlooks abuse like this. He definitely moves *against* those who use violence; He abhors violence against any person. "Don't you know that you yourselves are God's temple and that God's Spirit lives in you? If anyone destroys God's temple, God will destroy him; for God's temple is sacred, and you are that temple" (1 Cor. 3:16–17).

When faced with personal violence, David quickly turned to the Lord:

> Rescue me, O Lord, from evil men; protect me from
> men of violence, who devise evil plans in their hearts and
> stir up war every day. They make their tongues as sharp as
> a serpent's; the poison of vipers is on their lips. Keep me,
> O Lord, from the hands of the wicked; protect me from
> men of violence who plan to trip my feet (Ps. 140:1–4).

God does not turn away from pleas like this. But how can an abused spouse cope with a marriage marred by domestic violence or sexual abuse and still be faithful to Scriptures like 1 Corinthians 7:11 which commands spouses not to separate?

Separate from the abuser. Scripture acknowledges that there may be situations when a Christian couple separates (1 Cor. 7:11a). God knows that an unreasonably abusive relationship is not really a marriage as much as it is a murderous relationship fueled by hate and violence (1 John 3:15). God always provides a way of escape if our circumstances are more than we can reasonably bear so we can stand up under the pressure (1 Cor. 10:13). If counseling and reasoning have failed, then it is proper—and sometimes even absolutely necessary—for victims of abuse to separate themselves from their abusers for physical safety reasons.[11] It is time to move to a safe environment among church friends or a safehouse for victims of abuse. There is nothing wrong with avoiding further injury to oneself or other innocent family members. Separation allows time for sorting options out. It is reasonable after exhausting all other reasonable measures of protection.

Report the abuse to those competent to help. Abused spouses need help. This means notifying those who can be a positive force for change. The abuser needs proper confrontation. Governmental studies prove that women who reported their abusive husbands to the proper authorities were less susceptible to another attack within the following six months. More importantly, if one parent abuses children, the other parent has a moral and legal responsibility to protect these young ones. Failure to do so can forever scar a child and even bring possible legal action.

Seek comfort and counsel from faithful Christians. It is critical to find family members and friends who believe your reports of abuse and truly understand your situation. They must empathize with the trap a victim spouse faces by enduring continuing abuse. You need help in moving to a safe and secure environment without delay and without skepticism about your complaints.

Don't place undue reliance on the legal system. A Public Broadcasting System production, "My Husband Is Going to Kill Me," powerfully details the last month in a thirty-year-old woman's life. She sought help from friends, social workers, police, and the courts without success. Her husband forced his way into her home and held her hostage at gunpoint while trying to rape her. Eight days later, he shot and killed her in front of her two children in a Denver restaurant parking lot. Obviously the legal system was too slow or ineffective in dealing with criminal abuse in this particular case. You must fully utilize the protection of civil law to shield yourself from your abuser(s), but also be realistic. All the court injunctions and protective orders the legal system has to offer will not shield anyone against bullets, knives, or fists in extreme jeopardy like this. Take reasonable measures to protect yourself.

Churches should use scriptural discipline against abusive Christian spouses. Domestic violence and abuse cries out for the disciplinary procedures Jesus outlined in Matthew 18:15–17. This is not a problem for the abused spouse only. Everyone in the Christian community has a responsibility to help bring an abusive spouse to repentance (1 Cor. 5:2, 12–13; 12:24b–26). Certainly God wants reconciliation. But if there is a matter that God hates more than divorce, it is the shedding of innocent blood (Prov. 6:16–17).

Celibacy and Living without a Spouse

How can one cope with a life alone if reconciliation with one's spouse cannot occur and yet divorce and remarriage is not a scriptural option? Some acknowledge that the only option open to a couple living in an unscriptural divorce situation is reconciliation or mandatory celibacy. This thrusts formerly married spouses into a state of extreme temptation for sensual sin. First Corinthians 7:8–9 says that those unable to control themselves in a sensual way should marry rather than burn with passion.[12] Therefore, can 1 Corinthians 7:11 really mean what it says?

Those facing mandatory celibacy under the most conservative views of Scripture prohibiting remarriage include everyone who divorces without cause permitted by Scripture, spouses divorced for their own *porneia*, those deserted by a spouse for no scriptural reason, and Christian spouses abandoned by unbelievers. Some argue that this is a recipe for disaster in

119

the real world. It is too much to ask of too many distressed individuals. Who can make such a sweeping law over a complete class of individuals by requiring celibacy without consideration of whether these individuals can control themselves sensually?

But God can make such judgments about who must remain celibate—especially if it violates the marriage relationship. Using a pragmatic approach to avoid celibacy quite often violates what God commands in Scripture. The fact is that God denies sexual intimacy to many people. These include single persons who cannot find suitable mates or who find it expedient or impractical to marry. There are also *married* persons who cannot (or will not) fulfill their marital responsibilities. Celibacy is not an unnatural or extreme condition foreign to most human beings.[13] In any event, sexual tension cannot justify an unscriptural or improvident marriage. If it were otherwise, many parents would have their children marry at puberty to avoid fornication. Those who cannot control themselves sensually, such as rapists, also could justify their sin. God's command is clear that no one may take another person's spouse and live with him or her in adultery simply because one's passionate desires need satisfaction.

God surely knew of these difficulties when giving us the principles in 1 Corinthians 7:11, but His will is plain. Any spouse who separates from or divorces a mate without scriptural reason must remain unmarried or reconcile to his or her mate. Remarriage to another person is not an option. These persons are not being denied marriage. They have a choice—live separately or return to their marriage.

Jesus spoke specifically of celibacy in Matthew 19:10–12. It is extremely difficult for men and women to be celibate; for some it may seem impossible. But what does Jesus say? "All things are possible with God." This is not a trite or simplistic promise to us in coping with our difficult feelings and circumstances. God promises to provide us with the grace sufficient to meet our needs (2 Cor. 12:9). He also promises to keep us from being tempted above what we can bear. He provides a way of escape so we can bear up under the pressures we feel within us without committing adultery (1 Cor. 10:13). Jesus would not ask those in an unscriptural divorce situation to remain unmarried without His help.

We could review many other issues and controversies. Sometimes there are clear statements in Scripture, but when there is not, biblical principles exist that apply to issues not directly addressed. The best advice is to obey the truth as far as it is clear to us, regardless of our personal feelings. God always calls each of us to use spiritual judgment in prayerfully working out our problems. In doing so, we need to wrestle with some of these Scriptures rather than to ignore them. It is our task to move forward with confidence and trust Him—not to deceive ourselves into denial of His truth.

Some Personal Conclusions

As a divorcee, I have struggled with many of these issues of marriage, divorce, and remarriage over the past twenty years or so. I would like to share my own thoughts and conclusions with you now since these may help you sort out your own life. You may not agree with everything I believe.[14] You must decide what is best for you as God grants you wisdom. If your conclusions are heartfelt and, most importantly, consistent with Scripture, no one should chastise you for your convictions.

This is how I interpret the Scriptures on marriage and divorce:

- *I believe in the permanence of heterosexual, monogamous marriage where God permanently joins a male and female who leave their parents and cleave to each other.* No other "marriage" is natural or approved by God.
- *I believe marriage partners should not separate unless the emotional or physical well-being of any family member is unreasonably threatened.* No one should permanently separate a husband and wife in a valid, non-adulterous marriage. Temporary separations of spouses by mutual consent are, I believe, permitted (but not approved) by God. In addition, in severe cases of domestic violence, sexual abuse, or other destructive behavior injurious to the spouses or children, a separation to preserve the peace and prevent bodily harm is necessary and appropriate after exhausting all other measures (counseling, police action, court orders, etc.). However, each spouse should act faithfully and lovingly to move quicker, or slower, in separation as the situation requires.
- *I believe that those who have never married are free to marry (or not) anyone eligible to marry in God's view as they choose.* It is highly preferable for many reasons that Christians marry Christians, but God does not specifically require this.[15]
- *I believe that if any spouse (Christian or unbeliever) commits porneia, the other spouse may divorce and freely remarry.* The faithful spouse

121

may (not must) divorce the unfaithful spouse and remarry another person scripturally eligible for marriage.

- *I believe that anyone divorcing for reasons other than porneia (or other scriptural reason) cannot remarry without committing adultery as long as one's mate is alive and unremarried.* As a general rule that Jesus made applicable to all people, spouses who divorce for reasons other than *porneia* may not remarry without committing adultery while both spouses are still alive. (Christians may have a special exception if an unbelieving mate divorces and leaves the marriage.)

- *I believe that anyone committing porneia can repent, be forgiven, and remarry after any divorce if the other spouse has died, remarried, or committed porneia also.* The Scriptures do not tell us whether, or when, the unfaithful spouse may remarry while the faithful spouse is alive. If repentance occurs and reconciliation of the original marriage partners (which is highly preferable) is impossible, I believe the unfaithful spouse may remarry. If the unfaithful spouse repents and the other spouse has not remarried, the couple should make every effort to reconcile. But if the faithful spouse remarries after a scriptural divorce, and if reconciliation is not possible, it seems cruel and contrary to God's gracious nature to forbid remarriage to the formerly unfaithful spouse. It appears to serve no useful purpose and unnecessarily subjects that person to greater temptations from the world.

- *I believe that a Christian spouse divorced by an unbeliever may remarry another person (preferably another Christian).* In the limited instance where an unbeliever divorces a faithful Christian spouse for any reason, the Christian is "not bound" to the unbeliever. I believe the context of 1 Corinthians 7:15 does speak of breaking the marriage bond—not just freedom from any obligation to reconcile with the unbeliever. Although Scripture is not clear on whether this frees the Christian to remarry (unless the unbeliever dies or commits *porneia* through remarriage or otherwise), I believe it does—for several reasons: because a divorce by the unbeliever, recognized as valid by Scripture, has already occurred; because mixed marriages displease God and have the potential of compromising the Christian's faith; because a faithful Christian should not face the harsh option of forfeiting marriage versus reconciliation with an unbeliever; and because God has called Christian to peace within His family. I further believe that this Christian is much better off remarrying another Christian.

Why enter into another mixed marriage with an unbeliever that is displeasing to God? *I do not counsel anyone else to follow this belief. It is only a personal conviction.* If the unbeliever commits *porneia* or dies, however, the Christian is clearly free to remarry a scripturally eligible person.

- *I believe that anyone who marries a person who was not scripturally divorced commits adultery unless the former spouse of the divorced person commits porneia or has died.*
- *I believe that any remarriage by either spouse after any divorce scripturally breaks the prior marriage.* The remarriage may therefore continue unless it is inherently invalid (e.g., if incest or homosexuality exists). Even if the remarriage were to scripturally end, I do not believe God favors reconciliation of the spouses to the first marriage. I base my reasoning upon the principles of Deuteronomy 24:4. Though Christ fulfilled the law of Moses, this Scripture tells us that God abhors any remarriage of former spouses after an intervening marriage.[16] Also, I cannot believe God would condone more divorce in a questionable effort to restore the first marriage. For the sake of peace and to spare further heartbreak to innocents (children), it is better to stay in the remarriage and hope for the best. Each party to that remarriage should seek repentance and forgiveness, however. *Once again, I do not counsel anyone else to follow this personal conviction.* If a marriage or remarriage (Christian or unbeliever) is incestuous or otherwise unnatural due to homosexuality or some other scriptural prohibition, thereby making the marriage invalid in God's sight, sin continually permeates the relationship from start to finish. It has no redeeming qualities in God's view, and therefore should end.
- *I believe that an unscriptural divorce followed by remarriage to another person can be adulterous when entered into, but the prior marriage is immediately (and scripturally) broken and the adultery of the remarriage does not continue.* I realize that the Greek for "commits adultery" in Matthew 19:9 could be a continuous state of adultery. But it also could refer to a one-time act of sin that does not continue. Like murder, adultery is a grievous sin. But if it occurs and does not continue, I believe that God will forgive truly repentant hearts of the persons involved without ending the remarriage.

My intent in sharing these beliefs with you is merely to let you know of my personal convictions based upon the material presented in this book. They obviously are not Scripture or "commandments" anyone must agree with. They are simply conclusions drawn from one who loves the Lord deeply. Feel free to disagree and make your own interpretations as the Lord leads you, but do not neglect the Scriptures that are clear to you, even if they are difficult to accept or obey.

The Bottom Line: Where Is Your Heart?

Paul expressed so well the ultimate accountability each Christian has about these issues. Listen to what he shares about his own life:

> So then, men ought to regard us as servants of Christ and as those entrusted with the secret things of God. Now it is required that those who have been given a trust must prove faithful. I care very little if I am judged by you or by any human court; indeed, I do not even judge myself. My conscience is clear, but that does not make me innocent. It is the Lord who judges me. Therefore judge nothing before the appointed time; wait till the Lord comes. He will bring to light what is hidden in darkness and will expose the motives of men's hearts. At that time each will receive his praise from God (1 Cor. 4:1–5).

We are to make judgments about right and wrong within the church as Scripture guides us (1 Cor. 5:12). There are some matters that outwardly appear wrong or right, but God looks inwardly to our hearts (1 Sam. 16:7; 1 Chron. 28:9). No human can really know the thoughts and motivations of another's heart (1 Cor. 2:11). Therefore, when people who profess an obedient faith in Jesus make personal decisions in legitimately disputable matters of Scripture, who among us can condemn them? They cannot be condemned by matters of our own consciences (1 Cor. 10:29). If their hearts are not right in making any decisions about marriage, divorce, and remarriage, God is the judge—not us.

Which view do you choose? Many issues as to marriage and divorce are very clear in Scripture. Some, however, cannot be resolved conclusively from God's Word. Therefore, we should honor and obey those commands from God that are clear to us. In making decisions about disputable matters, we must exercise our best judgment in devotion to Him. But whatever we do should not serve our own selfish ends. Instead we should unselfishly give of ourselves and always seek to glorify God (1 Cor. 10:31).

And God is able to make all grace abound to you, so that in all things at all times, having all that you need, you will abound in every good work (2 Cor. 9:8).

Questions for Personal Reflection

1) Do I really understand God's original plan for marriage?
2) What personal conclusions have I reached about marriage, divorce, and remarriage? (Write them down and pray about them.) Are they consistent with what I have learned from Scripture?
3) If my marriage ends in divorce, what is my marital status in God's sight? Am I willing to remain unmarried if efforts toward reconciliation with my spouse fail?
4) In what areas of my life do I most need the Lord's grace and mercy right now?
5) Do I really believe that God understands my personal pain in going through a separation or divorce?

Part Three

Riding Out the Storm of Divorce

Be diligent in these matters; give yourself wholly to them,
so that everyone may see your progress. Watch your life
and doctrine closely. Persevere in them, because if you
do, you will save both yourself and your hearers.
1 Timothy 4:15–16

Rejoice in the Lord always. I will say it again: Rejoice!
Let your gentleness be evident to all. The Lord is near.
Do not be anxious about anything, but in everything, by
prayer and petition, with thanksgiving, present your requests to God. And the peace of God, which transcends
all understanding, will guard your hearts and your
minds in Christ Jesus. Finally, brothers, whatever is true,
whatever is noble, whatever is right, whatever is pure,
whatever is lovely, whatever is admirable—if anything is
excellent or praiseworthy—think about such things. . . .
And the God of peace will be with you.
Philippians 4:4–9

And surely I am with you always,
to the very end of the age.
Matthew 28:20

I love the old hymn, "God Moves in a Mysterious Way." The first verse says, "God moves in a mysterious way, His wonders to perform; He plants His footsteps in the sea, and rides upon the storm." Do you ask God why you are going through the troubles in your marriage? Do you blame Him for your pain and loneliness? Well, He is riding on the storm with you. There is hope. This hymn has more to say to us:

> Ye fearful saints, fresh courage take. The clouds ye so much dread are big with mercy, and shall break in blessings on your head. Judge not the Lord by feeble sense, but trust Him for His grace; behind a frowning providence He hides a smiling face. His purposes will ripen fast, unfolding every hour. The bud may have a bitter taste, but sweet will be the flower. Blind unbelief is sure to err and scan His work in vain. God is His own interpreter, and He will make it plain.[1]

Yes, God is near, and He cares for us. We need to seek Him out and rely upon His counsel to do the right thing through divorce from our spouses.

This part of the book offers practical solutions for many problems and issues facing us in separation or divorce: "tough love" in dealing with our spouses to help them to face the consequences of their own decisions; guidelines on seeking marital and personal counseling; options for reconciliation to save the marriage; and issues of concern in managing marital separation, property division, and child care.

How do we select a lawyer to advise us of our legal rights? What can we expect from the courts since lawyers and judges are typically emotionally detached and overloaded with work? How do we turn these disadvantages to our benefit so we can handle matters more responsibly and lovingly? Finally, how do we help the most innocent victims of divorce—our children—learn how to help them grow despite difficult circumstances?

Our example and influence on others is probably at its highest point during our separation or divorce. People watch to see how we work through our difficulties. By seeking the counsel of many advisors and striving to love unlovable people, we will find joy and freedom to move on. Spiritual crisis management should lead observers to think, "God is really with you!"

CHAPTER 8

Depending upon God Like Never Before

*In Part One, we reviewed how marriages fall apart
and examined the thoughts and attitudes of our hearts.
In Part Two, we learned of God's view of marriage,
divorce, and remarriage. In this part of the book, we use
what we have learned, preparing ourselves for action on
all fronts—at home, in the courts, and in life in general.
We begin by setting our minds and hearts on God in total
dependence upon Him. Facing the pain of our struggles
rather than running from them is essential.*

Fortunately, I have always been around Christians who are very serious about their commitment to Christ. Some years ago, a well-meaning Christian from another congregation came to a Bible study in my home. With all sincerity he asked us a shocking question: "I've heard some people say that you folks think you can walk on water. Is that true?"

We thought he was joking. (Lest you get the wrong impression, I can assure you that I can barely float and I have never walked on water.) Everyone chuckled, except for our friend. He was quite serious. We immediately sobered up and assured him that this was obviously the product of someone's very fertile imagination or a joke taken out of context.

Stories like this become believable if there are other extraordinary events happening. Our church was growing rapidly then. Men and women of all colors, sizes, age groups, and backgrounds were coming to Christ in a powerful way. That can be scary and intimidating to some who have not experienced this joy firsthand. But there was nothing special about any of the people involved. Nothing really remarkable except . . . they were *totally* depending upon God. When men and women put their faith into action, no wonder extraordinary events occur. This amazes onlookers so much that it is not surprising some believe secondhand stories like that of our friend.

The cross has a powerful effect on the lives of men and women today. When my wife and I were on our honeymoon in Israel, we visited Capernaum on the northwest shore of the beautiful Sea of Galilee. The city is in ruins now, but it was the place where Jesus spent much of His ministry during the first century—His home base. What really struck me about Capernaum's shores, however, was a large white cross set up right next to the dock. I was drawn to that cross, framed by weeping willow trees with the ruins in the background. It captured my attention for a long time as we glided by speedboat across the sea. I watched it reflect on the calm afternoon waters of Galilee. It moved me deeply—the cross on the water.

That cross reminded me of one windy night crossing of the same Sea of Galilee many centuries ago—the night when Jesus, the only One who truly walked on water, moved across the waters to join His disciples.

Looking to Jesus

In Matthew 14:22–33, the disciples left Jesus behind to teach the crowds. They launched out in a small fishing boat to row to the other side of the Sea of Galilee late one afternoon. That little vessel, cramped and powerless, was all they had to move across the lake.

Soon the winds and waves began beating strongly against that small boat. Constant rowing by the disciples became almost impossible—two lengths forward, one length back. They broke their backs rowing against the elements throughout the night and well into the fourth watch.[1] What a strain this was! They had been working hard to cross the sea for nine to twelve hours without stopping. Imagine the blisters that were popping up. No doubt some oars were dragging in the water during this journey!

Then, in their weariness and pain, the disciples saw Jesus walking effortlessly across the water. It was something never seen before—*or since*, for that matter. Thinking it was a ghost, they cried out in total fear. But Jesus calmly reassured them, "Take courage! It is I. Don't be afraid" (v. 27).

Peter did not hesitate. "Lord, if it's you," he yelled, "tell me to come to you on the water." If you were one of the disciples in the boat on that windy night and heard Peter's request, what would you have thought? Notice that none of the other disciples volunteered to join Peter. I might have said, "Peter, are you crazy? You can't walk on water. Who knows whether that's Jesus out there or not? But this boat is real. This oar is real. Hang onto this boat. Control yourself! Don't go chasing after visions."

But Peter was determined to leave the boat and be with Jesus. Rowing that boat was fruitless in comparison to breezing across the water with Jesus. His way was not working. Jesus had a better way. Peter wanted out!

Peter really wanted to do the *impossible*. People can't walk on water.

130

But everything is possible with God. Jesus told Peter, "Come" (v. 29). Without hesitation Peter got out of the boat, let it go, and walked toward Jesus. He did the impossible by putting his faith into action. He knew Jesus would not let him down. He kept his eyes on the Savior and focused on Him alone. He was single-minded in his dedication. James 1:8 tells us the "double-minded man is unstable in all that he does." No divided heart here—Peter did whatever it took to be with Jesus. But he could not have performed the impossible unless, and until, in faith he made a clean break with the boat and actually got out on the water. Only then was he able to experience the power of God.

Does surviving a separation or divorce appear an impossible challenge? Will family division shatter our lives forever? How can we love spouses who have ignored or rejected us? Do we have trouble controlling our tongues? Do we fall into lying, cursing, or gossip? Are we tempted to look for the easy escapes in life—drugs, alcohol, sex? Are we given to mental games, lust, or fantasy lifestyles? Do our insecurities paralyze us into feeling that no one loves us? There may be no true love in the world, but 1 John 4:16 tells us that God is love. Real love is a fruit of the Holy Spirit (Gal. 5:22).

No matter what our impossible circumstances are, Jesus calls out to us, much like He did with Peter: "Come to me, all you who are weary and burdened, and I will give you rest. Take My yoke upon you and learn from Me, for I am gentle and humble in heart, and you will find rest for your souls. For My yoke is easy and My burden is light" (Matt. 11:28–30). Having an active faith in Christ means believing in your heart, "I can do all things *through Christ* who gives me strength" (Phil. 4:13, emphasis added).

But Peter hit a snag when he took his eyes off Jesus and looked at the world around him. He lost his focus on Christ. The wind and the waves licked at his feet and reminded him, "You can't do this. Do you really believe you can walk on water? You're in way over your head on this one, Peter."

We can relate to this. The world is so much like a carnival arcade where the pitchmen bark at us, "Over here! Three balls for a quarter! You look like a winner!" Everything ungodly around us beckons, "Look at me!" Enough of this and we fall for it. We buy the lie and throw away God in the process.

Peter sank like a stone. He cried out to Jesus, "Lord, save me!" This was an earnest and urgent prayer. He knew he was in trouble, but notice that Peter did not try to reach back for the boat. He still moved forward to Jesus for salvation. Jesus immediately reached out His hand to raise Peter up from the depths, asking, "You of little faith, why did you doubt?" (v. 14). Why do we try to work out our own issues without moving forward in faith toward our powerful and loving God?

Peter's encounter with Jesus on the Sea of Galilee is so illustrative of the way many of us feel when facing a separation or divorce. Some want to be with Jesus but choose instead to keep on rowing their little boats of security and control. The going may be rough, but at least they are on familiar ground. Others know that pushing their own way through life is futile if God offers a better way. Those enlightened souls are the ones who make a clean break with worldly props and step out in faith to depend upon God. They experience the spiritual catharsis and rejuvenation in life that the boat rowers miss. But they too can fall into self-doubt and sink like Peter if times get tough. The key is to keep our focus on God (see Matt. 13:1–23).

The Problem of Avoiding Pain

Why do we not turn to God when our world is in turmoil? The simple answer is that we want to relieve our inward pain and restore order to our lives immediately. Is that necessarily wrong? No, unless our desperate search for fast relief pushes us toward worldly quick fixes—while also turning us away from God. In our race to numb the pain, we grab for the nearest anesthetic or rush for easy escapes rather than depend upon God for the cure. We do not have the patience to wait upon God.

When a crisis occurs and we become obsessed with relieving our pain, the world is always there to give us lots of "handles" to grab. Fire alarms, escape hatches, emergency brakes, ripcords, pills to take—all types of "saviors" to pull in a hurry when trauma hits us. Reaching out for God in a spiritual sense can be unsettling and uncertain. Sometimes God does not give us that feeling of flesh or metal that tells us we are connected with help. There are no flashing red lights confirming activation of emergency options. It can feel like walking in the dark around obstacles, listening to instructions from someone we cannot see.

What is wrong with relying on quick fixes? In reality, they are about as valuable as a trapeze artist's safety net lying on the ground. Many times our safety valves and best plans go awry. British writer L. P. Jacks tells of a horse doctor visiting a country fair who boasted of an invention that could make any animal swallow pills. Those wanting to challenge him on this brought him a mule. The doctor put a long glass tube down the mule's throat and prepared to blow a pill through it. But the mule coughed and blew first. The wrong patient got the pill! Sometimes we think we have the answer to our problems, but then something unexpected happens and we find ourselves worse off.

We are too quick to avoid pain instead of understanding *why* we hurt and *who* can really help us. Of course, being unable to immediately rid ourselves of painful circumstances is discouraging. But pain is God-given to protect us from hurting ourselves even worse and to lead us into depending upon Him. We just have not understood the message.

Much of our inner spiritual pain comes from a void within us. We know those personal, inward thoughts, fantasies, secrets, and private sins that no one else knows about us. In shame, we go into deep denial about where we are in life. We avoid probing questions and intimate contact with others. We hide in our secret gardens just like Adam and Eve did from the Lord. Outwardly to others, we know how to offer up evidence to make ourselves look good and exhibit a fake sense of well-being. But inwardly we know it's there—the pain of powerlessness, emptiness, and hypocrisy that will not go away. As we will see, it is a painful void which only God can fill. He knows how we really are on the inside (Ps. 14:2; 94:11; 1 Cor. 4:5; Heb. 4:13).

So what do we do about this? Instead of going to God, we constantly rearrange our lives and seek maximum comfort through escape from pain instead of learning contentment in spite of our circumstances. We *demand* that others love us and meet our needs, which is particularly tough in a marriage. Self-obsession with our own pain breeds selfishness. We expect our spouses to ignore their own pain instead and comfort us. Avoiding pain brings out the worst in us. It pushes God out of our lives. It does not satisfy us. It simply does not work in making our lives more fulfilling.

Facing the Pain

What is the answer? Instead of avoiding painful circumstances, why not use a major life crisis, such as a divorce or separation, as a catharsis for change? A family disaster shakes us mightily, down to the core of our existence. It strips away our self-protective layers and brings the issues bubbling beneath the surface into our conscious mind. We are vulnerable once again. Pain stares us in the face. There is no time or energy to pretend. But this is not necessarily something to avoid.

Life's trials build character and maturity. Norman Rockwell, the late artist whose pictures appeared for years on the cover of the *Saturday Evening Post*, was famous for capturing the essence of America in his paintings. When asked how he so vividly portrayed scenes from real life, even in his drawings of animals, he replied, "Whenever I need a dog model, I always get it from the pound. Dogs that have taken a beating from life have character." There's a lot of truth in that statement. Romans 5:2–5 tells us:

> And we rejoice in the hope of the glory of God. Not only so, but we also rejoice in our sufferings, because we know that suffering produces perseverance; perseverance, character; and character, hope. And hope does not disappoint us, because God has poured out His love into our hearts by the Holy Spirit, whom He has given us.

Life experiences help us mature, bringing God into our circumstances. As we resist the urge to fix matters but yield ourselves to His loving discipline, this produces perseverance, character, and hope in our lives.

Rejoicing in a Wilderness Experience

Before beginning His public ministry, Jesus fasted for forty days in the wilderness (Luke 4). Physically, He was alone and isolated, hurting and hungry. Then Satan tempted Him in every way. How did He resist? First, He never lost sight of His identity. He relied totally on His relationship with the Father, which was worth much more than the very best Satan had to offer. Second, He rejected Satan's invitations of thinly veiled greed and rebellion by relying on God's truth to counter these lies. This testing empowered Jesus to become the source of eternal salvation for all who obey Him (Heb. 5:7–9).

We, too, must welcome our own "wilderness experiences." These times remind us of our identity in Christ and our need to make daily choices to rely upon God like never before. We need Him—especially during tough times. Wilderness experiences toughen us up and clarify our priorities.

Like Peter walking on the water toward Jesus, now is our time to reach out for God. When sin and pain stalk us, it is time to face life honestly and to hunger for God. Depending upon ourselves is futile; instead, we can use our separation or divorce as a springboard toward total reliance upon Him.

Where Is Our Refuge and Strength in Tough Times?

> My soul finds rest in God alone; my salvation comes
> from him. He alone is my rock and my salvation; he is my
> fortress, I will never be shaken. How long will you assault
> a man? Would all of you throw him down—this leaning
> wall, this tottering fence? They fully intend to topple him
> from his lofty place; they take delight in lies. With their
> mouths they bless, but in their hearts they curse. Find rest,
> O my soul, in God alone; my hope comes from him. He
> alone is my rock and my salvation; he is my fortress, I
> will not be shaken. My salvation and my honor depend on
> God; he is my mighty rock, my refuge (Ps. 62:1–7).

> This is what the Lord says: "Cursed is the one who
> trusts in man, who depends on flesh for his strength and
> whose heart turns away from the Lord. He will be like a
> bush in the wastelands; he will not see prosperity when it
> comes. He will dwell in the parched places of the desert, in
> a salt land where no one lives. But blessed is the man who
> trusts in the Lord, whose confidence is in him. He will be
> like a tree planted by the water that sends out its roots by
> the stream. It does not fear when heat comes; its leaves are
> always green. It has no worries in a year of drought and
> never fails to bear fruit" (Jer. 17:5–8).

What cures can humankind offer to any distressed person compared
to what God delivers to us? Can we come close to harnessing the power
God has in His very nature? No problem we face is an obstacle for God.
People may rip us up behind our backs. Hidden agendas control. But God
is a steadfast rock. Like trees growing by His refreshing stream, we can
shoot out our roots into His living water. His refreshment will keep us cool
in the blazing heat of midday trials and the sorrows of life.

How do we depend upon God? How can we have the inexpressible joy
spoken of in 1 Peter 1:8 during a separation or divorce? We must get out
of our boats and keep our eyes on Jesus. We must resist the temptation of
self-protection and self-reliance and launch out in faith, focused on Him.

Dr. Larry Crabb eloquently states the goal of Christian maturity this way: "Christ wants us to face reality as it is, including all the fears, hurts, resentments, and self-protective motives we work hard to keep out of sight, and to emerge as changed people. Not pretenders. Not perfect. But more able to deeply love because we're more aware of His love."[2]

This is not an impossible ideal; it just seems that way. But that is the irony of having faith in God. The question is whether we are willing to let go of our lives to walk on troubled waters. Will we reach out for God, or for a quick fix from the world around us?

Walking by Faith—Not by Sight

What is it that gives us the confidence to depend upon God and do the impossible? Paul gave the answer in his letter to the Corinthian church:

> We do not want you to be uninformed, brothers, about the hardships we suffered in the province of Asia. We were under great pressure, far beyond our ability to endure, so that we despaired even of life. Indeed, in our hearts we felt the sentence of death. But this happened that we might not rely on ourselves but on God, who raises the dead (2 Cor. 1:8–9).
>
> But we have this treasure in jars of clay to show that this all-surpassing power is from God and not from us. We are hard pressed on every side, but not crushed; perplexed, but not in despair; persecuted, but not abandoned; struck down, but not destroyed. Therefore we do not lose heart. Though outwardly we are wasting away, yet inwardly we are being renewed day by day. For our light and momentary troubles are achieving for us an eternal glory that far outweighs them all. So we fix our eyes not on what is seen, but on what is unseen. For what is seen is temporary, but what is unseen is eternal. . . . We live by faith, not by sight (2 Cor. 4:7–9, 16–18; 5:7).

Do you see any common denominators between Peter and Paul in their devotion and dependence upon God? Outwardly, they groaned and felt burdened by life, perplexed, persecuted, and struck down. But inwardly, they renewed themselves by fixing their eyes on Jesus. They realized that life's death sentence taught them not to rely on themselves but on God. In doing so, nothing crushed them. They did not lose heart. They walked by *faith* in His promise, not by *sight* in a disapproving world.

What about us? Our marriages are coming to an early end. Our mates have left us. Confusion and fear grip our children in seeing their parents go in separate directions. Friends back away. Relatives take sides. As we watch these events coming at us, we may feel overwhelmed and hard pressed on every side. But who rides upon the storm? God calls us to look beyond our daily trials of faith and be confident with concentrated faith in His deliverance—no matter what. This is the essence of biblical faith: being sure of what we hope for and certain of what we do not see (Heb. 11:1). God gives us this faith through His Word (Rom. 10:17). In our trials and hardships we can know that if God is all we've got, He is surely all we need!

Preparing Ourselves for Action

There is no surefire formula or step-by-step process to depending upon God. If there was, too many would rely upon it as a legalistic recipe for righteousness. Personal growth comes in a variety of ways to different people—that is the beauty of God's grace. But whatever the experience, personal dependence upon God always begins with walking by faith and not by sight. It comes from a change of heart in total devotion to Him. Here are some useful suggestions to help us take that first step of faith:

Be Sensitive to Inner Hunger and Thirst

We have an inner need to feel significant; our lives must have meaning. We must make a difference to someone else, so we crave relationships with loving acceptance. God instills these needs within our souls to lead us to Him. Each person has a God-shaped void deep inside—an empty space that only God can fill. This emptiness creates a yearning and longing to be with God that most anyone can feel after our demanding schedules end for the day or after we turn off the television at night. It is always there, pushing us toward Him. We know how to turn away from these inward longings. We try to fill the emptiness by foolishly stuffing ourselves with food or sexual pleasures. We temporarily numb the pain of separation from God with drugs or alcohol. But these do not satisfy us. Our inward hunger remains; that inward yearning is always within us as long as we live.

We begin our spiritual growth by acknowledging our inward hunger for His love. When night comes and the place next to us in bed is empty, we will taste the bitter tears of loneliness. Sleepless nights will come. But we are well on the way to dealing with that pain by knowing this: only God can really comfort us in times like these. He gently tells us, "I know your pain. I share your sorrow. If no one else loves you in the entire world, I always will." Will we listen for His voice, or will we turn away to weak substitutes? If we seek comfort in this life through relationships, material wealth, or physical pleasures, the irony is that we move away from God. This is why Jesus tells us in Matthew 19:23-24 that it is hard for the rich to enter the kingdom of God because they may depend more upon creation than the Creator. We appreciate God when circumstances are good in life, but all the more when we lose those joys and still find Him meeting our needs for love and fulfillment. The abundant life Jesus offers us in John 10 is priceless.

Prepare with Prayer

When life's pressures are really boiling, too often we ignore one of our greatest painkillers—an active prayer life. Prayer is the ultimate heart tenderizer. It helps quiet our own inner voice and personal demands while opening our hearts to receive godly counsel.

There are times when I have felt so close to God in prayer, I could almost swear He touched me physically. But so many other times, I let the weariness of my day, television, and other distractions tear me away from Him. We become captive to schedules that constantly squeeze out time for private meditation and communion with God when we need it most.

Eloquence or the length of our prayers make no difference if our hearts are right. God knows our hearts. His Spirit intercedes for us (Rom. 8:26-27). After all, Peter made his drowning plea to Christ in three quick words, "Lord, save me!" (Matt. 14:30). Every word counted!

There is a major difference between the prayerful approaches of those who fulfill the minimum daily requirements and those with a desperate need to be with God. As Mike Warnke tells it, when life is going well, we calmly come into our bedrooms and lie down to pray. We use "King James" type prayers with all the "-ths" on the ends of our words and are flowery in our praise. But when we are in trouble, we hit the floor on our knees and cry out, "Lord, what are You doing to me? Haven't I been doing your will?!?" Challenges always strip away our masks to reveal our basic needs.

Remember Paul's encouraging words from Philippians 4:6-7, written from his jail cell? "Do not be anxious about anything, but in everything, by prayer and petition, with thanksgiving, present your requests to God. And the peace of God, which transcends all understanding, will guard your hearts and your minds in Christ Jesus."

In my own struggles, I found a definite peace in prayer. There is a real comfort in expressing the thoughts and attitudes of my heart to God. I do not worry about what He thinks of me; I do not fear Him recoiling in horror at my lack of faith. There is a real release in simply talking matters out. It is so encouraging to know that God hears and answers prayer.

Seek Guidance and Comfort from God's Word

Growth comes from drawing upon the right resources. Very soon after my wife announced that she was leaving me, I read everything I could find on divorce. I went to the Christian bookstores. I checked out the church library. I asked friends for copies of materials. I whipped through the Bible with the help of concordances. In my desperation, I believed that knowledge was power. To some extent this is true—if the focus is on knowing God. I quickly learned I was powerless to control my circumstances.

All was not lost, however. By immersing myself in the affirmation of Scripture from the different perspectives of many Christian writers, I also learned contentment. I knew there was hope. There were two ways to handle my situation—my way or God's way. The choices became clearer. God's advice made sense. His Word highlighted the traps and temptations in advance. The Bible truly became a light for my path (Ps. 119:105).

There is no substitute for setting one's mind and heart to do God's will on a daily basis than through consistent Bible study. Some time ago, *Newsweek* magazine ran a feature on mountain climbing. According to the article, more than 60,000 serious climbers live in the United States alone. But leading the pack was a very small elite group known as "hard men." For these individuals, climbing mountains and towering rock faces is a way of life. They revel in the ultimate climbing experience called "free soloing"—climbing without equipment or safety ropes. The only way to train for this very dangerous challenge is through daily dedication. Between climbs, these devoted men and women often hang on doorjambs by their fingertips to strengthen arms and hands.

Similarly, daily dedication to prayer and Bible study prepares us for our mountains in life. God reassures and strengthens us through this personal discipline. As the Bible tells us, "Everything that was written in the past was written to teach us, so that through endurance and the encouragement of the Scriptures we might have hope" (Rom. 15:4).

Focus on Jesus

When high rise construction workers walk narrow steel beams without supports many stories above the ground, how do they do it without falling? They focus on a point at the other end of the beam and walk straight toward it without looking down. When a farmer wants to plow his field evenly, he plants a stake with a red flag at one end of the pasture and plows from the other. By constantly watching the red flag as a reference point, the plow moves forward in straight rows. Perhaps this is some of what Jesus had in mind in Luke 9:62: "No one who puts his hand to the plow and looks back is fit for service in the kingdom of God." Whenever the risk is great and precision counts, as it does in a separation or divorce, clearly defined goals and focused progress toward success are critical. Looking to Jesus is the key.

When the Lord, through Moses, delivered the Israelites from Egyptian bondage, the people complained about their circumstances. Instead of focusing on the Lord's presence, in their hearts they looked back to Egypt. They preferred slavery to their oppressors over trusting their Deliverer for freedom. The result? Divided hearts compounded their sorrow.

In our marriage difficulties we can look back to "how things were" and yearn for the "good old days," or we can move forward in faith as God leads us. The choice is ours, but we must make a choice. As Jesus tells us, "No one can serve two masters" (Matt. 6:24). When we move forward, it should not be aimless, erratic, or inconsistent. Looking to Jesus gives our lives meaning, spiritual focus, and direction, bringing order to everything else.

Decisions come into clearer focus by simply asking ourselves, "What would Jesus do in this situation?" It is amazing how a parable or teaching of Jesus will come to mind that provides the right answer. But this means staying rooted in God's Word so these associations can guide us.

Focusing on Jesus helps keep worldly advice in perspective. During my separation, others urged me to "stop being so nice" to my wife. I should "cut her off" from some benefits. At times my anger *did* prompt me to be punitive or revengeful, but then I asked myself if Jesus would act this way. Often I saw my lack of love and forgiveness. This was not the type of person I am in Christ, nor was it what I wanted to be. If we cannot reasonably see Jesus doing what we want to do, it is time to explore other alternatives.

Resolve to Make Decisions with Godly Wisdom

As we prayerfully use our minds, thinking of how Scripture applies, comparing alternatives, weighing advice, and reasonably evaluating our desires, God gives us wisdom to make good choices.

Think of the competing choices you have faced. One alternative was pragmatic and easy, and the other more principled but difficult or costly. What decision did you make? As you read the biblical discussions on marriage and divorce in Part Two of this book, did you want to reject what the Bible says? If you want to remarry and an opportunity is there, will you do so if it causes you and your partner to commit adultery? If you are glad that your spouse left, what if he or she returns? If your spouse returns at an inopportune time, will you turn away?

Peter had a choice on the lake. He could play it safe and stay in the boat with the disciples, or he could launch out in faith on the water. Jesus said: "Come!" Peter obeyed. The apostle Paul had a choice. He could have been a meek evangelist and avoided many uncomfortable and even life-threatening situations, but he laid everything on the line for the Lord.

We have a choice. Will we retreat from painful situations and satisfy our selfish desires, or will we walk in faith by following God's direction in the Bible? Will we trust that He will make all matters work for the good as He promises? This book highlights many choices we face in a separation or divorce. Should we resist a divorce? Should we reconcile and forgive? Should we fight over material possessions in court? Hundreds of other dilemmas may arise. But when we find our answer from the Bible and spiritual counselors, we come to a point of decision: "Am I willing to trust God enough to deny myself and follow His way?" Too often we think we are doing God's will, but we are really doing *our* own will in God's name.

Reach Out for God

Some incorrectly believe that God has every event in your life mapped out for you like a travel agent's itinerary. Everything is fine as long as you make your appointed connections. But if you miss one, the itinerary is ruined. Any substitute plan will never be as good as the original. Only substandard Christianity awaits from then on as God puts us on a shelf. No wonder some divorcees who hold to this view feel hopelessness after their marriages fail. But God is not like that at all. Of course, we must face the consequences of our sins, but God is always ready and eager to forgive us from our past mistakes and restore us to new life (1 John 1:9). He proved it with David, after his committing adultery with Bathsheba and murdering Uriah, and with Peter despite his denying Christ.

The false notion that "God helps those who help themselves" comes from Benjamin Franklin in *Poor Richard's Almanac*—not from the God of the universe. Homilies like this only work to put God at a distance from so many of us who desperately need to reach out for Him. In truth, God helps the fatherless (Ps. 10:14), the poor and needy (Ps. 72:12), those who are weak in their faith (Mark 9:23–24), those who call on Him and seek His face (Ps. 27:8–9), and all believers in Christ (Heb. 13:6). It is more accurate to say that God helps those who *cannot* help themselves.

James 4:8 tells us, "Come near to God and He will come near to you." Even so, it is so tempting to hold on to our rowboats as the disciples did on the turbulent sea, trying to control our own circumstances.

There is another problem to avoid as well. Since we cannot physically touch God, we sometimes reach out for other people after our spouses have left us. We may demand that they love us to the same extent that our spouses or even God would—certainly an impossible task! We demand that others do for us what only God truly can. But people will fail and disappoint us. In desperation we may want others to love us so much that we neglect our own needs and sacrifice our identity for their approval. Instead of seeking healthy, interdependent relationships made by choice, in difficult times we feel compelled to become social chameleons. We blend into different environments and plead for love from others. This leads to the most unhealthy forms of codependency. But more than that, we move farther and farther away from God, our true source of strength.

Spiritual management of a life crisis like divorce means fostering our inward yearning for God into a passion that keeps us constantly moving forward, moving toward Him. Like those commercials of the man crawling through a hot, arid desert toward an oasis that promises him a tall, cold glass of iced tea, if we are truly aware of our thirst and need for God, we will not waste any time reaching for any substitute for the ultimate Quencher.

Total reliance involves being absolutely and totally committed to God. Evangelist Kip McKuen tells the story of a young Chinese Communist exchange student who attended college in the U.S. some years ago. This young man fell in love with American culture—especially Clint Eastwood movies. Fortunately, the good news of Jesus also touched his heart during his studies and he became a Christian. Since he would have to return to China some day, concerned Christian friends wondered about his commitment. What would he do, they asked, if a governmental official held a gun to his head and demanded that he renounce Christ? "Easy," he quickly replied, "I'll just tell them, 'Go ahead—make my day!'" That uncompromising commitment and faith to go with God regardless of circumstances is what we need to help us through separation and divorce.

We reach out for God by not forcing solutions that rid ourselves of stubborn problems and by ignoring quick and easy shortcuts. We yield to God by allowing time for Him to lead us. We trust in His promise in Romans 8:28 that all matters will work for the good of those who love Him.

We know how to make life very difficult for our spouses during a separation or divorce. And if we do not, there will always be others who do. It may be quick and easy to cut them off financially. We may know how to run them through the labyrinth of the courts for months or even years. We have the power to destroy their lives—but that is not fair or loving. It is not God's way. He guides us into loving the unlovable. His affirmation and unconditional love replaces what others have denied us. Seek His peace that surpasses all understanding (Ps. 34:11–22; Phil. 4:4–7).

Deal with Sin

Whenever we face a wilderness experience in life or an impossible challenge, every self-denial and resistance against temptation and sin we have made in our lives will come back to strengthen us. The reverse is also true: every self-indulgent sin, every shirking of responsibilities, every compromise with evil, and every ungodly word, thought, or deed will steal our power.

When we feel deprived by circumstances, sometimes we rationalize and give ourselves permission to satisfy sinful lusts. No home-cooked meals? Grab for the cookies and ice cream. No one paying the bills? Run up the credit cards. No one to clean house? Go out on the town and only come home to crash. No one to kiss goodnight? Chase after anything that lust fancies. We can reach for that forbidden fruit just like Eve did in the garden. But when we do, guilt and shame eat us up inside. Our consciences become so seared that we feel nothing—and we bear the consequences of our sins. We move away from God as we seek to please ourselves.

The strongest fortress against sin is breached with compromise. The Great Wall of China stretches for 1,500 miles. It was built to be impenetrable, but enemies breached the wall three times in its first few years. How? Not by knocking holes in the wall or climbing over, but by bribing the gatekeepers! God has given us the best defense against sin through His

Spirit, but He has made us the gatekeepers for our lives. It is our choice to say yes or no to sin. Our fortress is safeguarded or breached as we decide. And the bribes offered to us come when we are least expecting them.

Why did Satan come to Jesus in the wilderness? After fasting for many days, Jesus might be more vulnerable to temptations of the flesh. We are no different. Whenever illness strikes or the tragedy of a family death or divorce occurs, we are at our weakest point. We become prime candidates for giving in to the lust of the eyes, the lust of the flesh, and the pride of life. If we give in to our desires, we risk becoming hardened by sin and separated from God. It is absolutely essential that we rely on God's power to hold the line on sin.

Cultivate Humility in Assessing Ourselves

Some time ago, one of the homecoming queen finalists at a leading university decided to do some strategic campaigning. Students on campus often congregated in a courtyard after lunch. So this aspiring young lady staked out a spot and smiled in all directions at passersby. But everyone gave her the strangest looks and kept on walking. After being very perplexed and discouraged about this response for some time, the young woman finally asked a friend if she knew what the problem was. "Sure," replied the friend, "you've got a big wad of lettuce stuck between your two front teeth!"

To all the world, we truly believe we are the most reasonable, rational, and wisest persons around. But the truth is that quite often, everyone in the world may see our faults before we do, just like that young woman. This is why God tells us to have an attitude of humility (Phil. 2:1–11). We are to seek the counsel of many advisors (Prov. 11:14; 15:22; 24:6). We need God's help, as well as that of our trusted friends, to help us see ourselves objectively.

Take one day at a time. "Life by the yard is hard, but life by the inch is a cinch."[3] In Matthew 6:19–34, Jesus tells us that worry is futile. It will not positively affect the quantity or quality of our lives. God's advice? Easy does it by living one day at a time, knowing that He cares for us, and by seeking His kingdom first. Each day is a new opportunity to see our circumstances in a different light and to try new courses of action.

Daily prayer and Bible study are only the beginning. We must live out our faith. Visiting an encouraging Christian is always a lift. Church fellowship helps keep us on track. Sharing our faith in Christ and serving others—the simple act of giving—turns our minds away from self-pity and complacency. Even little details like keeping our bodies and homes clean can bring joy. Maintaining a daily personal journal or diary works well to keep a proper focus and perspective of where we are in our lives.

Bloom Where We Are Planted

Whenever tough circumstances trap us, our first instinct is to get out. Peter wanted to be with Jesus; he did not hesitate in getting out of that row-boat. But did you notice how Jesus responded? After rescuing him from the waves, He took Peter right back to the boat with the other disciples. Jesus easily could have taken Peter by the hand for a quick walk across the lake, but He chose to be with the disciples *in their situation*.

We either want to be free or in a happy marriage. But that is not where we are right now. Reality is in facing our circumstances and looking for the Lord to lead us *through* our difficulties.

Armilda Mathis remembers when earthmoving equipment tore up her backyard during a home improvement project some years ago. An enormous pile of dirt and debris filled the yard. Surprisingly, one day she saw something green coming out of that huge dirt pile—a tiger lily! She wanted to transplant it, but decided not to after marveling at how that little plant pushed so hard through all the debris. It burst into the sunlight and rain-water to beautifully flourish right on top of that huge pile. That little seed, crushed under the weight of all that junk, burst forth to triumph!

What a lesson for us. We can glorify God right where we are. We can shine through! Remember the eloquent words of Winston Churchill when England stood alone during World War II against Nazi tyranny? He said: "Though the British Empire should last a thousand years, men will say of her, 'This was her finest hour!'"[4] Triumph over an adversary is great, but to triumph over adversity is greatness. We will be remembered more for how we endured our difficulties than how we managed our blessings.

Hudson Taylor once noted that God uses people who are weak and feeble enough to lean on Him. Dr. Larry Crabb correctly emphasizes that a tough faith does not grow in a comfortable mind. Protection against pain blunts our capacity to love. Much as we dislike hearing it, sometimes it is good that we hurt; it keeps us going to God. When we try to look good and fool others, we only fool ourselves. It is easy to find scapegoats for our difficulties, but these do not *make* us what we are—they only *reveal* what we are in our hearts and minds. It is not so much what happens *to* us, but what happens *in* us, that helps us survive. As our faith turns dreams of deliverance into acts of obedience, God fulfills His promises.

Running the Race

My favorite "life verse" is Hebrews 12:1–3, summarized in this chapter:

> Therefore, since we are surrounded by such a great cloud of witnesses, let us throw off everything that hinders and the sin that so easily entangles, and let us run with perseverance the race marked out for us. Let us fix our eyes on Jesus, the author and perfecter of our faith, who for the joy set before him endured the cross, scorning its shame, and sat down at the right hand of the throne of God. Consider him who endured such opposition from sinful men, so that you will not grow weary and lose heart.

We are part of a long line of people who have struggled with pain and self-doubt. But they held onto their faith despite overwhelming circumstances—and they are watching us in the arena now, cheering us on.

A *Mayo Clinic* magazine once made this observation: "For the patients who have an especially difficult time after surgery, if they eventually recover, it is because there is a family member who gives them a reason to be strong and a reason to go home." We will survive divorce because we have a reason to be strong in this life and a reason to go home to be with God.

Questions for Personal Reflection

1) Specifically, in what ways am I depending upon God in daily life?
2) Am I honestly facing the pain of my situation or seeking to avoid it?
3) Will I seek biblical counsel and follow God's Word even if I disagree?
4) What are my goals in lovingly dealing with my separation or divorce?
5) Are my decisions focused on God or on my selfish desires?

CHAPTER 9

The Toughest Love of All:
Being Firm with Your Spouse

*Maintaining proper self-respect and dignity is a key
factor when facing the crisis of divorce. Using tough love
means being loving, yet giving firm and measured responses
to the decisions and circumstances affecting us. Respecting
boundaries and personal freedoms, while not being passive
and compliant about unwise decisions made by our spouses,
are critical concerns. We must not stand between the
choices our spouses make and the discipline arising
from the logical consequences of those choices.*

Divorce threats require action! Our spouses need unconditional love, but they don't need love that is permissive, passive, or weak. If our spouses act irresponsibly, it is time for us to set boundaries and encourage mutual accountability like never before. It is time for tough love!

Tough love is a firm and measured response to the decisions and actions of our spouses. It helps them feel the full weight of responsibility and inevitable consequences of their decisions and actions. Tough love sets up limits on what is acceptable conduct. It enforces clear boundaries between lives that are splitting apart. It is the courage of speaking the truth in love. Tough love reinforces options for repentance and forgiveness rather than revenge. It resists possessiveness and embraces the pain of being vulnerable in a positive way. Tough love encourages personal confidence and self-respect in moving on with your life. And it often means letting go of a spouse who wants to end the marriage.[1]

Some erroneously believe tough love contradicts unconditional love. They argue that unconditional love does not set limits on what is acceptable conduct. They view such limits as conditions in an effort to control the love object. They believe that unconditional love requires one to love others no matter what they do and without trying to change them. Not so! There is a difference between unconditional love for a *person* and unconditional acceptance of their actions. The former is biblical and loving, but the latter is not biblical at all. Unconditional love does not mean "anything goes." The Bible has numerous examples of loving the sinner but hating the sin.[2]

Tough love says: "I *love* you unconditionally as a person, but I cannot accept your conduct to the extent it adversely affects my life or harms you or others." Unconditional love for people and using tough love to set limits on acceptable *conduct* are not contradictory at all. They are consistent and biblically responsible in helping any person see a need for repentance.

Tough Love Survival Strategies

How is tough love put into action as we face the death of our marriages and impending divorce? Let's review some practical ways of being loving, but firm, with our spouses. This is not a one-sided venture. Our goal is to help both marriage partners during the crisis of divorce.

Loving Our Spouses in an Unloving Situation

Will Rogers remarked, "I never met a man I didn't like." Jesus never met anyone He didn't love—regardless of their problems or mistakes. He met the woman at the well in Samaria—even though Jews did not associate with Samaritans—to show that He overcame racial prejudice (John 4:1–26). He ministered to a man with an evil spirit to show His love to the mentally afflicted (Mark 5:1–20). Although the crowd was against Him, He stood by the adulterous woman until her accusers left. Then He compassionately but firmly urged her to change her life (John 8:3–11). He prayed for the forgiveness of those who jeered Him as He writhed in agony on the cross (Luke 23:34). The many ways that Jesus loved the unlovable are examples for us.

You may say, "But Will Rogers and Jesus never met my spouse!" Death of a marriage can make us cynical toward our mates. But when marriage partners divide, there is a "most excellent way" of dealing with the situation in love (1 Cor. 12:31). The apostle Paul wrote the Galatian church, "The only thing that counts is faith expressing itself through love" (Gal. 5:6).

What do we want to carry with us after the divorce is over? Can we take any pleasure in knowing that we have destroyed our spouses? Tough love distinguishes between taking firm action in dealing with imbalanced and sinful situations and never losing sight of the *person* and his or her worth. We can still love the person despite the predicament.

Defining Acceptable Conduct and Boundaries

Tough love means telling the person you love that there are limits to what conduct is acceptable in your relationship. You and your spouse have a right to define what that conduct will be like between you, using the Bible as a guide.

Real love is not a wimpy acceptance of others—sin and all. Lines have to be drawn—in love. Those in error must see what they are doing to harm themselves and others. We cannot avoid confrontation if these limits are to mean anything. The question is this: Do we have the courage to stand up for the truth and let the chips fall? It is easy to grovel and beg, or to compromise and appease. But the Bible tells us, "Faithful are the wounds of a friend" (Prov. 27:6, NASB).

Everyone remembers Bill Cosby as the funny but very wise Cliff Huxtable on television. It is almost inconceivable that one who portrayed the perfect father so convincingly could be anything less in real life. But this father of fathers was estranged from his real-life daughter Erinn some years ago through her abuse of drugs and alcohol. Cosby used tough love with her, truthfully acknowledging that his daughter was irresponsible and untrustworthy. "It's going to take her hitting rock bottom, where she's totally exhausted—that point where she can't fight any more," Cosby told the *Los Angeles Times*. "Right now we're estranged. She can't come here. She's not a person you can trust. You think that you're not a good parent because you don't answer the call. But you can't let the kid use you."[3]

Cosby loved his daughter deeply but refused to blame himself for this tragedy. He did not protect Erinn from herself while steering her to help. She had to realize that no one could change her against her will. It was up to her. She made the improvident life decisions; she had to straighten out her own life.

The key to Cosby's tough love approach was *setting limits* to what he did. Certainly he had the time, money, and resources at his command to make his daughter's life easier. Undoubtedly, it hurt deeply to see his daughter self-destruct. But he set limits to avoid interfering with the lessons of life that would turn her around for good if she allowed that to happen.

Setting limits and boundaries are vital in separation and divorce. It is too easy for spouses to entwine their lives and lose sight of where one's personhood ends and the other begins. To cope with the loss of our spouses, we must see ourselves as whole persons without them by our sides.

How do we set limits? Dr. James Dobson gives this excellent advice in *Love Must Be Tough*:

> By all means, unless there is business to be conducted, don't telephone a spouse who has separated. But if a call is necessary, state your reason for phoning after a few words of small talk and then get on with the matter at hand. When your business is finished, politely terminate the call and hang up. Do not, I repeat, do not get dragged into the usual brawls. If you explode as you did in the past, it will be evident that you are, as he suspected, the weak old pushover he has come to disrespect. There may be a moment for anger if he insults you, but in that case keep your response crisp, controlled, and confident. Throughout these exchanges, you must be careful not to behave in unloving ways. Remember that with God's help, you are attempting to build new bridges to this disrespectful, trapped partner. Don't burn them before they reach the other shore. Don't call him names, except to label his harmful behavior for what it is. Don't try to hurt him with gossip or even embarrassing truth. Don't telephone his family and try to undermine his position with them. Don't inflame hatred in the children of your union. And don't forget that your purpose is to be tough, yes, but loving as well.[4]

Tough love also makes these limitations and boundaries stick. If not, our efforts to stop unacceptable conduct will backfire and allow others to take advantage of us.

Helping others to face up to responsibility without protecting them from the consequences of their own decisions is what tough love is all about. Setting limits as to how far we can reasonably go in helping our spouses allows God to work His loving discipline in their lives.

Speaking the Truth in Love

Tough love courageously sees matters as they are and "tells it like it is" with sensitivity and love.

We all know that the word "love" is overused, misused, and abused.

Too many believe that love means never having to say you're sorry, as the movie *Love Story* made popular years ago. Still others think the true meaning of love is to look the other way and ignore harmful or sinful behavior of those close to us. This is a gooey type of "love" that accepts what is evil and false as readily as truth and righteousness. The Bible says, "Love does not delight in evil but rejoices with the truth" (1 Cor. 13:6). Ephesians 4:15 says that the *truth is to be spoken* in love.

In the guise of compassion, we can make excuses for our spouses. We can reinforce rationalizations in the process. Lovingly speaking that truth shifts the focus away from tolerance to accountability. Our spouses must know where they stand to properly assess their situations.

It is not wise to shield our spouses from the emotional turmoil that's going on inside. Nor should we take it upon ourselves to protect their reputations if divorce is what they want. This is not an authoritarian or retaliatory action on our part. It is a loving, measured response to whatever actions our spouses make. In essence, our spouses face their own consequences head-on without interference from us.

Speaking the truth in love is *not* an opportunity to vent our anger from a raw temper. Tough love is not screaming, accusing, and berating. It is not trading insults, accusations, or blaming, nor is it using labels or absolutes ("*You never . . .*" do this or that). Exercising tough love makes brief, specific, and firm requests about problems without indulging in insults, accusations, or blaming; addresses conduct in a positive manner without using absolutes, overgeneralizations, and labels, and without second-guessing motives; listens to and understands complaints by disregarding any negative statements while making every effort to find reasonable points of agreement; finds qualities and actions of others to compliment and reinforce; and does not hesitate to apologize for one's own mistakes.

Exercising Responsible Forgiveness Instead of Revenge

If there is ever a time when revenge against anyone is tempting to us, an hour in the divorce process might be prime time. Anger and resentment peak. The unjustness of a divorce eats away at us day and night. We ask ourselves a thousand times, "Why did this have to happen to me?" But all the tough love considerations discussed above have the wrong impact if revenge is our motive. There has to be a foundation of forgiveness and unconditional love.

Revenge and selfishness are self-destructive. If we thirst for revenge, we really do reap what we sow (Gal. 6:7). Revenge breeds counter-revenge. That circle of poison and hate between spouses destroys everything within its path. Like the modern proverb says, "Bitterness hurts the vessel in which it is stored more than the object on which it is poured."

My family has a classic story illustrating this truth. We all love ice cream. For years, ice cream on Sunday night was a special chocolate treat. It was a family tradition going all the way back to the dueling between my aunt and father in their teenage years. Wanting the leftover ice cream for herself after one particular Sunday's feeding frenzy, my aunt had a devious idea. She cleverly put a typewritten note in the freezer that boldly warned: "I spit on this ice cream." Imagine her surprise upon checking the freezer to find my father's hastily scribbled footnote: "I did too." Revenge works that way. You end up with nothing but a loss in every way.

Our spouses may wrong and hurt us; we may want payback. But God is the judge—not us. Any vengeance is His alone.

> Do not repay anyone evil for evil. Be careful to do what is right in the eyes of everybody. If it is possible, as far as it depends on you, live at peace with everyone. Do not take revenge, my friends, but leave room for God's wrath, for it is written: "It is mine to avenge; I will repay," says the Lord. On the contrary: "If your enemy is hungry, feed him; if he is thirsty, give him something to drink. In doing this, you will heap burning coals on his head." Do not be overcome by evil, but overcome evil with good (Rom. 12:17–21).

Real love, especially the tough love we are considering, begins with the knowledge that a better way exists. It ends with a *responsible* decision to take the high road of justice, mercy, and forgiveness.

As we hold our spouses accountable for their own actions and put aside our inner desire for revenge, our additional challenge is to pardon our spouses for how they treat us. There has to be a *release* of wrongs done to us in our hearts. Without it, we will dwell in bitterness and resentment even if we do not seek revenge. No one knows how difficult this is to do more than those who have suffered from years of physical or emotional abuse—yet it must be done for our own healing. We can still love that difficult person.

James Dobson stated the principle this way:

> I know it is easier to talk about forgiveness than to
> exercise it, especially when the hurt was inflicted by a
> marital partner. Nevertheless, that is what we as Chris-
> tians are required to do in time. There is no place for
> hatred in the heart of one who has himself been forgiven
> of so many sins. The toughness I have recommended in
> response to irresponsibility can be destructive and vicious
> unless it is characterized by genuine love and compassion.
> Our purpose must never be to hurt or punish the other
> person, even when retribution is deserved by him or her.
> Vengeance is the exclusive prerogative of the Lord (Rom.
> 12:19). Furthermore, resentment is a dangerous emotion.
> It can be a malignancy that consumes the spirit and warps
> the mind, leaving us bitter and disappointed with life. Ac-
> cording to psychologist Archibald Hart, "Forgiveness is
> surrendering my right to hurt you for hurting me."[5]

We have to crucify that bloodthirsty penchant for revenge within us.
It begins with forgiveness in our hearts, bathing ourselves with prayer for
the mutual benefit of our spouses and ourselves, and walking in absolute
dependence upon God.

Respecting Our Spouses' Right to Make Wrong Decisions

Tough love honors the freedom both marriage partners have to make
their own choices independently. God gives every human this right even if
spouses exercise that freedom irresponsibly to end marriages.

The sixties philosophers were correct about one matter: "If you love
something, set it free. If it comes back to you, it's yours. If it doesn't return,
then it never really belonged to you in the first place." Marriages frequently
end if one or both partners feel trapped in some way. This is not to justify
anyone's desire to leave the marriage if it is wrong, but some marriages
may be a jailhouse relationship. A true loving relationship always *invites*
one to stay; coercion confines and condemns.

If our spouses have made an irrevocable decision to divorce, we must
let them go without punishing them for it. If they no longer have to fight
us for freedom, they are better able to see their own errors. Battling and

grabbing on our part only diverts attention away from the truth. It keeps us in the headlines while the real issues in their hearts get buried in the back pages. There is real wisdom in returning good for evil, as the Bible says. The ones receiving unmerited graciousness have no one else to dislike but themselves. Doing anything less deprives our spouses of facing the full consequences of their decisions.

Becoming a Model of Confidence and Self-Respect

To have the maximum impact upon our spouses, tough love requires a firm and measured response in a calm and confident manner. They must see no equivocation or hesitancy in our actions. Acting decisively carries great authority and commands attention.

Let's face it: divorce is terrifying. We must face the fear of rejection, embarrassment, loneliness, single parenthood, and possible financial ruin. There is an uncertain future. We can dwell on it and sink like a stone, as Peter did in walking on the water to Jesus, or we can keep our eyes on the Savior and trust Him for guidance and deliverance (Matt. 14:22–33).

Tough love means viewing ourselves as whole persons, with or without our spouses. It means having the confidence and self-respect that we will make it with God's help. While being vulnerable in our love, we can appear self-assured and virtually fearless about the future.

Showing this confidence may require us to be less predictable in what we intend to do. It means restraint from foolishly speaking everything that is on our minds (Prov. 29:11). Self-confidence, self-respect, a confident quietness, and a wise and responsible independence should prevail as much as possible. It is setting a good example and being a positive witness to everyone watching how we handle our situation. Our goal is to reveal only what is necessary to help our spouses take an inward look. No annoyance or distraction on our part should interfere with that process.

Looking for Common Values

When either or both spouses have a fierce determination to see divorce through to the end, minds close to many issues. This leads to stonewalling tactics and unnecessary destruction. Instead, why not identify common values as a foundation for some compromise and mercy?

Our spouses will make some serious life decisions that will have a tremendously adverse impact on us. But are they evil? Do they really desire to make us hurt and suffer for the pure pleasure of it? Usually not. For right or wrong reasons, they are trying to achieve freedom and happiness for themselves. The divorce may not be as much of a personal attack as we believe. Therefore, looking for common ground without compromising our efforts at tough love can keep a bad situation from becoming worse.

Guy N. Woods relates the following incident from the Civil War. At the end of a day of fierce fighting, the deadly cannon and musket fire ceased. The stillness of a summer evening fell like dew on the two armies. Only a narrow river separated them. Softly at first, then enthusiastically, the Union soldiers began to sing "The Star Spangled Banner." As the final notes died on the evening air, the Confederates across the river struck up "Dixie." The men of the North followed with "Rally 'Round the Flag." The Southern soldiers answered with "My Maryland." This went on for many minutes as they challenged each other with patriotic songs. Finally, the night air carried the sad, sweet words of the song "Home, Sweet Home." Soon, both sides were singing the familiar refrain. At that moment all the bitterness of war was forgotten. Men on both sides were overwhelmed with thoughts of fathers and mothers, sisters and brothers, wives and sweethearts far away. Precious memories of home and loved ones surging through their breasts had—for a moment—transcended their differences and united them.[6]

Who does not melt at the thought of wanting a peaceful home? Our days as husband and wife may quickly end, but surely preserving some of the precious and irreplaceable gifts of home, such as children and each other's health, should keep the divorce from becoming a bloodletting contest. The stakes are high. Take the initiative. Why cause further damage to ourselves and our families as the divorce runs its course? Break the circle of poison. Despite how our mates choose to proceed, we still have a responsibility of loving them in a positive and constructive way (Rom. 12:10–19). As much as it depends upon us, God urges us to make every effort toward whatever leads to peace and mutual edification (Rom. 12:18; 14:19).

Unbinding the Ties That Bind

Love, even when it is "tough," really hurts. It makes us vulnerable. Sometimes to avoid pain, we may become hard and cold while hiding away from circumstances. As C. S. Lewis so accurately wrote:

> To love at all is to be vulnerable. Love anything, and
> your heart will certainly be wrung and possibly be broken.

If you want to make sure of keeping it intact, you must give your heart to no one, not even to an animal. Wrap it carefully round with hobbies and little luxuries; to avoid all entanglements, lock it up safe in the casket or coffin of your selfishness. But in that casket—safe, dark, motionless, airless—it will change. It will not be broken; it will become unbreakable, impenetrable, irredeemable.[7]

No one really wants to live like this.

If our spouses abandon us, we initially—in pain and fear—try to block their escape from the marriage. The personal rejection we feel then gives way to pleas for a "second chance" to reform. We condemn ourselves with our own guilty consciences. After all, this divorce would not be happening if we had been a good wife or husband, right? The cycle of denial, anger, guilt, bargaining, depression, acceptance, grief, and sorrow—and back into denial again—keeps us bound up tighter and tighter.

With our own lowered self-esteem and deep feelings of inadequacy, coupled with the panic of the situation, usually we either compromise and appease our spouses to win them back, or we just cling and grab onto them. But our self-respect and dignity is sacrificed, while our spouses feel absolutely suffocated and overwhelmed. Instead of being confident and whole, we perceive ourselves as incomplete without our spouses. We make ourselves a doormat for further abuse and punishment with little self-respect. When decisive action and mutual accountability are critical, who wouldn't be repulsed at someone groveling in the dirt? This is pathetic and sad.

If your spouse has made a firm decision and divorce is inevitable, cut the rope that lashes your ship to that of your spouse. Unbind the ties that bind. With prayer and counsel about your situation from competent advisors, let your spouse go if that is his or her desire. Use this opportunity to start a new life for yourself and move on. Do not let the social rejection by your spouse destroy your self-esteem. Look to Jesus, the Pioneer and Perfecter of your faith, rather than pine away for your spouse (Heb. 12:1–2).

Allowing the Crisis to Escalate

Tough love allows the natural consequences of questionable decisions to hit our spouses square between the eyes without holding anything back. We are not really creating or escalating the divorce crisis. In truth, we are moving out of the way to allow the choices our spouses make to proceed to their logical conclusions. Let's look at some examples.

Assume that you and your spouse sit down and talk for the first time a few days after your spouse demands a divorce. It is a Saturday night, and you are at home discussing the situation. Your spouse has not changed his or her decision. It is also clear that he or she intends to remain at home for a while. Although there are friends or family to stay with, your spouse still wants the comfort and convenience of staying in the same house with you.

After thinking and praying about everything you want to say, some confrontation is necessary. You explore various options with your spouse for one last time to see if a divorce is really necessary. You ask for a delay in the decision; no is the response. "Can we go to a marriage counselor?" "No." "Can we have a trial separation?" "No." No matter what you suggest, the answer is a predictable and swift "No." Prideful confidence may well up in your spouse by realizing you cannot do anything to stop the decision made. Then, at the height of this deadlocked conversation, you shift gears. "Well," you can calmly respond, "if you refuse to reconsider your decision, then I have no choice but to honor it. You have made your choice to leave me and our marriage. Therefore, you should move out right away."

This is an unexpected shock. If your spouse has not planned on leaving home right away (being a logical consequence of ending the marriage), a personal crisis arises. Financial problems, saying goodbye to children, and leaving familiar surroundings of home for a solitary life in a strange setting are all unpleasant consequences that demand immediate attention. But this brings the consequences of one's decision into sharper focus.

To blunt the shock, suppose your spouse tells you, "Well, I haven't even looked for an apartment. I'll need some time to look around and find something." This is often a smokescreen to buy some time and take the pressure off. You cannot let this loophole go by unchallenged. "Let's see, it's Saturday night. The early editions of the Sunday paper with the week's classified ads for apartments are at the corner store. I'll drive over and get you a paper to start looking tonight." That's tough love. You not only help your spouse feel the consequences, but you do so without delay.

Post-separation boundary encroachments are another area where consequences of the divorce crisis can lead to constructive discipline. For example, suppose your spouse is secretly coming back into the house after a separation to use the washing machine while you are away. You can confront this issue with passivity and compromise, or you can handle it with tough love.

The passive approach would be to joke indirectly to your spouse about the secret home invasions. This might bring the reaction, "Well, I'm sorry for using the washer if that bothers you." Then the anger and surprise may melt into tears or pleas of helplessness as your spouse plays for sympathy. "The only reason I used the washer is because I was out of quarters, and the washer at the apartment was tearing my clothes up." The tears and tension of the confrontation will cause the passive person to back down and immediately embrace the spouse to say, "It's okay."

But it's really *not* okay. Spouses who make the choice to put us out of their lives must be responsible for themselves without relying upon us. Tough love keeps boundaries clear and reminds the spouse of the consequences. Tough love would say, "Your clothes may tear up, but that's the way you'll have to live your life. This isn't punishment; it's a consequence of your decision to leave our home. There are more important issues at stake here. Our lives and emotions have been torn up much worse than your clothes."

Believe it—this type of loving firmness on your part will burn vivid memories in your spouse's mind for a long time to come, as well it should! In every way, this communicates to your mate that you are not being mean in what you say, but you do mean what you say. There is no groveling or passivity. You act diligently and use tough love responsibly.

After discussions like these occur, your spouse should always have time alone to think. Episodes like this will pinch the conscience. The mind will work overtime to arrive at one of three possible conclusions: Your spouse will either break the pride in his or her heart and reconsider the decision to divorce; will fall prey to excuses and more elaborate rationalizations to justify a divorce decision while making you out to be the "bad guy"; or, if true, will admit that the divorce is wrong but resolve to sever the relationship anyway. In any event, giving our mates time to think options through after making a reasonable ultimatum is extremely important.

Forcing loved ones to face the consequences of their decisions in this manner also blocks the emotional blackmail that may be coming our way. It turns those negative energies back upon our spouses where they belong. We step out of the way and let them face their own circumstances. This action escalates the crisis. Then the Lord's discipline will apply where it is needed most. Any codependency on our part is self-defeating at this point.

Our mates will never receive the right message or the blessings of discipline if we are always trying to protect them or relieve their pain. As the Bible says, "No discipline seems pleasant at the time, but painful. Later on, however, it produces a harvest of righteousness and peace for those who have been trained by it" (Heb. 12:11). Our spouses are better off by suffering natural consequences of their own actions. It is part of God's plan.

The Godliness of Letting Your Spouse Go

Some readers may be having trouble with this concept of speeding up a spouse's departure from a marriage. Should we not put up some fight to stop our mates? Would God want us to let our spouses walk out of the marriage too easily? Some will question whether the "tough love" approach of "letting go" is biblical and consistent with the nature of God. I believe it is. The Bible gives us some excellent examples of this.

In the story of the prodigal son, the son wanted to leave. So the father settled up and let him go. There was no begging or pleading to keep him at home. The father loved him—from a distance. But he let the son go. To the father, the son was dead and lost. He intentionally did absolutely *nothing* until the son took the initiative to repent and come home for reunion. The father's love reflects the nature of our loving God and shows us how to love the unlovable in the same way.

In Mark 10:17–23, Jesus met a rich young ruler who fell at His feet and asked how he could inherit eternal life. Jesus told him to keep the law's commandments, but added a personal challenge: "Go, sell everything you have and give it to the poor, and you will have treasure in heaven. Then come, follow me" (v. 21). The young man's face fell at these words. He had great wealth that he did not want to give up. The Bible says that he sadly turned away and left Jesus. Did Jesus run after this man? Some of us might want to say, "Hey, wait a minute! I was only kidding. You're a talented fellow that I want in this ministry. In fact, my followers will use your offerings more profitably too." No way! He let the young man go. He respected the man's decision for his own life, wrong though it was.

In John 6:60–69, many followers of Jesus could not accept some of His teachings. He let them go. He even turned to His disciples and asked them if they wanted to leave too. Jesus did not force anyone to follow Him. Much as He wanted to gather others to Him, He gave everyone a choice to make their own decision—and to face the consequences of that decision.

In Romans 1:18–32, we learn how people rebel and sin against God despite His warnings against such conduct. Three times in this passage, the Bible tells us that "God gave them over" to do what ought not to be done. We know that no one can snatch us out of God's hand or separate us from His love if we want to be with Him (John 10:27–29; Rom. 8:37–39). Even so, God will honor our wish if we choose to reject and disown Him to rebel in sin (2 Tim. 2:11–13; Heb. 6:4–8; 10:26–31). God will let us go if we consciously decide to leave Him.

Even in the context of marriage, 1 Corinthians 7:15 says that the believing spouse is to let the unbeliever go if he or she wants to leave. It is godly and right to let others go to do what they want, despite our disapproval or personal inconvenience. We cannot control them. We cannot protect them from themselves if they are competent to make intelligent decisions. This also provides us with a release from investing emotional energies into a dead relationship so we can move on with life.

From a practical standpoint, letting go means putting away the personal items and pictures that remind us of the death of our marriage. It can involve rearranging the house or moving to another place. Removing all of your spouse's personal effects and returning them is a constructive step that conveys a clear message that you are letting go. Even something as basic as finding another bed to replace the marriage bed will help. Letting go is critical to exercising tough love.

Writing a Tough Love Letter to Your Spouse

If nothing can be done to save our marriages, it is good to take time (and prayer) to put our thoughts in writing to our spouses. This allows us time to seek advice from trusted friends and family.

It also provides our partners with a tangible list of concerns that they can read and reread, over time. Once these thoughts and concerns are in writing, no one can reasonably argue that we said something to the contrary. We communicate our understanding in a clear and unmistakable fashion.

After writing this letter, do not mail it to your spouse. Deliver it personally. You might even want to face your spouse in a neutral setting (such as a marriage counselor's office) and read it aloud. This allows your spouse to see your calm, confident demeanor. He or she will see that your words are not angry in tone or written with a punitive frame of mind. Make sure that you address all the issues of importance to you. Above all, communicate a loving toughness by taking firm, measured actions.

Writing a letter like this is not easy. Remember, your letter should be a very personal expression of your own feelings and concerns. While the words you use will be your own, here are some major ideas and concepts you may want to express to your spouse:

- If true, honestly share that you did not consider living without your mate before the current crisis.
- If true, admit that you may have lost your perspective by being so close to the crisis. When it is difficult to see the issues clearly, mistakes occur—not by intent but by accident. Make this clear so your spouse will not misunderstand your actions.
- Acknowledge that if your spouse wants to let the marriage die, *you will let go!* This is a consequence of the decision to divorce. State your own declaration of independence in a firm but loving manner.
- Respect the freedom you and your spouse have to make personal decisions, but make the consequences of these decisions clear. A marriage requires mutual commitment. If your spouse wants to leave, you also withdraw your freedom given to him or her to share your life. If appropriate, let your spouse know that he or she can once again share a relationship with you upon recommitment—but not until then.
- If true, stress that divorce is not want you want—that it never was an option for you. You are not giving up on your spouse by allowing the divorce. You are simply honoring the decision he or she has made.
- State that you are going to be honest with people who ask about the marriage. If someone asks about your spouse specifically, you will tell them briefly about the situation without assigning guilt or blame. If the question is whether divorce is inevitable, you will respond that the decision is up to your spouse. If you disapprove of the divorce, you will express that but also confirm that you will not resist it.
- If divorce is inevitable, express the sincere hope that it will end peacefully. If possible, let your spouse know that you wish to settle your business affairs privately. Try to use lawyers only to advise of legal matters and to complete the court process.
- Your spouse may want to carve a friendship out of the terminated marriage. If you have strong feelings against this, clearly say so now.[8] Let your spouse know that when the door closes on the marriage, it is

over. When the divorce is finalized, you will do everything possible to remove all reminders of your spouse from your life. (These are tough words, but that is part of tough love.) Remind your spouse that this is necessary—not out of personal revenge but as a natural consequence of his or her decision to leave the marriage. *This is a key point.*

- If you believe your situation frees you to remarry, let your spouse know that you will consider marriage to someone else at the proper time.
- Reaffirm your boundaries while the divorce is pending. Commit yourself to having your lives untwined from each other as soon as possible. Discourage your spouse from calling except when delivering messages or to discuss winding up business affairs. Firmly resolve to live a separate life from your spouse if he or she does not want a married life.
- Humbly apologize for anything you have done to cause the crisis in your marriage. Be specific about any errors and express any regrets you might have. Seek the forgiveness of your spouse.

There are many other details we could go into.[9] However, by applying the tough love principles reviewed, you should be confident in making wise decisions. Be strong and courageous in doing so.

Questions for Personal Reflection

1) Do I really understand what "tough love" is all about? How can I apply it in practical ways to my own marriage?
2) Have I given firm and measured responses to whatever my spouse wants, or have I tended to be passive in my feelings?
3) Have I really let go of my spouse and respected his or her freedom of choice?
4) Do I have an attitude of forgiveness or revenge toward my spouse?
5) Have I set reasonable boundaries with my spouse, and have I respected those boundaries? Have I allowed my spouse to feel the full weight of his or her decisions—along with the corresponding consequences—without intervention on my part to make things easier?

CHAPTER 10

How to Find a Marriage Counselor

*If a marriage is in jeopardy, it is critical to secure the best
counseling help available without delay.*

Changing people for the better is the primary challenge of marriage counseling. As a child, psychiatrist Milton Erikson laughed as his father grunted and strained at pulling a mule into a barn without success. The mule refused to budge. Finally, exasperated and angry, Milton's father asked him if he could do a better job at putting the animal in the barn. Taking up the challenge, Milton ignored the futile efforts of straining against the mule, quickly stepped behind the animal, and yanked on his tail. Without hesitation, the mule trotted into the barn.

People do not like to change. Some, in fact, will not change, even if it means sacrificing a marriage in the process. Unless both spouses engage in counseling with a willingness to explore options, they frustrate the primary purpose of reconciling marriage partners. This makes it very important to find creative counselors who look for innovative solutions and know how to pull mule tails when other techniques do not work. These experts will give us the best opportunities to restore our failing marriages.

I made the fatal mistake of waiting too long to get in-depth marital counseling. I misjudged how my marriage was failing. Time and expense were always factors, but if we had secured the help we needed earlier, we might have saved our marriage. Unfortunately, my wife had decided irrevocably to leave the marriage before our first counseling session. She reluctantly agreed to go to joint sessions with me, but only for "divorce counseling." Though we were both Christians, another condition my wife imposed was that the counselor not have any religious affiliation.

What would you have done in this situation? Counseling is a risk. It can be a waste of time and money, except that it may prepare each spouse for avoiding similar mistakes in future relationships.

If your marriage is on the line and your partner is willing to receive counseling, select the best counselor available at the earliest opportunity. If you and your spouse cannot express personal feelings; if there is domestic violence, anxiety, or depression; if there is alcohol or drug abuse; or if there is loss of interest in the children—do not wait as I did to get competent counseling. But resist the urge to race into the world for help and relief. Quality counsel requires patience and thought. Rushing into the arms of unqualified strangers is foolish. Take time to think and plan wisely.

Where can you find wise counsel? Nothing can ever replace the confidence of relying upon God's wisdom in the Bible. The psalmist wrote, "Your statutes are my delight; they are my counselors. . . . I have more insight than all of my teachers, for I meditate on your statutes" (Ps. 119:24, 99). In Isaiah, Jesus is described as "Wonderful Counselor" (Isa. 9:6). In promising the Holy Spirit, Jesus said, "I will ask the Father, and He will give you another Counselor to be with you forever—the Spirit of truth" (John 14:16–17). Second Peter 1:20–21 tells us that Scripture does not have its origin in the will of man, but men spoke from God as this Counselor, the Holy Spirit, moved them.

"All Scripture is God-breathed and is useful for teaching, rebuking, correcting and training in righteousness, so that the man of God may be thoroughly equipped for every good work" (2 Tim. 3:16). How can anyone improve upon this? As a Christian, these verses tell me that wise counsel first comes from the Lord in the Bible.

From the very beginning, God's intent has been that *He* is our primary counselor, our first source of problem diagnosis. Insight into options and guidance in making the right decisions will always be most reliable coming from the One who loves us the most. Through Scripture, God also gives us guidance on the qualities of a competent marriage counselor (and legal advisor) to advise us.

Preparing Ourselves for Counseling
Come, Let Us Reason Together

Notice what God tells us about preparing ourselves to receive counsel:

We can be our own worst enemy. We think we know what is best for ourselves. Some marriage counselors urge, "Follow your heart." But God knows better. Through the prophet Jeremiah, He tells us, "The heart is deceitful above all things and beyond cure. Who can understand it?" (Jer. 17:9). Proverbs 14:12 reaffirms this point: "There is a way that seems right to a man, but in the end it leads to death."

Can you trust your heart right now with the emotions and stress you are under? Can you really be objective about your situation? Proverbs

12:15 clearly says, "The way of a fool seems right to him, but a wise man listens to advice." Follow God's advice and be very skeptical of your own judgments. Rely upon the advice of competent and trustworthy people.

Seek the wisdom of many counselors. God tells us to seek advice from others, but people are not God. How do we protect ourselves against ungodly advice? The Bible tells us: "For lack of guidance a nation falls, but many advisors make a victory sure" (Prov. 11:14). "Plans fail for lack of counsel, but with many advisors they succeed" (Prov. 15:22). "A wise man has great power, and a man of knowledge increases strength; for waging war you need guidance, and for victory many advisors" (Prov. 24:5–6).

Seeking advice from many different people we respect and trust reduces the risk of questionable counsel. If several competent counselors advise taking the same action, it often is a wise plan to follow. On the other hand, if an action receives mixed blessings from your advisors, it is best to rethink matters. As the saying goes, "When in doubt, don't do it." Competent advisors with different perspectives will protect you from well-intentioned people who may not have a godly view on a particular issue.

Develop a deep friendship with someone who will tell us the truth. We know God will always be with us, but we also need a close friend sticking with us during divorce. "A man of many companions may come to ruin, but there is a friend who sticks closer than a brother" (Prov. 18:24). We need the assurance of God *and* friends during these difficult times.

Treasure a confidant who will tell you what you *need* to hear rather than what you *want* to hear. Seek advice from someone who has nothing to gain except the satisfaction of serving you in your distress. "Perfume and incense bring joy to the heart, and the pleasantness of one's friend springs from his earnest counsel" (Prov. 27:9). Accept godly discipline faithfully applied by this caring friend. Make it easy for others to tell you the truth.

Follow wise counsel, even if against our own interest. We must train ourselves to be humble and accept godly advice. For example, if we receive wise counsel about settling a divorce in a manner that is expensive or disadvantageous for us, will we accept it? Pleasing God is more important than holding onto worldly goods, isn't it? If we reject godly advice meant for our good, we may reap what we sow and taste the bitter fruit of having our own way (Gal. 6:7–8; Prov. 1:29–33).

Eagerly desire to learn from our circumstances. We must allow our advisors to highlight our weaknesses and errors in judgment so we can learn from our mistakes. "Listen to advice and accept instruction, and in the end you will be wise" (Prov. 19:20). "No discipline seems pleasant at the time, but painful. Later on, however, it produces a harvest of righteousness and peace for those who have been trained by it" (Heb. 12:11). Use divorce as an opportunity for self-evaluation and deeper dependence upon God. Staying alert with an eagerness to learn transforms tragedy into triumph.

Qualities of a Good Counselor
Know the Person behind the Curtain

Remember that famous scene toward the end of *The Wizard of Oz* when Dorothy and crew finally met the wizard? All they heard on their arduous journey was how great and powerful the mighty wizard was. But while in his presence, the little dog Toto peeled back the curtain around a booth off to the side. It revealed a small old man using mechanical smoke and mirrors to project himself, larger than life, on a screen in front of his company. The hype was much bigger than the very human wizard.

Marriage counselors are not miracle workers or surrogate messiahs. Even those sensitive to biblical concepts in counseling make mistakes, but be wary of those who promise more than they can deliver. Here are some qualities any Christian or secular counselor should have:

The counselor must keep all discussions strictly confidential. It can be a voyeuristic seduction to listen to people divulge intimately personal thoughts, acts, and fantasies. It takes extraordinary restraint and discretion to preserve the client's trust and confidence in these circumstances.

Few feel comfortable sharing personal problems with another if there is fear of gossip. Sadly, this is why many Christian pastors are subject to being doubted as counselors. Even if a pastor is trustworthy, church members too often feel discomfort in knowing that a relative stranger within close contact knows such personal information about them. Consequently, they end up leaving the congregation. It is simply too great a risk that the minister will bring up their problems, directly or indirectly, in the Sunday sermon. For this reason, select a counselor with no ties to either spouse. This retards gossip and avoids bias.

The counselor must remain neutral and impartial. Even so, few counselors are completely immune from sympathy to the more acute pain of one spouse over the other.

The counselor should not bind personal opinions on whether a couple remains together or separates; that is for the couple to decide. What God has joined in marriage should not be torn apart by anyone (Matt. 19:6). The counselor should help the couple clarify issues and correct destructive or inappropriate behaviors. But the fate of the marriage rests with the husband and wife alone.

What happens if one spouse uses the counselor as an ally against the other? Sometimes counselors will temporarily align with one of the spouses to help the counseling process. But the best counselor will resist manipulations of others.

A good counselor patiently respects every ambivalence, point of indecision, and procrastination of clients until the individuals reach a personal catharsis and resolve to take a particular action. Even "riding the fence" (with the counselor's assistance) between continuing a marriage or divorcing is an enlightening experience for a couple.

The counselor must be a good communicator. Listening to what each spouse shares in a counseling session is critical to the success of the process. The counselor hears everyone out, not to give decisions like a judge but to clarify the issues so the couple can arrive at their own conclusions.

The counselor must be strongly empathetic. There is a big difference between empathy and sympathy. Empathy focuses on understanding the pain and problems of the client involved. It is the counselor participating in the client's feelings in order to see matters the way the client does for a time without losing objectivity. Sympathy, on the other hand, is not as helpful. It focuses too much on feeling the pain rather than on understanding its origin. Sympathy is not objective but subjective. The danger is that the pain can affect the counselor in the same manner as the client.

Many counselors would describe their job as being like a harpist. A harpist's fingers must become calloused so they do not bleed in stroking the strings and yet remain sensitive enough to feel the special qualities of each string. So the counselor must strike a balance: caring for others without falling apart in difficult circumstances.

The thing that people search for most in a counselor is a warm and understanding attitude. This determines whether the couple will *relate* to the counselor, which is crucial to progress.

The counselor must apply the proper balance between affirmation and confrontation. Most counselors guide a couple toward psychologically healthy behavior, but how this is done requires a sensitive and empathetic heart guided by keen perception and trained judgment. This occurs by either affirming a couple with encouragement to love each other, or by stressing personal accountability and responsibility for the voluntary choices made. But what is the proper balance between these two approaches?

The proper balance depends on what those being counseled can bear. Who drives ten-ton trucks over five-ton bridges? The bridge must support the load. Since it is often impractical to strengthen the bridge, the key is lightening the load just enough to cross the bridge without breaking it. This requires sensitivity and judgment. When dealing with issues like drug addictions or alcoholism, direct confrontation with a clear ultimatum and required response may be necessary. Others, however, may need affirmation and acceptance to grow. Wise counselors know *what* is needed and *when* it is needed.

Competent counselors are not omnipotent, but they do offer real help in a time of need unlike the Wizard of Oz. Competent counselors are *comforters*. In the New Testament this word means "to come alongside." Counseling is serving people by coming alongside them without manipulation on the part of anyone. Our task as those who are receiving their counsel is to remain alert to any personal failings of our counselors so these do not adversely affect our marriage relationships.

Finding a Qualified Counselor
Sorting Through the Maze of Abbreviated
Titles and Degrees

If you look through your telephone directory or see the business cards of counselors, be prepared. You will find a confusing jumble of initials and titles after names of counselors: "MD," "LMFT," "CAP," "PhD," "LCSW," "DO," "CST," "LMHC," "MA," "MSW," "PsyD," "ACSW," "EdD," "LMFP," and even more. What do these mean? What are the differences?

Private Practitioners

Psychiatrists have medical degrees (MD, doctor of medicine; or DO, doctor of osteopathy) with experience in mental health and treatment of diseases through medical internship and psychiatric residency work. Psychiatrists delve into human thoughts, feelings, and behavior to discover emotional and physical connections affecting behavior. Check into whether this person is board certified in psychiatry by the American Board of Psychiatry and Neurology (as about 50 percent of U.S. psychiatrists are), and whether psychotherapy is his or her primary practice. Also find out if he or she has a therapeutic specialty in working with adults or children, individuals or family, or group therapy.

Psychiatrists are not necessarily the best choice for marriage counseling unless some organic physical diseases (and related psychological problems such as paranoia, schizophrenia, or manic-depression) exist that require hospitalization or psychotropic medication.

Psychologists usually have doctorate degrees in psychology (PsyD), philosophy (PhD), or education (EdD) with a clinical internship of post-doctoral supervised experience.

Unlike a medical doctor or psychiatrist specializing in diagnosis and medical treatment of mental disorders, a psychologist is usually a person who studies psychological processes that affect behavior. Many psychologists are members of the American Psychological Association (APA). Some psychologists have PhD degrees (doctor of philosophy), which may be only a research degree, but clinical and counseling psychologists also have completed a doctoral psychology program with experience in applied areas. (Counseling psychologists deal with normal behavior, while clinical psychologists focus on pathological or abnormal experiences.)

Find out whether the individual is a licensed psychologist listed with the National Register of Health Service Providers in Psychology or the Academy of Clinical Psychologists. Therapeutic specialties can differ, so ask about the areas of counseling focus and experience as well.

Use of counseling psychologists in marital counseling is appropriate. Those with specialties in marital counseling are probably the best counselors to use. Try to find a psychologist who is a member of the American Association of Marriage and Family Therapists. This is usually a good indication of competence in the marital counseling area.

Clinical mental health counselors usually have a doctorate or master's degree in mental health (MA—master of arts, or MS—master of science) with several years of supervised clinical experience. They investigate the causes of mental illness and dysfunctional behavior in individuals, couples, families, and groups, and offer diagnosis and treatment of mental and emotional disorders. Licensure in the state of residency as a licensed mental health counselor (LMHC) is necessary.

Clinical social workers usually have a master's degree in social work (MSW) with two years of post-degree supervised clinical experience. State registration as a licensed clinical social worker (LCSW) is required. Listing in the Academy of Certified Social Workers (ACSW) is important.

The Register of Clinical Social Workers, first issued in 1976, defines a clinical social worker as one who is qualified to provide direct, diagnostic, preventive, and treatment services to individuals and families threatened by social or psychological stress or health impairment. In addition to psychotherapy, the clinical social worker reviews how the client interacts with others and the social environment.

One difference between a clinical mental health counselor and a clinical social worker—other than training and experience—is that the social worker uses a "person-in-situation" perspective in reviewing how people relate to their personal world. Mental health counselors use a more individualized approach in working matters through *within* the individual.

Marriage and family therapists are persons registered in their state of residency as licensed marriage family therapists (LMFT) and specializing in therapy for married and unmarried individuals and families. Similar to social workers, they diagnose and treat emotional and mental disorders and substance abuse within the context of relationships—in this case, marital or family systems or during marriage dissolutions. Their therapy involves joint meetings with husband and wife to devise active interventions that will rearrange family relationships to more healthy patterns.

These therapists are good for marriage counseling, but be aware that health insurance benefits may not cover this type of therapy unless the counselor also holds another mental health license permitting individualized diagnosis and treatment.

Always investigate the therapeutic specialties of any private practitioner. If substance abuse is a problem, look for a counselor who is also a certified addiction professional (CAP).

Church Related Counselors

Clinical pastoral counselors usually have at least a master of sacred theology (STM), involving at least sixty graduate hours from a seminary program in clinical pastoral education and an additional supervised internship in pastoral counseling. In contrast, pastors and ministers *without* clinical pastoral training who oversee the work of local churches may have a master of divinity degree (MDiv, requiring only one year of additional college education). But be aware of a pastor's limitations depending upon whether he or she has clinical training and experience.

After hearing a pastor preach on love and forgiveness in a caring, sensitive manner, many people think, "That's a person who can understand what I'm going through. I'd like to talk with him." His mere availability attracts members from his congregation who need counseling. But this creates a serious problem. While professional counselors can insist on appointed hours and hourly fees to discourage abuse of their time, church members feel they can meet with the pastor at any time—and for extended periods of time—without charge. This is why many pastors would love to put a bumper sticker on their cars: "I'd rather *not* be counseling." Consequently, many pastors devote only a small percentage of their time to personal counseling and frequently make referrals to others.

Be aware that many pastors without adequate counseling training and experience may not know when to admit that problems are more than they can handle. They sometimes feel as if they're letting Christ down by not continuing to help those with counseling needs requiring more service than they can give. Wise pastors will recognize, however, that Jesus is Lord and that He can work through other, more qualified counselors. Referrals can become an affirmation of this lordship by acknowledging personal limitations and making responsible referrals.

There are significant advantages to using pastoral counselors, however. Usually the pastor has numerous community contacts for referrals or agencies providing help to those in need. He or she will be more sensitive to those with limited financial resources. The best approach is to use pastors for temporary marriage difficulties, but for major separation or divorce problems, ask them for referrals to professional marriage counselors.

Church volunteers and support groups offered by ministers and churches are very inexpensive counseling substitutes. From time to time, churches will offer eight to ten-week training courses for those willing to help counsel others. The thinking here is that since many people are comfortable with talking to their friends about personal problems, why not have caring church members with time to serve available, primarily to listen? Just having another sensitive individual listen to one's problems can be very therapeutic in itself, even if that individual does not have a degree in counseling. But many of the same limitations for non-clinical pastoral counselors apply here as well. Unless there is an active and effective evaluation process with close supervision, those meeting with these counselor volunteers may not know what they are dealing with.

Public Mental Health Clinics

Aside from private practitioners and church related counseling, many counseling professionals work in local public health clinics or in the state-wide network of community mental health centers. Be sure to check the qualifications of individual counselors.

University/Medical Center Counselors

Professors often arrange for student counselors to provide supervised counseling services to the public as part of graduate training. Remember, these are counselors in training. Special state licensure requirements may apply to these services.

How Do We Contact Competent Counselors?

Personal recommendations. It is best to begin by asking Christian friends, neighbors, and business associates about counselors they know. Another excellent source is your pastor.

Local references. Check with the administrator of any employee assistance program available to you. If there is a university in your area, check with the psychology department for qualified graduates. Many local marriage support groups have individuals with a wealth of information about qualified counselors.

National references. In appendix E, you will find a number of useful sources of referral information. These organizations can provide you with contacts in your area that may be helpful.

Other counselors. Contact any marriage counselors you know and ask whom they would hire (present company excepted).

Counseling referral services. Many state counseling associations have referral services listed in your local yellow pages under "Marital Counseling Referral Services," or a statewide toll-free number.

Counseling clinics. Counseling clinics are new and low-cost means of providing counseling services. If cost is critical, consider this option.

Yellow pages. Many counselors publish their specialties in commercial yellow pages. Look for ads that provide useful information about the counselor. How long has he or she practiced? What professional licensure, experience, and certifications in the marital counseling area does he or she have? Does the listing express concern toward clients? Look for counselors close to your home or office to make meetings convenient.

Library resources. Secure the latest edition of the *National Register of Health Service Providers in Psychology* or the *American Psychological*

Association Directory to obtain the names of licensed psychologists. Check the *National Register of Certified Clinical Mental Health Counselors* and the *Register of Clinical Social Workers* listing social workers in your area. For Christian counseling contacts in your area, you may want to check with the American Association of Christian Counselors. Counselors writing for popular national magazines such as *Christianity Today* or *Psychology Today* may also provide referrals.

What to Ask in Interviewing Christian Counselors

Once we find appropriate candidates for our marital counselors, what then? It is time to conduct a brief interview with each candidate, asking questions about background and experience. In seeking a Christian counselor who uses methods consistent with biblical principles, consider the following additional questions:

- Do you believe that the Bible is the Word of God and a daily guide for your counseling? Do you *use* biblical principles in counseling?
- Do you use prayer during counseling sessions?
- What is your position on the permanence of and fidelity in marriage?
- Where are you insofar as your personal faith is concerned? How has God worked in your life and profession?
- What percentage of your practice involves separated or divorced couples? How many couples reject separation or divorce as options after receiving counseling from you?
- Do you have a particular specialty or personal Christian ministry that complements your work in marital counseling?
- What sort of counseling method(s) do you use? Which approach would your clients describe you as using: affirmation or confrontation?
- Do you emphasize forgiveness and reconciliation? Can you think of some particular suggestions that couples have found useful in overcoming resentment?

You may have more specific questions in mind, such as wanting to know the particular church affiliation of the counselor, when and how the counselor became a Christian, present marital status, and whether he or she has ever experienced separation or divorce. Just be sure to ask many questions and write down the responses for review before making any decisions.

Counseling Is Great, But Who Pays the Freight?

If separation or divorce is imminent, we need help right away. But how can we pay? As you interview counselor candidates, ask them to discuss payment options. Here are some general ideas:

Insurance benefits. Many health insurance policies and employee assistance plans pay for the services of *licensed* psychiatrists, psychologists, mental health counselors, and clinical social workers.[1]

Church resources. Many churches provide pastors and staff who will usually help with temporary counseling needs and arrange for referrals at little or no cost.

Community support groups. Local churches or community leaders may organize marital support groups with qualified professional counselors.[2]

Special fee arrangements. Many counselors will work out sliding scale fee arrangements. Rates are higher for those with good incomes and much lower for those with limited incomes. If you are unable to pay much, you may—for a few dollars per session—have the same quality time with a counselor that others must pay a hundred dollars an hour for (or more).

Barter of services. If you are a painter or do needlepoint, why not paint the counselor's house or make decorative pillows for the office in exchange for counseling time? Many professionals find this an attractive option that is almost like receiving cash.

Counseling usually is available and affordable if you look for it.

An Overview of Christian Counseling

Many prefer using Christian counselors, but even among them the methodology used can be very different. Some rely heavily upon biblical principles, making frequent use of the Bible and prayer during a counseling session. Others may not do so as often, but this does not mean their guidance is wrong. Just make sure you ask counselor candidates about training, experience, and Christian orientation, and how each of these influence the counseling methods used. The best counselor should have a balanced view between the importance and vitality of Scripture, personal accountability for one's actions, and the effects of one's experience in life and present environment.

Christian counseling sensitively attunes itself to the condition of one's heart as well as to outward actions. If, for example, there is an overemphasis on changing one's behavior without dealing with the heart, a legalistic "performance oriented" mentality may arise. It conveys the wrong message that "I am what I do." This paralyzes people, especially those already overwhelmed with guilt. But with the proper balance of changing the heart *and* the actions flowing from it, healing can come through counseling. The best Christian counselors foster a secure emotional and spiritual identity in others. They encourage constructive actions consistently flowing from the abundance of a heart strongly rooted in a personal relationship with God through Jesus Christ.

Christian Counseling Formats

The general format used by many Christian counselors is a five-stage process beginning from the initial consultation: 1) setting a firm foundation on Christian principles and creating a spiritual environment of love and acceptance; 2) identifying and assessing the problems in intimacy, communication, unresolved conflicts, divided commitments to the marriage, and individual spiritual maturity; 3) looking at problems and issues through direct or indirect scriptural and psychological analysis of each spouse's needs and desires, relationships within the family unit, and each individual's life cycle; 4) reviewing plans and goals with a godly perspective and focusing on spiritual Christian growth and maturity; and 5) moving on to a balanced and healthy physical, emotional, and spiritual life.

The Christian counselor consistently encourages husband and wife to acknowledge and express their emotions and feelings to test their frequency and intensity. Each spouse is encouraged to use empathy toward the other in trying to understand each person's basic outlooks on life that affect feelings and behavior. Each learns to summarize the other's statements to reinforce accurate understandings. The counselor uses biblical principles in addressing each person's needs, applying them in specific and practical ways. The couple also receives the counselor's encouragement to study Scripture and to pray for new insights and personal discovery. With the help of the Holy Spirit—the ultimate spiritual healer—each spouse puts positive, loving, redirected lifestyle changes into action. As you can see, Christian counseling is "psychotherapy-plus." It goes further than secular counseling methods by using the resources of Scripture and relying upon God's interaction.

Preparing Yourself
How to Receive the Greatest Counseling Benefits

Marital counseling may be the last opportunity to make or break a marriage. Here are some excellent ways to experience personal growth during the counseling process regardless of the outcome:

Keep a personal diary or journal. We learn more about ourselves while with our spouses and counselors than ever before. Do not miss this excellent opportunity to examine the thoughts and attitudes of the heart.

Journal writing helps us to get in touch with our feelings in a soothing and relaxing way. It is a rewarding time of solitude for personal reflection. It also provides us with a record of our difficulties and how we worked through them. We gain perspective in reviewing our thoughts later.

Find a suitable notebook with looseleaf features (rather than spiral bound) to add material easily in any section.[3] Always look for a quiet, safe, comfortable place to write without distraction. You need not write every day, but do not lose the continuity of your thoughts and feelings. Always keep your journal in a secure place for privacy. If you prefer to handwrite journal entries, consider using different color felt-tip pens to express different perspectives or match the mood you are in when writing. This makes it easier to find particular sections in reviewing your notes later.

[NOTE: You also need to know that personal diaries and journals could be obtained by lawyers and courts as part of any divorce litigation discovery procedures under some legal circumstances. Despite this risk, many facing divorce believe the psychological benefits of journaling outweigh the possible detriment of surrendering these private writings to public inspection. They simply keep private matters private and do not let anyone else know that these journals even exist. Another possible legal protection is to make prior arrangements with one's marital counselor so that these journals are part of one's therapy, thereby possibly protecting the same through doctor-patient privilege. Even so, you need to be aware of this potential risk.]

Prepare with prayer. Praying before and after a counseling session is essential. Counseling involves delving into the heart, so why not keep in touch with the only One who truly understands each person's heart?

Pray for openness to see whatever we need to change. David expressed this attitude in Psalm 139:23–24: "Search me, O God, and know my heart; test me and know my anxious thoughts. See if there is any offensive way in me, and lead me in the way everlasting." Attending counseling sessions with this godly attitude will surely bring answers!

Strive to communicate like never before. Any relationship that does not allow for communication, negotiation, and conflict resolution will die. Counseling will determine whether spouses can reach compromises and solve problems, or if they are better off terminating the relationship entirely.

In giving the counseling process the best chance of success, there are a few important communication skills to use. Keep harmful emotions in check. This does not mean to suppress feelings, but keep anger or depression from becoming uncontrollable and destructive. Keep the counseling setting open for calm, rational discussion.

Try to see matters from other perspectives whenever possible. What is affecting our spouses' choices and desires? What do they want? How do they want to achieve their goals? To be sure we understand their concerns and feelings, paraphrasing what they shared *before* expressing any response reassures them that we listened and focused on the issues of concern to them. Patiently consider any personal objections to the issues and discuss them openly, face-to-face.

Avoid giving anyone mixed messages by promising one course of action and doing another. This requires thoughtful planning of what we share in advance to assure consistency.

We must keep anything our spouses share during a session in strict confidence. This reinforces trustworthiness and restores confidence.

Lay aside any attempts at power or control tactics in communication such as: attacking our spouses rather than the problem; trying to win an argument rather than solving the problem; presenting "final" solutions before any input is given; focusing on one solution to the exclusion of other options; trying to break a spouse's will rather than appeal to what is fair; or threatening action unless our spouses agree with our analysis.

Whenever possible, we need to communicate acceptance of our spouses and agreement with legitimate complaints without belittling or stereotyping them or rejecting their views. Naturally aggressive, power-oriented persons must focus on non-coercive persuasion. Introverted, less expressive persons may need to work on communication of feelings so others will understand their needs and desires.

Be sensitive to gender differences in communication. Psychologists once believed that communication between the sexes would improve by removing gender differences. More recently, however, they realize that men and women are distinctively different in communication by creation.

Men work in environments of power and achievement with hierarchies of control and authority. They are more action-oriented. Their communication focuses on achieving status, preserving independence, and avoiding failure. Men are less likely to talk about problems unless they want advice. Women, on the other hand, strive to connect with others through relationships to preserve intimacy and avoid the loneliness of isolation. They often talk about problems to seek understanding and sympathy more than to find solutions. Women are more willing to be vulnerable and to reveal weaknesses and secrets to achieve intimacy.

Women will give supportive cues to someone sharing with them by saying "Oh, yes," or "Yeah," as others are talking, meaning that they understand the speaker. Men are typically the opposite, limiting affirmations only to those statements with which they agree. Women may apologize to make a connection with others, as in, "I'm sorry this happened to you— just as if it had happened to me." Men are slow to apologize for anything unless there is good reason. If a wife says, "Honey, I want to spend time with you," a husband may see this as nagging. He may feel controlled by his wife's effort to create intimacy.

These gender differences can lead to major misunderstandings between spouses, and can work against each spouse in a counseling session. Therefore, try to empathize and listen carefully to statements made. Summarize your understanding and confirm with your spouse that it is correct.

Be gracious and loving in giving constructive criticism. There are right and wrong ways to give criticism. Some say that all criticism is inappropriate because it is meant to change the other person. But expressing our feelings about what the other person does that bothers us is always appropriate. For constructive criticism to be useful, serve it up with generous helpings of honest, sincere appreciation of others and a genuine interest in their welfare.

Our tendency may be to attack our spouses with impatient criticism without first having our objective in mind and without considering their feelings. As a result, they feel pain, resentment, confusion, or rebellion with our approach. Matters become worse rather than better.

Before criticizing others, we must always begin with ourselves. Why do we feel the need to criticize? What do we want to accomplish? Is there any reason it would be inappropriate to criticize our spouses on a particular issue? Are we being hypocritical? Do we have all the facts, or are we just assuming matters to be true? Can we give examples to help our spouses understand? Are we just laying problems on our spouses, or are we also offering solutions to consider? Are we making insulting comments disguised as "helpful suggestions"? If we do not know the answers to these questions, it is best to wait until we do. Above all, if we criticize only to vent personal anger, to hurt or demoralize our spouses, or to give advice that we pridefully believe will impress them, it is best to keep silent.

Next, we should consider our spouses. Helpful criticism requires planning. This guards against assaults on self-esteem, sarcasm, undue blame, or accusations. How do we want our spouses to respond? Is our criticism positive, or will it undermine their confidence? Once criticism is given, the receiver has control of any response; therefore, the delivery is important. Are the time, place, and emotional state of our spouses appropriate to receive criticism? Justifiable and well-thought-out criticism, if delivered harshly to a sensitive person, may cause more harm than good. Tone of voice can make a difference.

How will our spouses receive our criticism? If we do not know, consider asking them. What about their education and experience? Will they understand the words we use? Why risk a misunderstanding by using "dollar terms" if "nickel words" will do the trick? Finally, nothing irritates more than having a critic report to the counselor, "I have a problem with her," rather than look the person in the eyes and say, "We have a problem between us." Face the source of the problem directly.

After criticism is given, be open for any responses. Discussion about the problem should communicate a cooperative spirit and flexibility in considering options and solutions to a problem. If possible, look for incentives to make positive changes more appealing. Above all, emphasize any positive qualities of the criticized person so they will have reason to feel good.

Be gracious and loving in receiving criticism. Before reacting to criticism—constructive or otherwise—we must be sure we understand our critics and thoughtfully consider the complaint. Our responses should be given calmly with sensitivity to our critic. This is extremely difficult, but if we can do it gracefully, our attitude will mean more to our critics than our response. Acknowledge justifiable criticism with a request for help and suggested changes. If the criticism is not valid, then be honest in saying so and dismiss it if it merits no further investigation.

As we respond to criticism, a good counselor will watch for defense mechanisms that may keep us from dealing with the truth. Everyone uses coping mechanisms for self-protection, but it is unhealthy to shield ourselves forever from painful truths. Defenses often conceal hidden inner feelings. The counselor will explore these to help us feel more secure.

What defense mechanisms should we expect? Three common ones are: 1) identity defenses rooted in low self-esteem that affect our self-image; 2) emotional defenses to mask pain, such as crying or anger or depression to cover over feelings of insecurity or inadequacy; and 3) mental defenses to avoid taking action, such as denial, rationalization and excuses, avoidance, distancing oneself from painful situations (leaving the room), or projecting our own faults onto others. These defense mechanisms keep us from looking at ourselves honestly and dealing with the underlying feelings.

Marriages often self-destruct from the cumulative effects of thousands of small decisions, unfair or insensitive remarks and responses, unresolved differences, and emotional apathy. Marriages last when couples have a willingness to listen, the humility to apologize, the selflessness to provide physical and emotional support to one's mate, and an eagerness to reach out and give a comforting touch when the other hurts. Counseling may be your last chance to restore these critical elements to your marriage and help you and your mate focus on what is important in your relationship. Make every effort to put the past behind you, strengthen trust and commitment, and cultivate intimacy.

Questions for Personal Reflection

1) What kind of counselor do I want? What does my spouse want? Can we compromise?
2) Do I need personal counseling aside from marriage counseling?
3) Am I willing to find the best Christian counselor I can afford?
4) Have I prepared myself for counseling with an open mind?
5) Am I ready to give and receive criticism in a loving manner?

CHAPTER 11

Separation and Reconciliation

It is possible to survive a marital separation and still leave open the chance for reconciliation. There are many practical ways to make an unpleasant separation run smoothly.

"Tear down the wall!" That was the cry of then President Ronald Reagan to President Mikhail Gorbachev of the USSR while standing by the famous Berlin Wall.

For years it had stood as a cold, gray barrier between the German people. Topped with barbed wire, twenty-six miles long and ten feet high, policed by guards with every incentive to shoot border crossers without hesitation—it was an icon of tension, hatred, and division. Then in November 1989, with the decline of communism, people came from everywhere wielding pickaxes and hammers to bring the wall down. What a joyous event it was! Germans from East and West met and mingled with each other for the first time in decades. Families rediscovered one another; friends hugged warmly. It was a special time of reunion and celebration.

Today, all that remains of that awful wall is one short stretch left up as a reminder of what once kept loved ones apart. On that section, artists have painted a colorful mural in sharp contrast to the colorless, drab gray barrier it once was. Visitors to Berlin see this concrete and steel monument . . . and remember. Traffic now freely passes beneath the 200-year-old Brandenburg Gate that closed after World War II. Barriers have given way to open gates symbolizing the unity of the people.

Who does not rejoice when loved ones once divided reunite? We can see this same joy in the father greeting his wayward prodigal son. Whenever reconciliation sweetens the air, it is intoxicating.

In my own life, the Berlin Wall's collapse had a particular irony. It happened about four months after my wife left home. My heart was yearning for some sort of reunification between us. Of course, much as I desired it, she had made it clear that our marriage was over. But I did not lose my deeper awareness of how important reconciliation is with loved ones. It reminded me of others in my family separated by walls and barbed wire spun from lonely or wounded hearts.

I began reaching out to my father. We had always been together when I was growing up but never really close. Before becoming a Christian, I felt bitterness toward him for his harsh discipline during my childhood. But now I wrote my father a letter from my heart. In it, I referred to the Berlin Wall. I asked him, in as loving but firm a manner as I could, to help me tear down the wall between us. I let him know that my love for him was complete. There was no bitterness or blame for anything between us in the past. I asked his forgiveness for my shortcomings and unloving remarks. My marital separation sensitized me to how I had put others down too often without respecting their personhood and feelings. I wanted to express my love for him without waiting another day to do it. It would always be on my conscience if I never shared these matters with him clearly and lovingly.

In many ways I expressed to my father what I tried to express to my wife during our separation. I earnestly wanted to make peace with all those who had turned away from me. I could not stop loved ones from leaving, but I could tear down the wall within me that kept them from coming back.

How about you? Why not use this time of separation or divorce to bring peace to other broken relationships? By filling our hearts with reconciliation, we open ourselves to many new options.

Initial Separation Decisions
Leaving the Door Open for Future Reconciliation

How can we remove walls of hostility arising during separation or divorce? How can we encourage reconciliation? Decisions made during separation greatly affect any future reconciliation. Exploring different options with thought and prayer *before* completing a separation can resuscitate or suffocate a marriage. Tough love and letting go allows our spouses to leave, but it also leaves a door open for a while should they choose to come back. Our goal now is to act lovingly in ways that foster peaceful reconciliation without compromising our tough love positions or becoming compliant.

A Personal Experience

Someone has said that a bitter experience was what put the "prod" in the prodigal son. Experience makes a person bitter or better. It brings a note of familiarity to our mistakes. In this spirit, I want to share the experience of how separation from my wife occurred. I hope that it will help and encourage you to deal with your own situation lovingly and creatively.

It was 2:00 a.m. on a Thursday in late July 1989. My wife came home from theater rehearsals to announce, "I'm not happy. I want an immediate divorce." How could this happen? In her fifth anniversary card given to me earlier that same month, my wife had expressed how happy she was with me and our marriage. So this sudden announcement shocked me deeply. I asked her if she was in love with someone else. She admitted that she was.

I reasoned with her that if she loved someone else and did not want us to be accountable to each other, it would be best for her to move out. That was tough love.[1] At first she wanted to live in our guest room indefinitely, but agreed to move out when we arranged for her own place.

She would find an apartment right away. I would not influence her decision on where to live. But we both thought it best to find a place nearby so moving would not be a great burden for her. I also thought it would be easier for her to come back if she had a change of heart.

While I disagreed with my wife's lifestyle change and desire to end our marriage, we both knew that we had to work together. We had to untie our lives carefully to limit any more damage to ourselves and others than was absolutely necessary. So through anger, hurt, disappointment, and distrust, we had to forge a reasonable working relationship to let each other go.

After she located a modest apartment, we agreed she would prepare a budget for all her living expenses. Since she worked in a low-pay school-teaching position, we decided I would pay her living and moving expenses for six months so she could prepare to support herself later.[2] Before seeing her budget for the support period, I decided to borrow whatever money was necessary to meet her expenses in full.[3] I gave her a check for this sum immediately after she moved out.[4] She would then be solely responsible for all her needs during the six-month period.

We went to a local discount store together so she could pick out a television, telephone, and some small appliances to help her get on her feet.[5] Since we had two cars at the time, she took her car, in good working order and debt-free, and I kept mine. She secured separate auto insurance. I continued her coverage under my health and dental plan at work and paid for the premiums from my income.[6] I encouraged her to have a complete physical and dental exam (covered by insurance) before she left home.

Finally, we agreed that she could take from the house any furniture and kitchen utensils she needed for her apartment, and that any personal belongings she could not take with her could remain at the house until later.

The separation went smoothly. She carted her belongings to her apartment on her own. I borrowed a trailer and only helped her with the heavy items.[7] Everything was peacefully in place within a month.

We did not see one another other than at meetings with our counselor. We had no romantic involvement and very little communication away from the counselor. I carefully sorted out any mail not forwarded to her apartment and put it on the front door step for her to pick up.

With the counselor's help, we agreed to boundaries. I would not go to her apartment, nor would she come to the house. She would surrender her keys to the house; I would not have any key to her apartment.

Through mutual cooperation, we avoided more grief and expense than was absolutely necessary. Your situation may be different. With many couples who separate, problems can pop up quickly. A common source of conflict is who keeps control of the marital home.

The Ultimate Catch 22
Who Moves Out of the House?

Everyone suffers if warring spouses stay under the same roof. But if neither moves out, what happens? This simple question fires up a pot full of boiling legal, emotional, and psychological issues.

One spouse wants a divorce, which often invites anger and hostility. Each mate is uncooperative and unpredictable. There may be constant arguments. Neighbors and friends hear the latest gossip of the house as depressed spouses seek sympathy. If one spouse changes the locks on the house, the other breaks in. Each sleeps restlessly at night in different parts of the house. Anxiety and distrust are constant bedfellows.

As this war continues, each spouse feels isolation in the home. Both feel hopeless and frustrated. For sanity's sake, the marriage counselor urges one spouse to leave the house right away. But the lawyers warn that doing so may constitute abandonment of the marriage and a waiver of property claims on the house. Worse still, spouses leaving children with the parent at home may jeopardize custody rights.

To avoid losing legal rights, the advice is to stay in the house, endure the conflict, and seek personal stress therapy. This pits the counselor against the lawyers. The therapist sees the lawyers as playing opportunistic power games bent on "winning" the battle for their clients, no matter what the cost to the entire family. The lawyers believe the therapist is using emotional concerns to sacrifice key legal and financial issues that may jeopardize the future of each spouse for years to come. Conflict usually breeds even more conflict.

If domestic violence occurs, judges can and do remove violent spouses immediately from the home by court order and force if necessary. But since no one can photograph emotional abuse as they can bruises on a body, though the trauma may be as great, the legal process is not much help. After all, anyone can fake psychological anguish to win control of the house.

What is the answer? To break the deadlock, one spouse often gives up and moves out. Life is too short to endure this emotional suffering. Staying in the same house pending a divorce just will not work in most cases.[8]

If a move-out is inevitable, why not speed up the process? Encourage the spouse willing to move out by agreeing in writing that he or she can do so without prejudice to any legal rights? Take control of the situation. Make an agreement that minimally outlines temporary custody of children, visitation rights, child and spouse support. Preserve the rights of each spouse to contest exclusive occupancy of the home and permanent child custody at any future trial. Leave disputed property division for later. Just cover the basics and restore peace to the home. Have the therapist and lawyers cooperate with one another (without violating any rules of confidentiality) for the best interest of everyone concerned. Use each professional as an advisor, but you must make the decisions.

Separation: Personal Survival Strategies

Separation is, of course, a major life adjustment—many times under tight schedules and overwhelming emotions. Wise, quick planning with minimum expense and personal harm is crucial. This requires advance strategies about finances, living arrangements, and custody of children, among other issues. Both spouses need to commit to fair play and consider the needs of everyone concerned without being vindictive. Both must work together toward a common goal—becoming free enough from each other to live independent lives, if only temporarily. Surprises disrupt the process and push a couple farther apart. It is time to be alert and prepared for anything that could arise.

Timing

> There is a time for everything,
> and a season for every activity under heaven:
> a time to be born and a time to die,
> a time to plant and a time to uproot,
> a time to kill and a time to heal,
> a time to tear down and a time to build,
> a time to weep and a time to laugh,
> a time to mourn and a time to dance,
> a time to scatter stones and a time to gather them,
> a time to embrace and a time to refrain,
> a time to search and a time to give up,
> a time to keep and a time to throw away,
> a time to tear and a time to mend,
> a time to be silent and a time to speak,
> a time to love and a time to hate,
> a time for war and a time for peace (Eccles. 3:1–8).

Knowing when to ask that special person to be yours for life was important. Setting the wedding date and arranging honeymoon details on time required a lot of thought and planning. Having children or making career moves at the right time in a marriage can make or break a relationship. Now we come to separation and divorce. It is usually the result of poor timing—not doing enough, or giving enough, when the time was right.

Sometimes a temporary separation can be healthy for a marriage. It is a time of testing. Each spouse has time alone to cool down and mull over issues. Perhaps they will miss daily contact with each other. Absence does make the heart grow fonder sometimes. It can provide new insights and perspectives into reasons for discontent within the marriage. If separated spouses remain unhappy, perhaps other personal dysfunctions are the root cause of unhappiness rather than the marriage relationship itself.

When is the best time to leave home? It is not good for a couple to agree on separation but then continue to live with each other. The hurt and stress of rubbing shoulders in the same house will do more harm than good. It also reinforces denial mechanisms already working in the non-initiator spouse. Smooth changes are best. A complete move-out within a month after making a decision gives each spouse a reasonable adjustment period.

Try to know when your marriage reaches the point of no return. It helps both spouses to let go of each other and to work on a fair settlement without tearing one another apart. Resist a separation or divorce if there is any hope of reconciliation. But blocking it through manipulation, vindictiveness, or selfishness risks destroying the lives of all family members.

Emotional Adjustments and Grieving

With separation, major life adjustments and grieving are inevitable. The spouse leaving home feels anger at the task of making another place home. Starting from scratch in a strange, lonely apartment tests anyone's patience. There is a flood of emotions with every visit to fast-food joints or each microwave meal eaten alone. Child care overwhelms single parents. Sons and daughters rebel without the restraint of the missing parent. Each spouse shares a profound sense of isolation and loss. Each may feel abused, unloved, and inferior. Both may envy those with good marriages and secure, happy homes. There is a sense of shame in wondering how others view the couple.

These feelings are natural. The grieving process is healthy, providing a release of emotions that enables us to cope. Yet there are many reasons to be thankful. Blessings come in good health, food, and shelter—in family and friends. America gives us the best opportunities in the world for life, liberty, and the pursuit of happiness. Above all, we have access to the God of all comfort if we seek Him. There is no reason to despair.

Relationships with Family and Friends

Separation or divorce changes other personal relationships. Those disagreeing with any marital split keep their distance. Some in-laws continue family relationships, while others withdraw. Everything changes rapidly, and intolerable attitudes come from unexpected sources.

I initially kept my marital problems private. Only my family and a close friend from church knew. I rationalized that others could overreact to the news. Why allow unpredictable reactions of others to ruin a chance of reconciliation? I kept my daily routines, but I did not lie about my situation. I just avoided the issue if any probing questions came up. But soon others began asking questions that were difficult to avoid. Parties and events came up, and everyone expected to see my wife. Friends wondered why they were not invited to the house anymore. I found release by letting concerned friends and coworkers know about our separation.

How much should others know about a separation? A good approach is to reveal only those facts each person should know at the time—nothing more. We can advise those sincerely concerned enough to help in prayer and encouragement without violating the privacy of the marriage. Keeping gossip and sensationalism to an absolute minimum is critical. If we handle disclosures with love and integrity, our spouses will trust us more. It fosters a safe setting for reconciliation.

When should those at work know about the separation? Some fear disclosure will bring different treatment, subtle ridicule, or alienation. They believe the boss should only know if the situation disrupts work performance. But is this realistic? We work seven to ten hours a day, five days a week. Are we so composed that the stress of separation will not show? With the pressures of work, rare is the separated person who does not lose patience a little quicker or become distracted and forgetful. We are naive to think we can hide our troubles indefinitely. Also, we may miss opportunities for coworkers to provide us with reassurance and advice when we need it most.

Helping Children to Understand

How will children react, adjust, and mature? Will it affect their growth into responsible adulthood? How can one parent fulfill the role of a mommy and a daddy? How can the same parent brush a daughter's hair in the morning and teach a son how to fish or play baseball in the afternoon? Will children feel abandoned? How will children survive tight money situations or parents' lack of time to give them what they need?

Difficulty in answering these questions forced many couples in the past to stay married "for the children." But this is risky and harmful. Children of alienated spouses sense the friction and emotional divorce between parents. If tension and arguments fill the home, every child feels the sting of knowing that mommy and daddy are mad at each other. That lack of warmth can harm their development. If peace does not prevail in the home, it is best to explore other options quickly. "Better a dry crust with peace and quiet than a house full of feasting, with strife" (Prov. 17:1).

Children need quality time with each parent during any separation; reaffirmation of self-worth and confidence that his or her feelings matter; assurance that parents will not lose them in the shuffle; and reminders that the separation is not his or her fault. Times of simple fun—playing games, pitching a baseball, going to a movie or a local amusement park—mean so much to hurting sons and daughters. Keeping good relationships with children is a key to any reconciliation.[9]

Separation: Financial Survival Strategies

Some divorcees jokingly lament having an "out of money experience." But of all separation issues, two pressing needs receiving the least attention are children and the money crunch.

When a family splits into two households, usually each home has a lower standard of living. This often requires both spouses to work. Lifestyles may change radically. Each spouse must cut back on costly gifts for birthdays, weddings, and holidays. Thrift shops, discount stores, and garage sales are common fare. Bartering with others may be necessary.

Lines of credit, small loans from banks, family, and friends, or even benevolence from a local church brings temporary financial relief. If money is tight, separations may have to wait until Christmas bonuses or tax refunds arrive. In emergencies, welfare benefits keep disasters away.

As short-term money problems ease, long-term budgeting and spending controls are essential. What jobs will help us become self-supporting? How can income increase through additional jobs, babysitting, or other services? What educational training and expense do we need? How can we cut expenses without sacrificing basic needs? Who makes the payments on personal and joint debts of both spouses? Must creditors consider loan extensions or more flexible payment plans?

It is foolish to drift into the future without budgeting. Careful spending begins with computing assets and liabilities and determining net worth. The money and property each spouse expect from a divorce settlement should be considered carefully with help from lawyers and accountants. Use dollars and sense.

Before spending, make life needs a priority. Postpone purchases of luxury items (vacations, jewelry, televisions, entertainment systems) until savings reserves increase. It is tempting to be selfish if money is short, but try to make ends meet with what you have without hoarding resources.

Use of Credit

Prudent use of credit will give temporary financial relief. If credit balances carry over from month to month, apply for credit cards from issuers offering the lowest interest rates.

If your spouse has maintained all the credit cards, find out whether the credit bureau has any credit rating information on you.[10] Frequently, it will not. Consider setting up separate, personal credit privileges without delay. Secure a charge card from a local store, or even apply for a small loan ($100 or so) and repay it promptly. This should be enough to get a credit history. Being financially independent helps spouses deal as equals.

A favorable credit history is vital if the separation becomes overly expensive and credit is a necessity. Be careful not to open more than three to four charge accounts within a short period. Credit providers may believe you are churning applications for a spending spree and will deny you credit.

It is wise to cancel or convert any joint charge accounts to the name of one spouse alone. Write the card issuer about how to do this. If you cannot change a joint account, try to terminate it or notify the issuer in writing (keeping a copy for your file) that you do not want any liability for future charges made by your spouse. Try not to allow your spouse's financial irresponsibility to affect your credit rating—especially if vindictive behavior exists. Separate charge accounts solve this problem.

If a credit application is denied by a creditor, always request an explanation for the denial under the Equal Credit Opportunity Act (ECOA). Correct any errors before they go on your credit record.

Spouse and Child Support

How can you receive support from your spouse? Support comes in two major ways: 1) pursuant to a private settlement agreement or court order for one spouse to pay; or 2) by selling assets. If spouses cannot agree on the timing and amount of support, try mediation.[11] Nonpayment of support by a spouse who can afford to do so is seldom excusable.[12] If you need emergency support, courts have procedures for verifying financial need and ordering payment from a financially stable spouse.

The amount of support varies, depending upon many social and economic factors bearing upon each spouse.[13] Usually a reasonable percentage of the paying spouse's net income (gross income less taxes, social security, mandatory pension contributions, insurance payments, etc.) supports a spouse and children while still leaving enough to live on.[14]

Support for children depends upon their actual needs until attaining the age of majority (eighteen to twenty-one years old). It may include payments for a college fund, treating extraordinary health problems, insurance premiums, and similar expenses. Custodial parents of children usually must bear some expense in providing for their needs and household expenses. This may reduce child support payments.

At the time of separation, each spouse should agree on a fair and workable support schedule. But be careful. In agreeing upon a schedule, a legal precedent could be set that would continue after the divorce. Therefore, make sure that the sum is reasonable and will not cause undue hardship on either spouse over time.

Remember that child support payments are usually separate obligations from visitation rights. If the custodial spouse denies or hinders visitation, support payments should continue. Seek court relief for missing visitation time. A court may suspend support payments directly to the custodial spouse for this interference, but do not do so without a court order.

Separation: Physical Survival Strategies

Health Matters

Those leaving home should have medical and dental checkups *before* separation or divorce ends any group insurance benefits available to a couple. Even after moving out, each spouse should cooperate with the other to reduce rising insurance expense. Try to keep both spouses and children covered on the same policy offered through any employer unless and until the coverage ends or alternate, comparably priced insurance is available. For critical situations, apply for Medicaid benefits (although this protection does not cover some matters).

Personal Appearance

You may be thinking, "Come on, I need advice on my situation—not my choice of wardrobe!" But the stress of separation or divorce can make us forget about some very obvious needs. For instance, it is tempting to neglect personal hygiene until it affects our health. If finding work is a concern, a neglected appearance is certainly counterproductive. Above all, consider this: is returning to a marriage with a slob attractive?

Maintain a balanced diet and engage in a vigorous exercise program. Staying physically fit and mentally alert are important for good health and self-esteem. Keeping hair and nails neatly trimmed or styled does wonders. Hot showers help relieve tension. Care like this increases our self-assurance and reduces stress. Keeping a regular schedule from week to week restores equilibrium to life during times of turmoil.

Review your wardrobe; try new outfits. Avoid clothes that remind you of special times with your spouse. This is part of letting go. If finances are a concern, swap clothes with friends or go to a thrift shop. Buy interchangeable items that allow for assembly of different outfits.

Separation: Legal Survival Strategies

Domestic Violence Situations

Document incidents of violence and abuse through police or objective, unbiased witnesses without delay. Prepare yourself to answer these questions: What happened? When? How frequently did any violence occur? Was either spouse provoked to violence?

Never let possible loss of legal rights keep you trapped in a home with physical violence. It is simply not worth protecting property rights if your life or the lives of your children are in jeopardy.[15] If the situation is absolutely intolerable, make an immediate separation. Let the mediators and lawyers give you advice on protecting your legal rights later.

Try to move in with blood family members rather than live alone; this discourages unwanted visits from an abuser. It also provides a calming influence if jealousies of any romantic involvement with other persons are irritating the abuser. Always avoid bringing any potentially violent situation into the homes of those who are housing any abused victim. Spouses experiencing domestic violence should not meet unless it is at the office of a marriage counselor, responsible church leader, or mediator.

Many experts believe it is best to report all instances of domestic violence promptly to local police or appropriate community action groups. In many states, you may secure peace bonds, court injunctions, psychiatric intervention, exclusive possession of your home, imprisonment of your spouse, and other assistance to stop the abuse.

Seeking Legal Advice

Use lawyers constructively for advice during separation and divorce.[16] Remember, your lawyer is only an advisor. Listen to the advice, then make a decision best for you and your family. If you need to talk to your spouse, get advice and then do so. Do not let your lawyer intimidate you. If it happens, hire someone else. You can disagree with your advisors.

Avoid fighting your spouse through lawyers. An attorney's posturing in the case will often increase anger and mistrust.[17] Escalating the battle means everyone loses except the lawyers. Use attorneys for advice on legal issues, and use neutral third-party mediators for property settlement issues. This promotes reasonable negotiation and increases reconciliation possibilities.

Always try to get legal advice before leaving home. Moving from home can jeopardize your legal rights. Leaving children behind with the other spouse can affect custody decisions in court. Also be aware that if the non-initiator spouse leaves home, the initiator receives immediate relief—the spouse gone and complete control of the home. This may tempt the initiator to delay a formal divorce for a long time. If so, the non-initiator is in limbo and at a severe disadvantage in negotiating settlement issues.

Ask your lawyer to provide you with a reasonable estimate of spouse and child support you might receive and how property distributions occur under your state laws without delay. This will allow for budgeting with realistic expectations and will avoid future disappointment.

Finally, do not gloat over legal victories; this only invites revenge.

Protecting Assets

There is a major difference between prudently protecting assets and hiding assets to avoid accounting for property division. If either spouse does not account for *all* assets as part of any settlement, it could jeopardize the legality of any settlement agreement.

How are assets protected? There are instances when it is proper, even necessary, to safeguard your property. The classic example is guarding against one spouse running to the bank to withdraw the balance in joint savings accounts or cleaning out the safe deposit box. If this is a concern, contact the bank immediately. Change the names on the savings account if possible. Inventory the contents of everything in the safe deposit box in the presence of a neutral witness or bank employee (not family or friends). Transfer valuables to a personal safe deposit box. Make your lawyer or accountant an additional keyholder to assure access. Protecting assets involves locking property down until the parties agree on a proper division. But only take defensive actions like these *after* receiving legal advice.

Protecting assets may mean carefully checking business records maintained during the marriage and making sure that these match with the assets itemized in any settlement or at trial. This discourages anyone from hiding assets. Cross-referencing records helps in finding any missing items.

Separation Agreements

Before any separation occurs, it is wise to have a *written* understanding of everything agreed upon. A lawyer can prepare a formal separation agreement, but a letter agreement between husband and wife is fine if it clearly sets out their basic understanding. Always receive legal advice before signing *any* agreement with a spouse, however. With so many pressing emotional issues, it is easy to overlook important matters.

The spouse providing financial support will want to make sure that all such payments are tax-deductible if possible.[18] To qualify these payments, there are several very important steps to take. Be sure to contact a competent tax advisor before making any support payments.

What does execution of a separation agreement or letter mean to each spouse? Attorneys know that many spouses already view themselves as "divorced" even if the marriage continues. Therefore, some will encourage the couple to complete the divorce without delay. Since the separation agreement divides up property, it is better to complete the distribution before circumstances change. What happens, for example, if one spouse keeps an automobile at separation, then wrecks it without adequate insurance? If one spouse keeps stock that doubles in value a few months later, will this cause a dispute during a later divorce? This is why it's a good idea to make any property divisions stick, regardless of what happens. Each spouse should assume the risk of changes like these in pursuit of peace.

Separation agreements memorialize a time for reflection before rushing toward divorce. Each spouse knows that this time away from the other is necessary. Each agrees to part for a while and consider options. Each needs time to try and save the marriage, not to end it early.

Inventorying Property

The spouse leaving home will never have a better chance to inventory everything than before the separation occurs. Itemize valuable property in the house and carefully note who owns what. Check records on all major assets (real property, stocks, and bonds, etc.) to determine the date and circumstance of each purchase, current value, and name(s) on the titles. Both spouses should locate and inventory deeds, certificates, and other legal evidence of these assets. Photocopy all title instruments to prove their existence if improperly sold, "lost," or stolen.

Separation: Housekeeping Survival Strategies

Splitting Up Personal Belongings

Wait to divide major assets until a property settlement or divorce occurs. Dividing personal property during a separation is an immediate challenge. How can you split the pet hamster or cat? Who keeps the family photo album? Even pots, pans, blenders, and the microwave oven may cause fights. Each spouse can feel selfish and guilty about taking utensils from the other after years of being together. Each household item passed over is another replacement that must be purchased, but property is not as important as the marriage. With reconciliation, these items come back home anyway.

One solution for splitting household goods is for the spouse keeping any basic utensils or appliances to make sure the other has items of equal usefulness purchased from a discount store.

What about dividing very special or deeply personal items? Each spouse must negotiate. If she keeps the china and silverware, he should keep the exercise equipment or stereo. But always ask: is this item worth fighting over if it shipwrecks any hope of reconciliation?[19]

Housing and Moving Expenses

After one spouse decides to move out, find separate housing without delay. The first night may be a short-notice event. Motel rooms, apartments, homes of friends or family, or even a guest bedroom in the same house are the usual choices. If a move occurs suddenly, leave a note unless domestic violence is a concern. Give a contact address and telephone number, but not necessarily the actual location moved to. Promise to call back shortly to discuss further separation arrangements.

Having control of the home is an advantage, unless it means losing peace of mind or reconciliation opportunities. Weigh the options. Leaving a house in a quiet neighborhood for a noisy apartment complex requires sacrifice and adjustment. Do what is best for everyone concerned.

Housing costs require careful budgeting. Competitive pricing of apartments is always a good idea. Absent homeowners may have attractive offers for housesitters. Realistically budget moving, utilities, and maintenance expenses. Will rent in a new location be equivalent to the monthly rent or mortgage payment at home? Will landlords require first and last month's rent, plus deposits for utilities and telephone? How about the first grocery bill to stock the kitchen? Is it easy to find furniture? Will family or friends lend needed items? Each spouse must work hard to keep the cost of maintaining two households down.

If finances will not allow for two households, the moving spouse can move in with friends or family or seek temporary placement by caring church members. Emergency shelters run by the Salvation Army or women's resource centers are also available for a short time in critical situations.

The physical move works best when both spouses cooperate. If this cannot happen, family or friends can help load up belongings. Avoid using any third-party romantic interests—it is inflammatory, inviting problems and unnecessary stress. Renting a trailer or borrowing a friend's van will significantly lower moving expense.

Maintain boundaries in living arrangements. If it is necessary for husband and wife to meet, do so at a neutral location. Since leaving home may limit any future re-entry, reserve the right to re-enter in any separation agreement. Re-entry is reasonable if it is for legitimate purposes after advance notice and at reasonable hours. Even so, legally enforcing this right is not an easy challenge.

Transportation

If a couple has two cars at the time of separation, it is easy for each to take one car for personal use. If there is only one car, the spouse having custody of the children should probably keep it for school days, doctor visits, and trips to the supermarket. The other spouse may have to borrow the car from time to time or use vehicles of family or friends. In some cases, both spouses may have to purchase a used car, lease an inexpensive vehicle, or use public transportation.

Car maintenance should be undertaken wisely. Many tasks like oil changes, tire rotation, and minor adjustments can be done personally or by friends who have repair experience. Always secure recommendations from trusted friends about the most inexpensive and reliable garage mechanics. If possible, each spouse should have independent auto insurance policies. This is more expensive than a single policy, but if one spouse is accident-prone, separate policies protect the other spouse.

Separating the Mail

Privacy between spouses is an issue every time the mail arrives. Credit card statements, canceled checks, and bank statements open one's life up in embarrassing ways. Letters from attorneys delivered to the wrong spouse can be a temptation to prying eyes. For the spouse who leaves, it is wise to have all mail sent to the new address without delay.[20] Have sensitive mail delivered to a personal post office box or marked "personal and confidential" and sent to a trusted friend to assure privacy.

Employment Considerations

The unemployed spouse should make realistic appraisals of his or her abilities and experience. Is it possible to work during the day and go to school at night? Is the employed spouse better off in an existing job, or by upgrading to a new position? These factors are difficult to evaluate. Each is a function of local economic conditions, personal experience and skills, personality and emotional stability, as well as good timing and fortune.

Child custody may require arrangements with employers for flexible working hours. If a spouse cannot afford childcare, family or friends from church can help in rotation for a time.

In the short run, keep a job that pays the bills. For fulfillment in the long run, however, evaluate whether job pay is fair, the work environment is pleasant and encouraging, and your mind-set is positive about what you are doing. Nothing wears a person down more than a dead-end job. Do not limit your vision in exploring different work opportunities. If possible, face new challenges. Finding new jobs with higher pay and without jeopardizing existing relationships and responsibilities invigorates a person.

Tax Returns

Separated but not yet divorced spouses should decide whether to file income tax returns jointly or separately. Check with a tax advisor about the differences in tax savings.[21]

There are many other tax planning issues as well. For example, which parent will be able to claim dependency exemptions for children?[22] The timing of the separation or divorce and who qualifies for head-of-household status can make a big difference in taxes.[23] The tax basis in property transferred as part of a property settlement can lead to a large surprise tax bill when the property is sold later on.[24]

Tax returns carry important privacy considerations.[25] They contain revelations of one's business and private financial affairs. This leads some to file a separate return during a separation, even though the taxes may be disadvantageous. But it is unlikely that anyone can complete a divorce settlement or trial without first exchanging copies of all tax returns—joint or separate—with his or her spouse at some time.

If your spouse is uncooperative in filing a joint return, do not wait. File a separate return. With joint returns, spouses should indemnify each other for any additional tax liabilities arising from inaccurate or incomplete information. Each spouse remains individually liable for the taxes, penalties, and interest owed, but the indemnity may provide a useful claim in any court-ordered settlement or divorce decree.[26]

The best tax advice is this: do not do *anything* without talking to a competent tax advisor first.

Separation: Social Survival Strategies

Dating

During separation, dating between spouses by mutual consent is an excellent way of exploring reconciliation. Although it often happens, it is probably not wise to have sexual relations with each other. This gives mixed messages and fosters false hopes of reconciliation if none exist.[27] Naturally, if one spouse forces sexual relations against the other's will, this is criminal violence.

Avoid casual dating of other people during separation. It is always wise to avoid the appearance of impropriety and not provoke jealousy. A night activity with a friend of the opposite sex may be completely innocent, but a marriage still exists. Hints of adulterous activity can severely jeopardize a divorce settlement.[28] An imminent remarriage could also adversely affect spouse support. Even extended time away from responsibilities (child care, timely bill payments, house maintenance) can lead to claims of neglect or waste of marital assets.

Surveillance

If your spouse is involved with someone else, it is natural to want to know the truth about the situation. Although it carries risk, many believe that hiring a private investigator is necessary and appropriate. But beware. Resist the urge to record any telephone conversations between your spouse and a lover. In most cases, it is illegal.[29] Not only will any recordings not be admissible in court, but you could be liable for extensive damages to your spouse.[30] Use surveillance of any kind *very* reluctantly.

Dealing with Gossip

It is inevitable that people will talk about us behind our backs during a separation or divorce. Unfortunately, they will also embellish the truth. Be ready for this if reports of something your spouse said or did comes back to you. Speaking or receiving lies and bearing false witness against another person is a very serious matter with the Lord (Ex. 20:16; Prov. 6:16–19). Lies crush one's spirit and destroy reconciliation opportunities. People suffer unjustly from these accusations, just as Joseph was imprisoned by the lies of Potiphar's wife (Gen. 39:7–21). Do not entertain those wishing to gossip by listening to them. *Assume the best* rather than the worst of your spouse until the truth is properly verified by several witnesses through following the steps Jesus set out for us in Matthew 18:15–17.

Divorce Support Groups

Individual counseling is very necessary in sorting out so many of the issues of separation or divorce. Each spouse needs to develop an accurate picture of the situation. Support groups are a great way to receive encouragement and meet fellow survivors who can share our pain. This helps us work through the grieving process. Since group members are at different stages of recovery, new members usually find another person who can offer particular empathy and hope. While groups typically have new topics each week, the structure is such that if a group member has an immediate crisis, the group can minister to that need and provide support in a powerful way. (I *highly* recommend attending a DivorceCare support group session offered through Church Initiative. See appendix "E" for more information.)

There are many ways to plan a necessary marital separation wisely with opportunities for reconciliation. Your situation may have special considerations that requires advice and creative thinking of your own. Avoid burning any bridges. Keep options open for a reasonable time. Reconciliation is what God desires most if spouses can forgive each other.

Preparing for Reconciliation

The missionaries to the Auca Indians in South America had a real problem. Since there was no equivalent word in the Auca language for "reconciled," they struggled with how to share the concept of Christian reconciliation with these people. One day a translator traveling with some Aucas through the jungle came to a narrow, deep ravine. The missionary thought they could go no farther, but the Aucas quickly took out their machetes and cut down a large tree so that it fell over the ravine. This bridged the gap, permitting everyone to safely cross the chasm. The translator learned that the Aucas had a word for "tree across the ravine," which seemed quite appropriate to describe the concept of reconciliation.

A tree across a ravine. Is there any way to bridge the gap between us and our spouses right now? How willing are we to put our machetes to work to span the chasm between our mates and ourselves?

Consider the effort of Robert and Linda Bernecker of South Florida who divorced after four years of marriage. A year after their son, Wesley, was born, Linda was fed up with Robert's long hours at the family nursery and at church. She packed up her bags and left with their son in March 1991. After being divorced for eleven months, Robert hoped for some sign of reconciliation from his ex-wife. Then, on the morning of January 30, 1992, he received one—a huge billboard by U.S. 1 that read: "Robert, we want our family together. Can we come home? Linda & Wesley." Linda had spent $1,200 for the sign to be put up that morning at 9:15. By 11:30, Robert was on Linda's doorstep. Two weeks later the sign was still up by the highway with Robert's response nailed across the top in big letters: "Yes. Yes. Yes."

I like that story. But realistically we know that our situations may be entirely different. Even so, we must be ready for reconciliation just as the father was in the parable of the prodigal son. Reconciliation tears down walls of hostility to restore friendship and fellowship. Our love for God and our spouses should compel us to follow the example of Christ, the peacemaker.

> For he himself is our peace, who has made the two one and has destroyed the barrier, the dividing wall of hostility, by abolishing in his flesh the law with its commandments and regulations. His purpose was to create in Himself one new man out of the two, thus making peace, and in this one body to reconcile both of them to God through the cross, by which he put to death their hostility. He came and preached peace to you who were far away and peace to those who were near. For through him we both have access to the Father by one Spirit (Eph. 2:14–18).

This passage literally refers to how Christ reconciled Jews and Gentiles, fulfilling the law of Moses with His sacrificial death on the cross. But it also speaks beautifully about reconciliation. Read the passage again. This time, imagine that you and your spouse are the ones spoken of in these verses. Christ desires to reconcile each of us with our spouses. This is one reason why He died on the cross.

We are to emulate God (Matt. 5:48). If so, are we ready to forgive and reconcile? (Rom. 5:10; 12:14–21). Jeremiah 3:1 tells us of God's marriage to Israel. Even after a divorce occurred, God showed His great desire for reconciliation (Jer. 3:8, 14–16). Through it all, He remembered His vows to Israel (Lev. 26:42–45). He remained faithful to His covenant. But how can we prepare ourselves for reconciliation in a godly way?

Reconciliation begins with commitment. It is not weak or cowardly to desire reconciliation because it is righteous. Committing ourselves to submission rather than trying to overcome our spouses requires the utmost in courage and graciousness. The easy way out is to keep distance between our spouses and ourselves when they want to return. It is a heroic and faithful act of obedience to open the door again. Are you ready?

Reconciliation flows with forgiveness. Intense, unresolved anger and the failure to forgive will kill reconciliation. Reconciliation is a two-step process: confessing and forgiving personal wrongs that led to separation, and negotiating a mutually satisfactory resolution to issues of conflict in the spirit of Matthew 18:15–17.

Anger and resentment build a wall of stone between spouses, a dividing wall of hostility as foreboding as the Berlin Wall once was. But Jesus tells us, "Love your enemies and pray for those who persecute you, that you may be sons of your Father in heaven" (Matt. 5:44–45). If that is how we are to treat our enemies, how much more should we respond to our spouses returning home in repentance. Tear down the wall! The Lord is compassionate and gracious, slow to anger, abounding in steadfast love. He will not always accuse, nor will He harbor His anger forever. He does not repay us as our sins deserve (Ps. 103:8–10). Are we willing to do the same with our spouses? Give peace and reconciliation a chance.

Reconciliation grows with wisdom. Rejoice with any reconciliation, but take matters slowly with wise counsel. Separation required transition and adjustment; so does reconciliation. This may require weeks, months, or even years, with lots of prayer, biblical counsel, and encouragement. Each spouse must fall in love with the other again. Bringing back those old, close feelings that once bonded us to our spouses prepares us for good times in the future. For the sake of the marriage, it is best to define mutually acceptable standards of behavior, such as no physical abuse, drugs, or alcoholism. It is good for each spouse to commit to giving mutual respect in communication with courtesy, honesty, and openness when discussing and resolving issues that create problems. Set a date for reviewing the process of reconciliation so that both spouses can step back and make sure good progress is being made. Promptly define and allocate household responsibilities as soon as reconciliation leads to a shared home once again.

Reconciliation never ends. Amen!

Until reconciliation becomes a reality—if ever—accept circumstances the way your spouse desires. After a separation occurs, there are inevitable times of fantasy. Both spouses may imagine reunions. The mind can run through endless "Boy, what-a-fool-I-was-for-leaving-our-marriage" dramas. I really believed that my marriage would survive. I thought my wife would experience life alone and come back home. But it was not to be. Eventually, I reached this peaceful, personal resolution: "I hope that she will return to the marriage, but I will live each day as though she will not."

My prayer is that you and your spouse will lovingly reconcile your marriage if possible. Using some of the suggestions outlined in this chapter should create a better setting for this if attitudes of love and forgiveness are the motivation for every action. But just tear down the wall!

Questions for Personal Reflection

1) Is there any dividing wall of hostility between my spouse and me that I can tear down?

2) Do I find myself wanting to remain angry with my spouse for power, control, or revenge? Have I considered the needs of my family and what is in their best interest?

3) Have I prayerfully considered a reasonable plan of action for completing an amicable separation from my spouse and children?

4) Am I willing to give up on some property issues to keep family peace and encourage future reconciliation?

5) Am I ready to accept the truth that my marriage may be over and to face the reality of having to move on with my life without my partner?

CHAPTER 12

Biblical Property Division and Settlement Negotiation

*Creative and practical solutions using biblical principles
are the best way to overcome property division problems
and agree on a fair and reasonable settlement. The key is
to mediate rather than litigate with your spouse.*

Aside from the divorce itself and child custody issues, a battle for control is most often waged over property division. The key to success is to keep property issues from becoming too much of a priority.

We think of our "assets" as everything we own—cash, property, and investments. The term comes from an old French word, *asetz*, meaning "enough." It means having enough wealth left to settle any debts of a deceased person. After you divide your property with your spouse, will you have enough assets left to move on with your life? If so, be willing to compromise. Be flexible and avoid further resentment.

The old French proverb is true: "Money is a good servant, but a bad master." Property can distort our view of the more important things in life.

> But godliness with contentment is great gain. For we brought nothing into the world, and we can take nothing out of it. But if we have food and clothing, we will be content with that. People who want to get rich fall into temptation and a trap and into many foolish and harmful desires that plunge men into ruin and destruction. For the love of money is a root of all kinds of evil. Some people, eager for money, have wandered from the truth and pierced themselves with many griefs" (1 Tim. 6:6–10).

We should strive to measure our wealth not by the things we have, but by the things we have for which we would not take money. Our peace of mind is worth more than possessions. Further destruction of relationships and resentment that could last for years is too great a price to pay for the family car or some china.

You Are in Charge—Not Your Lawyer

If your lawyer has a never-give-an-inch outlook, you will needlessly sacrifice settlement opportunities. Few lawyers will tell you this, but this attorney believes that if there is any reasonable way to settle your affairs, do so diligently. Certainly seek legal advice, but do not allow your attorney to come between you and your spouse unless it is absolutely necessary. If you can speak amicably with your spouse, keep the lawyers on the sidelines as much as possible. Confine them to an advisory role. Using your attorney as the sole pipeline of communication with your spouse or his or her attorney is expensive and possibly counterproductive.

Lawyers feel the need to control your case in responsibly protecting you from unwise commitments or waiving any legal rights. But the ultimate responsibility for your own destiny is yours and yours alone. *You* must bear the consequences.

Therefore, remember your personal priorities and stick to them. It is up to you to do what is best for everyone concerned. Take every opportunity to resolve your divorce quickly and without undue strife over material possessions. This chapter will help you to do just that.

How Do Property Disputes First Go Wrong?

Think back briefly to the beginning of your marriage. In preparing for a property settlement, reflect upon how property ownership issues affected you even before your wedding.

Management of Finances

Did you and your spouse consistently deal with your finances and property in a particular way? Did you combine all of your earnings and then pay bills, or was there a mutual agreement as to who paid certain bills? Was it understood that certain investments were personal to one spouse?

Some spouses do not have much experience in handling finances. In counseling many church couples on financial matters, I found that joint checking accounts and the use of one checkbook by both spouses were often arguments waiting to happen. Inevitably, one spouse would have the checkbook when the other needed it. The other spouse would write a check and forget to record it in the register, so the account would be overdrawn.

This can be trouble enough during a marriage, but add the complications of divorce, and it becomes quite difficult to trace funds.

Other spouses use independent checking accounts. In this way, if one spouse is negligent in handling money, it does not put the family finances in jeopardy. Records that indicate who paid for certain expenses are very useful when both parties can account for personal and marital funds.

Title to Property

How is your real and personal property titled? Who held the title at the time you married? Was the title changed during your marriage?

There are many reasons spouses change title ownership to major real and personal property investments. Aside from the obvious desire to show solidarity among mates, there can be significant tax and personal liability considerations in having the title owned by one or both spouses.[1]

Titles to automobiles and boats should seldom be in the name of both spouses for liability reasons. Any entry of a judgment against both spouses subjects any jointly held property to confiscation (if the property is not otherwise exempt by law, such as a family homestead). Title to these assets is persuasive in deciding what the parties receive in a property settlement. But many spouses believe that liability issues are a higher priority. They put different assets into individual names and view each asset as separately owned property.

Premarital Agreements

A premarital agreement between spouses outlines how property is to be divided, spouse support, and other matters in the event of any future divorce.[2] When spouses are not equal financially, such agreements can protect the wealthier spouse from any exploitation.

There are obviously several drawbacks to using a premarital agreement. To a young couple in love, the entire issue can communicate "I don't trust you." The underlying message is that you are planning for a marriage that may not last "until death do we part." For Christians, premarital agreements can send an even stronger negative message. Christians can and should view their marriage as lasting for life. If an agreement can be sensitively discussed by a couple before marriage, it is useful if needed or conveniently forgotten if not. However, if the agreement only fosters bitterness and emotional turmoil just before a marriage, it is probably best to forget it.

Perceived mistrust can also become a self-fulfilling prophecy. If a spouse perceives mistrust, he or she may act accordingly. To spouses who are business-oriented, an agreement may be good. Although not pleasant to think about, planning is prudent—like making a will or buying life insurance. For inexperienced mates, though, it can be emotionally devastating.

But guidelines in premarital agreements can resolve issues in advance—before emotions are running high and property division is a hotly contested issue. Think about it. Why not decide these matters at the start of a marriage when each party is lovingly cooperative? Partners begin with a partnership agreement. If spouses resolved property matters in advance, divorces would be over in a short time. Many believe it is desirable for a couple to discuss these matters early in a serious dating relationship. This is especially true in states where the laws are not fair to both spouses.

If you are facing a divorce now, find out if any existing premarital (or antenuptial) agreement governs your property rights. Did you ever sign such an agreement? If so, have your attorney review it immediately and advise you as to your rights and responsibilities. If it is not fair and reasonable to you, the courts may be able to intervene and provide you with relief.

For the remainder of this chapter, we will review alternatives for resolving property disputes. First, we review how the courts may distribute your property. Then we propose a biblical plan of private settlement.

How the Courts May Divide Your Property

Marriage as an institution has undergone radical changes in the civil law. More states are moving toward a "no-fault" divorce standard with an equitable distribution of all *marital* property (in many instances, simply splitting assets 50/50).

In making divorces easier to secure, the civil law is retreating from the centuries-old legal view that marriage is a union that cannot be broken except in very limited instances. Today, more courts view a marriage as a type of business partnership. As such, marriage vows are similar to a partnership agreement that can be breached like any contract. (We know this is not the way God looks at marriages, but it is the way the civil laws are evolving.)

Under these "no-fault" laws, property division calls for equal treatment of men and women. Since the marriage is similar to a business partnership, both spouses contribute to the accumulation of property during the marriage. Husband and wife either generate income or provide the family with services such as homemaking or childrearing to keep the property.

Even so, discrimination against women unfortunately still exists in the judicial system. This is not to suggest that this is fair, but it is reality. Many courts have trouble viewing a homemaker as an equal partner with the "breadwinner" earning most of the family income. Thus, husbands often receive court awards of about three-fourths of the property bought or improved during the marriage, while the wives receive the remaining fourth of the same assets. Some judges even require a wife to prove she contributed more to the marriage than the husband before receiving an equal distribution of assets.

Why are women shortchanged like this? First, the wife's one-fourth share is about the same as a dower right under the oldest U.S. laws (originally coming from England, known as the "Common Law").[3]

Second, contributions by husbands who are breadwinners are much easier to measure economically than a homemaker's work. Finally, male judges may identify with the husband's role in marriage more than the wife. Both spouses should account for this gender bias if property rights are not privately settled.

Your lawyer should advise you of the property distribution laws in your state.[4] In states using equitable distribution standards for dividing property in divorce, a court may go by the following general rules in dividing marital assets and non-marital assets:[5]

"Marital assets and liabilities" include the following:

1) Assets acquired and liabilities incurred *during* the marriage by either spouse individually or jointly by both of them;

2) Increases in value of non-marital assets (described below) resulting from the efforts of either spouse during the marriage or from use of marital funds or assets or both;

3) Gifts between husband and wife during the marriage;

4) All vested and nonvested benefits and funds gained during the marriage in retirement, pension, profit-sharing, annuity, deferred compensation, and insurance plans;

5) All real property held by the spouses as joint property for the marriage, whether bought prior to or during the marriage.

"Non-marital assets and liabilities" include:

1) Assets acquired and liabilities incurred by either spouse *prior* to the marriage, and assets acquired and liabilities incurred in exchange for such assets and liabilities;

2) Assets acquired *separately* during the marriage by either spouse by gift, bequest, devise, or descent (other than between the husband and wife themselves) and any other assets bought in exchange for such assets;

3) All income earned from non-marital assets during the marriage (unless the income is treated, used, or relied upon by the spouses as a marital asset);

4) Assets and liabilities excluded from marital assets or liabilities by agreement of the spouses, and by inclusion of the same among the non-marital assets and liabilities as part of any property settlement.

The courts will use these factors (or others like them) to put all of the marital assets into one pot. The judge may assume that this pot of marital property will be split 50/50, but real life does not always work this way. Before distributions occur, courts frequently adjust the 50/50 split.[6] Ultimately, the parties receive a percentage of the marital assets and whatever non-marital assets belong to either of them as separate property. Judges have wide discretion in considering all the factors.

If a judge decides your property rights, two results usually occur. First, you can never be sure of the final award. Court decisions are rarely the same in similar cases. This uncertainty is troublesome. Second, you can be certain that no one will be happy with the court's decision. This is why private settlement with your spouse is better. You have more control over how your property is split. Judges will encourage private settlement, and the law allows for it. Take advantage of this opportunity. Here's how to do it:

A Biblical Plan for Property Division

Now that you have a general idea of how the civil law may deal with your property, let us look at a plan of action to settle your matters privately from a biblical viewpoint.

Preparing Yourself for Action
Biblical proposals can be radical and difficult to accept. Before we

discuss the following suggestions—and they are only suggestions for you and your lawyer to consider—you should expect your lawyer, family, and friends to resist these measures. Although the proposal below applies Scripture to resolution of a property dispute, it can be risky and costly from a worldly perspective.

Why take these risks? I believe these actions are a strong Christian witness to your spouse and others. If you believe that God is prompting you to do anything suggested here, and you can see scriptural support for it, you should exercise faith and proceed. The only exception to this is if a specific, valid legal reason exists for not doing so (beyond your lawyer's personal feelings). You have a higher allegiance to act in love and be gracious in following God's counsel over what the world tells you to do. Also, people are more important than property lost in any bargain. Possessions will come and go, but people last a lifetime.

You must be strong and act on the courage of your convictions. You will almost certainly be misunderstood, at least in the initial stages. But in the end, you and the Lord (and those sensitive to spiritual matters) will know that you acted lovingly and responsibly. Be a faithful steward of your resources. Settle your property disputes God's way.

Begin with prayer. Actually, *bathe* yourself in prayer. "Do not be anxious about anything, but in everything, by prayer and petition, with thanksgiving, present your requests to God. And the peace of God, which transcends all understanding, will guard your hearts and your minds in Christ Jesus" (Phil. 4:6–7). No plan of action should begin without seeking the Lord's blessing. Make Him your partner.

Believe in your plan. Once you believe that your plan is good for everyone concerned (not just yourself), set your sails and steer a straight course. "Do not those who plot evil go astray? But those who plan what is good find love and faithfulness" (Prov. 14:22).

Plan your work, and work your plan. After you have prayed about your plan and sought good counsel about the details, commit yourself to following through with whatever you decide is best. However, avoid being rigid and inflexible about this. Divorce by agreement between spouses requires negotiation. Few can make progress in negotiations if one party remains inflexible. Allow for some flexibility in your plan of action and change course if necessary.

Make no judgments where you have no compassion. Keep in mind the "big picture" as you determine what settlement strategies to follow. Do not get caught up in "winning" at all costs. Sometimes you win by losing on some issues. Sensitivity and empathy will help you know the time to give in.

Step 1: Meeting Personally with Your Spouse

Set up a pre-settlement meeting with your spouse. Speak directly with your spouse as quickly as possible when it becomes clear that divorce is inevitable. Establish that you want to discuss a fair and reasonable property settlement. Meet before any lawyers stand in the gap between you.

Set up a time to meet quietly in comfortable privacy away from distractions. If possible, meet on neutral ground in a friend's apartment or a conference room at church, for example. If not, meet wherever you or your spouse lives. Allow your spouse to make this decision. Keep children away and make sure you are alone. Take the telephone off the hook or divert calls to an answering machine or voice mail. Use restaurants or coffee shops as a last resort, because servers will always interrupt at the worst times. Also, it is important to protect your privacy.

Make a full disclosure of assets and liabilities. Before you meet, have copies made of the papers to everything either of you own jointly or separately. Offer copies to your spouse, but never release original documents in your possession unless your lawyer approves. Organize your papers into files labeled for each subject, such as "Automobiles," "Insurance," or "Stock." This shows your good faith and makes discussions easier to follow.

Important documents to photocopy and deliver to your spouse are:

- Income and expense reports showing money spent during the past three years;
- Federal and state tax returns for the past three years;
- Current statements from all checking and other accounts (with the account numbers blacked out for security protection);
- Statements as to stock owned by you alone or jointly with your spouse;
- Information as to any pension and retirement plans;
- Appraisals and invoices of all personal property;
- Automobile titles;
- List of all real property and any appraisals for these properties;
- Insurance policies.

Carefully write a letter inviting a settlement. Before you meet, send a letter to your spouse expressing your views and goals for the property settlement. This will help you organize your thoughts and allow others (family, trusted friends, your marriage counselor, etc.) to review your plan in advance and provide constructive criticism. Your attorney also should review the letter before it goes to your spouse. But writing a letter helps your spouse understand your goals and objectives.

Important points to cover in your settlement invitation letter. What should your letter say? Obviously, it must be sincere, natural, straightforward, and scrupulously honest.[7] Here are some suggestions to consider in writing your letter:

- Let your spouse know that, due to the subject matter, your letter must have a "businesslike" tone. Acknowledge that you know all papers given to your spouse will be shown to an attorney.[8]
- State the purpose of your letter. Your goal is to explore important property settlement issues. Ask your spouse to keep your letter and documents *strictly confidential*—except for attorneys, family, and friends who are already aware of your situation.
- If true, confirm that the documents delivered with your letter are, to the best of your knowledge, accurate as to your financial situation. But urge your spouse to double check everything with an attorney. Also, confirm that your spouse's lawyer will be responsible to advise him or her of legal rights—not you. Then catalog the documents delivered with a brief explanation of the importance of each one.
- For the purposes of settlement, confirm relevant facts—not opinions—about your marriage.[9] Early agreement on these facts will limit legal time and expense of discovery in depositions and in court.
- Acknowledge that you are listing the facts to the best of your recollection so your spouse will not feel like you are trying to rewrite history. Encourage your spouse to correct your statements if anything is in error. Do not state any "facts" that will assign blame to your spouse or put him or her on the defensive. Keep them as innocuous as possible.
- Since your spouse will receive your letter in advance of your actual meeting, confirm your prior appointment to meet privately at a specified time and place to answer any questions and provide any additional information that may be necessary.
- Even if your spouse accepts the matters in your letter and agrees on a

211

settlement amount, be sure that the lawyers review your agreements before they are final.[10]

- Be sure your letter and documents give a *full* disclosure of every major asset each spouse owns, either jointly or separately.[11]

Give your spouse an advance look at your letter and documents. Several days before your meeting, deliver your letter and copies to your spouse. No one likes surprises with important information. Give your spouse time to review the materials and prepare responses in time for your meeting.

Conduct the meeting in a firm but loving manner. Take an extra copy of your letter and documents with you to the meeting. Use your letter as a script to share matters with your spouse. Go through each point or paragraph slowly. Make sure that your spouse clearly understands everything. Look at the documents that apply to a particular paragraph in your letter. Note any objections or questions your spouse raises by writing notes to yourself in the margin of your copy of your letter. Do not argue objections. Show a willingness to listen. Express your sincere desire to understand your spouse's concerns. Writing these down helps your understanding.

As you deal with the issues, remind your spouse that divorce is not what you want—if true. Confirm that you are discussing these issues as a consequence of his or her own decision—not yours. At each juncture, the "tough love" approach should be applied firmly and lovingly.

After reviewing everything in detail, encourage your spouse to tell you what he or she wants in settlement first. Ask your spouse to be specific since you want to agree on as many points as possible. At this meeting it is best to simply note what your spouse says for further thought and prayer before giving a response. However, if it is timely and proper to counteroffer, do so. You never know whether another opportunity to discuss these matters in such detail will come again without direct intervention of lawyers.[12]

Many spouses quickly settle their property affairs in this first step. If not, the temptation is to run to the attorneys and battle matters out in court. From a Christian perspective, however, several important intermediate steps should be taken before lawyers actively intervene. Step 2 engages wise Christians who can be objective and fair in promoting a settlement.

Step 2: Church Mediation

If you and your spouse deadlock on Step 1, consider the advice the apostle Paul gives to Christians in 1 Corinthians 6. This Scripture warns against Christians going to law against one another. This is exactly what happens in a divorce. God's counsel is to seek mediation within the church.

> If any of you has a dispute with another, dare he take it before the ungodly for judgment instead of before the saints? Do you not know that the saints will judge the world? And if you are to judge the world, are you not competent to judge trivial cases? Do you not know that we will judge angels? How much more the things of this life! Therefore, if you have disputes about such matters, appoint as judges even men of little account in the church! I say this to shame you. Is it possible that there is nobody among you wise enough to judge a dispute between believers? But instead, one brother goes to law against another—and this in front of unbelievers! The very fact that you have lawsuits among you means you have been completely defeated already. Why not rather be wronged? Why not rather be cheated? Instead, you yourselves cheat and do wrong, and you do this to your brothers (1 Cor. 6:1–8).

If your spouse does not respond with a settlement offer in Step 1, apply 1 Corinthians 6 to your situation. Seek help and counsel from spiritual men and women in the church.[13] This also follows the counsel of Jesus in resolving disputes in Matthew 18:15–17.[14] It is biblical and right.

Advise your spouse in writing of your mediation proposal. Begin the process by sending your spouse another letter similar to the following (but obviously revised to fit your own situation):

> Regretfully, since we cannot settle the property matters amicably, I propose that we promptly try the dispute mediation procedures encouraged in 1 Corinthians 6:1–8 and Matthew 18:15–17.
>
> We can agree between us now, if you want to do so, that this church mediation shall be non-binding on either one of us, nor shall our participation jeopardize our legal rights or be used as evidence in any legal proceedings

between us. Instead, this mediation shall serve solely to help each of us determine what is fair and reasonable for a mutually acceptable settlement with other Christians to assist us.

I propose that we quickly convene a panel of unbiased Christians to review the documents exchanged between us and anything else the panel needs to review. After this review is completed, the panel will advise both of us of suggestions for a fair settlement.

My proposal for the panel members are:

1. Mr. Smith. Mr. Smith is an elder in a different congregation from the one we have attended. Mr. Smith is a local attorney who has never represented either of us. He is a family law specialist. I believe you will find that Mr. Smith is a fair-minded individual. He is intimately familiar with civil law on domestic disputes and biblical principles as well.

2. Preacher Jones. Mr. Jones has served as the minister at another congregation for many years. He knows neither of us. Therefore, he should be very objective in reviewing our property affairs from a Christian perspective.

3. Miss Doe. Miss Doe is a member of our own church. We have worshiped together for years. She is a longtime family friend. She is one of the few persons from church who has remained in regular contact with both of us during our difficulties.

Each of these individuals is very familiar with the biblical principles involved. They have the highest integrity and embrace a loving Christian spirit in settling matters of this sort. All of the panel members have graciously agreed to listen to whatever you and I want to share. They assured me of an objective review of our property situation and help with a fair settlement if that is what both of us want. We will not be pressured in any way.

Therefore, I would like to deliver a copy of our papers to the panel members by the end of this week. In the spirit of being open and both of us making a full disclosure, please accept this letter as an invitation to you (and your attorney, if you wish) to participate in this church mediation. It is an excellent opportunity for us to quietly present our property division problems to unbiased individuals for their comments and suggestions without undue embarrassment to ourselves or others.

If you prefer not to meet, I will ask the panel to review my file and to take whatever information they have from you into account in making their recommendations. While these recommendations will not be binding upon either of us, I will seriously consider their suggestions in making a settlement offer to you.

Above all, I reaffirm my sincere desire for a fair and mutually acceptable settlement. We should keep the emotional pain and legal expense of our divorce to a minimum.

Please respond to this proposal soon so we can begin mediation.

Mediation considerations. In sending this type of mediation proposal, be mindful of certain matters:

Be sure to choose a panel that is objective and balanced. Notice the balanced makeup of the panel members suggested in the sample letter above.[15] Remember, this is only an example of how to select a panel. Yours will be different (for example, with no attorneys). If your spouse is willing to do so, you might invite him or her to suggest panel members first. Just make sure that your panel has balance and includes responsible members who will provide an impartial forum.[16]

If your spouse fails, neglects, or refuses to participate in church mediation, ask the panel about what to do next. You are responsibly seeking the counsel of many advisors (Prov. 11:14; 15:22; 24:6). Even if church mediation fails, the court will appreciate your initiative to settle matters rather than rush to litigate or coerce a settlement from your spouse. It will help your legal case if the judge asks whether you tried to mediate or settle your dispute.

Finally, before you deliver a copy of your papers to the panel, notify your spouse in writing of your intention to proceed on your own if your mate will not participate. This shows your sincerity in doing nothing in secret and reaffirms that the invitation is still open to your spouse to meet with the panel.

What about paying panel members? Panel members should appreciate your distress and be willing to help. Most dedicated Christians will have the unselfish spirit of Galatians 6:2: "Carry each other's burdens, and in this way you will fulfill the law of Christ." However, Galatians 6:6 says, "Anyone who receives instruction in the word must share all good things with his instructor." Also, 1 Timothy 5:18 says that every worker is due his (or her) wages. Take these verses to heart. Pay them for their time.

If you cannot afford to pay these panel members, then personally do something special for each of them with love and thanksgiving. Too often we forget to say thank you to those who help us. We focus too much on our own problems and overlook this common courtesy.

What sort of response can be expected from a Christian panel? Often it is recommended that the husband and wife equally split all of the marital *and* non-marital assets, regardless of how state law divides these assets.[17] This is because many Christians believe a husband and wife should be equal partners in a marriage's resources. Although they may make differing contributions, they should share equally in the assets. There may be other ways to divide assets of a marriage and abide by biblical teaching. However, to share the assets equally is completely in line with biblical principles and gives every appearance of being right.

Some may not like this recommendation, saying that it is "not fair." According to the world's standards, it may appear eminently unfair to divide assets in a biblical manner.[18] But Christians are asked to settle disputes according to the Word of God—not the world's standards—in ways that amaze the world. This may be one reason why Paul included the teaching that it is better to *suffer* wrong than to *do* wrong (1 Cor. 6:7).

Another objection might be: "You are rewarding the spouse breaking the marriage." This may appear to be the case on the surface. But according to biblical principles, a spouse seeking a divorce is merely receiving his or her spouse's share of the marriage assets as an equal partner.[19]

You may not agree with everything your panel suggests. Make sure, however, that your panel's suggestions are supported by God's love and grace and confirmed by Scripture.

Step 3: Making a Settlement Offer to Your Spouse

After you receive your panel's recommendation, and if your spouse has participated in the church mediation process, you may be fortunate enough to settle matters. But if your spouse did not participate and has never told you what he or she wants in settlement, it is time for you to take the initiative in making a settlement offer.

Settlement strategy. Up until this point in your negotiations, you should not make any settlement offer to your spouse. There are several reasons for this. First, it is good to express graciousness by not trying to influence or control what your spouse may want. You show that you are secure in allowing this freedom. Also, you can truthfully testify in court that you gave your spouse every opportunity to tell you what he or she wanted.

Second, it is wise to let the other party open with an offer and set the parameters for negotiation. If it is too high, you can protest. If it is too low, then you have some leeway to be generous.

Third, if your spouse feels intimidated by the settlement process, it gives him or her a sense of control by setting the pace for negotiations.

Finally, prompting your spouse to make an offer reinforces "tough love." It helps him or her to take responsibility for sorting out financial difficulties.

But if your spouse has not responded to anything thus far, the time has come to shift gears. You should take the initiative to settle your dispute by making an offer. (If this still brings no response, then "tough love" will require a firm, measured response in reducing your offer, as we will see. Eventually you will offer no more than what the courts will impose in your effort to avoid further litigation.)

Prepare and personally deliver a final settlement offer to your spouse. Write another letter to your spouse setting out a firm and final settlement offer. Seek counsel from your attorney and other advisors before it is delivered. Make sure it is an offer you will honor and not regret. Also prepare and enclose a memorandum outlining how you arrived at your offer so your spouse can understand its fairness. Deliver your settlement offer letter personally to your spouse. Try to meet on a Saturday morning. You want the positive impact of your offer to sink in over the weekend before your spouse runs to the attorney on Monday for negative reinforcement. Make it clear in your letter—as well as verbally during your face-to-face meeting with your spouse—that your offer is fair and reasonable and that you do not want to argue.

Include a definite but reasonable period for your spouse to accept your offer. If you do not receive a clear acceptance of your offer within this period (or any extension you grant), then consider it rejected.

What to say in your settlement offer letter:

As you have lived your life on your own and separate from me, you may have wondered whether I still care about you. This letter will show you that I do. I want to share this letter directly with you without our attorneys communicating for either of us.

You know that divorce is not what I want. I am only honoring your wishes. It is futile, however, to let attorneys battle over our affairs and make the emotional turmoil worse than it is now. For peace of mind, we should give God every opportunity to speak to our hearts. We should be gracious (giving to each other what we do not deserve) and merciful (not giving to each other the judgments we do deserve).

Toward that end, in the spirit of grace and mercy, I want to propose the following to resolve our property dispute:

[Put the details of your settlement here.]

I prepared, and enclose, a memorandum for our attorneys to review that outlines how I arrived at this offer. The bottom line is exactly the same as if we took everything we own and split it right down the middle.[20] You actually come out with a little more than half, but this is okay with me. It is certainly much more than what any court would award after very expensive litigation, as any reasonable attorney will confirm to you.

My motivation in making this offer is to limit the considerable expense for both of us to litigate this matter. I would rather try to be generous with you than for strangers to profit from our unfortunate circumstance and our failure to resolve our differences in a Christian spirit. We need to live in peace. I have peace in my heart in giving this to you.

My hope is that you will prayerfully consider these matters right away. Be sure to discuss everything with your attorney before you respond. (Both of our attorneys are receiving a copy of this settlement proposal in the mail.) This offer is the very best that I can do, so please let your attorney know that this is not an "opening bid" to go higher. Our attorneys will not be able to improve upon it.

Please let me know by [date] if this offer is acceptable to you. Otherwise I will have to withdraw it.

Considerations of your settlement offer. In sending this settlement offer letter, be mindful of these issues:

First, be sure to discuss the matter with your attorney *before* delivering your letter. You will be warned that this is not a wise legal move. Also, your spouse *will* think that this is an "opening bid" that can be negotiated even higher if greed is a motivation. However, these are no reasons to ignore God's counsel. Trying to resolve disputes in a gracious and loving manner is the right way to achieve personal release from emotional bondage. Be a person of faith and courage. Be bold in moving forward with your offer unless your attorney gives you very sound legal advice for not doing so.

Second, a detailed memorandum showing how you valued your property and divided your assets is critical. Your spouse and the attorneys must understand your reasoning and independently verify matters.

Third, to protect yourself against having your settlement offer being used against you in any future court proceeding, ask your attorney about putting a legend at the top of your letter similar to this:

THIS SETTLEMENT PROPOSAL IS CONFIDENTIAL TO THE PARTIES, THEIR FAMILIES, COUNSELORS, AND LEGAL ADVISORS. AS SUCH, THIS PROPOSAL SHALL NOT BE USED AS EVIDENCE IN ANY PENDING OR FUTURE LITIGATION BETWEEN THE PARTIES, AND IS SUBMITTED SOLELY TO FACILITATE AMICABLE RESOLU-TION OF THE EXISTING DISPUTES OF THE PARTIES.

Make your words stand; keep final offers final. Anticipate that your spouse or the attorneys will seek an increase in your offer, but resolve to stand firm (within reason). Unless there is an obvious error or oversight, do not change it. If you do, it will be difficult to stop the upward pressure.

Give your spouse a definite time (ten days or so) to review everything and respond. If there is a good faith request to extend this period, and you are willing to do so, grant a short extension (seven days). If more time is requested, grant another brief extension, but with a condition. *Reduce your offer* by a certain amount every day of the second extension until your offer is accepted or time expires. This warns others not to exploit your generosity, and it confirms that time is of the essence to accept.[21]

If your spouse does not accept your offer, do not give up. One more step may avoid a trial.

Step 4: Voluntary Civil Law Mediation

Church mediation, discussed in Step 2, is the better forum for resolving disputes among Christians. If that is unsuccessful, however, do not dismiss all mediation measures. Try civil law mediation.

What is civil law mediation? It is an informal but structured non-adversarial process in which a third-party facilitator encourages resolution of a dispute. The goal is to help the parties reach a mutually acceptable and voluntary agreement. It is different from arbitration (where arbitrators are decision makers) or a trial (where the judge determines questions of law, and judge or jury decides questions of fact). Civil law mediation offers more flexibility in providing creative solutions to disputes. The parties have more control over their own destinies. There is a big difference between a judge telling you, "You will do it," and voluntarily agreeing in mediation to a settlement by saying, "I am willing to do it."

The role of the mediator is to guide the parties toward an acceptable settlement of a dispute. He or she helps parties by identifying issues and clarifying needs that are critical to a solution of the dispute, while exploring alternatives for the parties to achieve their goals. The mediator is not a fact finder, nor does this person make decisions or offer opinions about the issues. The parties involved make the decisions.

Civil law mediation may begin by court order or by voluntary request of the parties to a dispute. Voluntary mediation can occur even before filing suit for divorce. It is not legally binding unless the parties reach a mutually acceptable agreement reduced to writing and signed by everyone.

All civil law mediation proceedings are strictly confidential. Each party has the privilege of disclosing any information. The mediator is bound to secrecy unless statements relate to commission of a crime.

The mediator's fees are usually split between both parties. Usually, the mediator is an attorney or retired judge charging hourly rates. Check with your local court mediation office for specific fee information.[22]

Civil law mediation has a good record in resolving disputes. When you also consider the fact that mediation is less expensive and more certain than litigation, and that mediation conferences are scheduled much quicker than hearings before a judge, the advantages are obvious.

How does civil law mediation work? The process begins with the filing of an application for voluntary mediation by either party, or by a pre-trial court order entered to promote settlement. The application or court order notes the issues requiring mediation. A mediator is assigned to the case, and scheduling of a mediation conference usually occurs within forty-five days.

If the parties to the mediation have attorneys, they may come to the conference with their clients. If one party is represented and the other party is not, the party with a lawyer is often encouraged to consult with counsel outside the conference room or by telephone so no one feels intimidated or at an unfair disadvantage. The mediator usually tries to put the parties on equal footing as much as possible.

Most mediation conferences begin with all parties attending an orientation session. The mediator makes introductions and explains the confidential nature of the proceedings. Then a general session begins with each party making an opening statement outlining positions on the issues. Once the parties state the facts and define the issues, the general session may continue or private sessions with each party (called a *caucus*) may occur as needed.

Since flexibility is a key element of legal mediation, the mediator has discretion to meet privately with each party. Strengths and weaknesses in each side's arguments and alternative approaches to break a deadlock are explored. If resolution is more likely in private sessions, the mediator will "shuttle" offers back and forth rather than continue a general session.

The mediation process continues for as long as both parties are willing to participate. If the parties reach a settlement, the mediator helps them prepare a settlement memorandum. If they are unable to agree, the mediator declares the mediation at an impasse and concludes the session.

Key considerations of civil law mediation. First, nonadversarial mediation, without pressures of litigation, is an ideal opportunity for each party to correct misconceptions and communicate effectively. Use this time wisely.

Second, all discussions should be issue-oriented rather than presented as personal attacks. Separate emotional issues from economic concerns. This is not the place to vent feelings, although some expressions of personal frustration are appropriate at times.

221

Third, timing is critical. Mediation is timely after each party knows enough about the other's positions but before heavy litigation begins.

Fourth, selection of a mediator is important. The approach of individual mediators in facilitating negotiations between the parties, controlling attorneys, and bridging gaps in negotiation deadlocks varies from person to person. Is the mediator certified to handle a property dispute of this sort? Many qualities you look for in a lawyer (chapter 13) should also be present in the mediator.

Fifth, mediation proceedings are confidential, but some matters revealed in conference can be explored through discovery in the divorce.

Sixth, if mediation reaches an impasse, maintain control of your strategy. Many cases settle days or even weeks after the actual conference. Be patient.

Finally, if you reach a settlement, reduce it to writing *without delay* so you and your spouse can sign it (along with the attorneys, who also sign to confirm they advised you of your legal rights).

Mediation strategy. You should enter mediation ready, willing, and able to be flexible about settlement. However, remember not to contradict or rescind limitations that you have already imposed, such as withdrawal of the settlement offer made in Step 3. Work up a new settlement offer if you must, but do not reopen closed offers or you will lose credibility.

Use mediation to settle based upon what the civil law would grant to each party. The time for generous offers must end in Step 3.[23] The mediator will use the law to make settlement suggestions. Therefore, find out the most likely result a court would give and strive to settle within those parameters.

Remember, if your spouse has not cooperated in Steps 1–3, civil law mediation is the only forum for settlement left before trial. Play by the rules, but settle only as the law provides.

Settlement Sundown

If you have followed each step up to this point and your efforts are unsuccessful, it is unlikely that your case will settle. You have done all you can to resolve your dispute. Advise your attorney to prepare for trial without delay. The time has come to let the court decide this matter.

Do not give your spouse another chance to accept any rejected or withdrawn offer in Step 3, or you may be perceived as weak and indecisive while setting yourself up for another round of negotiation games. Stick to your promise to go to court. However, it is still better to settle your affairs without going to court if you can. Therefore, leave on the table the civil law mediation offer to settle based upon a court's expected ruling arrived at during Step 4. Nothing more than that. (If your spouse accepts that offer, you can expect that it will be with much regret for not taking your *first* settlement offer. That can be good for your spouse, however. It may be part of the Lord's discipline in his or her life. In the meantime, you have been a faithful witness by doing your best to please God by loving Him and your spouse).

Settlement Agreements

Your attorney obviously will have to help you prepare your settlement agreement. Do not ever try to do this on your own! Your attorney (and tax advisor) should carefully review and approve an agreement tailored to your specific needs.

Questions for Personal Reflection

1) Are there any matters relating to my finances or ownership of property that would help decide who should receive specific properties?
2) How would the equitable distribution guidelines apply in my case?
3) Do I have reasonable expectations about settlement? Are the marital assets being split equally? Who will receive the non-marital assets?
4) What are the advantages and disadvantages of settling with my spouse now versus going to trial? How much in legal fees and costs would I incur in both instances?
5) Have I tried Steps 1–4 in trying to settle matters with my spouse?

CHAPTER 13

How to Hire and Manage Lawyers

In a divorce, your lawyer is one of your primary advocates. You may not have the emotional objectivity or stamina to make many important decisions while the legal process is going on. Therefore, it is crucial to be patient and wise in carefully selecting the right lawyer. By making this major choice well, other decisions fall into place.

If you have been unsuccessful in reaching a settlement with your spouse, your relationship may be breaking down fast. You must fill the void quickly with an attorney—often a total stranger. You must trust this person to work with you and your spouse and protect your legal rights. How will your lawyer handle your intimate marital problems before a judge in a public courtroom? Even as a lawyer, I was very apprehensive about this process in my own divorce. It is time-consuming, intimidating, and expensive!

With many emotional and deeply personal matters demanding your attention, a divorce may be the first time anyone has sued you. It hurts even more to see your spouse as the aggressor. It also may be the first time you ever really needed to hire an attorney. Where do you find one? How do you make a wise choice? How can you control the expense?

Regrettably, there is a crisis of confidence in my profession and a negative public image. Despite that concern, however, you need a trustworthy lawyer to help you. Like many others in a divorce situation, you may dread the personal risk of giving up some control over your affairs to a lawyer. You may feel vulnerable, exposed, and threatened by revealing unflattering secrets to your legal counselor. You may feel insecure and not fully confident you can trust him or her. Will your lawyer needlessly run up your bill? Will he or she be difficult to contact, fail to explain what is done for you, or confuse you with legal jargon? These concerns create anxiety.

Remember, keep calm. Don't panic. This chapter will serve as a short primer on how to hire and work with your lawyer. We will review some tips and suggestions that will make this responsibility much easier for you from start to finish. We also will look at some ways to limit your legal expense that most attorneys will never tell you. You have enough to handle in focusing on the deeply personal aspects of your divorce. Let me help you make the task of dealing with your lawyer a little less intimidating.

Vital Personal Qualities of Your Legal Counselor

Finding the right lawyer is critical to making life less traumatic during a divorce. You must feel comfortable with and trust whoever is going to represent you.[1] If someone does not inspire confidence, then keep looking. Seeking a competent lawyer is not enough.[2] Consider the personal qualities your lawyer should have before you start interviewing candidates.

From a legal standpoint, you should reasonably expect your lawyer to provide you with high quality legal work; consistently give quick reaction time handling your case and responding to questions and concerns; offer you advice in simple English; counsel you on options and relative risks involved in reaching your goals within the law; and, above all, offer solutions to problems that keep litigation and your legal expense to a minimum.

On a more personal level, look for these qualities in your lawyer:

Scrupulous Honesty and Integrity

Lawyers are traditionally "officers of the court" in a judicial system pledged to a continuing "search for truth." Since some lawyers today do not cherish honesty and integrity to the same degree as their predecessors, the legal profession has lost public confidence. Most lawyers, however, are honorable men and women. With good references and a wise selection, you can easily avoid the few undesirables.

Honesty and integrity will keep your attorney from routinely assuring you that everything is fine when caution about issues and problems is needed. Honesty requires frank discussions and accurate appraisals of your case instead of unfounded promises. It is very tempting amid tough economic times and cutthroat competition for business to put the client's best interest aside.[3] Those who fall prey to this flaw cultivate various deceits. They exaggerate legal qualifications, dodge responsibilities, pad bills, unnecessarily run up legal time, and tell "white lies." Some believe that "lies are necessary in order to live," to paraphrase Nietzsche. But in his 1847 address to the Charleston, South Carolina, Bar Association, Daniel Webster rebuked this attitude: "Tell me a man is dishonest, and I will answer he is no lawyer. He cannot be, because he is careless and reckless of justice; the law is not in his heart and is not the standard and rule of his conduct."[4]

A dear friend, who endured a very expensive divorce lasting more than four years with numerous appeals, told me her case could have ended much sooner had she known of the pitfalls. Her attorney used charm, power, and authority to influence her decisions. Whenever she had doubts about strategies, her lawyer assured her: "Don't worry about it. That's why you hired us." As my friend worried about the mounting expenses and moving on with her life, she was told, "You're charming, intelligent, and sophisticated. You'll be married again in two years." After many months, however, her lawyer threw up his hands and announced that nothing more could be done. She was to sign a settlement much less favorable than one she originally wanted to accept, or find another lawyer.

Without honesty and integrity, you and your lawyer, your case, and your credibility with the court will suffer. A good, honest lawyer will give you the respect and loyalty that are vital to your relationship.

Sensitive and Perceptive Communication

If your attorney is unable to write clearly or speak persuasively, the best legal arguments will be to no avail. Look for lawyers who speak with clarity, precision, focus, and persuasion. Note those who strive to help people understand issues rather than give a prepared speech. If your lawyer is arrogant or filled with vain pride, he or she will not be genuine in dealing with others or listen with empathy. Such a person has too many personal problems to help you. Does your lawyer have a sense of humor? When inevitable frustrations arise in your case and you become impatient and anxious, will your attorney react with appropriate humor and assurance?

Good communicators come in both genders. Some feel female lawyers are more supportive than male attorneys. Others believe male lawyers will gain more power and control over the case, the courtroom, and the judge. Do not overrate these concerns, however. Gender is less of a consideration than legal competence and positive personal attributes.

Good Judgment and Common Sense

Those knowledgeable about hiring lawyers often rank good judgment about human nature above technical knowledge of the law. A brilliant lawyer who gives impeccable legal opinions may alienate others and destroy your case. There is no substitute for life experiences and the maturity that comes from understanding how and why people think and act as they do. Your lawyer should have empathy for others, and understand issues and motivations. Will your attorney see only your side of matters instead of the "big picture"—the needs and desires of your spouse, opposing counsel, witnesses, and the judge? If you find a lawyer with rigid preconceptions rather than one who is a good listener, that person is not for you.

Like anyone else, attorneys' egos and emotions may get out of hand at times. Professionals in the law sometimes get caught up in the action and competition. Look for a lawyer who keeps the ego in check and jealously holds onto a rational perspective of your case. The best lawyer will be a person who exercises mature judgment, reflects on decisions before actions are taken, and relies heavily on moral as well as legal reasoning.

Disciplined Toughness

While your lawyer must be objective, perceptive, communicative, and rational, you do not want an attorney who is wishy-washy or fearful of difficult negotiations. Your attorney should be tough but fair, one who feels comfortable negotiating settlement agreements or addressing the court. When circumstances require aggressive action, your lawyer must rise promptly to the challenge. If your lawyer does not inspire this confidence in you, others will see this weakness and exploit it to your disadvantage.

Disciplined toughness does not mean having an arrogant or belligerent attitude. Some describe the proper balance as being a "velvet-covered brick." There should be a sensitivity and tenderness to the heartbreak of the parties to a divorce, but a firm and uncompromising stand against dishonest exploitation or unnecessary cruelty in the legal process on anyone's part.

Creativity in Finding Constructive Solutions

This goes beyond molding the facts into an argument that will win at all costs. A good lawyer will always be solution-oriented with the goal of reducing time and expense through reasonable compromises, especially whenever volatile situations can be easily defused. Why run up legal bills arguing over an inexpensive household item? A wise lawyer explores alternatives to resolve issues quickly through concessions on other important issues rather than major on the minors.

A lawyer having the personal qualities listed above is rare but not impossible to find. He or she does not have to be a Christian, but it certainly helps.[5] Christian lawyers may understand your motivations better.

The Role of Your Lawyer as
Comforter and Healer

Find an attorney who is a comforter. A gifted lawyer gently consoles clients who are stressed out, angry, broke and broken, hurt and confused as they face poverty, destruction of their families, bills, and other stresses.[6] The client is shielded from opposing counsel, unnecessary case complications, and people who will foment strife and derail settlement.

Former Harvard law professor Arthur Miller once said, "Lawyers owe complete allegiance to their client, very little to the system, and none at all to the adversary." Some clients praise lawyers who intimidate and browbeat their opponents as being good, hard-nosed litigators. Their goal would be to crush your spouse financially and otherwise. But when the case is over, the lawyer gets paid and goes home. You, however, find a wedge of hostility and distrust between you, your spouse, and family members that poisons relationships for years to come.[7] The better approach is to hire a reasonable and fair attorney regardless of whom your spouse chooses for a lawyer.

Look for a legal counselor who is a healer—one who treats you and your opponents with kindness, courtesy, respect, and humanity. Find an attorney who uses the law with logic, fairness, reason, and empathy to restore, remedy, and reconcile social and personal wounds as fairly and peacefully as possible.

In his confrontation of King David in 2 Samuel 12, Nathan gave an excellent example of what a lawyer's demeanor should be. Read verses 1–14 and note the ways in which Nathan met confidentially with David to deal with an intolerable situation. He marshaled the facts and was aware of the problem, but he listened to understand David's attitude. He was creative in helping David face his own responsibility in a very firm yet loving manner. Notice Nathan's character and integrity as he courageously challenged the king. As a result, David experienced a personal catharsis and repented.

Some individuals in the legal profession are conflict resolvers, healers, and peacemakers. These comforters sweetly oil our social systems and keep everything from coming to a grinding halt. Search out these lawyers.

In describing the lawyer as a "counselor," it is important also to understand an attorney's limitations. Your lawyer should be supportive and encouraging, but he or she is not a mental health professional. Do not expect your lawyer to be your therapist. This is especially tempting for vulnerable clients who idolize their lawyers as invincible knights in shining armor. Seek counsel for personal, nonlegal problems from mental health professionals. Besides, you pay your attorney more per hour to listen than your therapist.

Therapists encourage communication between disputing parties. They discourage withholding of personal information in order to determine root causes of any denial or self-deception. They allow clients to learn from the consequences of their own decisions without judging whether an action is right or wrong. Lawyers, however, want clients to empower them to make the decisions. A lawyer counsels clients against any decision that has an adverse consequence. After all, courts will judge actions taken by either party to a divorce with the intent of assessing damages. Therefore, use your lawyer wisely. Seek legal advice on issues which have a legal or financial consequence. Use a therapist for personal problems.

The Selection Process

After knowing what to look for in a lawyer, you are ready to begin the selection process.

How to Find a Lawyer

Personal recommendations. The easiest way to look for a lawyer is by asking friends, neighbors, and business associates. Your family counselor, psychologist, or pastor also might have some names. This is good—as long as you know whom to ask.

To save time in running down false leads, ask those who are recommending personal divorce lawyers whether their attorney was supportive of their position and attentive to their needs. Were they kept informed as to the progress of their case? Were fees and costs reasonable? Did the attorney further alienate the former spouse? Most importantly, would they use their attorney again without hesitation?

There are some drawbacks to personal referrals, however. You may not want to ask those close to you for names of divorce lawyers if you want to keep matters quiet in the early stages. Also, your friend's case may be very different from your own. Does the lawyer practice in family law regularly? Your friends may not be sure about this. Make sure that those giving you recommendations are thinking of your best interest.

Local references. Check with your employer's lawyer. Court reporters, clerks at your local courthouse, secretaries, and law clerks for judges often know good attorneys. After all, they see the lawyers in action. If there is a law school in your area, check with the alumni office for qualified graduates.

Other attorneys. Ask attorneys you know who practice in other areas of the law for suggestions. Also, call several family law attorneys and ask whom they would hire (present company excepted).

Lawyer referral services. Lawyer referral services sponsored by local bar associations are also excellent sources. In 1992, more than 53,000 clients were referred to the 600 attorneys who participated in the Florida Bar Lawyer Referral Service.[8] In the years since, hundreds of thousands of clients have participated successfully in state lawyer referral services. Your state bar association often has a referral service listed in your local yellow pages or a statewide toll-free number.

Referral services have some disadvantages. Sometimes these services are training grounds for recent law school graduates or incompetent lawyers with few clients. While the American Bar Association encourages the use of "recently admitted and less experienced lawyers" for lower cost service and personal dedication, be careful. Not all services maintain high standards. Many of them charge your lawyer a referral fee (usually about 10 percent of the lawyer's fees). Ultimately these fees are charged back to you. Finally, these services recommend lawyers on a lottery system rather than by expertise or price. Carefully check out the qualifications and personal demeanor of any lawyer recommended to you.

Law clinics. Legal clinics are a low cost source of legal services. Advertisements typically tout completion of uncontested divorces for a few hundred dollars. The attorneys' competence is not emphasized because you will not spend much time with a lawyer for that low fee. Do not expect to interview and consult at length with attorneys in legal clinics because they make liberal use of forms and non-lawyer paralegals and secretaries. Use this alternative at your own risk. However, if cost is critical and your divorce is uncontested, this is an option.

Prepaid legal plans. See if you are covered by a prepaid legal services benefit through an employee assistance plan. According to the National Resource Center for Consumers of Legal Services, 71 million Americans are in such legal services plans, which are similar to prepaid dental or medical plans. Typical plans allow for free initial consultations, with further work handled at reduced rates and/or a cap on fees. Review different plans endorsed or sponsored by a reputable organization, such as the American Bar Association (www.abanet.org). These provide affordable legal services, but limitations could affect your choice of attorney. Also, the quality of services may differ between plan clients and other clients of the attorney, although ethically this is prohibited.

Yellow pages. Relaxed restrictions on lawyer advertising now allow attorneys to publish their specialties in the yellow pages. Look for ads that provide information such as the length of time the attorney has practiced, as well as his or her professional experience and certifications to practice. Does the listing express concern toward clients or promise reliability, speed, and intelligence? Use listings to shop prices among lawyer candidates. Look for attorneys close to your home or office to make meetings convenient. Remember, however, that advertisements and listings in the telephone book can be misleading. Be skeptical of whatever you cannot independently verify.

Martindale-Hubbell Law Directory. The Martindale-Hubbell Law Directory is a multi-volume legal directory alphabetically listing most lawyers in the U.S. and Canada. With this directory, available at your local library or law school, you can look up the biography of licensed attorneys and learn of their education, honors, and personal background. (Obtain additional lawyer locator information at www.martindale.com.)

There is this added attraction: Martindale-Hubbell develops ratings for individual lawyers by asking for confidential opinions from members of bar associations—including judges—who have some knowledge about the attorney. Two ratings are given. The *legal ability rating* evaluates the lawyer's ability in his or her city and takes into consideration experience, nature of practice, and qualifications. The *general recommendation rating* considers faithful compliance with standards of conduct and ethics of the legal profession, professional reliability, and diligence. The directory gives an "AV" rating to the most highly regarded and qualified lawyers.

Use this valuable directory to find family law attorneys in your area. Before your interviews, make notes on all of your attorney candidates. If you can afford it, try to hire an "AV" rated lawyer, although lawyers with that high rating will be among the most expensive. A "BV" rated lawyer, being the next highest rating, is also a good attorney but should be less expensive.

Other resources. Marquis publishes "Who's Who in American Law".

with a helpful biography on listed attorneys, although only a few selected attorneys are listed and no expertise ratings are given. The American Bar Association also lists many attorneys with family law litigation experience in its "Directory of Litigation Attorneys." Both publications are available at most law libraries or universities.

Community action agencies such as Parents Without Partners, Legal Awareness for Women, and special interest groups have information on attorneys. Local divorce support and recovery groups meeting at churches or community centers are also helpful resources.

In your search to find a qualified attorney, resist the urge to hire the first impressive lawyer you interview. Shop around. Ask many questions. Most lawyers will meet briefly with you to discuss your case and their qualifications for free or a nominal fee. (Be sure to confirm this in advance.)

Interviewing a Lawyer

Before scheduling an appointment with a lawyer candidate, specify that this is a "get acquainted" interview. Ask for the attorney's résumé, firm brochure, or newsletter. This will acquaint you with his or her qualifications and achievements. The purpose of the interview is to secure background information about the attorney, the general nature of your case, and his or her availability to handle it. Be sure to ask about any materials you should bring to the conference. Also ask in advance about the range of fees. Lawyers do not like to waste time attending an initial meeting if the client cannot afford the work.

Before your interview, outline the facts of your case.[9] Prepare a detailed list of questions to ask the lawyer. Be frank in divulging all of the legal facts, good and bad. Since your interview is confidential, your candor will allow the lawyer to provide you with an accurate assessment of your case.[10]

When you meet, be on time. Also be sensitive to the lawyer's time. The attorney may begin by asking you to describe your legal problem briefly, then will listen to your explanation. After all, you and the lawyer will be evaluating each other in this interview. The attorney needs to know whether you will be a cooperative and pleasant client.

After you describe your case, ask the attorney about any obvious strengths and weaknesses in your case. Ask what strategy the lawyer would use. Find out how long it may take to complete your case based upon the lawyer's previous experience. As different lawyers answer your questions, you will see how well this candidate knows the law and focuses on the issues.

Ask whether the lawyer can work on your case right away. Will the attorney be personally handling your case or assigning it instead to another lawyer or paralegal? How will he or she keep you informed about your case? What fee arrangements and billing procedures apply? Make notes of all responses. If the lawyer has no objection, use a tape recorder.

Also be sure to ask the attorney for personal references to check out.[11]

After a few of these interviews, you will see differences among the lawyers you meet. Quite often your decision will be obvious. There will always be some candidates who impress you more than others.

Financial Matters

Regardless of which attorney you select, you must understand fee arrangements and be aware of how to keep your legal costs reasonable.

Negotiating Fee Arrangements

How fees are set. Attorneys fees are often negotiable, although most experienced lawyers do not want to lower their fees.[12] Most lawyers set their rates based upon these factors: time, labor, novelty, the difficulty of the legal issues involved, and the legal skills necessary to work the case properly; the likelihood that acceptance of the case will prevent other employment, either because of time or conflicts of interest; the customary fees usually charged in the area for similar legal services; the amount involved and results obtained; the time limitations imposed by the client or circumstances; the nature and length of the professional relationship with the client; the experience, reputation, and ability of the lawyer performing the services; and overhead (library costs, secretarial help, office rent, and costs of equipment, etc.). The lawyer will be very familiar with what can and cannot be done in setting a reasonable fee for your case. Even so, negotiate for lower fees. Above all, make sure fees are in line with what other local lawyers charge for doing the same type of work.

Most attorneys realize that the practice of law is no longer just a service profession but is also a business. No one can ignore business considerations and practice for very long.[13] Therefore, many attorneys are diligent in advising their clients up-front what they charge. You should expect regular bills during the case, as well as a collection system for late payments.

Types of fee arrangements. There are three traditional methods for setting fees: fixed fees; hourly rates for work of uncertain duration; and contingency fees (a percentage of whatever a lawyer wins for the client).

Fixed fees are unusual in litigation cases because no one can reasonably foresee when and how the case will end. Although fixed fee arrangements may force the lawyer to work more efficiently and prevent misunderstandings about the final bill, lawyers know that clients can take advantage of them by excessive calls and conferences. Consequently, the lawyer may lose interest in the case and assign it a low priority.

Contingency fee arrangements in dissolution of marriage cases are illegal in most states. Such arrangements create many conflicts of interest at the expense of shattered marriages and broken lives. Therefore, you should expect your lawyer to charge a negotiated hourly rate for your case.[14]

Retainers. Many lawyers want an advance retainer or deposit against your fees and costs. You should receive full credit for this retainer against your legal expenses. Negotiate now for a refund of all unearned portions of the retainer when your lawyer's representation ends.

Legal representation agreements. Fee and representation requirements are usually written into an agreement or letter signed by you and your lawyer.[15] Carefully read this agreement. It will control how you and your attorney work together in handling your case. If you have any questions or concerns about the lawyer or the work involved, have your understanding written into your agreement. These agreements help avoid misunderstandings and assure effective communication about mutual expectations.

Billing statements. You have a right to know about work completed on your behalf in enough detail to be sure that fees are reasonable and comply with your fee agreement.[16] If you do not ask for a detailed bill, many attorneys will simply send a short, one-page statement that states "For Services Rendered" and list a lump sum fee due. This saves time for the attorney, but even the most honest of lawyers can make mistakes in figuring fees. Without a detailed bill, you cannot correct those errors. Therefore, always ask for a statement with a daily accounting of tasks performed, hours per task, individuals who did the work, and the hourly rate for each.[17]

In examining your fee statement, be aware of a few overbilling problems like these: overuse of conferences among lawyers in the same office about your case; repeatedly passing your file on to new lawyers who will bill you for reviewing your case; overstaffing your case by having more than one person attend hearings and depositions; overresearching issues and padding legal research hours; charging a high hourly rate for existing computerized form documents usable in many cases; charging for services at improper rates such as billing secretaries as paralegals, paralegals as lawyers, and lawyers not yet admitted to the bar as admitted lawyers; billing for workproduct that cannot be produced to you; markups on fixed costs such as computerized legal research, photocopying and facsimile charges, meals, and airline tickets; and summarizing depositions to an unwarranted degree. If you prohibit these matters in your fee agreement, you avoid many expensive misunderstandings during your case.

Billing frequency. Most lawyers bill on a monthly cycle under the theory that regular billing helps assure regular payment. It also reduces your shock in receiving one enormous bill at the end of your case. However, billing at the end makes it easier to talk to your lawyer about adjusting the bill if the result is worse than expected due to decisions he or she made.

Payment of fees. Most lawyers have a precise system for collection of fees. After thirty days, the lawyer may send out a second statement. A letter follows after forty-five days, with a personal telephone call after sixty days. Slow-paying accounts receive low priority for the lawyer's time if other clients pay promptly. Also, although lawyers do not like to arbitrate or litigate fees with clients, they will do so if the potential loss is large enough to warrant it. Be wise and promptly pay your bills within thirty days. Your lawyer will appreciate you as a client and work harder for you.

How to Cut Your Legal Fees and Costs

Developing a strategy and budget. Many variables are difficult to control in a divorce, such as whether your spouse and opposing attorney will settle, fight discovery, or use delay tactics. Developing a strategy and budget for your case—and updating it before major hearings or conferences—will provide you and your attorney with a clear understanding of the proper level and limits of the work.[18]

Try to set a maximum fee cap on the case that should not be exceeded without prior written approval. This helps you monitor expenses and avoid surprises in your final bills.

Your lawyer should watch fees and expenses to make sure you are billed fairly under your fee agreement. Before your budget for legal expenses in any phase is exceeded, you should be notified promptly so that you can decide whether to revise your budget or modify the strategy. Then you can give your prior written approval of the excess amount.

Encourage your lawyer always to be alert for a creative or less expensive way to proceed—even if the work is within your budget—and to discuss these matters with you promptly. Above all, in developing a strategy and budget, use a laser rather than a shotgun in addressing your issues and problems. Be precise and efficient.

Cost limitations. Ask your lawyer to be sensitive to the costs of multiple representation at meetings and hearings, high staffing levels, rotating persons onto matters with which they are unfamiliar, and training young lawyers on your case.

Since your lawyer can handle most of your case in the office, the need for overnight travel is slight. However, if out-of-town travel is necessary, have your lawyer agree that only one attorney should travel; expenses for lodging, restaurants, or transportation should not be extravagant; and charges for airfare should be at the coach rate only.

If you require extra or unnecessary legal work, such as excessive telephone calls or conferences or filing unwarranted court pleadings, you should expect to pay for these. Similarly, your lawyer should agree that if work completed is not budgeted or approved, is not properly done, or requires correction, you will not be billed. Find out what your lawyer's minimum billing increment is.[19] Lawyers often charge in tenths or quarters of an hour. If you are charged a quarter-hour for a two-minute phone call, prepare for this call and use the full fifteen minutes to your benefit.

Does your attorney double-bill you and other clients for work benefiting everyone?[20] If so, object to this and work out a fair fee allocation.

Assist your lawyer in finding documents or information to lower your legal expense. Offer to locate witnesses, secure property appraisals, and copy lengthy documents at discount copy centers.

Develop a friendly working relationship with your lawyer's secretary. You will receive information about your case at no additional cost, since time for secretaries is not usually billed to clients and they are quite familiar with cases. Happy secretaries will also work to keep your case a priority.

Hourly rates almost always include your lawyer's overhead, which should not be added separately onto your bill.[21] Reimbursement of expenses to third-party suppliers should be at documented, actual cost.[22]

Unless agreed upon in advance and in writing with your lawyer, try to avoid or limit paying for these costs:

- Administrative time by the attorney;[23]
- Secretarial overtime, unless it is a legitimate emergency for your case alone;

- Time spent preparing bills and discussing billing matters with you;
- Photocopies made internally in excess of a good faith estimate of actual cost;[24]
- Internal office messenger expense in excess of the cost of comparable outside services;
- Meal costs, except for a reasonable cost if a matter necessary to advance your case must be discussed with an outside party during the meal;[25]
- Auto mileage in excess of a reasonable cost per mile (AAA rates or IRS allowances).[26]

Communication. When you meet or talk with your lawyer, be prompt. Organize papers and have information ready with a list of carefully thought-out matters you need to discuss. Avoid deluging your lawyer with information unless it is requested. Always listen carefully to your lawyer's advice. Promptly follow the instructions carefully.

Tell your lawyer you do not want "surprises." As the expert, your attorney should expect and warn you in advance of matters that may affect you or your case so that you can properly prepare yourself.

Make sure your lawyer does not negotiate away any of your rights or give away any personal information without your prior written approval.

Tell your lawyer that you will not call unless you have an important legal concern. (Remember, you are not your lawyer's only client.) Your attorney should return telephone calls within twenty-four hours unless he or she is out of town or reasonably indisposed.

Keep your case files up-to-date. Ask your lawyer to copy for you significant memoranda or pleadings prepared on your behalf so that you can monitor your case progress. This also allows you to stop any activities that may be too expensive or overly combative with the other side.

Encourage your lawyer to alert you to anything you do that interferes with your case. Similarly, advise your lawyer that you want to discuss any of your concerns directly with him or her as well.

If your questions cannot be answered within fifteen minutes by telephone, write your attorney a letter. This will give him or her time to focus on your needs and give you a more thoughtful response. Letters allow you to share more information with your lawyer in a shorter period of time while also documenting your concerns. Always keep a copy of your letter for your files. Use it as a checklist when your lawyer responds.

Disagreements and termination of representation. If you have any disagreements with your lawyer, discuss problems directly without delay. Face-to-face discussions are biblical and good practice (Matt. 5:23–24; 18:15–17).

If you and your lawyer cannot agree on a fair settlement of the dispute, your attorney should agree to promptly secure court approval to withdraw so you can secure alternate counsel without jeopardizing your case.

Pay your first lawyer a reasonable fee to the date you change lawyers. To avoid disputes about fees in this instance, have your lawyer agree in advance to arbitration or mediation of the dispute. If this is not available, then you and your attorney can pursue whatever legal remedies are available.

If your lawyer has violated rules of professional conduct (such as missing filing deadlines or misappropriating trust account funds), you should consider filing a formal complaint with your state bar association.[27] This association also may have a client security fund to reimburse you if your funds or property have been embezzled by your lawyer.

Be a Good Client

As a client, you should receive high quality, cost-efficient representation. This means receiving written work that is easily understood and reflects a thorough treatment of options and risks in your case; advice responsive to your goal of settling the case or completing the divorce quickly; and reasonable bills for fees that are competitive with those charged by other lawyers.

Your lawyer expects prompt payment for services rendered. Do not deny him or her a reasonable fee.

You are your lawyer's eyes and ears. Be cooperative and accessible for consultation whenever necessary. Do not be a pest. Avoid any unreasonable interference with your lawyer's work.

You and your lawyer always should act in a manner that shows good faith and inspires trust.

Remember, you are in charge. It is your money, so it is your decision. Keep up with the progress made on your case. When your lawyer gives you options to consider, make decisions promptly after receiving advice.

After you hire a qualified attorney and have guarded yourself against the matters in this chapter, you will be in good shape to let your lawyer protect your interests in a calm and reasonable fashion.

Questions for Personal Reflection

1) What qualities are important to me to find in my legal counselor? What practical help do I expect from my attorney?

2) Did my attorney meet my requirements?

3) Does my lawyer understand my situation? Do I feel comfortable in communicating with my lawyer over an extended time period?

4) Is my lawyer honest and straightforward in answering my questions? Is my attorney reasonably available to me whenever I need help? Does my lawyer keep me advised of what is happening?

5) Am I pleased with how my case is being handled by my attorney and with the results obtained? Do I feel that my case is important to my attorney, or a low priority? Are my expectations of my attorney reasonable?

CHAPTER 14

When Your Case Goes to Court

*What happens if every effort at settlement and
reconciliation has been unsuccessful and court action
is unavoidable? You face dealing with the legal system.
It is important to know what to expect during the stages
of a legal proceeding, from the beginning of the case
through trial and enforcement procedures, to help
matters run smoother along the way.*

"There's a rogue at the end of my cane!" That's what the notorious judge known as "Bloody Jeffreys" remarked as he pointed his cane at the man on trial. The man looked at the judge and replied, "At which end, my lord?"

This humorous anecdote from James V. Bennett in the *Journal of American Judicature Society* is not far off the mark about the judicial process. Going to court with a spouse inevitably leads to "he said, she said" complaints. Each spouse blames the other; each tries to put the other in the worst possible light. Someone said that love is the quest; marriage, the conquest; and divorce the inquest. The legal process shows how true that can be.

If a trial is unavoidable, love and forgiveness must continue. This is no small challenge. You may face a spouse doing everything possible to take you to the cleaners in court. But if we lose sight of Jesus, we will sink into turbulent waters as surely as Peter sank on the Sea of Galilee. Our lashes at others with legal whips will end up becoming stripes across our own backs.

Over 2,500 years ago, the prophet Isaiah lamented:

> No one calls for justice; no one pleads his case with
> integrity. They rely on empty arguments and speak lies;
> they conceive trouble and give birth to evil. They hatch the
> eggs of vipers and spin a spider's web. Whoever eats their
> eggs will die, and when one is broken, an adder is hatched.
> . . . So justice is driven back, and righteousness stands at a
> distance; truth has stumbled in the streets, honesty cannot

enter. Truth is nowhere to be found, and whoever shuns evil becomes a prey (Isa. 59:4–5, 14–15).

No wonder Jesus warned:

> Settle matters quickly with your adversary who is taking you to court. Do it while you are still with him on the way, or he may hand you over to the judge, and the judge may hand you over to the officer, and you may be thrown into prison. I tell you the truth, you will not get out until you have paid the last penny (Matt. 5:25–26).

These are wise words from those familiar with the justice courts of men. With fallible people being what they are, little has changed over the years. Many courtrooms have a sign reading, "We who labor here seek only the truth." But too often there is distortion of truth. These days, many people perjure themselves by lying under oath. Many judges shrug their shoulders at the exposure of a lie and tolerate it rather than take action by enforcing the penalties for that crime. Actually, the justice system is fair and balanced; people are the problem. Impartial judgment is difficult for anyone.

Pursuing divorce in today's civil courts is no exception. In the 1989 dark comedy *The War of the Roses*, actor/director Danny de Vito, playing a lawyer, narrates the tale of an awful divorce battle. A husband and wife fight over who will receive the house in property settlement. They make a suicide pact of mutually assured destruction and fiendishly carry it out. The moral of the movie is: "Civilized divorce is a contradiction in terms."

Real life is not far from this. Consider the case of Los Angeles millionaires Stanley and Dorothy Diller.

Their divorce took more than seven years. They disputed every issue possible. The case required 110 court hearings and a marathon trial lasting forty-nine days. The divorce continued until the case transcript had consumed 5,165 pages in twenty volumes more than six feet high. Attorneys fees exceeded $3 million as appeals were taken all the way to the U.S. Supreme Court. Trial Judge Robert Fainer described Dorothy Diller as "a frightened, bitter woman" who was "obsessed" that her husband was hiding assets. He described Stanley Diller as "an avaricious, covetous, and stubborn man." No judge could stop this couple from grinding out the litigation without concern for the time and costs of doing so. In fact, if spouses fail to agree, this type of result is possible in almost any divorce case.

Despite these horror stories, most divorce cases can move smoothly through the courts—especially in states with no-fault divorce laws. Where did these divorce laws come from?

Sign of the Times: No-Fault Divorce

After decades of divorce between warring spouses with imbalanced bargaining positions, California tried a new approach in January 1970. Before that time, divorce required one spouse to prove the other was at fault for ending the marriage. Judges did not grant a divorce until proof of misconduct justified it. As a result, tragic and embarrassing personal problems like alcoholism, cruelty, desertion, adultery, felony convictions, impotency, or insanity shocked the courtroom. In searching for divorce grounds, the finger-pointing, exaggeration, and deceit by each spouse had no end.

But then California Governor Ronald Reagan signed the first no-fault divorce law in the United States. Courts could now grant divorce if the marriage was broken by irreconcilable differences or incompatibility between the spouses. No-fault was an effort to make the divorce process more rational and fair. It reduced the economic and emotional trauma.[1] (As of 2006, forty-six states have adopted no-fault standards as the sole basis or additional ground for dissolution.[2]) In the years that followed, divorces became less scandalous. But this did not end the hostility and revenge arising over child custody and visitation, spouse and child support, and division of assets.[3]

Housewives with custody of children were financially unequal with working husbands, so no-fault often led to inequities. Spouses sold homes to divide sale proceeds, which displaced families. Jobless spouses received little or no financial support after dividing marital assets. Women, especially those unskilled or unable to work, began a slide down the economic ladder while the standard of living for men with comfortable incomes rose.

Legislators around the U.S. review many alternatives for reform each year. Due to the economic imbalance between husband and wife, they seek to include a spouse's business assets and professional benefits among the marital assets for division. They seek more penalties to enforce child support debts. They attempt to protect the disadvantaged spouse through greater post-divorce support awards.

In addition to these reforms, family court divisions handling only family law cases are being created.[4] These help judges develop special sensitivity for the emotional side of divorce, while making them "experts" in family law issues and more consistent in their rulings. The divisions also provide better protection for victims of domestic violence.[5] Family law cases, accounting for almost 50 percent of all court cases filed in many states, move on a "fast track" in these new divisions. This should cut the time for completion of typical cases substantially. Before going to court, find out what reforms exist in your state to avoid unrealistic expectations.

Preparing for Civil War

Before engaging in a civil divorce, we need to ask ourselves a few questions.

Making Our Decision

Is it worth the turmoil to go to court and "win"? Even under no-fault laws, each divorce case has the potential for becoming unmanageable. Litigation requires a lot of time and effort, coupled with restless nights. Is it worth it? If not, we need to factor that into our last settlement offer and explore a compromise one last time. Even if we "win" in court, is it worth the further bitterness and resentment our spouses, family, and friends may feel toward us? To be sure: "If a wise man goes to court with a fool, the fool rages and scoffs, and there is no peace" (Prov. 29:9).

Is our cause just and reasonable? Is it worth the time, expense, and trouble of litigation? Are we unjustly withholding benefits from our spouses? "Do not exploit the poor because they are poor and do not crush the needy in court, for the Lord will take up their case and will plunder those who plunder them" (Prov. 22:22-23). Imagine "winning" our court litigation only to find the Lord standing against us at the end! Be wise, compromising within the limitations of tough love. Even if this shortchanges us to a tolerable degree, fairness is what counts.

Have we fully considered the court issues in advance? We know matters about our spouses that no one else but the Lord knows. If we wanted to be mean and vindictive, we could hurt and embarrass them handily. But this is a double-edged sword. They can do the same to us. What do we gain by revealing titillating information? Gossip makes anyone look exploitative and hateful. Witnesses to court conduct—family and friends—will never forget how each spouse dealt with the other. "What you have seen with your eyes do not bring hastily to court, for what will you do in the end if your neighbor puts you to shame? If you argue your case with a neighbor, do not betray another man's confidence, or he who hears it may shame you and you will never lose your bad reputation" (Prov. 25:8–10).

Before the action begins, advise lawyers if there are any personal matters that you will not reveal. Do discuss any confidential matters that may have a bearing on the case privately with the lawyer, but if no good legal reason exists to use that information, let it go no further than the lawyer.[6] Stick to the minimum facts necessary to resolve the issues. Avoid personal attacks or innuendo against anyone unless the truth demands it.

Have we fully investigated the facts? Never make decisions without first having the facts. It is reckless and unfair to make any assertion that will harm someone unless it serves a reasonable purpose and the truth is verified. When in doubt about the accuracy of anything, forget it.

Can we maintain self-control throughout the trial? "A fool gives full vent to his anger, but a wise man keeps himself under control" (Prov. 29:11). If anger is needed, let it be a controlled, focused response that concentrates precisely on the issues. Now is the time to remain patient. Be willing to bargain without becoming compliant or retreating from tough love positions. Always keep the big picture in mind. Remember that God desires reconciliation of a marriage if it is possible and safe to do so.

The Legal Process of Divorce: A Sword and a Shield

Will we fight the good fight as Christians, even in court? In a court system premised on a search for truth and the fair administration of justice, we possess a shield for use as a defensive weapon. Meanwhile, attorneys are our swords, using the law to exercise our legal rights. And yes, we need to use all of this armor responsibly.

But for Christians, the best armor comes from the Lord (Eph. 6:10–18). We may be in the courts of man, but we do not lay aside our spiritual armor. To the contrary, we buckle the belt of truth around our waist. We keep the breastplate of righteousness in place. We take up the shield of faith to extinguish the flaming arrows of evil sent flying at us. We take up the sword of the Spirit, the Word of God, and strengthen ourselves by moving forward with wisdom and grace.

As a Christian, I found Psalm 37 to be particularly encouraging in preparing for my own litigation. "Delight yourself in the Lord and he will give you the desires of your heart. Commit your way to the Lord; trust in him and he will do this: He will make your righteousness shine like the dawn, the justice of your cause like the noonday sun. Be still before the Lord and wait patiently for him" (Ps. 37:4–7). Read through this beautiful psalm many times during the legal process. It is very encouraging.

Trust your lawyer and keep alert to what is going on in court. Don't try to be your own lawyer,[7] but do be diligent about keeping up with your case and try to learn more about the court process. This is important so you can discuss case strategies intelligently with your lawyer.

Remember that each state has its own laws. In court, each judge interprets those laws differently. Attorneys also try differing methods to use state laws and court systems effectively. This makes it impossible to predict any result in a divorce case conclusively. While there are some similarities in legal proceedings, which we will review in the remainder of this chapter, this book obviously cannot be a comprehensive guide to the many legal considerations that may arise in your case. Always ask your lawyer about your own state laws.

Orderly Justice: The Phases of a Divorce Trial

Phase 1: The Complaint and Summons

A divorce action begins with one spouse filing a *complaint for divorce* or *petition for dissolution of marriage* with a state court that can make decisions for both spouses (that is, the court that has "jurisdiction" over the case). A complaint is a legal paper (called a "pleading") that describes the facts and grounds for seeking a divorce and asks the court for certain relief.[8] The *plaintiff* or *petitioner* spouse files the complaint, while the other is the *defendant* or *respondent* spouse.

The court issues a *summons* after filing the complaint. The summons, with a copy of the complaint attached, commands the defendant spouse to file a legal response to the complaint within a specific time (usually twenty to thirty days after receipt of the summons).[9]

What does receiving a summons and complaint mean? It could mean you have a contested divorce. What is the difference between a *contested* and *uncontested* divorce? If there are any issues not agreed upon by both spouses, a contested divorce exists. The plaintiff asks the court to decide these matters. Since the lawyers and the court have to review many facts and the law on all disputed issues, contested divorces are obviously much more expensive and time-consuming. Uncontested divorces, where the spouses resolve all the issues and merely seek approval from the judge, are much quicker and more economical.

Does it matter which spouse files for divorce first? From a biblical standpoint, no Christian should file for divorce unless there are scriptural reasons for doing so. From a legal standpoint, it does not make much difference who files first in most states, other than receiving any psychological satisfaction by moving to end a dead marriage. However, if one spouse needs immediate support, wants child custody, or desires possession of the home, a quick filing helps secure temporary court relief sooner. This settles any disputes about these issues while the divorce continues.

Phase 2: Answer to the Complaint and Counterclaim

Within the period specified in the summons, the defendant spouse (through an attorney) will file a response admitting or denying the specific statements or *allegations* in the complaint. This response is an *answer*.[10]

If the defendant spouse believes that he or she has some claims against the plaintiff, the defendant may file (again, through an attorney) a court pleading called a *counterclaim*. Like the plaintiff's complaint, it states certain facts and then requests court relief for many issues.

Phase 3: Discovery of Facts and Production of Documents

The attorneys will need to verify the facts in the *complaint* and any *counterclaim*. They must review documents and records of each spouse. This is called *discovery*. Each attorney files detailed lists of what they need to review in a court pleading called a *request for production of documents and records* or a *notice of discovery and inspection*. This pleading states the time and place to produce everything for review and copying.

One of the first documents most attorneys want is a *financial affidavit* or *net worth statement*. This is like a financial balance sheet, except that it includes much more detail as to personal expenses and assets. Because this pleading is usually a sworn statement filed with the court, accuracy is very important.[11]

During discovery, each attorney may secure appraisals of property, businesses, and other assets. Current, accurate values are needed to make a fair division of marital assets. If child custody is an issue, each spouse may undergo psychological studies to make sure home settings are suitable.

Attorneys can ask questions in two ways about the case and documents produced. First, the attorneys exchange written questions (*interrogatories*) for each spouse to answer and file with the court. Second, each attorney can ask questions of the adverse party spouse and his or her witnesses face-to-face and under oath, using a *court reporter*. This is an *oral deposition*.

Phase 4: Legal Motions and Hearings

If attorneys disagree on how to resolve certain matters in the case, they seek decisions from the judge by filing a *motion*, describing the problem and the requested relief. The opposing attorney may file an objection, called a *response*. The judge schedules a *court hearing*, hears each attorney's argument, and makes a ruling (an *order*) resolving the matter.

Initial hearings may involve requests for temporary support and/or child custody. Attorneys will ask the judge to grant *temporary orders of relief*. Who will have possession of the home? How much should one spouse pay to support the other until completion of the trial? This is where a good attorney can make your life more bearable, or vice versa. Consider attending the hearing to make sure the judge knows all the facts.

If payment of attorney's fees and costs is a concern, often there is no choice but to secure temporary advances for these fees through the court from the wealthier spouse. But this gives the spouse receiving relief an enormous legal advantage. The wealthier spouse will not want to give someone pushing litigation forward potentially unlimited funds to fight. This also may remove any incentive on the part of the spouse receiving relief to settle the case early. The attorney for the needy spouse may lose the chance for payment, however, if a prompt request for financial relief from the judge is not made. Then lack of funds may force an unfair settlement.

The judge can act on other emergency matters as well. If one spouse secretly tries to dispose of marital property, or if domestic violence exists, the attorneys can set an expedited (or speedy) hearing before the judge. The judge enforces the order by police protection and arrest of violators if necessary. These emergency rulings are *temporary restraining orders*, *temporary injunctions*, or *orders of protection*. But they only provide for punishment of violators after the fact, not before it happens. They do not block a spouse from unexpectedly barging into the home one afternoon, kidnapping children or stealing assets, and leaving the state in a matter of hours. Although law enforcement carries out the judge's commands, too often the real damage is complete and irreversible.

The motion and hearing phase is expensive and time-consuming. Because of the severe backlog in many courts, attorneys may not obtain a hearing that requires extended argument for weeks or even months after their request. To address this problem, many judges set twenty-five or more "short" motions for hearing in quick order one right after another. This is a *motion calendar*. Sometimes this brings numerous attorneys to the judge's chambers waiting to have their motions heard. To get through the calendar, the judge only allows five to fifteen minutes for each hearing.[12]

Ask your attorney which hearings are critical to the case. Many attorneys fight over technical legal matters or *civil rules of procedure* that may make little difference to the spouses. Some attorneys spend time filing motions for orders they know are difficult to obtain or perhaps even improper, solely to delay the case. Watch your attorney, and tell him or her not to waste time and money on procedures that do not advance each party's goals.

Phase 5: Pre-Trial Conferences and Court-Ordered Mediation

After filing the complaint and answer and after all discovery is completed, the case is *at issue* and ready for *trial*. Any attorney can file a *notice for trial* or *note of issue*, asking the judge to schedule a trial date. Do this early. Due to court backlogs, it can take months—or more—to get a trial date.

Before trial, the judge will want the parties to try one last time to settle all disputed matters by attending a *pre-trial conference* or *court-ordered mediation* to discuss the issues. If nothing else, it narrows down the issues for trial. Conferences of this type are an excellent way to explore alternate solutions for settlement. The pre-trial conference judge or *mediator* reminds each spouse that proceeding with trial will give neither one everything he or she wants. Winning is not the goal, but rather arriving at a fair settlement that will give each spouse something. It is better for parties to settle than allow a dispassionate judge to rule on so many personal matters.

At a pre-trial conference, the parties have an informal opportunity to see how the judge is reacting to various issues in the case. It is a chance to see whether the judge's view is accurate or misplaced.[13] Use these pre-trial settlement discussions to determine whether proposed settlements are better than what the court is likely to order if the case goes to trial. Those in the legal system view this opportunity as the *sweet spot*—a time about sixty days before a scheduled trial date when a case is most likely to settle.

Phase 6: Trial

There are several distinct parts of a civil trial:

Opening statements. Trial begins as the lawyer for each spouse gives an *opening statement* to the court. They summarize disputed issues and explain how the evidence supports a decision for their respective clients.

Plaintiff's evidence. The plaintiff's attorney begins proving up the allegations in the complaint by calling witnesses to testify and by putting documents into evidence as *trial exhibits*. A trial exhibit is any physical evidence that supports a point in the case being proven. The attorney usually has a detailed outline about the order for questioning each witness and the use of trial exhibits. Interviews of each witness occur before trial to coordinate testimony so the case presentation will go smoothly. Questions by the plaintiff's attorney may be given to "friendly" witnesses in advance. No witness must ever give any false testimony; that could result in *perjury*.

In some divorce cases, the plaintiff spouse may be the only witness called if the case can be adequately proven without using anyone else. Friends and relatives of a spouse do not usually testify unless character or integrity issues arise. Sometimes the plaintiff's attorney calls the defendant spouse as an adverse or hostile witness to complete proof of the plaintiff's case. This does not mean he or she is abusive. It merely means the court gives more leeway to questioning by the attorney.

The plaintiff's attorney questions each of the plaintiff's witnesses, called *direct examination*. Then the defendant's attorney may question the witness further in *cross-examination*. If the testimony is particularly damaging to the defendant's interests, the attorney tries to find any errors or show that the witness is not believable. This entire process of questioning witnesses tests the accuracy of testimony before it affects the outcome of the trial.

Defendant's evidence. After the plaintiff's attorney completes the plaintiff's presentation, the defendant's attorney proceeds with the other side of the case issues. Use of witnesses, including examination by both attorneys and introduction of trial exhibits, occurs in the same manner as for the plaintiff. The task of the defendant's attorney is to counter any damaging arguments of the plaintiff, while also showing the court why the defendant's case is more reasonable to believe.

Plaintiff's rebuttal. The plaintiff's attorney then has another opportunity to present additional witnesses and evidence to contradict the defendant's case (called a *rebuttal*). Many times this step is not necessary unless the defendant's attorney has brought up new evidence or especially damaging witness testimony requiring clarification or further challenge.

Defendant's rebuttal. In fairness, if the plaintiff's attorney presents new witnesses or evidence in rebuttal, the defendant's attorney is then also given a chance for rebuttal.

Closing arguments. The attorneys for both sides then summarize the evidence for the court once again in a manner most favorable for their respective clients in *closing arguments*.

Final ruling. The court then makes a decision on each of the disputed issues after taking the evidence into account, called *rulings*. The judge may give these rulings on the same day that the trial ends or elect to take matters *under advisement*. This means the judge wants to think some more about the case and make the rulings on a later date by advising the attorneys.

Phase 7: Judgment for Dissolution or Decree of Divorce

After the judge has made the final rulings on the disputed issues at trial, or if the spouses settle before the judge makes any final rulings, the judge and both attorneys work together on writing up a *judgment for dissolution* or *decree of divorce*. This is the final ruling of the court. The judgment confirms the legal dissolution of the marriage.[14]

This judgment may include *findings of fact* and *conclusions of law* advising each spouse how the court decided each disputed issue. It advises of division of disputed property, amount and time for payment of spouse or child support, and any other matters not settled by the spouses. Custody of the children usually is given to one spouse, with specified visitation rights given to the non-custodial spouse. Unless either spouse files an *appeal* to an *appellate court* quickly (usually ten to thirty days after entry of the judgment), both spouses must abide by whatever the judge has ordered.

Before the judge enters a judgment that may be adverse to your interests, consider seeking a settlement on each of the following matters with your spouse, if possible:

Spouse support. The judge sets the amount of any spouse support after considering many factors such as: the standard of living during the marriage; the duration of the marriage; age and the physical and emotional condition of each spouse; financial resources of each spouse (including the marital and non-marital assets given to each person); time necessary to get an education or enough training to find appropriate employment; contribution made by each spouse to the marriage (such as homemaking, child care, education, and career building of the other spouse); and all sources of income available to each spouse. Additional consideration of marital misconduct (adultery, illicit cohabitation, homosexuality, etc.) may occur in some states to limit or even deny the amount of spouse support the errant spouse receives.[15] Thoroughly discuss these matters with an attorney based upon the laws of your state. If your spouse will not agree on the proper application of all these factors, make sure the judge knows all relevant facts by having your lawyer file a post-trial motion if necessary.

Child custody. Child custody decisions under no-fault laws often bring unexpected results. Under the old law, judges usually assumed that mothers are better at child care than fathers.[16] Under no-fault, however, there are no such sex-based presumptions, although gender bias still exists. The law presumes each parent can care for the children without evidence to the contrary. The judge therefore may rely upon recommendations of a court-appointed expert giving an impartial appraisal of custody matters. This expert will look for the most stable environment for the child.[17]

Tax considerations. Awards of cash to even up property distributions or to supplement spouse or child support obligations can have significant tax effects on each spouse. Watch out—this is a time bomb! The paying spouse will want the payments characterized as spouse support, while the spouse receiving support will want to do the opposite. Support payments deductible by the paying spouse are usually taxable income to the receiving spouse. Each spouse should check with tax advisors and attorneys so all payments are allocated fairly before the judge signs the judgment.

Phase 8: Compliance with the Court Judgment

With entry of the *judgment*, the last phase of the legal process is compliance with its terms and conditions. Like the dissolution of a business relationship, this is called *winding up*. It is a time for the attorneys to oversee property distributions and make the spouses legally independent.

The attorneys work to transfer real estate and personal property and to change bank accounts and insurance policies in accordance with the judgment.[18] Debts on mortgages, personal loans, and lines of credit or credit cards are paid off or accounted for. The attorneys get releases of the spouse not required to pay each debt if possible.[19]

Upon completion of these matters, the legal process ends. The attorneys or the court only become involved again if one spouse refuses to abide by the judgment. If so, various enforcement measures may be necessary.

Usually the judge reserves the right to issue further *court orders* to force compliance through the seizing of property or income of the uncooperative spouse, fines, or imprisonment. Obviously, if a spouse is not abiding by any court order, contact your attorney immediately to arrange for the judge to apply the proper enforcement measure.

A Closer Look at Discovery and Trial

Now that we have gone through an overview of the entire legal process of divorce, let's briefly go back to both the *discovery* and *trial* phases, looking at some ways that we can help our attorneys and secure favorable results in our cases.

Use Scrupulous Honesty and Integrity

How we present ourselves to opposing counsel at oral depositions and to the court at any trial can have a major effect on our cases. In fact, a good impression at an oral deposition may determine whether a trial becomes necessary at all. If we show honesty and integrity in testifying under oath, opposing counsel may find that further legal action serves no useful purpose.

What are the purposes of taking personal testimony? Opposing counsel has several goals in mind: to find out truth useful to the attorney; to discover leads to new evidence; to discredit or impeach our credibility by showing inconsistencies in our statements; and to test our honesty, candor, and responsiveness in ways that might affect the judge.[20] Therefore, *always* tell the truth, under oath or otherwise, when a question is legal and proper. With all the checks and balances in the legal system to verify truth, the chance of a lie or misstatement going unchallenged is minimal. Lies cause major embarrassment, destroy credibility, and subject one to perjury charges. Even more important, they destroy your Christian witness.

How to Be a Good Witness at Oral Depositions and at Trial

How can we be good witnesses in court and make the best impression on others? Here are a few ideas:

Appearance. Do everything possible to be attractive. Clothes should be modest, simple, and clean—nothing flashy. The key is not to dress down for sympathy or overdress to be impressive.[21] It is also smart to remove any jewelry that you have a temptation to play or fiddle with when nervous.

Keep your hands away from your face. If this is a problem, try holding something such as a pen or a purse, without using either one. Do not write anything or doodle during questioning. This gives the impression that you may not be concentrating fully on the questions.

Attitude. The goal is a relaxed and natural outlook. Have an attitude of sincerity, helpfulness, and cooperation with everyone. Do so without patronizing anyone or being overly eager. Opposing counsel may try to test your patience with sensitive questions or even by being somewhat rude. Do your best not to respond in kind unless the circumstances warrant appropriate anger. Be courteous and firm without being hostile or rude. Avoid defensiveness or being suspicious. It may affect your tone of voice or facial expression and work against you if the questioner exploits it.

Awareness. Do your best to stay alert. Be on guard and cautious without being obvious about it. Listen for objections to questions that your attorney may raise *before* answering. If you are talking when he or she objects, stop talking immediately. An objection is a danger signal. Follow the directions of your attorney or the judge carefully before continuing.

Concentrate on the questions asked of you. Look your questioner in the eyes without gazing around the room. Avoid any arguments with your spouse or the opposing counsel—especially at trial if the judge can overhear you. Be aware of how you are feeling. If you feel fatigued or grow uncomfortable during questioning, immediately inform your lawyer and ask for a brief recess. Sometimes your attorney may sense that you are becoming tired if you are too talkative or argumentative and may request a break for you.

Communication. During oral depositions, you may stop the questioning at any time to speak privately with your attorney. The court reporter's transcript of the questions and your answers will not reflect what you say or how long you speak before continuing your responses. Neither can opposing counsel ask you or your attorney about what you discussed. But try to keep such discussions to a minimum. Above all, never talk with your attorney about the case when opposing counsel can overhear you or if the court reporter is still transcribing. At trial you will not have the opportunity to stop during questioning. Also, since the court will be watching your responses, any delays in answering questions may make you appear evasive.

Be careful not to say anything to your spouse or opposing counsel during any recess or any period when the attorneys stop the court reporter from taking notes by asking to talk "off the record." Avoid any small talk. Opposing counsel may be polite, but he or she is not really your friend. If you say anything inappropriate or damaging to your case, opposing counsel can later question you about it.

Conduct. Always arrive early at the proper place for giving testimony. Be courteous, serious, even-tempered, and self-controlled. Naturally there should be no profanity (unless you are quoting others in giving testimony), temper tantrums, sarcastic or facetious remarks, or inappropriate joking. Being argumentative, evasive, or flippant with the examining attorney is also inappropriate. Always wait patiently to respond to any questions until the questioner has completed each one. Keep a straight face with a pleasant smile if appropriate, without smirking, grimacing, or reacting to questions that may be rude, repetitive, annoying, or stupid. Your attorney's job is to keep your questioner in line through objections to offensive questions so you can concentrate fully on your testimony. By being thoughtful, polite, fair-minded, and cooperative, you will help yourself and frustrate any effort of opposing counsel to get you stirred up emotionally or to cause you to lose your focus.

Fact-oriented testimony. Dedicate yourself to making the facts clear and easily understandable. Lawyers pride themselves on using precise language and nailing down details to bring clarity to situations. Your lawyer will tell you that facts are the key to persuasion. Facts, not arguments, win cases. Therefore, commit yourself to the elegance of simplicity in testifying only to what you have seen and know for certain to be true.

Avoid talking about what you've heard others say to you (hearsay) unless asked about these remarks. If the attorneys do ask about what others have said to you or in your presence, quote the exact words used as best as you can recall. Be careful to recite the same language even if it is personally offensive to you. Do not be ashamed or shy. Everyone understands that these are not your words but those of another person.

Your testimony is not the time to give your subjective opinions about matters. Answer the questions specifically asked of you. Say no more than is necessary to give a proper answer. Do not guess or speculate about answers you do not know. If you think something "probably" happened, it is also possible that it did not happen the way you think. Stick with first-hand knowledge from a clear memory—not speculation. Even if you think you know exact information such as dates, times, or financial information, state that you are giving your best recollection only; documents or records might have the precise information. If asked about a particular document, do not speak from memory. Ask to see the document before answering.

Honesty. Your primary duty as a witness is to testify about the facts you know accurately—even if it hurts. Carefully consider your answers. Have them clearly in mind before you speak. If you are uncertain, take a moment to think matters through as long as it does not become a habit. If you did not actually witness events, state that you do not know the answer.

Never be misleading or untruthful. You will lose your credibility. During your testimony, if you recall that a prior response was in error, incomplete, or open to misunderstanding, immediately advise your lawyer. Anyone can make mistakes, but mistakes do not correct themselves. Overlooking mistakes can cause embarrassment or damage to your case. Timely corrections can show that you are doing your best to be careful in your testimony.

Preparation. Do your homework about the facts within your knowledge. Think about the sequence of events and important circumstances. This information will prepare you to be a good witness. Confidence in knowing what you are going to say will also reduce anxiety. But do not overthink your testimony or memorize responses. Having fancy answers prepared in advance makes you appear slick and shifty, and you lose the gift of spontaneity.

Your attorney will probably give you an instruction sheet or video to help you prepare for testifying. The two of you should have some personal time together to discuss specific aspects of your case. It is irresponsible not to prepare properly. Therefore, when opposing counsel asks you if you have discussed your case with anyone, promptly state that you have.[22] There is nothing wrong with talking to others if you tell the truth.

Responsiveness. Answer all the questions that are asked of you unless your attorney objects and instructs you not to answer. If your attorney makes an objection and the examining lawyer tells you to answer the question anyway, do so unless your attorney tells you not to respond. Always respond if a judge instructs you to answer a question. If you do not want to answer for a personal reason, such as violating another person's confidence or injuring their reputation, state your reluctance and the reason. Ask for permission not to answer. But be direct in responses to unchallenged questions. Answer as many questions as you can with yes or no, without explanation if possible.

The inquiring attorney will ask about the issues in dispute in your divorce case—spouse or child support, property division, and child custody matters, for example. These questions usually begin with "Who?" "What?" and "Where?" Opposing counsel does not ask many "How?" and "Why?" questions. These questions open the door for the witness to give testimony about many matters. This can be very damaging to his or her case. But if you receive a question leading off in this manner, be wise and give a response that justifies your case.

Before responding, make sure you fully understand the question. If not, have the question repeated. You are under no duty to guess at what the examining lawyer is trying to ask or to interpret imprecise or unclear questions. Watch out for questions with terminology having more than one meaning. Ask that the questioner define any confusing terms before answering. If a question is long or complex with compound clauses (as we attorneys often use), ask the attorney to rephrase the question into a more simple one. Be cautious about answering questions using absolutes like "always" and "never." Loaded questions like these nearly always require clarification.

Be alert for questions containing factual assumptions that you are uncertain about or know for certain are not true.[23] Correct all false assumptions before answering the question.[24] Also be alert for questions that paraphrase your answers. Sometimes lawyers take your thoughts and restate them in ways that change your meaning. Listen carefully. If the rephrasing is wrong, correct it. You are entitled to stand by your prior remarks.

Understanding. Once again, do not lose sight of the big picture of everything going on in your separation or divorce. Through your attorney, you should try to be a guide and teacher to help your spouse, the attorneys, and the court understand the facts. Do your best to encourage them to work with you in arriving at a fair and reasonable outcome in your case. This is why your direct input through your settlement efforts and testimony at various points in the legal process is so important. You must believe that you are going to show the way of reason in a spirit of love and forgiveness.

Answers to Common Questions About Divorce

Q. How much financial support (alimony) can one spouse with custody of the children expect to receive from the other? What can be done if a spouse never makes support payments?

A. The court sets spouse support after consideration of several factors, as we discussed earlier. The most important factors are the lifestyle that each spouse was accustomed to having during the marriage, the financial resources of each spouse, and the duration of the marriage. In no-fault states, any support awarded after equitable distribution of marital assets is likely to pay only for education or learning job skills (called "rehabilitative alimony"). This probably would not last more than a couple of years at the most. Child support awards are more generous. The court takes into account what is reasonably necessary to provide for the child's needs, usually until he or she legally becomes an adult (18 to 21 years old, depending upon the state).

While each case may vary considerably, those entitled to support (and not everyone is) quite often receive about one-third of the net income of the spouse compelled to pay. Generally, judges will not award spouse or child support that is more than the other spouse can reasonably afford.

The court usually retains power in the judgment to enforce payment of spouse or child support. This is done through holding the nonpaying spouse in contempt, levying fines, imprisonment, and income deduction orders that take money out of the spouse's paycheck.

If the spouse quits a job to frustrate income deduction, the court can order him or her to seek employment. The judge can enter another judgment for unpaid sums and authorize foreclosure on other assets the spouse may own. But the reality is that judges do not act swiftly enough to use these remedies effectively.

As a result of the unresponsive court system, some enterprising people have set up self-help organizations such as the national Association for Children for Enforcement of Support (A.C.E.S.) in University Heights, Ohio (toll free, 800-738-2237, www.childsupport-aces.org). This nonprofit group helps mothers collect child support through information and help in locating ex-spouses, obtaining orders to pay, and other efforts with an excellent success rate. Self-help is effective if carefully used with proper legal advice.

The cries of many deprived divorcees are moving state legislatures to enact more reforms every year. Some states are moving toward permanent support for spouses. This is especially true for those in long-term marriages to help equalize post-divorce standard of living for both spouses.[25]

Q. What is the best way to maintain custody of any children? What if the noncustodial spouse secretly takes them away?

A. The best way to keep custody of children is to always keep them physically with you. Try to have the court grant you temporary custody immediately. No matter how great the inconvenience or how expensive it might be, do your best to hold onto your children if custody is vitally important to you.

The court usually awards custody of children to the parent who can adequately provide them with a stable environment that is in the best interest of the child.[26] Since staying in the home means that schools, friends, and other attachments will not change, the spouse having possession of the home has an added advantage in securing custody.

The custodial spouse must allow visitation by the noncustodial parent unless the court denies that right. Hopefully, both spouses will work together on this as the judge has ordered. If the noncustodial parent violates visitation rights or kidnaps the child, in most states this is a serious felony punishable by fines or imprisonment. Enforcement of the law usually is rapid throughout the United States if law enforcers find the location of the spouse in possession of the child.

Q. How can a spouse remove personal property from the house if the other spouse denies entry?

A. The judge can issue a break order to get into the house. The judge can order the police to escort the denied spouse to the home with a locksmith to open the house and remove the items.

Q. If one spouse is committing adultery, what should be done?

A. First, confirm if it is true. Is there a motivation to commit adultery and an opportunity to satisfy that desire? Hire a responsible private investigator to legally document the adulterous conduct.

From a legal standpoint, courts in no-fault states do not consider adultery when granting a divorce or in equitably dividing marital assets. But extreme marital misconduct can affect support obligations and child custody matters. Also, if the judge allows evidence of adultery, this information can be useful in testing the truthfulness and credibility of the immoral spouse through impeachment of false testimony.

From a Christian perspective, we have already reviewed the significance of adultery in depth in Part Two of this book. It is a key factor in determining whether the faithful spouse can scripturally divorce and remarry. Therefore, always make some effort to find out the facts. Wise and careful use of an investigator's reports can prompt repentance and help the immoral spouse face the truth.

Q. Can a spouse have a divorce judgment or settlement agreement modified if matters change?

A. If both spouses agree to a specific change in a judgment or settlement agreement, the judge will usually enter a court order approving the change unless it is illegal or affects the rights of others, such as young children. If no such agreement occurs, the spouse seeking a change must file a petition for modification with the court describing the need for an amendment. After proper notice to both spouses, the judge decides whether the change is proper after a court hearing on the matter.

Usually the only matters changed are the amount and term of spouse and child support payments or child custody and visitation rights (unless fraud exists which adversely affects the judgment or settlement agreement). Any significant change in the relative financial positions of the former spouses after entry of the judgment (or the signing of any settlement agreement) can have a significant impact on whether the judge grants relief. Be aware, however, that many settlement agreements may specifically prohibit any court from changing any provisions except those concerning inadequate child support obligations. If so, it will be very difficult to change these agreements. Usually, property distributions are not modifiable.

Q. How can someone deal with divorce court without any money?

A. If the other spouse can afford it, apply to the court for temporary support and attorney's fees. If both spouses are poor, check in with local Legal Aid offices or the State Bar Association. If you need legal help, there are always resources available for help.[27]

Questions for Personal Reflection

1) Am I willing to face an uncertain future in court as opposed to doing whatever I can to settle matters with my spouse now?
2) Do I need to protect my legitimate rights in court, or am I simply making matters difficult for my spouse, motivated mainly by power, control, or revenge?
3) Have I prayerfully considered the effects that civil litigation will have on my spouse, my children, my family and in-laws, friends, and the church?
4) Do I understand how a judge's decision in my case will affect my own life goals and needs?
5) Even if I "win" my case, am I willing to show compassion and empathy to my spouse and make reasonable adjustments if necessary?

CHAPTER 15

Helping Children Grow through Separation or Divorce

What happens to our children and their special needs?
What are their greatest fears? How can these be overcome?
What are the greatest mistakes parents make with their
children in separation or divorce? How can a single parent
take care of the home and meet each child's needs?

Hungarian pianist Andor Foldes, exceptionally skilled at age sixteen, was experiencing many personal struggles when Emil von Sauer, one of the most renowned pianists of the day, came to Budapest. Von Sauer was further distinguished by being the last surviving pupil of the famed concert pianist and composer Franz Liszt. It excited Foldes when von Sauer asked him to give a recital.

With great enthusiasm, Foldes played some of the most difficult works of Bach, Beethoven, and Schumann. After completing the works, von Sauer quietly walked over and kissed him on the forehead. "My son," he said, "when I was your age, I became a student of Liszt. He kissed me on the forehead after my first lesson, saying, 'Take good care of this kiss—it comes from Beethoven, who gave it to me after hearing me play.' I have waited for years to pass on this sacred heritage, but now I feel you deserve it."

What an honor to give and to receive a kiss of honor and blessing! Our children need blessing and acceptance from us, just as we needed it from our parents and grandparents—not necessarily a kiss of approval for good performance, but just a warm acknowledgment that we love each child and appreciate him or her as an individual.

What did the father do first when he saw the prodigal son coming home? He ran out to the boy and kissed him (Luke 15:20). Our children learn to love God, themselves, and others by first experiencing love from God and their parents (see 1 John 4:19). This means having vision for our children. We need to believe in them during the short time we have to shape their young lives for the future.

Author Erma Bombeck expressed it this way:

I see children as kites. You spend a lifetime trying to get them off the ground. You run with them until you're both breathless . . . they crash . . . they hit the rooftop. . . you patch and comfort, adjust and teach. You watch them lifted by the wind and assure them that someday they'll fly. Finally they are airborne: they need more string and you keep letting it out. But with each twist of the ball of twine, there is a sadness that goes with joy. The kite becomes more distant, and you know it won't be long before that beautiful creature will snap the lifeline that binds you together and will soar as it is meant to soar, free and alone. Only then do you know that you did your job."[1]

Children are our heritage, blessed by God Himself. They are innocent and humble, examples of how we should approach God in complete trust and dependence. In Matthew 18:1–5, the disciples asked Jesus, "Who is the greatest in the kingdom of heaven?" How did Jesus respond?

He called a little child and had him stand among them. And he said: "I tell you the truth, unless you change and become like little children, you will never enter the kingdom of heaven. Therefore, whoever humbles himself like this child is the greatest in the kingdom of heaven. And whoever welcomes a little child like this in my name welcomes me."

Often children get lost in the shuffle with busy adults, but Jesus knew their worth, affirming the high regard God has for them. Therefore, we must have an urgency about giving our children our very best. As Gabriela Mistral cautioned us:

We are guilty of many errors and many faults
but our worst crime is abandoning the children,
neglecting the fountain of life.
Many of the things we need can wait.
The child cannot.

Right now is the time his bones are being formed,
his blood is being made,
and his senses are being developed.
To him, we cannot answer "tomorrow".
His name is "today."[2]

After caring for ourselves, our children and their needs must be our first priority. More than ever now, we need to kiss and bless them. They must feel loved.

The Most Innocent of Victims

As the powerful forces and emotions of separation and divorce whirl, children twist and turn in a world of bewilderment, confusion, and fear. What will they do when Daddy leaves? Why is Mommy crying all the time? Why can't we be a happy family like other children at school? Given their fears of abandonment, even if we try to give our children a kiss of blessing, we risk the perception that it's a "Judas kiss" (Luke 22:47–48) if we are walking out the door.

Life can be very cruel to children. Who can forget that strikingly sad picture of young John-John Kennedy bravely saluting the 1963 funeral procession of his slain father as it moved slowly amid muffled drumbeats through the streets of Washington, D.C.? How could he fully understand that he must grow up without knowing his father's continued embrace and blessing? Even to the day of his untimely death in an air crash some years ago, young John Kennedy confided in interviews that he remained deeply wounded because of losing his father.

If separation or divorce is like a death to us, we can only begin to imagine the devastating impact it has on our children. They may bravely bear up under the pressure and turmoil, but they still pay the price. They are losing a loved one—an irreplaceable parent. Other children have suffered emotional, physical, or even sexual abuse from a parent. This absolutely suffocates them. In desperation, they must break free to survive.

Consider Gregory Kingsley, an eleven-year-old Florida boy, shuffled back and forth between an abusive father and a neglectful mother from the time he was four. His alcoholic father beat him, once throwing his younger brother through a plate-glass door during a drinking spree. His mother left Gregory and his brother at a temporary shelter for almost a year. Two months after picking the boys up, she returned them to the shelter for another year and a half. From the time he was eight, Gregory had been in and out of foster homes. He once told a social worker that all he wanted was a "place to be." But Gregory had taken enough abuse. In what may have been the first case of its kind in American history, Gregory filed suit in 1992 seeking to "divorce" his natural parents so his foster parents could adopt him.

This lawsuit shocked the legal community. Traditionally children had no part in a custody decision. They were "property" of their parents.[3] Judges in most states use personal discretion in making custody decisions in the best interests of the child, but quite often the court's decision is contrary to the child's own wishes. With most custody laws favoring reunion of family, some courts have returned children to abusive and neglectful parents. Although Gregory's adoption was approved, his case shows that children have been pawns in divorce for too long.[4] Parents, churches, courts, and legislatures must learn what is truly in a child's best interest.[5]

Dealing with Our Guilt over the Distress of Our Children

If you are a parent who is in touch with your child, you already feel the incredible weight of this responsibility. You are particularly susceptible to guilt in this area if your children suffer.[6] Each parent thinks about many missed opportunities when weariness tuned out a child's pleas for attention. If children suffer at school, fall into drug usage, or rebel at authority, many parents blame themselves.

When this guilt arises, it is important to keep matters in perspective. A possible root of our guilt is that we want to protect our children from the harsh realities of life. If we do not, we believe we have failed. But is this true? Is keeping children free from physical and emotional pain really in their best interest? Is it better for them to learn about survival in life?

Despite our greatest overprotective efforts, our children still cut themselves with rusty nails, break their arms on the slide, get intimidated or beaten up by schoolmates, have dearly loved pets hit by cars, lose their playmates to fatal illnesses, and have nights with bad dreams and tears. Hardships bear equally upon adults and children to remind us of this truth: facing pain is part of growing up in life. Parents need to face unavoidable situations with grace and dignity, without guilt. Our children watch for this in us.

The act of separation or divorce does not begin the pain children feel.

The genesis of their pain comes at the first hint that Mommy and Daddy may not love each other anymore. Angry words from shouting matches in the parents' bedroom or the kitchen always work their way through walls to the child's ear. Fights between adults in the front car seat always roll over the little ones in the backseat. This often happens long before any separation or divorce occurs.[7]

Life is not perfect, nor are any parents. We are weak, flawed, selfish, immature, and sinful people. Children need to learn this truth. But we can turn bad situations into good learning experiences for children as we cope and try to solve problems in ways that minimize the damage. If a divorce is unavoidable, we can still strengthen existing family bonds among those who must depend upon each other.

Breaking the News to Our Children

When the time comes to talk to our children about a pending separation or divorce, here are some practical matters to consider:

If possible, have your spouse join you in talking with each child. This reassures a child at the point of one of his or her greatest fears—abandonment. It salvages some continuity of the parenting relationship out of a disintegrating marriage. If the child sees Mommy and Daddy talking calmly together, he or she perceives both parents as caring and loving. If both parents make clear that they believe it best to separate, joint communication helps the child face reality rather than falling prey to denial in a fantasy hope that separation will not occur. This also keeps the child from pitting one parent against the other and making an emotional situation worse.

It is best for both spouses to agree on a joint statement for the children that is truthful and tailored to their level of understanding. Find some common ground and understanding that will comfort, not frighten the children. This common understanding beforehand is important to reduce the chance of hostility arising between parents while talking to each child.

If joint communication is not possible, speak privately with each child. This requires diplomacy, love, and understanding. Speak honestly with the child about the situation. Avoid any negative putdowns of the absent spouse, but do not cover over any obvious faults already known by the child.[8] Instead, foster a compassionate concern in the child for both parents. A mother may sensitively tell a child, "Mommy and Daddy are having a very difficult time. But Daddy is having a tougher time and needs your special love just now. We all need to work very hard so everything runs smoothly. You can encourage us a lot by letting Mommy and Daddy know, in your own way, that you love us and want to help."

Find a good time and place to talk. Schedule the talk for a day when any hostilities are in check. Engage in prayer and personal reflection before the meeting. Since work and schooldays put pressure on everyone concerned, consider talking on a Saturday morning. This gives children time to think matters over with a minimum of distractions and to talk more as they sort feelings out through the day. Find a private place to talk—away from telephones and other activities. The child's bedroom, with favorite toys at hand, might be a safe and familiar place to talk.

Talk to each child individually. This provides the most personal and intimate atmosphere for discussing whatever the child is struggling with most. Tailor the message to each child's maturity and personality.[9] This is a time for honesty in communication, not a Pollyanna type of brush-off. Consider other immediate life changes affecting each child. Deal with these in a positive, reassuring way. Show empathy. You might say, for example, "I understand that you feel hurt and angry about this turn of events. That's okay. It means a lot to me to know how you feel. But let's think together of some ways we can help each other to have happy times once again." Each child needs a personal time with the parents. They need to know you will listen and understand. A family conference is also very helpful to talk about the issues.

Be sensitive to the age differences of each child. The children of today are different from their peers in earlier generations. With the influence of television, video games, and the Internet, they are less likely to listen effectively and keep their attention focused without frequent reinforcement. This makes the parent's task of damage control more challenging. Divorce especially disorients and confuses infants and toddlers. Changes in normal surroundings and people upset their lives, so comforting them requires extra sensitivity.

For children up to two years old, they are learning sounds and the familiar voices of their parents. Obviously, reasoning with a child this young is not practical. Child psychologists believe that warm reassurance and holding of the child by each parent as often as possible is good therapy.

Children between two and four years old are beginning to develop problem-solving and listening skills with speech development in identifying words as concepts. Their thinking focuses more simply on "I want" and "I need." So rather than be abstract and conceptual, respond accordingly. Confusion will be the most disturbing factor to children this age. Therefore, reduce anxieties by keeping favorite toys within easy reach and, as best you can, continue with familiar activities.

Preschoolers between four and six years old are beginning to use language to map out their own behavior. By now, they have created that inner voice that says, "I want to go outside and play, then come home in time for dinner." But they still have trouble distinguishing between fantasy and reality. In a divorce situation, these fantasies conjure up abandonment scenarios, creating a growing fear of the unknown. These youngest ones may believe the divorce is their fault. It is good to address them in nondirect and nonthreatening ways such as, "I know a little boy who feels like his daddy doesn't love him anymore just because he doesn't see him every day. But when a boy's dad goes away, sometimes his dad just needs some time to be alone for a while. He still loves his little boy as much as ever!"

Early elementary school children tend to doubt whether parents are right in their judgments. They may have settled into a simplistic lifestyle of loving those who love them and hurting those who hurt them. But they may experience depression or loneliness with the loss of a parent. They suffer the most long-term damage arising from separation or divorce because of their critical development stage and their acute need to rely upon the family for strength and security. Empathy with a child of this age is important. If true, assure the child of frequent and predictable visits with the missing parent.

Parents can address late elementary school children between nine and twelve with more ease. These children can understand divorce problems. Their conscience has emerged with a willingness to live up to the expectations of others. They are more likely to be honest for the sake of preserving a good self-image. Reputation is a valuable personal asset. But they are not adults. They are not mature enough to fully handle the emotional aspects of the divorce. They need help in working through their grief.[10] Consider this approach: "Honey, you may find yourself feeling angry one minute and sad the next. That's very normal to feel. That's a way you can know that you're dealing with a situation like this."

Finally, adolescents and teenagers are better able to see their relationship within the family and society. But they struggle with changes in their families—especially at a critical point of adjusting to their changing bodies.[11] They can feel crunched by all the changes that are competing for their attention. But they are better able to explain their feelings and express their anger. They may shun personal responsibility for the divorce, preferring instead to blame the parents for not maintaining the marriage. Respect their emerging autonomy, but use sensitivity on how much information they can handle.

Body language is important. For all children who can express themselves, it is always good to listen intently to the concerns shared, then repeat those concerns to the child to show understanding. Sit at eye level and within arm's reach of the child. Be as expressive and consoling as necessary with loving touches and hugs, while being sensitive to how the child reacts.

Important points to make to each child. First, the *attitude* of each parent will convey more than any words said to the child. Children search for reaffirmation from each parent. They must hear that Mommy and Daddy still love them, and do not blame them for the marital split. Do not overanalyze the problems; keep it simple. Confirm the truth in a comforting way: "Mommy and Daddy both love you very much. We always will. But we have had some problems with each other that make us believe we will be happier if we lived in separate places. This is not your fault, not at all. Neither of us is upset with you. You will still see each of us as often as we can get together. Mommy will still be your mommy, and Daddy will be your daddy. That will not change. Each of us will be here for you when you really need us. But Mommy and Daddy will not be living in the same house for now."

Give each child as much time as necessary to express feelings. It is tempting to move from meeting to meeting with each child since the discussions will be emotionally challenging and difficult, but resist the urge to do so. This is not a time to be impatient with a child's expression of feelings. Let each child know that you will listen for as long as it takes. Encourage each to let everything out—questions, angry words, fears, and anything else that is troubling him or her.

Each child should feel free to express concerns as he or she believes reasonably appropriate. Some children share inner feelings best by drawing pictures. Others respond to role-playing with parents.

This brings to mind the humorous story of a little boy who never cried as a baby or even spoke one word, for that matter. Although this baffled the doctors, his family slowly became used to his demeanor over the years. Then suddenly at dinner one night, the now ten-year-old child blurted out, "This dinner is awful!"

"You can speak!" his amazed mother yelled. "Why haven't you said anything in all these years?"

The boy thought for a while and then said, "Well, up to now the food's been pretty good." Given time, each child will let you know where the hurt is.

A Child's Greatest Fears
And How To Overcome Them

It is wise to use good discretion in talking to children about a separation or divorce. But we must also try to understand their fears. Fears shape their perception of reality more than our words. Here are some common fears, as well as some suggestions on how to help a child work through each one:

Abandonment: "My Parents Are Leaving Me Alone"

This is a basic survival issue for children. The child believed parents loved each other and brought him or her into the world to love. If they stop loving each other, will they stop loving the child as well? Can the child trust Mommy and Daddy anymore? As children see parents become depressed, angry, and absorbed in legal negotiations, dealing with financial problems and devoting themselves to longer hours at work to make ends meet, this is perceived as rejection. It confirms their fears of abandonment. The child may become very clingy and difficult to leave at school or even temporarily with a babysitter. Even going to bed at night while feeling these strong emotions can bring upsetting nightmares. Children believe parents will leave them alone and unloved forever. The darkness of their bedrooms echoes what they feel inside. How can we reassure them and dispel this fear?

Keep in touch with the child. Listen and allow ventilation of feelings. Be willing to spend quality time talking about his or her concerns. Encourage open discussions. Avoid immediate, critical, or judgmental reactions to whatever the child says. Patiently consider the child's statements, and gently respond as appropriate. Use relaxed body language that says, "I am going to hear you out for as long as you need to express yourself because I care for you." Offer up facts and reassurances that confirm you will always try to be there for the child. Provide freedom for the child to cry if needed.

Provide assurance. If true, assure the child that everything will be taken care of, that there is no need to worry about food or shelter. Either a parent or friend or close relative will be there if the child needs comfort.

Keep your promises. Avoid exaggerating the future or making impossible promises. Giving the child the false impression that he or she will receive unlimited time and attention whenever the child desires will reinforce feelings of abandonment. Instead, try to explain that the pressures of any given moment may mean less time with a child. However, the child must know that these responsibilities of yours will not lessen your love for the child.

Recreate security. Encourage relatives and friends to recreate a circle of security for the child. The child needs to see familiar faces. Regular contact with the usual friendly visitors in the home provides a sense of continuity. This helps fill the gap left by the missing parent.

Encourage visitation. If possible, encourage frequent visitation and quality time with the noncustodial parent. Each parent should try to keep normal schedules rather than making each visit a special event.[12]

Communicate often. Set aside frequent family times with children to talk about whatever is on their minds. Encourage positive discussions by opening with lead-off questions like, "What happy times would you like to have?" "How do you feel we could work together to make our family better?" or "Why don't you share something good that happened to you today?"

Be vulnerable. Let your child know who you really are as a person, not just as a parent. Include the child in daily activities whenever appropriate.

Self-Blame: "The Divorce Is All My Fault"

Consider a child's perception of the world.[13] They see that unpleasant results are usually caused by misbehavior. Therefore, when parents split up, the child may believe it's because he or she was naughty. "If I had been a good kid, Mommy and Daddy would not divorce." After all, the child thinks, parents often mentioned his or her name during fights.[14] This leads to self-punishment, guilt, and self-pity. If the child lives with one parent, he or she perceives this as personal rejection by the other parent. If the parents continue to suffer with each other, the child feels the need to suffer as well. What can be done?

Reinforce love. Both parents should reinforce—as often as necessary—that the divorce would have occurred regardless of any involvement by the child. Merely saying, "It's not your fault," is not enough. Stress that the problems in the marriage are personal between Mommy and Daddy. Both parents should reaffirm their mutual love for the child.

Do not criticize. Avoid criticizing your spouse in front of your children. It only reinforces self-blame.

Teach them about disappointment. Use separation or divorce to teach children that life can be unfair and disappointing at times. Help them understand that everyone is powerless to control many unfortunate events—like the weather, for example. But with God's help, anyone can be flexible and cope with whatever happens by being positive and learning to adjust.[15] Think of personal examples of how good changes came from bad situations (as summarized by Rom. 8:28). Teach children that nothing in this world—not even a marriage—can be anyone's sole source of security. This is why belief in and daily dependence upon God is so important.

Be fair. Avoid making the child feel disloyal for loving a noncustodial parent or grandparents.

Cooperate. As much as possible, cooperate with your spouse on coparenting the child. Whenever possible, try to agree on child-rearing goals. Cooperation conveys the healthy message that, although the parents lead separate lives, the child will survive and life will go on. Focus on taking care of the child's needs rather than looking back to the dead marriage.

Look for the positive. Search for any positive side of separation or divorce. Acknowledge negatives, but try to look for any benefits.[16] Create a sense of adventure and excitement about a new life.

Peer Pressure: "What Will My Friends Say?"

The child may be jealous of others who have both parents at home. He or she may be ashamed about living in a divided household. Since school-children can often be very cruel in their joking and ridicule, the child may fear exclusion from circles of friends. Shame also comes in believing, "I am the only one having this awful pain inside."

Divorce happens. Stress that divorce happens unexpectedly to people, just like an auto accident or an illness. It's not what people want or would like to happen, but it is not a matter of shame for the child.

Appropriate sharing. Encourage the child to talk privately with close friends about the divorce. But ask the child to limit public discussion. Stress that discussing feelings with another child of divorce is okay, but getting into specifics of family discussions is not.

Notify teachers. Some believe advising the child's teacher of the divorce is helpful. The teacher may arrange for a time in school to discuss divided family situations hypothetically to reassure all students. This also might work well in a Sunday school class at church. It allows children to see that their peers have divided families and that they are not alone.

Anxiety about the Future: "What Will Happen to Me Now?"

Fear of the unknown can be a struggle. When the most personal aspects of a child's life—his home, parents, and livelihood—are in a constant state of flux, it can be terrifying. The child knows that parents are keeping some marriage matters private. The fear is that parental secrets will lead to terrible news. Children dread this, fearing a painful surprise. This compounds their worries and anxieties, exaggerated even more as the child notices the additional worries of parents. Insecurity comes out in endless questions about what will happen, where parents will be, and who will take care of everyone.

Reassure your child. Give your child enough information to assure him or her that matters will be under control and taken care of in an orderly fashion. Try not to allow a child's lack of information to propel negative thoughts out of proportion to actual circumstances. Give reassurance and comfort by letting your child know in advance—whenever reasonably possible—where everyone will be going and what will be happening to the child and significant others.

Prepare for changes. If a move is necessary, visit the new location beforehand. Help the child adjust during a transition period. If the child must attend a new school, arrange for a visit during school hours and walk around with a teacher.[17]

Discuss visitation. Make sure the child knows the visitation schedule of the noncustodial parent. Give him or her reasonable input on when and where to meet. If possible, keep the telephone number of the noncustodial parent available and encourage frequent calls.

Keep traditions. As much as possible, have both parents attend significant school events or birthday parties for the child. Try to keep traditional family gatherings such as Thanksgiving or Christmas if possible.

Avoid uncertainty. Keep any new changes within reasonable limits to avoid further uncertainty or chaos.

Start a scrapbook. To encourage stability and consistency, help children make a scrapbook of their lives with photographs, birth certificates, special mementos and awards, drawings, and a narrative focusing on happy times and achievements. This reminds them that life will continue on in many ways as it has in the past.[18]

Encourage decision-making. Helping your child make decisions appropriate to his or her age and maturity develops individuality, decision and problem-solving skills, and self-sufficiency.

There are many fears and anxieties a child may experience. This is only natural since the child is losing a familiar family structure—something vital and precious to healthy development and maturity. When the structure breaks down, the child may feel like he or she is falling into an abyss. Even worse, some children fail to realize that the chaos and panic will not last forever. But consistent love and attention to a child's needs will help him or her cope and mature with a minimum of difficulty.

Custody Arrangements and Payment of Child Support

Even with understanding children's fears, we can make mistakes in custody and child support matters that will affect the perception of children and reinforce their fears, directly or indirectly.

Custody of children[19]

State legislatures and courts traditionally have believed it preferable for young children to stay with their mothers under the legal "tender years doctrine." In recent years, however, this is no longer a foregone conclusion. With no-fault divorce laws in most states (discussed in chapter 14), courts in theory are to treat husbands and wives equally. This theory of equality has generally carried over into a related shared parental responsibility doctrine that equally favors fathers and mothers in custody arrangements.[20] The key is in objectively determining who is the principal nurturing parent, both physically and psychologically.[21] The court then rules on a custody arrangement that is in the *best interests of the child.*

Each parent must make an honest self-appraisal as to who would be best to foster the child's growth and development:

- Who derives more pleasure from spending time with each child?
- Who is more likely to have quality time to spend with each child in the future?

- Will a career be given priority over care of the children?
- Given the child's age, who can provide better care for a toddler, pre-schooler, pre-adolescent, or teenager? Are there any special parenting bonds with particular children?
- Who does the child feel more comfortable with?
- Who can better provide for the children financially?
- Will a move from the existing home environment be necessary?
- Will disruptions occur in a child's relationships or recreational activities?
- Which custody alternative provides each child with the most free access to both parents? What other people are significant in each child's life other than the parents (grandparents, step-parents, etc.)?
- Which arrangement provides the most continuity of a parent-child relationship?
- Has there been any physical, sexual, or emotional child abuse?

Tough questions like these need reasonable answers before making any custodial arrangements.

Types of Child Custody Arrangements

Although there can be several different variations, here are the most common forms of custody arrangements:

Temporary custody pending a final divorce. If the parents are unable to agree on a satisfactory custody arrangement that preserves the peace and is in the best interests of each child, a court will make this determination as a first priority upon the filing of any divorce action. Quite often this results in leaving the child where he or she is presently residing, pending completion of the divorce. If the child is still in the family home and is happiest there, that will carry great weight. This may assure continued ties to friends, schools, and neighborhood activities with the least amount of disruption.

Permanent sole custody with one parent. This is a rather rare, extreme arrangement where one parent has exclusive custody of children without any visitation rights by the other parent. It is primarily used only when one of the parents has been particularly violent, abusive, or self-destructive.

Permanent primary custody with one parent. Although the laws have changed, the courts still favor—as a matter of practice—granting custody to the mother as the principal nurturing parent more than the father. The noncustodial parent has periodic visitation rights. Both parents have input on major decisions such as education and religious upbringing, but the parent having primary custody makes the most important daily decisions about the welfare of the children.

Permanent split custody between parents. Children live with a different parent for certain times during a year, while the other parent maintains visitation rights. Both parents have more input into important daily decisions about the children. This arrangement works best when both parents live relatively near each other but when frequent contact for short periods is impractical or unwise for the child's development. One obvious disadvantage, of course, is when the child must adjust to new environments, schools, and friends with each move.

Permanent joint custody with both parents. This has been an increasingly unpopular form of custodial arrangement.[22] Many child psychologists also question its effect on children. In this arrangement, each parent shares in the care and nurturing of children in reasonably equivalent ways throughout each year. In theory, it creates an environment as close to the original family unit as possible after separation or divorce.[23] Some believe this arrangement has the best chance of reducing a child's natural fears of abandonment, self-blame, and anxiety about the future. But more recent experience in California, Florida, and elsewhere has led to mixed results. It is not always a workable arrangement in practice.[24]

Non-parental custody. This type of custody arrangement, where a child is placed with relatives or even unrelated foster care families, is gaining more attention in the courts. When parents have not been an active force in a child's life or where abuse is present, circumstances are such that substitutes (neighbors, relatives, friends) often make time and effort to help the child. If a significant bond exists between a non-parent and the child, and the parents are unable or unwilling to properly care for the child, courts are becoming more sensitive to these relationships—although it is a troublesome and problematic matter to take one's children away to live with a non-parent. Grandparents and great-grandparents are receiving more rights to custody and visitation if it is in the best interests of the child.[25]

Important Legal Factors

Both parents should see the wisdom of cooperation and compromise in making a good custody decision.[26] Settling this issue privately or through mediation (discussed in chapter 12) is best. If a judge makes the custody decision, the result may be unpleasant for everyone.[27]

In making a custody decision, the judge must make legal and very public determinations about each parent. This can prove very embarrassing or provide a severe blow to one's ego beyond the obvious pain of having a stranger decide custody rights for one's children. Therefore, try to work out an acceptable arrangement with your spouse in advance.

If parents fail to agree on custody matters, what can they realistically expect if a court decides these issues? For children under the age of six who usually stay at home with a nonworking mother, the mother will *generally* receive custody unless there is good reason for the court to deny it. For school-aged children between six and twelve, the judge is still most likely to favor the mother. Custody of teenaged children can vary, with the father having much more leverage—especially if teens express a personal preference in this regard.[28]

When loss of custody is a grim reality for a parent, unfortunately many do almost anything out of desperation to keep a child. Tactics include abduction or bad-faith relocation out of state[29], fabricated sexual abuse charges,[30] and parental alienation and manipulation.[31] Needless to say, these tactics absolutely destroy families in the most public way. It is too great a price to pay. If you are not fortunate enough to receive custody of your children, abide by the court's decision while seeking relief through the judicial system. Try to increase visitation rights, and patiently wait for a future modification of custody.

Regardless of the custodial arrangement, in most cases the custodial spouse must allow visitation by the noncustodial parent unless the court denies that right. If the noncustodial parent violates visitation rights or kidnaps the child, the custodial parent must act *immediately* by taking proper legal action.[32]

Child Support

How will each parent care for the children financially? What is a fair allocation of the expense for this care between each parent? What is the cost of supporting each child? How much will housing, food, clothing, transportation, medical and dental care, education (grade school and college), entertainment, allowances, counseling, and unusual or extraordinary expenses arising from special physical or emotional needs cost? Despite a divorce, both parents must shoulder the responsibility of providing for their children regardless of their financial circumstances. The children should not suffer economic deprivation while struggling to cope with the separation or divorce of their parents. Nor should they have their emotional and economic well-being threatened by seeing parents argue about support matters.

This obligation of child support usually continues until the child legally becomes an adult.[33] In making child support awards, courts usually consider the net income of *both* spouses. Some states add both parents' net income together for a combined net income. Then the court determines each parent's percentage share of child support by dividing each parent's net income by the combined net income to arrive at a percentage. The court then multiplies the minimum amount of support needed for each child by each parent's percentage to arrive at a monthly amount.[34]

One particularly controversial and expensive item of child support is whether children must receive a college education. If one or both parents can afford to pay for this education, the courts may order support. However, this is a matter of discretion rather than an absolute right for each child.[35]

But what can parents do if there is not enough money to go around? The children, who cannot provide for themselves, must come first. This may mean postponing the purchase of a new home, canceling vacations, or getting a second job. It may mean exhaustion of a "nest egg" savings account or even an emergency fund account. Loans from family or friends and borrowing money from a bank or on a line of credit may be necessary. Whatever it takes to keep the children afloat, it must be done.[36]

Then there is the problem of parents who ignore child support responsibilities. In August 1992, the U.S. Commission on Interstate Child Support issued its report on this problem after a two-year study authorized under the 1988 Family Support Act.[37] The commission concluded that America's state-based system of collecting child support was a "cumbersome, slow-moving dinosaur fed by paper." Each year, the report said, the judicial system failed to collect about one-third of the approximate $15 billion dollars of child support ordered or promised for about 11 million children. The Commission further noted that too many parents were escaping child support responsibilities by relocating to other states. Even so, the commission considered but rejected federalizing child support payment enforcement.[38]

What is the answer to this serious problem?

We hear and read about children living in substandard housing, inadequately clothed, with no insurance, while noncustodial parents live in relative luxury, paying little or no child support. Your situation may not be as drastic, but missing child support payments still present a problem for many divorcing families. Your children need and deserve this support!

Experts estimate that about 51 million Americans have child support obligations—either owing it or receiving it. About 85 percent of custodial parents are mothers. Meanwhile, U.S. Census Bureau figures for 1996 indicate that only 39 percent of all custodial parents in the U.S. received the full amount of court-ordered support. An almost equal proportion—37 percent—received no support at all from noncustodial parents. Another quarter only received partial payments.

Steven J. Silver, an Arizona assistant attorney general and head of that state's Enhanced Enforcement Unit, has prosecuted hard-core child support violators for years. "What is really appalling and painful to watch is the damage people do to their children," he notes. "It's going to affect these kids throughout their lives in their own ability to have trusting relationships, and it's going to affect their own parenting skills."[39]

Some noncustodial parents with court-ordered child support obligations mistakenly believe this obligation ends if or when a custodial parent makes more money or remarries a wealthier person, reducing the need for financial assistance. Not true! The legal obligation remains on *both* biological parents to support their children. Other noncustodial parents think they're excused from paying support to their biological children if they remarry and have stepchildren to support. Also not true! Parents still must support their biological children despite any added responsibilities for supporting stepchildren. Children, unlike baseball cards, cannot be traded with other parents!

The problem of "deadbeat parents." What about the truly hard-core cases—"deadbeat parents" who fail, neglect, or refuse to obey a court order directing payment of child support? This includes parents who can afford to pay child support but don't do so, those who are voluntarily unemployed (or underemployed), and still others whom lawyers humorously refer to as suffering from "R.A.I.D.S." (Recently Acquired Income Deficiency Syndrome). A true deadbeat parent makes *no* child support payments rather than reduced payments. Florida Judge O.H. Eaton, Jr. elaborates:

True deadbeats have no money or assets. They live off the income of others, usually day-by-day, or they rely upon the generosity of friends for assistance through the hard times. Deadbeats believe they have nothing to lose. They have no job. They have no status. They have no property. They perceive themselves to be creatures deserving of sympathy due to their pathetic state which was caused by the custodial parent who now is to blame for the whole thing. The usual civil remedies such as income deduction orders and writs of execution or sequestration do not produce needed monetary support. To add to the frustration, the custodial parent is usually destitute, or nearly so, and cannot afford counsel. Sometimes the court files in these cases are voluminous because the deadbeat [represents himself in court] and is making a career out of dragging the custodial parent to court over trivial matters, thus jeopardizing employment and putting the custodial parent even more at the mercy of the deadbeat. . . . It is not rational to refuse to pay child support. It is not rational for an able-bodied person to refuse to earn a living in order to avoid paying child support. Deadbeat parents justify their irrational behavior as a way to get back at the custodial parent, or to get the custodial parent back.[40]

Many deadbeat parents do have the necessary funds for support, but refuse to pay because they're angry with their ex-spouses. They ignore the fact that child support is a vital contribution to the physical and emotional well-being of their *children*, and selfishly put their own needs first. If a divorce decree requires an embittered noncustodial parent to carry medical insurance for his/her children, that parent may try to withhold information on the policy, use sloppy handling of insurance claims to "get even," or allow the policy to lapse. But the children who lose critical medical coverage suffer the most!

Unmet child support obligations create great frustration and volatile emotions for everyone concerned—even judges. After dealing with deadbeat parents in court for many years, Judge Eaton believes attorneys and courts should get tough by using indirect criminal contempt proceedings to force these parents into meeting their legal support obligations—pay up or go to jail! He believes having a deadbeat parent arrested, booked, and fingerprinted, followed by prosecution before a jury (many of whom themselves regularly pay child support) is an "eye-opening event" for a deadbeat parent. (If a custodial parent is destitute, Judge Eaton notes that invoking the criminal process usually is without cost to the custodial parent, since taxpayers pick up the tab.)

New child support enforcement laws. Since defaults on child support obligations reached epidemic levels in the latter half of the twentieth century, Congress took action by enacting the following:

• The Personal Responsibility and Work Opportunity Reconciliation Act of 1996 (PRWORA—Pub. L. 104-193, 110 Stat. 2105 (1996)) ended welfare as we knew it for the past sixty years. It also included some significant child support enforcement amendments, including establishing new federal and state registries for support orders. It enhanced interstate enforcement by requiring all states to enact the Uniform Interstate Family Support Act (UIFSA), (which is complementary to the Full Faith and Credit for Child Support Orders Act (FFCCSOA—28 U.S.C.A. §1738B)) by January 1, 1998 to keep federal funding for child support programs. (By April, 1998, this was done.) The Act also expanded use of the Federal Parent Locator Service, and required states to enact tougher enforcement measures, such as authorizing the placing of liens on occupational and professional licenses.

• The Debt Collection Improvement Act of 1996 (Pub. L. 104-134, 110 Stat. 1321-358 (1996)) denies federal loans to parents who owe child support, and intercepts federal payments to parents to pay child support debts.

• In 1995, the Child Support Recovery Act (CSRA—18 U.S.C.A. §228 (1995)) created a federal offense for those willfully failing to pay legal child support obligations for a child who lives in another state. The Deadbeat Parents Punishment Act of 1998 (Pub. L. No. 105-187, 112 Stat. 618 (June 24, 1998)) strengthened the CSRA, and also makes nonpayment of child support a federal felony, punishable by fines and up to two years in prison and mandatory restitution. Defendants can be convicted—even upon showing they couldn't pay the full amount ordered—if they also failed to pay the portion they could afford![41]

Congress' intent is to centralize collection and distribution of support funds in each state, provide for automatic wage-withholding orders each time a child support order is entered by a court, streamline enforcement of orders across state lines, and use recent technology advances to track parents trying to hide their assets from child support enforcement agencies.

These laws are *tough!* Congress wants all states to get serious about making "deadbeat parents" pay child support so children no longer have to suffer the consequences of their failure to do so. Federal prosecutors also are becoming more aggressive in criminally prosecuting those who repeatedly flout state court child support orders. In August 2002, they arrested 102 deadbeat parents in twenty-nine states who together owed more than $5 million in unpaid child support.[42] Even so, collection of child support remains a serious problem in America.

Both biological parents—custodial and noncustodial—have a spiritual, legal, and moral obligation to take care of their children. Deadbeat parents still try, naturally, to find legal loopholes to "beat the system." But those loopholes are rapidly closing. And certainly there are no loopholes in parenthood obligations before God!

What's really broken here? It isn't child support defaults and legal obligations—it's *parenthood*. David Blankenhorn, author of *Fatherless America* offers this insight: "Our current deadbeat dad strategy fails even to acknowledge our society's crisis of family fragmentation and declining child well-being. For what is broken in our society is not the proper police procedures to compel small child-support payments from reluctant men. What's broken is fatherhood."[43] Secular sources agree. A few months after Blankenhorn made these comments, New York Bar Association Matrimonial Law Committee Member Sy Reisman made this observation:

> There is nothing simple about divorce, and the seething anger that surrounds the imposition of [support] cannot be diverted even with the legal arsenal Washington is considering. If we are really serious about tackling the multibillion-dollar problem of deadbeat parents, we need to look at how visitation and custodial rights are handled by the courts. The strongest weapon we have for solving the deadbeat parents problem is to ensure they have ample access to their children and a significant role in their upbringing.[44]

So why do many noncustodial parents (with fathers comprising about 85 percent of that group) fail to pay full support? Quite often, it's because they feel cut out of their children's lives![45] It's not morally right to do this, and support obligations should be met regardless of feelings, but we still need to understand how noncustodial parents view their circumstances so we can work out an appropriate solution. And it's a fact that when noncustodial parents don't feel disenfranchised from their children, they do pay more support.[46]

(For more information on collection of child support, as well as additional options and alternatives for collecting it, refer to the companion volume to this book, *Making A NEW Vow: A Christian Guide to Remarriage and Blending Families*, by Joseph Warren Kniskern.)

Throughout this book we have encouraged both spouses to cooperate and compromise as much as tough love will allow. It is best for everyone concerned to avoid having the courts intervene and make decisions over the most personal family matters. This is particularly true of child custody and support matters. Try to set aside your own interests for a time. Instead, focus on the needs of your children, who will be forever scarred if their parents ignore their interests.

The Worst Mistakes Divorcing Parents Can Make

Mistake No. 1: Making Our Spouses Enemies of Our Children

Fighting in front of children and blaming a spouse for a divorce is a recipe for disaster. With all the fears, panic, guilt, anger, resentment, and loss of physical and emotional security that children experience in a divorce or separation, excessively or unfairly criticizing a parent can destroy everyone concerned.

Consider the case of Richard and Laurel Schutz, a classic case of parental alienation syndrome. After six years of marriage, the Schutzes divorced in November 1978. The former Mrs. Schutz received sole custody of the couple's two very young daughters, while Mr. Schutz had visitation rights.

Between 1981 and 1985, the mother moved with the children from state to state without telling Mr. Schutz before each move. When Mr. Schutz finally found his children, he discovered that they "hated, despised, and feared" him.

Mr. Schutz went to court for help. The judge determined "the cause of the blind, brainwashed, bigoted belligerence of the children toward the father grew from the soil nurtured, watered, and tilled by the mother." The court further found that "the mother breached every duty she owed as the custodial parent to the noncustodial parent of instilling love, respect, and feeling in the children for their father. She slowly dripped poison into the minds of these children, maybe even beyond the power of this Court to find the antidote." Consequently, the judge ordered the mother "to do everything in her power to create in the minds of [the children] a loving, caring feeling toward the father ... [and] to convince the children that it is the mother's desire that they see their father and love their father."

The mother was not content with this decision, however. She appealed the judge's ruling all the way to the Supreme Court of Florida, arguing that the First Amendment to the U.S. Constitution guaranteeing free speech protected her from any legal obligation to undo the harm she had already caused the children. The Florida Supreme Court agreed that she had freedom of speech. But the father of her children— and the state of Florida— had a stronger interest in encouraging a good relationship between father and child. If it were otherwise, the court reasoned, any such encouragement would do no good if the mother could undo it. No one required the mother to express opinions that she did not hold (a practice disallowed by the First Amendment). She was, however, required to take those measures necessary to restore and promote the frequent and positive interaction between father and children, and to refrain from doing or saying anything likely to defeat that end.[47]

Sadly, the real victims in the Schutz divorce were the children. Despite the efforts of the judicial system, will they ever appreciate their father fully? Who suffered most from the damage done by the mother's vindictive behavior? Sowing seeds of resentment and bitterness in young, impressionable minds of children against a parent reaps a whirlwind (Hos. 8:7; Gal. 6:7–8).

Focusing on an ex-spouse's behavior diverts attention away from the real concern for any parent: the children's welfare. Personal resentments between parents almost always fall upon the children. They become wounded pawns in the process. If an ex-spouse continues being hostile and harmful to the children, legal action like that taken by Mr. Schutz is necessary as a last resort. Ideally, however, each parent will separate the differences of opinion and the wounds of the past from any parental decisions, always making them for the best welfare of their children. This calls for compromise, cooperation, and a mutual resolve to avoid using the children as hostages in games of manipulation and blackmail.

If one parent is viciously running the other down, the child will know what is happening. But a parent might tell a child, "Your Mom believes I'm not a good father because we play video games together. I have a different opinion about this. I care about you and want to participate in whatever interests you. But if it's ever a problem for you, please let me know so we can work everything out in the best way for you." It is not necessary to counter each unfair criticism.[48]

Mistake No. 2: Withholding Visitation Rights or Child Support

The custodial parent needs child support payments from the noncustodial parent. When no payments come, the custodial parent then resorts to "payback" by holding the children hostage from the other parent when he or she comes for a visit. Some parents entitled to receive support believe that withholding visitation until a spouse fulfills prior commitments is reasonable. But the usual outcome is that the needs and wishes of the children become a secondary concern in a game of manipulation, control, and one-upmanship between parents.

And it doesn't usually end there. If the noncustodial parent is shut out for visitation or not allowed to participate in significant events of the children, intimacy fades over time. A vendetta between parents leads to estrangement from innocent children. Parent and child drift apart, and love dies. Eventually some noncustodial parents quietly believe, "*It's* not *my* kid." The noncustodial parent rationalizes by thinking it's better not to pay child support. After all, the custodial parent probably spends payments on personal whims rather than for the children. The real conflict is between the parents, but it cuts the children up in the crossfire.

A good example of how children are often casualties caught between warring parents is the case of John and Esther Lock of Chicago, Illinois, as reported in *Newsweek* of May 4, 1992. The Locks had been through more than 100 court hearings about their divorce and child support matters over nineteen years. The state of Illinois figured that Mr. Lock owed his former wife more than $160,000 in child support for their four children. This was certainly an intolerable situation.

How was the situation handled? In February 1977, Esther Lock was doing all she could to keep the electricity on in her home while eating a "white diet" of rice and cereal. Health insurance lapsed for nonpayment of premiums. Meanwhile, Mr. Lock was then a dentist living with his new family in an affluent suburb of Highland Park. This infuriated Esther Lock so much that she gave her two teenage sons overnight packs and deposited them on their father's front porch in subzero weather. She knew that Mr. Lock did not want the children, but she decided to use them in a "scare tactic" against their father. Result? John Lock called the Highland Park police with the request that they come remove two young trespassers from his yard. (Mr. Lock later stated that one of the boys was trying to kick his door down.) Revenge this destructive is worse than the original wrong.

What a tragedy when spouses go to war using their children as the ammunition. Instead of putting marital differences aside and fulfilling their important roles as parents, expediency and revenge burn and consume everything in their path.

Breaking out of this pattern means returning good for evil. Use the legal process for enforcing rights of visitation or child support in a reasonable and responsible manner as a last resort. Regardless of how your spouse acts, do your best to fulfill your side of the bargain for the sake of your children. The Bible warns each of us: "If anyone does not provide for his relatives, and especially for his immediate family, he has denied the faith and is worse than an unbeliever" (1 Tim. 5:8).

The marriage between husband and wife ends, but the relationship of each parent to each child continues. Do not use children as arbiters of adult disputes or as messengers of threats or bad news between parents. Negotiate differences away from the children. Make it work. Be willing to compromise for the children's best interest and welfare.

Mistake No. 3: Using Visitation Exchanges as a Battleground

For parents who live separately, it is tempting to catch up on hostilities when the noncustodial parent comes to pick up a child for visitation.

Visitation wars often begin in the divorce proceedings. An inattentive parent may fiercely contest custody in favor of the other, not because of desire for the child, but solely to oppose the spouse and use later concession of custody as a bargaining chip for other concessions on spouse support or property settlement. When visitation schedules are set up, one parent will intentionally "forget" scheduled appointments to inconvenience the other. He or she will discourage the children from visiting the noncustodial parent. Negative remarks bombard the kids, or competing activities arise to create a conflict with regular visitation. Parents bribe children with better entertainment or by slacking off on discipline to make the other parent appear mean or unreasonable in the child's eyes.

But consider how everyone is struggling with an enormous load of emotional turmoil during visitation. The failed marriage haunts every visitation encounter. Everyone suffers with having to share responsibilities. The noncustodial parent may have a powerful desire to visit but wrestles with the understandable reluctance and anxiety of doing so. Each parent has at least some unhappiness or nostalgia when the child is picked up at the family home. Each parent receives a fresh reminder of the divorce with the lonely sight of an empty room while the child is visiting the other parent.

The only answer is to call a truce. Compromise for the sake of the children. Look for ways to make visitation work. Hold each parent up in the sight of each child. But be honest. If the custodial parent is not being reasonable and interferes with visitation, the excluded parent cannot allow the child to think that missed visits are neglect. Tell the children the truth, depending upon their age and maturity.

If visitation pickups of children are often scenes of arguments between parents, arrange for pickups away from the home at the house of a friend or relative. If visitation appointments require cancellation for good reason, involve the child by explaining the situation directly and making alternate arrangements promptly. Few matters disappoint a child more than being dressed and ready for pickup by a noncustodial parent who does not show up or even call.

Some visitation problems are inevitable for the best of parents. Consider the classic case of two sons who left their mother in Virginia for a visit with their father in California. The boys felt frightened and anxious about their first flight out to the West Coast. Weeks later, however, they returned to their mother happy with beach tales and boasts of staying up late watching cable movies. Obviously mother and father have different lifestyles now. This created unavoidable friction in parental authority and discipline.

There are no easy answers for visitation problems. Each parent should strive for balance in fun times, discipline, completion of chores, and normal parental lifestyles. Spoiling the child to best the other parent causes the child to suffer tremendous psychological damage and alienation. It also creates a false impression in the child's mind that "good times" will never end. But this distorts reality; the holiday atmosphere will not last. A "Disneyland Dad" or "Mall Mom" using visitation time to impress children and outdo each other with gifts and parties loses more than he or she gains.[49]

Mistake No. 4: Forcing a Child to Choose the Custody Parent

This is a most unfair position for the child. Even if the child is mature enough to give input into such a decision, it capitalizes on fears that the disfavored parent will see the child as disloyal. What will this parent do? Does the child risk losing that parent's love, affection, and support? If spouses cannot agree on custody matters, let the court decide the issue based upon the recommendations of examining counselors and experts. This takes the child off the hook and relieves significant guilt.

Mistake No. 5: Parents Using a Child as a Messenger or Arbiter

The greatest temptation is to pump the child for information for use against the other parent. If a third party lover exists, a parent may want to know from the child what this person is like. This traps the child in a classic "Catch-22" situation—having to choose between disloyalty in spying on one parent, or alienating the other by refusing to answer questions. Parents succumbing to this temptation debase themselves in front of their children and lose respect.

Or dealing with another issue, how does a child feel taking this message from a mother to a father: "Tell your father that I don't know how he can look you in the face when he hasn't paid your support"? Or when one parent says to a child, "Now I ask you, who's right—me or your mother?"

Children caught in this double bind situation must disengage with the help of one or both parents without delay. A child should be given permission—even encouraged—to say to each parent, "It hurts me that my parents cannot love each other, but I do love each of you. Carrying mean messages hurts me very much. Please talk directly with each other and do not ask me to do this any longer."

Sometimes children struggle with understanding divorce situations and ask questions like, "You hired a lawyer to go to court against Daddy, but he says he can't afford to hire an attorney. Why?" Don't avoid the question. Help the child work through the problem by responding, "Divorce is a very complicated legal process, so your dad and I need an attorney to help us do things right." Downplay the adversarial nature of divorce in favor of constructive cooperation between parents.

Mistake No. 6: Forcing Children to Deal with Separation or Divorce Too Quickly

Chastising a child for not recovering from the shock and trauma of a divided family as quickly as an adult can is unfair and insensitive. A related problem is telling the child that he or she must now step into the role of the missing spouse—an unreasonable and unrealistic burden for the child. The child has enough of a challenge in working through personal feelings. It robs a child of joy. Let the child recover at his or her own pace. Give each child the individual time and help needed to work through grief and loss.

Train Up a Child in the Way He or She Should Go

In divorce or separation, we must deal with our children without the daily teamwork we had in the past with our spouses. What is the best approach to help these kids grow? What can we do? How do we give and "be there" for our children when we may feel depleted, bereft, angry, empty, and lonely ourselves? What does God tell us?

"Train a child in the way he should go, and when he is old he will not turn from it" (Prov. 22:6). This means much more than making them memorize Scripture and attend church. It means loving discipline. It means patiently taking enough time to really *know* a child individually and intimately. It means pruning and shaping a child's life at every opportunity.

It involves helping him or her to work through the traps and pitfalls in life. Like woodworkers, it means studying the grain and contours—how the child was created—knowing that only the contours that run with the grain endure, that all others eventually break under life's pressure.

Notice that the verse says we are to train up the child in the way he (or she) should go—not necessarily where we as parents decide we want the child to go. God has made each child unique and complex. He made a way for this child to go in his or her own search for a personal relationship with the Creator. This may not follow our path. It may not be the way of our parents. Other children we know who "turned out well" may dance to a different drummer. We are to seek our child's way, the way that is best for him or her.

Do you remember that touching scene at the 1992 Summer Olympics in Barcelona, Spain, when twenty-six-year-old British runner Derek Redmond pulled a hamstring muscle in the 400-meter semifinal race. Although he fell to the track in excruciating pain and was eliminated from the competition, Redmond forced himself to get up. He hopped and limped in his lane toward the finish line in an agonizing fashion as the entire stadium gave him a standing ovation. But it was too painful for him to continue, and he collapsed again . . . until his father, Jim Redmond, leaped from the stands, embraced him, and helped him to his feet. They inched forward over the final eighty meters—a father and his grimacing, tearful son—until they crossed the finish line together. Jim Redmond simply said, "All I could do was help him. That's what fathers are for."

Our children are running the race of life. They will fall down; they will get beat up at times; they will lose races. But like Jim Redmond, our task as parents may be to help them finish *their* race.

In practical terms, how can we find the best way for a child to "grow and go" after going through the trauma of separation and divorce?

We must not overburden ourselves with guilt about any trouble a child has. Some upsets and complaints are natural events of childhood. Stormy times in life arise—with or without divorce.[50]

Children will undergo the grieving process (discussed in chapter 2) in their own way and at their own pace. For some, there may be regression to earlier childish ways, but this is part of coping with the anxiety and insecurity of the loss they feel. Give them time. Let them work through life as they need to. Be there for them.

Respect a child's personhood. Children respond best with affirmation, love, and respect as people. We must not assume that we know how our children think or feel. Listen to them. Make every effort to consider their feelings in making decisions affecting them. Depending on their age and maturity, they should experience the joy and responsibility of making some of their own decisions—and facing the consequences of those decisions. Children who feel free to express themselves, even at the expense of discipline for their inappropriate conduct at times, will often grow up into adults who are secure, joyful, and more effective in life by being themselves.

Adversity brings strength and growth. Hard times cause anyone to stretch and grow beyond present circumstances and experience. It is not wise to protect a child from unavoidable, troublesome times. Instead, encourage your children to weather the storm with reliance upon God.

Each child needs to experience a constant, consistent, biblical love (1 John 4:7). Biblical love expresses itself in forgiveness, acceptance, and security. It roots itself in a firm commitment to the child regardless of circumstances, brings constancy in the face of change, and inspires godly wisdom to fend off the fickle fallacies of this world. This is a love that never fails (1 Cor. 13:8). It lifts the worth of the individual far above any failings in performance. The father in the parable of the prodigal son is the epitome of how our loving God receives us. We need to strive for that same love for each of our children.

We also need to watch our example as parents. "He who fears the Lord has a secure fortress, and for his children it will be a refuge" (Prov.14:26). Our children need to see God in our lives. Parents characterized by praise and thanksgiving continually offered up to a loving God in an active prayer life make their mark in a child's eyes. Children need to see a parent's life confidently moving forward with clear purpose and direction. Then they will crave the sweet fruit the Holy Spirit offers—love, joy, peace, patience, kindness, goodness, faithfulness, gentleness, and self-control (Gal. 5:22–23).

When we make mistakes with our children, we need the humility to apologize to them. Our personal spiritual maturity means more to our children and to our God than wherever our children are spiritually at any given time.

Putting all these principles into practice is the best legacy we can leave to our children as we release our string and let the kites sail off on their own at the proper time. Give them your kiss of blessing.

Questions for Personal Reflection

1) Can I take care of my children's emotional, physical, material, and spiritual needs alone? Do I honestly believe that my ex-spouse is a good parent?
2) Am I fully aware of the psychological impact my separation or divorce will have on my children now and in the years to come? Can I reasonably separate disagreements with my ex-spouse from issues involving the emotional well-being of my children?

3) What will my future relationship be like with my ex-spouse and children? How can I foster a loving, caring feeling in my children toward my ex-spouse without compromising my convictions? If my ex-spouse remarries or has a serious relationship, can I accept that person's positive influence on my children, or will I always see him or her as a competitor?

4) Do I want custody of the children so I will not feel alone, or because I can be a parent to them in a way that is in their best interest?

5) Based upon what I have seen in my child's life, what is the way that God would want him or her to go in growing up into adulthood?

Part Four

The Dawn After Divorce:
A New Life!

No one sews a patch of unshrunk cloth on an
old garment, for the patch will pull away from the
garment, making the tear worse. Neither do men pour
new wine into old wineskins. If they do, the skins will
burst, the wine will run out and the wineskins will be
ruined. No, they pour new wine into new
wineskins and both are preserved.
Matthew 9:16–17

But now, by dying to what once bound us, we have been
released from the law so that we serve in the new way of
the Spirit, and not in the old way of the written code.
Romans 7:6

You were taught, with regard to your former way of life,
to put off your old self, which is being corrupted by its
deceitful desires; to be made new in the attitude of your
minds; and to put on the new self, created to be like God
in true righteousness and holiness. . . . "In your anger do
not sin": Do not let the sun go down while you are still
angry, and do not give the devil a foothold. . . .
Get rid of all bitterness, rage and anger, brawling and
slander, along with every form of malice. Be kind and
compassionate to one another, forgiving each other,
just as in Christ God forgave you.
Ephesians 4:22–24, 26–27, 31–32

When the divorce is over, it is time to let go of the past and move on with your life. It is not going to be easy, but having vision for yourself and those around you is where you begin.

Lucy and Charlie Brown put life in a nutshell in a "Peanuts" comic strip some time ago. Lucy said that life is like a deck chair. Some folks place their chair so they can see where they are going. Others place it so they can see where they have been. Still others place it so they can see where they are right now. Charlie Brown's reply: "I can't even get mine unfolded!"[1] It's easy to feel as though life is leaving you behind. But pick up the pieces from where you are right now and face your future with optimism. There are better days ahead!

In his book *The Enormous Exception*, Earl Palmer wrote that the San Francisco Golden Gate Bridge, constructed right on the San Andreas fault, was built to sway about twenty feet at the center of its one-mile suspension span. This flexible sway is a key feature to the bridge lasting so many years. But that's not all! By design, every part of the bridge's concrete roadway, steel railings, and crossbeams are hinged from one welded joint to another, all the way through the vast cable system, eventually tying every single part to the top of two great towers standing tall from two enormous land anchor piers. Because these towers bear most of the weight, they are deeply embedded into the rock foundation in San Francisco Bay. The secret to the longevity of the bridge, then, involves these two things: flexibility and foundation.

As you get a new start in life, ground yourself firmly in the Lord. Be willing to adjust to new situations and circumstances without being tied to the past. Close the circle on your marriage and divorce. With sorrow over the divorce decision that has become irreversible, you must leave it behind and let go. Strengthen yourself from what you have learned so you will be a better person tomorrow.

There are ways to guard your heart from unwise involvement with your spouse. Giving yourself time to heal and refresh in many practical ways will help a lot. You may not be able to believe it today, but you will learn how to trust people again. Avoid some of the common mistakes in getting a fresh start as a single person. Consider remarriage possibilities very carefully. We will close out by reviewing the most important principles threaded throughout this book so that you can truly become free to live a new life.

CHAPTER 16

Letting Go and Rebuilding Self-Esteem

*How can we rebuild our lives after a separation or
divorce? We need peace and stability after the turmoil.
We need a return to normalcy. It is time to move on in life
with hope and vision by letting go of the past and having
eager anticipation for better times in the future.
Finding practical ways to unchain ourselves from
the baggage of past failures and to learn from our
mistakes is the best way to do just that.*

In the early morning hours of Monday, August 24, 1992, Hurricane Andrew slammed into the Florida coastline just south of Miami, packing winds gusting to 214 miles an hour. A family friend peering through the darkness with infrared night-vision goggles at the peak of the storm said that the swirling hurricane clouds overhead spawned tornados as far as the eye could see. They looked like spaghetti hanging down from the sky—a storm within a storm. It was a terrifying time! Homes and buildings shattered like glass and became a whirling dervish of wreckage. Friends desperately looked for any safe refuge from danger, fleeing from room to room as their houses collapsed around them.

In the aftermath of Hurricane Andrew, the midday sun confirmed everyone's worst fears. "The Big One" that Miami had dreaded for so many years had finally hit. It looked like an atomic bomb blast rivaling that of Hiroshima and Nagasaki. Experts who assessed the damage proclaimed it the most destructive natural disaster ever to hit the continental U.S. It left all of us in a state of shock. Hundreds of thousands—homeless overnight—wandered aimlessly through an area of almost total devastation about eight times the size of Manhattan. Only a few hours of hurricane force winds on Monday morning had caused property damage in the tens of billions of dollars. Miraculously, fewer than thirty people died in the storm, unlike the tragic, deadly aftermath of Hurricane Katrina, which devastated New Orleans more than a decade later.

What does experiencing a natural disaster like this have to do with surviving separation or divorce? A lot! The emotional turmoil and stress during and after a hurricane are remarkably similar to that suffered by one going through a divorce. It leaves you stunned. Hyper-vigilant one moment, numb the next. Not knowing where to turn for help—and not really even wanting to try—a thousand details instantly call for your immediate attention. It's like climbing a mountain merely to get started once again.

Disasters and divorces produce stress beyond what many people can imagine. Both spring from experiences beyond the realm of everyday life. Both involve threats to life, property, and possessions. Bad life experiences like these bring anxiety, nightmares, or sleeplessness and other disturbing symptoms that can last for years after the trauma is over.

Fear compounds the trauma. For disaster survivors, there's the fear of another disaster or the fear of looting. People who should seek shelter after a natural disaster sit instead with loaded guns on top of piles of debris and rubble that used to be homes. They desperately try to guard and preserve what little remains of their lives and its emotional attachments. For those coming out of a divorce, the tendency is to withdraw and become isolated. They fear getting involved romantically with anyone.

So whether it's a disaster or a divorce that has stripped away your relationships and property, the same mental attitude sets in. You want to sit on top of whatever you have left and protect it from further loss.

In all stressful experiences, there can be anger and short tempers with other people. As anger turns inward, those who hurt can become depressed and despondent. Many say to themselves, "I can't win. Why try anymore?" They experience fatigue and complacency, a loss of appetite and concentration. It is very difficult to feel pleasure in doing anything. Some lose their sense of having a personal future or a place in the community. In natural disasters, of course, insurance can replace much or all of the lost or destroyed property. But in a divorce disaster, there is no such insurance. What we have lost may have taken a lifetime to achieve. The losses can be staggering to those with meager financial resources. Divorce pierces them with many griefs.

What is the answer? How can we cope while feeling overwhelmed like this? The key is to adjust to the storms in life by allowing them to lift us up rather than tear us down.

When a storm is approaching, an eagle flies to a high spot and waits for the winds to come. As the storm hits, the eagle sets its wings so the wind lifts its body up to soar above the raging currents. The eagle does not escape the storm; it uses the storm to lift it higher. It rides upon the storm.

If we wait upon the Lord, we also can mount up with wings as eagles (Isa. 40:31). Letting go sets our wings to catch the wind.

How Long Does It Take to Recover?

After a divorce, the first question many ask is, "How long will it take me to get over this?" There are no easy answers. How long does it take to fall in love? For some, it can happen almost overnight. For others, romance takes years.

The same is true with falling out of a relationship. How long will it take? Forget experts who say that divorce recovery takes one month for every year, or one year for every five years of marriage. Recovery takes as long as *you need*. But take heart—you *will* recover! Remind yourself that the tough times will pass. Life will be happy once again. Routines will return to normal.

But recovery begins with the right attitude, by viewing changes in our lives as challenges and opportunities rather than threats. Then, when we are ready, we rebuild our lives to regain a sense of normalcy. We commit ourselves to our remaining family and friends, our work, and our church. We cling to our spiritual values rooted in our personal relationship with God. We strive to regain control over our lives. In doing so, we let go of what cannot be changed. We heal at our own pace.

Closing the Circle: Letting Go of the Past

We mark marriages with formal, public ceremonies full of joy and celebration. But when it ends, too often spouses leave each other with a slammed door and a muffled curse. There is no closure of feelings and emotions. The shattered relationship is left in pieces.[1] But an important first step in bringing closure to a relationship is through letting go of our spouses.

Letting go does not mean we stop *loving* our ex-spouses. Loving the unlovable is the essence of unconditional love. But letting go leads us to a crossroads. We accept the truth that it is time to stop investing further emotional energy into a relationship where at least one party refuses reconciliation.

How Can We Let Go?

To let go is to accept reality, not deny it. "No-fault" divorce laws may reduce some of the public blame and accusation, but we still feel the sting of embarrassment and failure as we helplessly watch our marriages die. We married with the expectation that the relationship would last "till death do us part." We would live with our spouses, work and laugh together, raise our children to be loving and responsible citizens, and die in each other's arms. But now, that will not happen.

With these failed expectations, the lingering effects of divorce can frustrate or delay acceptance of the reality that our marriages are over. Prolonged court proceedings keep the wounds open. Custody and visitation of children remind us of the union that once was. Even pets are ties to the past. Many want to run away from the turmoil. But this will not heal a broken heart if we do not accept reality.

To arrive at peaceful acceptance of our situations, we need an awareness of where we are in our own grieving process (discussed in chapter 2). We must deal firmly with whatever hinders our effort to let go—guilt, fear of rejection, and low self-esteem. Each of us must make a very personal psychological inventory of where we are in our lives. Our goal is to move through the grieving process to a point of full acceptance of our situations. Where that point of personal acceptance *is* depends upon you.

Acceptance of your divorce begins with making the most of your situation.[2] It means taking a good hard look at your life to find out what is best for you. The following anonymous poem, entitled "The Man in the Glass," illustrates how we need the integrity and courage to be honest with ourselves:

When you get what you want in your struggle for self,
and the world makes you king for a day,
just go to a mirror and look at yourself,
and see what that man has to say.
For it isn't your father or mother or wife,
whose judgment upon you must pass;
the fellow whose verdict counts most in your life
is the one staring back from the glass.
Some people might think you're a straight-shootin' chum,
and call you a wonderful guy,
but the man in the glass says you're only a bum,
if you can't look him straight in the eye.

He's the fellow to please, never mind all the rest,
for he's with you clear up to the end.
And you've passed your most dangerous, difficult test
if the guy in the glass is your friend.
You may fool the whole world down the pathway of years,
and get pats on the back as you pass.
But your final reward will be heartaches and tears
if you've cheated the man in the glass.[3]

We can fool others. Perhaps we can even fool ourselves by pretending to be someone we're not. But ultimately we must confront ourselves honestly. And certainly, we will *never* fool the Lord. Therefore, as we let go of the baggage that weighs us down in life, there are some things we need to hold onto—consistency with our values, honesty in dealing with others, acknowledging our true feelings, and the courage to stand up for what is right.

To let go is to admit powerlessness, not to control people and events. Some believe that letting go feels a lot like bungee cord jumping. You step off your high perch and feel as if you are totally out of control as you spin helplessly to the ground. Then, just before you reach bottom, that invisible cord snaps you back and spares your life. It is really unnerving to be so out of control and powerless. But this inner urge for self-protection keeps us from stepping away from people and situations that enslave us.

We may desperately want to chain ourselves emotionally to former spouses who want nothing more to do with us. But we cannot control what others do with their lives. This is why using "tough love" is such an important part of letting go. Limiting communication with spouses who are leaving a marriage restrains our temptation to jump in and control their lives against their will. If they want out, forcing them to stay only makes them more determined to leave. We increase our pain by not releasing people and events that must be set free. As hard as it is to do, let them go.

Take each day one at a time. Bend so you won't break.

To let go is to make the most of ourselves, not to blame our ex-spouses. We may want to blame our ex-spouses for everything. We yearn to find a scapegoat to ease our guilt. We want to view ourselves as nurturing and responsible mates. Our spouses are the unreasonable and angry ones unjustly attacking us. But deep down we know this is not right or fair.

How do we honestly feel about our ex-spouses, our children, and our former in-laws? Think about each person. What is their attitude toward us? How about our attitude toward them? We need to let it out. Get rid of blame that only distorts how we view ourselves. Then, as we purge ourselves of this desire to point a finger at others, let us consider how we can become better persons.

Acceptance of our circumstances and making the most of ourselves mandate that we act responsibly by acknowledging our own mistakes. As some have said, "Bless those who curse you—they may be right!" Our focus shifts more toward how we will live, and less toward what our ex-mates do.

To let go is to permit former mates to face reality, not to protect them. In using tough love, we allow others to make mistakes. They must have this freedom to affect their own destinies without unwelcomed interference from us. Let them learn. Do not soften the blow of consequences flowing from any bad decisions.

It is sad to see others make wrong choices in life. In an interview for *Rolling Stone* magazine, Pat Boone recalled the last time he saw Elvis Presley. The two accidentally ran into each other in the Memphis airport while boarding different planes. "We hugged, and I slapped his stomach because he was really overweight," Boone remembered. "He said he was going to Vegas, then asked where I was going. I told him 'Orlando,' and he said, 'Man, that's the wrong way. But you were always going the wrong way, weren't you?'"[4] These are words Elvis might have wanted back. If others stubbornly decide to self-destruct, we cannot protect them from themselves.

But there is another viewpoint to consider. Edmund Burke once remarked, "There is a limit at which forbearance ceases to be a virtue." How true! We must not become sappy wimps who look the other way while our ex-spouses make poor decisions which affect us or our children. By irresponsibly "turning the other cheek" through accepting emotional or physical harm without complaint or accountability, we leave ourselves vulnerable to manipulation by unscrupulous people who may attack and control us. Unconditional love does not mean unconditional acceptance of whatever wrongs others commit. There is a responsible way to "turn the other cheek." There is a faithful way to overcome evil with good (Rom. 12:21). It comes through having the integrity and love to disrupt sinful practices of others by encouraging them to do what is right rather than ignoring them meekly. Let them make their own decisions, but urge them to do what is right.

To let go is to forgive ex-spouses while keeping past wrongs in perspective, not to forgive and forget. This is not double-talk. It is responsible love. To "forgive and forget" is a myth—it is impossible. A playwright once said that God gave us memory that we might have roses in December. If we truly could forget events in our lives, think of how we could lose precious memories of good times we want to remember. Can we ever really forget our past?

Some years ago, an over-zealous youth cleanup crew ventured into the prehistoric Bruniquel caves in southwest France to remove some modern graffiti. They proudly displayed the spic-and-span walls until curators discovered that the kids had also scrubbed away Cro-Magnon paintings thousands of years old! Fortunately, God created us so that our personal memories cannot be scrubbed into oblivion as easily as those paintings!

The truth about what has happened to us in the past is this: we cannot change it, and we will never fully forget it. When we try to forget wrongs others have done to us, we could be trying to rewrite our personal history to make it less disappointing and distressing. But this is not reality. It blurs our focus. It causes us to lose perspective. We fail to learn from our own mistakes.

And yet, we should quickly put behind us bad memories that stir up bitterness, resentment, or despair. After all, some people remember things with a string around their finger. Others do it with a rope around their necks. Holding grudges is like the army who carried heavy cannonballs wherever it went out of fear of meeting up with the enemy and having nothing to shoot with. Aren't grudges just as heavy? There comes a time when we need to take our cannonball grudges and stack them up on the courthouse lawn after our divorces are finalized.

The principles of letting go and keeping a proper perspective on the past intimately tie into a correct understanding of biblical forgiveness. Contrary to popular thought, forgiveness is not overlooking wrongs of others while pretending that everything is fine. Being hurt and angry because others have sinned is not contrary to having a forgiving heart. Anger actually helps us focus on *correcting* the wrong (when we can) for the benefit of others trapped in sin. It is a continuing desire to see justice done by restoring and rebuilding—to the glory of God—what has broken down.[5]

To let go is to grow wiser and live for the future, not to regret the past. Marla Hanson was a very beautiful, talented actress and model with a career that was skyrocketing some years ago. But all this changed in an instant when she was brutally attacked and stabbed. After receiving more than 100 stitches in her head, no amount of make-up could ever hide the hideous scars that cut across her face from her nose to her left ear and from the right corner of her mouth. After many months in recovery and rehabilitation, someone asked Marla whether she felt self-conscious about her disfigurement. "Everyone has scars," she replied. "Mine show. Most others carry theirs on the inside."

How true that is! It is foolish to think we will ever again be the persons we were before our separation or divorce. This tragedy left a mark upon us that we will carry for the rest of our lives. But as healed survivors, our inner scars should not enslave us in self-pity. Instead, let them propel us forward with experience and hope. As the apostle Paul testified, "We also rejoice in our sufferings, because we know that suffering produces perseverance; perseverance, character; and character, hope. And hope does not disappoint us, because God has poured out His love into our hearts by the Holy Spirit, whom He has given us" (Rom. 5:3–5). The scars of our painful past remind us how much we have to live for.

To let go is to say good-bye to relationships tied to our marriages, not to cling to them. This is a sad part of losing our spouses and marriages. The time comes when it is best to say good-bye to some who cannot really accept us as single persons.

This is particularly true of our in-laws. You may find that you can maintain relationships with your in-laws after divorce. If so, and if you can still fully accept your divorce situation as a newly single person, you are most fortunate. If you have children, you may not have much choice—you cannot cut their ties with relatives. But if children are not involved, do not deceive yourself and rationalize the thoughts and attitudes of your heart. Check your feelings to see if preserving relationships with in-laws interferes with your own recovery. It may be best for everyone concerned to lovingly cut the ties with in-laws and those friends who maintain a strong bond with our ex-mates. Bring a closure to these relationships.[6]

A related problem arises when our ex-spouses ask us, "Can we still be friends?" Answering yes or no depends upon individual situations. Again, you may be able to handle a friendship, but I suspect that most people will have trouble with it. Ending a marriage is serious business. This is not a matter easily ignored or brushed away with time. From a practical viewpoint, you probably will find it awkward to continue a friendship. There are so many feelings and emotions that could arise. How will you handle hearing favorite old songs or going to memorable restaurants or parks? How will you feel watching your ex-mate become romantic with another person? How will he or she react to your new relationships? We should not deceive ourselves into thinking we can handle this emotional bombshell for a long time after the divorce is final—if at all.

These are only suggestions. Ultimately, the decision about how to manage post-divorce relationships with ex-spouses and in-laws requires much prayer, advice from competent counselors who are familiar with the situation, and sensitivity to everyone concerned. Do what is best for you. Just be sure to fully let go, and continue with your personal grieving process and recovery into a new life.

To let go is to strive for new beginnings, not to isolate ourselves. A return to normalcy is our goal in letting go. We need to get into the groove once again at work. Go to church ready to give and encourage others. Enjoy a movie or play, or just relax with a funny situation comedy on television. Get fulfilling outdoor hobbies going—jogging, swimming, biking. Feel the warmth of the sun.

New beginnings start at home. This means putting away reminders of a former spouse—pictures, wedding albums, and other momentos.[7] It also means avoiding telephone calls, letters, and personal visits from ex-mates.

New beginnings flower forth from a positive attitude. Reflect on everything you appreciate in life. Imagine yourself achieving your goals and dreams as a single person. Count your blessings. Think about what you value most in life. Write a poem expressing your feelings. I found digging in the dirt around my house and planting new shrubs and flowers tremendously uplifting.[8]

New beginnings also mean taking care of ourselves. Strive for consistent bedtimes and wake-up times. Use routines in a healthy way. When life has been a jumble of change and uncertainty, routines can provide comfort and order. Stay away from alcohol. Eat a balanced diet. Limit use of sugar, salt, and caffeine, which can compound stress by leading to fatigue and irritability. Stick to a regular sleep schedule. Try different stress-management techniques regularly—prayer and meditation, exercise and relaxation. My sister suggested I join her in power walking through the neighborhood on a regular basis. I did and found it to be a great stress reliever.

Isolation for long periods of time after a separation or divorce can be counterproductive. As you complete the grieving process, join humanity once again. Don't become invisible. Whenever anyone invites you out to anything—go!⁹ Be flexible and try something new. Thrive on life! Obviously the process of letting go is much easier if we have something good in our lives to build upon for the future. If we involve ourselves in a good church congregation, hold a fulfilling job, or have a strong support system of family and friends to encourage us, we are rebuilding our lives.

To let go is to strive for peace, not to exhaust ourselves in life's rat race. Remember the promises that technology wizards made to us? Cellular telephones, modems, fax machines, laptop computers, and similar wonders would make life easier. They promised us more free time for ourselves and our families. *It was a lie.* Instead, technology merely extended the boundaries of where and when we work, extending them into our quiet times, evenings, weekends, and vacations. It pushed people to negotiate deals on their car phones, draft memos on portable computers as they jetted from city to city, and fax or email documents from homes and hotels all over the world. Peer pressure from those working longer hours often leaves us no choice but to keep grinding harder and faster, too, with no apparent escape.

As part of renewing our personal lives after a separation or divorce, it is critical that we do not ride through one storm only to fall prey to another. This is not a time to "lose ourselves in our work." Take it slow. Be very conscious of not overcommitting to matters for a while. Strive for balance in life. Seek the peace that surpasses all understanding.

To let go is to fear less and love more. It is natural to fear new relationships; we do not want to experience the pain of rejection once again from someone else. But we also fear a suffocating loneliness that comes when we shut others out of our lives. The way of escape is to love others as we love ourselves. It is practicing the "golden rule" of doing for others what we would have them do for us. We need to be more "other-centered" by helping those who are less fortunate (Phil. 2:4–7; Isa. 58:10).

By loving and serving others, we help ourselves form new friendships.

> "Two are better than one, because they have a good return for their work: If one falls down, his friend can help him up. But pity the man who falls and has no one to help him up! Also, if two lie down together, they will keep warm. But how can one keep warm alone? Though one may be overpowered, two can defend themselves. A cord of three strands is not quickly broken" (Eccles. 4:9–12).

To let go is to trust in ourselves less and rely upon God more. Are we ready to take counsel from the Lord that we may not like? Are we truly committed to putting our faith into action—no matter what?

An old story tells of the man who fell off a cliff only to stop his fall by desperately grabbing a small bush growing from an outcropping. After screaming for help, the man noticed an angel sitting leisurely on the cliff's edge. "Will you trust me to save you?" the angel asked.

"Yes!" the man pleaded, "I'll do anything you ask—just help me!"

"Anything?" the angel said thoughtfully. Growing more impatient with each moment, the man agreed, "Yes, anything!"

"Okay," came the reply, "if you want to be saved, let go of that bush!" After a short pause, the man yelled, "Is there anyone else up there who can help me?"

Most of us can empathize with this man. We want help, but we want it to come our way—when and where we want it. It is not always comfortable to lay ourselves aside at times and trust God enough to do what He says. And yet, it is the only sure way out of the valley of the shadow of death we often find ourselves in after a separation or divorce. Is your separation or divorce drawing you toward God right now, or is it pushing you away from Him?

God is the Author of new beginnings. It is time to let go of our ex-mates and in-laws—and let God work in our lives.

Self-Esteem: Rebuilding for the Future

How do our self-image, self-esteem, and self-acceptance affect recovery from separation or divorce?[10] Each of us carries a portrait wherever we go, a picture far more important than any in our wallet. It is our *self-image*. The problem is that we act in harmony with how we perceive ourselves, and our perceptions are not always correct. We may be very secure and capable individuals, but if we do not like the person we see, then we think no one else likes us either. If we see ourselves as failures, then we will fail—no matter how much we want to succeed. But if we view ourselves as capable and confident persons, we will face life with more optimism, performing nearer to our abilities. "As a man thinks in his heart, so is he" (Prov. 23:7, KJV).

Self-esteem is an expression of how well we feel about the difference between our self-image and how we wish we could be. As children, we see the world favor beautiful, talented, popular, wealthy, or smart people. We desire that for ourselves. But when we compare ourselves to others, we fall short and become discouraged. This gap between our self-image and the ideal we hoped for pushes us toward not being thankful for who we are. We do not fully appreciate the talents and abilities God has given us. And the more this gap bothers us, the more it works against us to lower our self-esteem. If, however, we have more realistic expectations for improving ourselves according to the gifts God has given us, we increase our self-esteem.

Self-acceptance is arriving at a point of approval and respect for how God created us as we are. We see ourselves more as God sees us, rather than trap ourselves into comparisons with others. This does not mean that we condone sin in our lives. Instead, we recognize that we will make mistakes. And we humbly receive God's grace as an eternal invitation to do what is right.

Whatever you've heard about self-esteem—good or bad—you can be sure there are many others who will tell you that what you've heard is wrong. Psychologists, theologians, and many others have been engaged in a long-standing debate about this issue. Is focusing on increasing one's self-esteem a sin or a virtue? Certainly there is a difference between those attributes of self-esteem that are good, and those that are self-serving and humanistic in promoting a self-sufficiency in human potential while ignoring God.

I do not endorse self-worship or self-centeredness. We are not the center of the universe. God does not cater to us like a cosmic bellhop. Rather, we acknowledge our sinfulness and our need for God's forgiveness—in true humility rather than self-degradation. We seek to improve our self-image in a healthy, biblical way that reflects God's glory. We strive to conform to the example of Jesus Christ. As we grow in Christ, we claim the calm assurance that who we are and what we do are the good fruit of God's grace and redemption. Our desire in this life always should be to reflect His glory.

We can see the effects of low self-esteem. Have failed relationships, poor performance, unrealistic expectations, and a lack of joy plunged you into despair? Low self-esteem robs us of joy in life. It brings a pessimistic outlook, where we worry or expect the worst. It steals away our confidence in dealing with other people. It makes us self-conscious about our appearance, performance, or status in life. Instead of feeling comfortable with who we are and our identity, we are enslaved to the opinions of others. Low self-esteem can make life a living hell.

If we struggle with low self-esteem, what happens when an unwanted separation or divorce assaults us? Our spouses have, in some way, made it clear to us that we have failed, that we do not measure up in their eyes. It is the ultimate personal rejection. It may shatter our self-image. Certainly it is difficult to have self-acceptance when those who know us better than anyone else on earth are throwing us away. How do we recover? How can we rebuild our self-perception in a healthy and biblical manner?

Reaffirm Your Identity: Get to Know Yourself Again

After going through a separation or divorce, what is your self-image like? Maybe you are seeing that too much of yourself was bound up in trying to please your ex-spouse, no matter what the cost. Do you see yourself as half a person simply because you are alone now? Do you feel the need to check up on your spouse so urgently that you are ignoring your own needs? As you manage all the details of housing, finances, relationships, and caring for children, have you lost touch with yourself?

For a while it is only natural that we examine ourselves and ask anew, "Who am I?" The key is to focus on the right answers. Allow God and faithful Christian friends to reassure you of the truth about yourself. Be careful to avoid those who will steer you astray.

Take note of how Jesus used His identity to fight against Satan. As He was fasting in the wilderness before beginning His public ministry, Satan came forward to tempt Him. The *coup de grace*, Satan thought, was to challenge Jesus to doubt His identity. "If you are the Son of God . . . " were the words he used repeatedly in speaking to Jesus (Luke 4:1–13). But it was of no use. Why? Because Jesus knew who He was in relation to the Father. He was (and is) the Son of the living God. He did not need to prove it to Satan or anyone else. Instead, by holding firm to His identity and purpose, He could avoid distractions and fulfill His mission of seeking and saving the lost (Luke 19:10). Can we have that same sense of security in knowing who we are in Christ? Can we have the same assurance of looking forward to a home in heaven with the Father? Absolutely!

For some, knowing one's identity has always been a question of doubt. This is easy to understand since, from childhood, we pay more attention to what our parents, teachers, relatives, friends and others see in us than how we think and feel about ourselves. Too often we try to live up to the expectations of others while ignoring our own needs. Sometimes it is difficult to express our feelings or know whether what we feel, say, or do comes from us or from the influence of others. We filter and restrain our words and actions because we fear that we cannot truly be ourselves. As we feel these powerful emotions, the pressure grows to compromise who we are. Slowly but surely, we lose track of our values, principles, and identities. Eventually we are not sure who we are anymore.

Why not escape this negative trap by reminding ourselves of who we are in Christ without comparisons to others? In 1 Corinthians 15:10, Paul spoke of his own self-image this way: "By the grace of God, I am what I am." He told us the truth when he said, "Each one should test his own actions. Then he can take pride in himself without comparing himself to somebody else" (Gal. 6:4).

What is a biblical definition of a healthy self-image? As author and lecturer Josh McDowell puts it, we need to see ourselves as God sees us—no more, and no less.[11] Who are we? We are His children.

> How great is the love the Father has lavished on us,
> that we should be called children of God! And that is what
> we are! The reason the world does not know us is that it
> did not know Him. Dear friends, now we are children of
> God, and what we will be has not yet been made known.
> But we know that when He appears, we shall be like him,
> for we shall see him as he is (1 John 3:1–2).

Reject the negative, ungodly messages that have caused you to believe you have little or nothing of value in your life. Why not remind yourself of how you have changed with God's help?[12]

Healthy self-esteem begins with an accurate self-image free from the bias of others. By faith we accept who we are—right now—as God sees us.

Treasure Relationships: Know That You Are Still Loved

What good is knowing our identity unless we can share ourselves with others? We still have basic emotional needs that require satisfaction. We need to belong. We yearn for the security of knowing that someone unconditionally loves and cares for us. We earnestly seek a feeling of worth and acceptance by others. We need to feel competent and confident about who we are and what we do in life.

Our most important relationship, of course, is with God Himself. Do we see Him as a friend, or an adversary? Do we believe God loves us unconditionally? (John 3:16; Eph. 2:4–8).[13] Nothing will ever separate us from God's love in Christ Jesus! (Romans 8:38–39) How does that assurance make you feel? We are *individually* valuable to God (Ps. 8:3–8; Matt. 6:25–33). God does not love us because *we* are valuable; we are valuable because *He loves us.* He knows more about us than we know about ourselves—even down to how many hairs we have on our heads (Matt. 10:30). Jesus tells us not to worry about what we will eat, drink, or wear. God knows that we need daily care. If He takes extra care to feed sparrows, aren't we much more valuable than a little bird?

God also gives us the assurances we need to love others. He knows that we cannot really love others if we do not love ourselves. It is not wrong to love ourselves so that we can love others more deeply (Matt. 22:37–39; Eph. 5:28). Therefore, God loves and forgives us so that we can forgive, love, and accept ourselves and others. As we repent and confess our sins, God continues to forgive us daily (1 John 1:9; Ps. 32:5; Rom. 8:1). If God forgives us, why do we condemn ourselves? (see Eph. 4:32; Romans 8:31–39). As we in faith accept these truths and act to serve others, we find that our minds will focus less on ourselves, and more on others. As a result, our self-image and self-esteem improve. We see that we have a purpose in life beyond ourselves. We become more like Christ as we enjoy God's blessings, working alongside Him and by His power in His ministry to humankind.

Keep Separate Who You Are and What You Do

Test scores measure our talent in the educational system. The business world measures our ability by how big a salary we can command or how well we do our job. In sports, success is measured by how well we move farther, faster, and higher than anyone else. Former tennis great Chris Evert recalled how her performance consumed her this way: "Winning made me feel like I was somebody. It made me feel pretty. It was like being hooked on a drug. I needed the wins, the applause, in order to have an identity."

We blur our vision of ourselves if we always define ourselves in terms of what we *do* rather than by who we *are* as individuals. External performance standards are woefully inadequate measures of the intangibles of one's personhood and life—the content of one's character. But somehow we believe the lie that failing to excel in socially important areas means we are worthless.

We make bad decisions. We make mistakes—sometimes even big mistakes that make us feel stupid and incompetent. But *we* are not mistakes.

309

And we are not alone in doing stupid things. After all, as Albert Einstein once remarked, "Only two things are infinite: the universe and human stupidity, and I'm not sure about the former."

To the contrary, we are created and loved by God. He has given us a renewed sense of competence. We can do all things through Christ who strengthens us (Phil. 4:13; 2 Cor. 3:5). Why mourn our shortcomings in life? God's power is made perfect within us through our weakness (2 Cor. 12:9–10). Having a realistic view of ourselves means using our strengths while accepting our weaknesses. It means appraising our talents and abilities separate and apart from who we are as persons. Biblical self-esteem is the assurance that we can be the best we can be, without being better than everyone around us. We no longer have to compete with others in trying to stay younger or more slender than the next person.

But as we separate ourselves from our performance, beware the other extreme. All the biblical and healthy self-affirmations in the world are ineffective in raising our self-esteem if we are violating our consciences and habitually living in sin. We remain responsible for confronting and crucifying the sin in our lives with the power God gives us. Even so, putting off the sinful nature is not the same as putting ourselves down.

Remember, our priority is not merely to cultivate healthy self-esteem but to know Jesus Christ and become transformed into His likeness. A godless existence chases after self-esteem as an end in itself. Even well-intentioned people in the church can key on goals and results rather than the source of success—Jesus Christ. Inevitably, this leads to a trap: people seek praise and glory for themselves rather than glorifying God because of what He has done in their lives. But the essence of Christian humility comes with knowing who you are, knowing who *made* you who you are, and giving God the glory for all of it.

Regain Confidence in Your Judgment

The decisions we make in life will both positively and negatively affect our self-image and vice versa. If we violate personal values and standards, we sear our consciences, lose self-respect, and undermine our self-esteem.

When we make poor decisions, we can be sure that there will always be someone around to let us know it. If you saw the movie *City Slickers*, you may recall that comedian Billy Crystal played a midlife city dude bored with his nine-to-five job. He decided to recharge his batteries by signing up with two buddies for a cattle drive out west. While at a remote campsite on the drive, Crystal bragged that he had some gourmet coffee and promptly chunked the beans into a battery-powered grinder. The noise stampeded the herd as Crystal and his pals desperately clambered up nearby trees. The tough veteran trail boss, Jack Palance, calmly watched the whole scene from a distance. He took a hand-rolled cigarette from his mouth, tossed it in the dust, and mumbled one acidic epithet: "City folk."

Have you felt the heat of criticism from others like this after doing something stupid? Did it freeze you into inaction?

Someone once asked a wise sage to define the secret of success. "Good judgment," he said. When asked how to get good judgment, he answered, "Experience." When pressed on how to get experience, his response was, "Bad judgment." As Clarence Day once said, "Information is pretty thin stuff unless mixed with experience."

We feel good when we make proper decisions. It affirms us in positive ways. Others respect us and our judgment. But making bad decisions and learning from them is what makes us wise. The challenge of experience makes us stronger persons better able to deal with troubles in the future.

How can we make decisions that will build up our self-esteem in a biblical, healthy way? First, we must consider what we really need, not merely what we want. How will satisfying this need affect our future? Consider options and run them through to logical conclusions. Are the results what we really intend them to be?

Second, it is good to ask ourselves these questions: Will any behavior or attitude enslave me if I take this action? Will taking this action make me a better person and become more Christlike? Will taking this action be constructive and edifying to others and move them closer to God? Will taking this action make me feel guilty or believe that I'm doing something wrong? If we can honestly answer these threshold questions in a positive manner after seeking the counsel of many competent advisors—and still feel clear, calm, and enthusiastic about a course of action rather than fearful of its outcome—then we are moving in the right direction.

Those with healthy self-images feel relaxed about their decisions and behavior, know their personal boundaries, and are not fearful of the choices they must make each day.

Live in Harmony with Who You Are

Knowing what it means to have a positive self-image and how to build up our self-esteem is very important. But living it out is crucial. To put our thoughts into action, we must decide to change our lives with God's help. This means putting what we know to be true into practice in every area of our lives—work, church, relationships, parenting approaches, and the way we feel about ourselves. It means changing the way we look at ourselves, focusing more on our positive qualities. We must re-examine our relationships and avoid destructive patterns. This means either ending harmful alliances or transforming them into productive forces for change.

If negative thoughts come, identify the sources of those thoughts and sort out truth from fiction. Consider the validity of each message. Dispute it; challenge it; contradict and reverbalize it. If change is necessary, take action. But if the message is inaccurate, unrealistic, or distorted, release and discard it. Seek objective feedback from knowledgeable and competent advisors who can give us an honest appraisal of what we need to change.

What is our goal in rebuilding our self-esteem? What is our dream? What are we really striving for? I have found few experts who have defined what it means to have healthy self-esteem better than Dr. David E. Carlson in his outstanding counseling treatise, *Counseling and Self-Esteem*:

> I possess self-esteem when I think about what I am doing, saying, and believing with discernment, not with condemning judgment. I allow myself to recognize and admit deception and dishonesty to myself and correct them. I act with integrity, saying no when I want to say no and yes when I want to say yes. I take full responsibility for what I say, think, feel, and do, accepting the consequences of my behavior without denial, rationalization, or attempts to escape. I see with my own eyes, not what I am told is there. I hear with my own ears, not what I am told to hear. I feel with my own heart, not what I am told to feel. I ask with my own mouth, not what I am told to ask. I act with my own intentions, not just doing what I am told to do. I trust myself as the final arbiter and decision maker, not letting others decide for me. I use others as a resource and have the courage to make my own decision. I explore, discover, and understand myself, not criticizing, putting down, or chastising myself. I accept God's love, his value affirmations, and his forgiveness of me, not wanting God to tell me I am better than others.

Self-esteem is the result of facing my pretensions and acknowledging my longing to grow beyond the need for repentance. It is accepting my mortality, limited wisdom, and power, and groaning for what I am—a sinner in need of God's grace and mercy each day. . . .

Self-esteem, from a biblical viewpoint, is acknowledging and rejecting my grandiosity. It is not religious or moral superiority or pride in being better than others. It is pride in being God's adopted child. It is humility in being chosen and called by God.[14]

But remember that in order to live in harmony with who we are, as Dr. Carlson has described so well, we first must treasure our identity in Christ. We must discover and cherish our unique, God-given talents and abilities, relying upon the power we possess through Christ to be all we can be before we can do all we can do. If we do not, we will fall into despair whenever our actions fall short.

With God's help, take personal responsibility for your own low self-esteem (Gal. 6:5). Your past and present life may influence you negatively, but you can be a creative force in forming positive thoughts, actions, and feelings. Ignoring this responsibility traps you into living in the past.

Strong self-esteem provides us with the resilience we need to endure life's difficulties. We learn to accept ourselves through understanding God's love. This allows us to develop love and acceptance of others. In turn, loving others allows us to see ourselves more clearly, experience God's love in a new and fresh way, and gain an ever deeper understanding of God's love and acceptance for us. This cycle goes on and on for as long as we live.

Having a biblical, accurate self-image—and building a healthy self-esteem from it—testifies to this eternal truth: "I have been crucified with Christ and I no longer live, but Christ lives in me. The life I live in the body, I live by faith in the Son of God, who loved me and gave himself up for me" (Galatians 2:20). We are new creatures in Christ. We have a new identity as Christians. We have been resurrected to a new life. If we claim in faith to love ourselves because God first loved us (1 John 4:10), then we will have a godly view of ourselves. If we believe, however, that we are the center of our world, we will continue to suffer from low self-esteem. It's as simple as that.

Having the Peace That Surpasses All Understanding

We have let go of our failed marriages. We have honestly appraised ourselves by reaffirming a biblical self-image and striving for healthy self-esteem. But we still yearn for peace in our lives.

At 3 a.m. the night that Hurricane Andrew struck, one of the last hymns played on the local religious radio station in Miami before its radio tower toppled was the beautiful "It Is Well with My Soul." Remember this comforting lyric? "When peace like a river attendeth my way; when sorrows like sea billows roll; whatever my lot, Thou has taught me to say, 'It is well, it is well with my soul.'"[15]

H. G. Spafford originally penned these words on a ship in the North Atlantic many years ago as it was passing over the sunken wreckage entombing the bodies of his loved ones. But on that night in August, 1992, as the winds roared over south Florida, it was a final reminder that God gives us peace in our souls that can withstand any hardship in life, a peace that surpasses all understanding.

After the hurricane, military helicopters hovered like flies over the devastation in Dade County. But up in the blue sky, something beautiful floated over the wrecked home of Homer Knowles. It was a kite with a twenty-five-foot tail that looked like a bright, flickering rainbow! There it was, hanging effortlessly in the breeze above the huge holes in his roof.

Knowles had already had a tough year in 1992. He had been a pilot with Pan Am until the airline folded several months earlier. But now, while cleaning up after Andrew, he took a break to fly his kite. "I bought this kite fifteen years ago in San Francisco," Knowles told a reporter from the *Miami Herald* just after the storm. "I found it in a closet cleaning up. I decided I'd come out and fly it."[16]

That's the spirit we need after going through a separation or divorce—looking for the beauty in life. Renewal. Hope. Trying new things. A joyous peace despite all that has happened. Through any tragedy or traumatic life experience, there is still something eternal that wells up in our mortal hearts. Call it faith, the "survival instinct," or whatever you want. But there is something that God in His love has placed within each of us, constantly whispering and reassuring us, "I will survive. I will live on to love others and receive their love. I will rebuild my life."

Jesus said this about having peace during trouble and hardship just before He went on to the agony of the cross: "Peace I leave with you; my peace I give you. I do not give to you as the world gives. Do not let your hearts be troubled and do not be afraid. . . . I have told you these things, so that in me you may have peace. In this world you will have trouble. But take heart! I have overcome the world" (John 14:27, 16:33).

David touched the heart of God with these comforting words:

> God is our refuge and strength,
> an ever-present help in trouble.
> Therefore we will not fear, though the earth give way
> and the mountains fall into the heart of the sea,
> though its waters roar and foam
> and the mountains quake with their surging.
>
> There is a river whose streams
> make glad the city of God,
> the holy place where the Most High dwells.
> God is within her, she will not fall;
> God will help her at break of day.
> Nations are in uproar, kingdoms fall;
> He lifts his voice, the earth melts.
> The Lord Almighty is with us;
> the God of Jacob is our fortress (Ps. 46:1–7).

How do we find this peace that surpasses all understanding? Here are a few keys:

Understand and Embrace the Source of Joy and Peace

This means truly understanding who God is and who we are in our personal relationship with Him—the source of real joy and peace. God is Lord. We are His sheep, His servants. If we reverse these roles, we will never have peace. Only the forgiveness and love flowing from the cross of Christ opens the way to peace.

At the correctional center in Guelph, Ontario, police constable John Bolton noticed a cross around the neck of a prisoner arraigned for attempted robbery. Bolton took a closer look at the necklace, since he knew the prisoner was not particularly religious. As he did so, the prisoner tried to cover up a strange protrusion from the top of the cross, nervously dismissing the entire piece as only a good luck charm. But the keen-eyed constable noticed that the ornament looked suspiciously like a handcuff key—and he was right! After confiscating the cross, Bolton discovered that it would open almost any set of handcuffs. That cross had the power to set the prisoner free; so too with the true cross of Christ.

Our abiding love for God will maintain our peace. "You will keep in perfect peace him whose mind is steadfast, because he trusts in you" (Isaiah 26:3). What did Jesus tell the expert in the law who asked about God's greatest commandment? Love the Lord your God with all your heart . . . your soul . . . your mind . . . your strength . . . [and] love your neighbor as yourself (Mark 12:30–31). Keeping this greatest commandment brings us to a place where "love and faithfulness meet together; righteousness and peace kiss each other" (Psalm 85:10).

Our focus on Christ is crucial for seeking God's peace. Over and over again, we forfeit peace in our lives by looking away from the Lord. We focus on ourselves and the world around us. We need to fix our eyes continually on Jesus, the author and perfecter of our faith (Hebrews 12:1–3).

Develop an Attitude of Optimism, Joy, and Hope
Paul told us:

> Rejoice in the Lord always. I will say it again: Rejoice! Let your gentleness be evident to all. The Lord is near. Do not be anxious about anything, but in everything, by prayer and petition, with thanksgiving, present your requests to God. And the peace of God, which transcends all understanding, will guard your hearts and your minds in Christ Jesus. Finally, brothers, whatever is true, whatever is noble, whatever is right, whatever is pure, whatever is lovely, whatever is admirable—if anything is excellent or praiseworthy—think about such things. Whatever you have learned or received or heard from me, or seen in me—put it into practice. And the God of peace will be with you (Phil. 4:4–9).

Pessimism can destroy anyone's peace and confidence. Former NHL coach Harry Neale remembered some of the problems he had with his hockey players in Detroit: "I heard my best center say to my best defenseman during the national anthem, 'Every time I hear this song, I have a terrible game.'"

Or how about the farmer who had the brilliant dog? His neighbor was so negative that whenever it rained, he worried that it would flood. If the sun was bright, he fretted that it would scorch his crops. So to help turn the fellow around, the farmer trained his dog to walk on water without telling his neighbor of this rare talent. When the two of them were duck hunting from a boat one day, the farmer ordered his dog out onto the lake to retrieve their prey. The dog bounded across the water, picked up the ducks, and hopped quickly back into the boat without a drop on him except for his paws. "What do you think of that?" the farmer asked. "Can't swim, can he?" grunted the neighbor. Pessimists miss out on life.

Some joke that optimists believe that today is the best of all days; pessimists fear the optimists may be right. But which type of person would you really like to be?

Optimists are more at peace than pessimists because they project positive expectations. They see problems as opportunities merely disguised as trouble. They refuse to say they are no good at anything but that they are getting better. They do not fail; they learn. They give credit wherever it's due. They encourage cooperation and reduce conflict. Optimists see themselves as having some control over their lives. They accept responsibility. They speak decisively, and communicate effectively in a way that makes others feel good just to be around them. They firmly believe that the only limitations on what you can accomplish are those you impose upon yourself.

Moving toward recovery and inner peace means changing our mindset. As Paul urges us, rejoice in the Lord! Do not be anxious about anything, but turn everything over to Him in prayer. Think of whatever is true, noble, pure, lovely, and admirable, not negative and discouraging things.

If your attitude is bringing you down, reassess all of your long-standing beliefs. Listen to your inner voice. How do you talk to yourself during the day? Is it negative? Is it accurate? Ask yourself why you feel bad. What belief causes this feeling? Is your value system realistic, logical, and an accurate reflection of the truth? Think of your strengths and weaknesses. What can you thank God for giving you? Are you afraid to fail, or do you accept failure as part of learning and growth?

The key is to allow God's vision for us to become a daily reality, imagining ourselves doing great and wonderful feats. Hold onto those dreams! Anchor your mind on them. Make the details vivid. Let it really make an impact on you! Say to yourself—out loud—"I can do all things through Christ who gives me strength!" Say it again. Say it a third time, but this time emphasize the words "all things." Then say it one last time with emphasis on who gives you the strength to do this.

Believe it, then do it!

Strive for Patience in Adversity

Perhaps you have heard the story of the truck driver who stopped at an all-night restaurant in Broken Bow, Nebraska, some time ago. The waitress had just served him when three swaggering, leather-jacketed motorcyclists started bothering him. One grabbed a hamburger off his plate, while another took a handful of his french fries. The third picked up his coffee and began to drink it. Remarkably, the trucker calmly rose from his seat, picked up his check, paid the cashier, and left without a word. As the waitress watched his big truck move away in the night, one of the cyclists remarked snidely, "Well, he's not much of a man, is he?" The waitress replied, "I can't answer that, but he's not much of a truck driver. He just ran over three motorcycles out in the parking lot!"

This is not the type of patience we need—merely waiting for an opportunity to even the score. No, peace comes from the realization that God gives us enough in life that we can release our need to seek revenge. We trust the Lord to strengthen us with His power so that we can have endurance and patience (Col. 1:11). "Be patient, then, brothers, until the Lord's coming. See how the farmer waits for the land to yield its valuable crop and how patient he is for the autumn and spring rains. You too, be patient and stand firm, because the Lord's coming is near. Don't grumble against each other" (James 5:7–9). The Lord will give us what we need, when we need it (see Matt. 6:25–34).

Accept That Pain Is Unavoidable

God does not insulate us from the trials of life; pain is inescapable for everyone. It does not matter how capable we are, how faithful or righteous, or how sincere we are in our love for God and others. Suffering grief from the trials of life strengthens us. Irritation almost always precedes revelation.

When a painful crisis comes, we suffer and are sorely tempted to point the finger at God. This is nothing new. Job experienced disappointment with God (Job 29–32). So did Elijah (1 Kings 17:20). Jeremiah and Habakkuk did, as well (Jer. 12; Hab. 1:2–4). But it was his suffering that turned Elijah from fearfully fleeing King Ahab toward Mount Carmel, where he glorified God by destroying the false prophets of Baal (1 Kings 17–18).

Why does God allow bad things to happen? Edgar Valdes's home was badly battered during Hurricane Andrew. But when his daughter asked him if God had sent the storm, he told her it wasn't God but only part of nature. "I guess I felt like I had to defend God's image," Valdes told a reporter from the *Miami Herald* as tears streamed down his cheeks. "Sometimes you need to have the roof down to see the sky."[17]

In his pain and anguish, Edgar Valdes held onto a valuable truth. We can get so caught up in the regimen of our lives that we box ourselves in and shut God out. Sometimes God uses our troubles and hardships to get our attention. Trials in life remind us that we cannot make it without Him.

The Scriptures confirm that Jesus was made perfect through suffering. "In bringing many sons to glory, it was fitting that God, for whom and through whom everything exists, should make the author of their salvation perfect through suffering" (Heb. 2:10). How was He able to avoid the disappointment that we experience? Hebrews 12:2 tells us that Christ, "for the joy set before Him endured the cross, scorning its shame, and sat down at the right hand of the throne of God." He knew why He had to suffer—to bring reconciliation between God and man—and looked forward to the joy in pleasing and glorifying the Father.

What did Paul conclude about the purpose and meaning of his troubles?

> We do not want you to be uninformed, brothers, about the hardships we suffered in the province of Asia. We were under great pressure, far beyond our ability to endure, so that we despaired even of life. Indeed, in our hearts we felt the sentence of death. But this happened that we might not rely on ourselves but on God, who raises the dead. He has delivered us from such a deadly peril, and He will deliver us. On Him we have set our hope that He will continue to deliver us, as you help us by your prayers (2 Cor. 1:8–11a).

Have you despaired of life itself at times? How did you feel as you watched your mate walk out the door for the last time? Have you felt the "sentence of death" in your heart during your separation or divorce? We may see our troubles as failure or confirmation of some inherent worthlessness we feel inside. Or we may kick against the goads and refuse to change, as Saul once did (Acts 26:14). We may insist upon circumstances we can live with. We may lock ourselves into a defensive posture, become more hurt and confused, then wonder why we suffer so much. But the testing of our faith is part of God's plan for our lives.

> Consider it pure joy, my brothers, whenever you face trials of many kinds, because you know that the testing of your faith develops perseverance. Perseverance must finish its work so that you may be mature and complete, not lacking anything (James 1:2–4).

> In this you greatly rejoice, though now for a little while you may have had to suffer grief in all kinds of trials. These have come so that your faith—of greater worth than gold, which perishes even though refined by fire—may be proved genuine and may result in praise, glory and honor when Jesus Christ is revealed (1 Peter 1:6-7).

As J. Oswald Sanders has said, "Peace is not the absence of trouble, but the presence of God." God can banish that sentence of death from our hearts and renew us. He can deliver us from any peril. Peace and joy come in keeping pain and suffering in perspective, seeking God's face through it all.

Be Content with What You Have

Oscar Wilde once wrote that there are two great tragedies in life: not getting what you want, and not wanting what you get.

Beckah Fink tells the story of a young man from a wealthy family who was graduating from high school. The custom was for parents to give their graduates an automobile. After months of looking at cars, the boy and his father found the perfect auto. The son was sure that it would be his. So imagine his disappointment when, at graduation, his father handed him a gift-wrapped Bible. The boy angrily threw the Bible down and stormed out of the house, never to return until his father's death brought him home again many years later. As he went through his father's possessions that he was to inherit, he found the old Bible that had been his graduation gift. Opening it, he found a check inside bearing the date of his graduation, made out in the full amount needed for the car they had chosen together.

Contentment with what we have is vital to having peace that surpasses all understanding. We are by far our own worst enemies in this. Paul reminds us, "But godliness with contentment is great gain. For we brought nothing into the world, and we can take nothing out of it. But if we have food and clothing, we will be content with that" (1 Tim. 6:6–8).

Paul also underscored this secret to a peaceful life:

> I have learned to be content whatever the circum-
> stances. I know what it is to be in need, and I know what it
> is to have plenty. I have learned the secret of being content
> in any and every situation, whether well fed or hungry,
> whether living in plenty or in want. I can do everything
> through him who gives me strength (Phil. 4:11–13).

The green grass on the other side of the fence in life always allures us. But with God's peace in our hearts, perhaps we will feel like the farmer who became discouraged with his spread and hired an auctioneer to sell it all. The auctioneer walked around the farm taking inventory, and then published an enthusiastically worded auction notice in the local paper. When the farmer read the notice, he realized right away that it described everything he had ever wanted—and promptly took his farm off the market.

The writer of Hebrews tells us: "Keep your lives free from the love of money and be content with what you have, because God has said, 'Never will I leave you; never will I forsake you.' So we say with confidence, 'The Lord is my helper; I will not be afraid. What can man do to me?'" (Heb. 13:5–6). In divorce, we learn contentment when we focus on what we *have* rather than on what we've *lost*. We waste what we *do* have when we allow ourselves to get upset over what we *do not* have. Be content with and thankful for what you have, and peace is around the corner.

Seek the Fellowship of Other Believers

Did you know that the Sequoia trees of California, towering as much as 300 feet above ground, have unusually shallow root systems? Their roots reach out in all directions just under the surface to get moisture. Due to this quirk of nature, you will not find a Sequoia tree standing alone very often because high winds would uproot it. How do these beautiful trees survive for centuries? They grow in clusters, intertwining their roots and providing support for one another against the storms. And just as the Sequoias rely on the strength of each other, we too must rely upon our brothers and sisters in Christ.

The beauty of encouragement and fellowship is that everyone needs it in times of trouble. After Hurricane Andrew, volunteers dropped off relief supplies and donations by the carload and truckload outside the Broward Mall near Fort Lauderdale for those suffering farther south. But the entire operation was set up so that these good Samaritans could not leave the area without passing by a second crew of volunteers, whose job was simply to applaud—that was all. And it meant so much.

Even our friends and family who come to our aid during a divorce crisis need that applause. They need to know that their help and concern counts. It means something to us.

Deeply Involve Yourselves in Life and Rebuilding

After Hurricane Andrew, what turned the people in south Florida around more than anything else was an immediate commitment to rebuild. Time after time as people who lost their homes and businesses were interviewed on television, the remarks were always the same: "We will rebuild!" Community leaders picked up on this optimism and formed the "We Will Rebuild" Committee. This commitment to renewal and hard work was contagious. It inspired hope and vision for the future.

And now, all these years later, their vision has become a reality. All areas devastated by Andrew stand proudly rebuilt in the Florida sun, fresh and new!

After our divorces are final, we must have the same commitment. We must follow God's leading and rebuild our lives. "So then, those who suffer according to God's will should commit themselves to their faithful Creator and continue to do good" (1 Peter 4:19). We must accept what has happened to us in the death of our marriages and go on from there. Joy and peace in life come from cultivating an attitude of gratitude (1 Thess. 5:18). We rebuild to return to the normal rhythms of our existence, to give of ourselves to others, and to creatively look for new happiness. As we weave our lives back together again, we enjoy the very best life freely offers us—a beautiful sunset, good friends, an ice cold soda on a steaming hot day, or a jump in a crystal clear lake.

We rebuild our lives, not as *victims* of our past but as *victors* in Christ. He is our supreme hope of glory. Peace and joy come in fully understanding and accepting this: no matter what comes our way in life, God's favor lasts throughout and beyond our lifetimes. We may weep during the night, but rejoicing comes in the morning (Ps. 30:5).

A Closing Prayer for Us

In his excellent book *Growing Through Divorce*, Jim Smoke includes the following prayer that beautifully captures the essence of recovery and renewal after divorce:

PRAYER FOR THE DIVORCED
God, Master of Union and Disunion,
Teach me how I may now walk alone and strong.

Heal my wounds;
Let the scar tissue of Thy bounty cover these bruises and hurts
That I may again be a single person adjusted to new days.

Grant me a heart of wisdom,
Cleanse me of hostility, revenge, and rancor,
Make me know the laughter which is not giddy,
The affection which is not frightened.

Keep far from me thoughts of evil and despair.
May I realize that the past chapter of my life
Is closed and will not open again.
The anticipated theme of my life has changed,
The expected story end will not come.

Shall I moan at the turn of the plot?
Rather, remembering without anger's thrust
Recalling without repetitive pain of regret,
Teach me again to write and read
That I may convert this unexpected epilogue
Into a new preface and a new poem.
Muddled gloom over, tension days passed,

Let bitterness of thought fade, harshness of memory attenuate;
Make me move on in love and kindness.
(Original Source Unknown)[18]

We are starting over. And the future is bright if God is lighting our way. Do not be afraid to let go of the past. Embrace your new identity in Christ. Feel confident about the gifts and talents God has graciously given you. Be content with what you have. Seek His all-surpassing peace.

Questions for Personal Reflection

1) Have I really let go of my former spouse? Do I find myself thinking of my ex-spouse only occasionally? Do I feel emotionally upset when I do think of him or her? Am I still making excuses to talk to my former spouse? Do I still feel bound to a romantic relationship with my spouse?

2) Am I overly sensitive to others' opinions? Am I self-conscious about my appearance, performance, or status? Am I striving to be like somebody else rather than enjoying others for who they are, while still respecting who I am? Do I have a fear of being alone? Do I fear intimacy with others because it may lead to rejection or another failed relationship? Do I have a problem in accepting the love of God or other people? Am I able to express my emotions? Do I anticipate or worry that the worst will happen to me?

3) Do I have a generally pessimistic outlook on life? What is my present outlook on the future and my ability to grow and change? How do expectations of myself and others affect my behavior, thoughts, feelings, and the desire to move forward? What would my best friend tell me about these matters?

4) What have I learned from the mistakes I made in my marriage? What have I done to change? Do I see myself growing and becoming a stronger and wiser person? Have I forgiven myself? Have I exercised biblical forgiveness to my ex-spouse and others who have wronged me?

5) How do I feel about my life after divorce? Am I truly content with what's left to me after the settlement? Have I asked myself what Jesus would do now? What is keeping me from experiencing a peace that surpasses all understanding in my life?

CHAPTER 17

Becoming Free in Deed

We cherish our freedom as formerly married,
single persons. We do not enslave ourselves with
excuses or regrets. We break free from mistakes
of the past to experience life anew.

As the Communist regime in the USSR crumbled in 1991, ABC News reporter Ted Koppel interviewed President Gorbachev on the eve of his resignation. He wondered what Gorbachev might be thinking in reflection on the end of his political career after bringing so much reform to his country.

Gorbachev considered Koppel's question thoughtfully for a moment. Then he remembered the story of an ancient king who asked his advisors to explain the meaning of life. After twenty-five years, they presented the king with fifty railroad cars of books examining his question. Not having time to read them all, the king ordered his advisors to shorten their response. After fifteen more years, the counselors returned with five railroad cars of books on the meaning of life. Knowing that he was getting older, the king grew impatient and demanded that his experts shorten their answer to a few words. The advisors left for another five years, only to return as the king was on his deathbed. They presented him with a small piece of paper that simply read: "People are born. People suffer. And people die."

My hope is that the message of this lengthy book has been more encouraging than that received by the ancient king. If I were to condense all that we have shared together into a few words, I would offer you this: "People marry. Some divorce. But Christ offers all divorcees hope for a new life."

The Giver of Life

Divorce is not a life or death experience, although it may feel that way at times. But it sure gives us a new perspective on "life." Even the word—"life"—carries a certain mystery. Life is the most precious gift God has given us in Jesus Christ. "In him was life, and that life was the light of men"

(John 1:4). It is more than food and shelter, more than just an experience. An astute observer of life once said, "Man can give medicine when sickness comes, food when hunger comes, help when weakness comes, love when loneliness comes. But when death comes, man can give only sympathy, only compassion, but never the gift of life. Only God can do that."[1]

We were not given life by the Lord on a whim to see how we would handle it. We have a reason for living. What we do, say, think, and feel is a response to what He has given us. We have done our best to complicate matters with all our cars, bars, and movie stars. All the materialistic trappings blind us from the beautiful simplicity of what God initially created in us. But God still tends His garden. He still speaks to our hearts through the example of His Son and the discipline of the trials we face. Do we hear Him? Are we tuning out the noisy channels of this world enough to listen?

If life were simple, everything would be black or white. We would succeed or fail. We would not agonize over decisions. It would be easy. Roman gladiators toasted each other on the evening of a contest with, "Eat, drink, and be merry, for tomorrow we die." Then they fought each other to the death in the Colosseum the next day. When you are a gladiator, you win or you die. No gladiator had two bad days in a row! But fortunately, life is not like that. We have options. We can survive trials to live another day.

Although it may feel like death, divorce will not kill us. But if we allow it to happen, a special part of who we are can die.

In her book *It's Always Something*, written as she was dying of ovarian cancer, actress Gilda Radner made this observation: "While we have the gift of life, it seems to me the only tragedy is to allow part of us to die—whether it is our spirit, our creativity, or our glorious uniqueness." Instead of cutting our losses in divorce and moving on to save the truly precious qualities of our lives, we lose our freedom by fighting spouses, lawyers, judges, and in-laws. It is so true that "some men die by shrapnel, some go down in flames, but most men perish inch by inch, playing little games."

The Giver of Life has given us freedom of choice so we can enjoy life. This is an awesome responsibility. We can call our own shots. What should our response be? To follow in the footsteps of Jesus by loving Him and others as He has first loved us. We are His sheep. Every word we utter and every action we take should be an offering of thanksgiving to God for His love and mercy. He changes us into the likeness of His beloved Son from one degree of glory to the next (2 Cor. 3:18).

Your life is not over if you are a divorcee. You can give; you can love once again. You are God's creation. He will never cut off His personal relationship with you as you continue to seek Him. Watch for His direction. See Him move spiritually among His people. If you continue to submit to God, then you will respond by doing what is right and best for everyone.

No Enslaving Excuses or Regrets

What have we learned together? Remember to keep the big picture in mind. When marriage vows break, we accept the realities of separation and divorce. As difficult as it is, we embrace our emotions and face the pain. We humble our hearts and admit our mistakes. In the spirit of the parable of the prodigal son, we learn to let go—but with a willingness to reconcile upon repentance.

In our private struggles, we freely choose to go with God. In faith we depend upon Him for guidance. We use tough love—not for revenge but to help others face the consequences of their own decisions. When facing the turmoil of the legal process, our message is to mediate, not litigate. We strive to settle matters with our spouses quickly, if reasonably possible.

Post-divorce survival and recovery—the toughest part of a divorce—means taking personal responsibility for getting our lives and emotions back on track. We learn to let go of the "couple lifestyle" in favor of singleness. With God's help, we rebuild our self-esteem.

But the foundation for all that we have discussed is this vital point: we need to come to Jesus for the peace that surpasses all understanding. This means experiencing and using our freedom in Christ to glorify God.

Making excuses for what has happened to us can make us appear silly and childish. One notable excuse-maker was former Dallas Cowboy placekicker Rafael Septien. His excuses for missed field goals were legendary. Septien once muffed four out of five field goal attempts against the Houston Oilers. Rejecting the traditional excuses such as, "It was a bad snap," or "My holder messed up," Septien took the blame by confessing, "I was too busy reading my stats on the scoreboard." Later that year after missing another field goal in Texas Stadium, Septien complained, "The grass was too tall." (This might have been plausible if the field hadn't been made of artificial turf!) Other classics that Septien dreamed up for shanked shots included, "The thirty-second clock distracted me," and "My helmet was too tight and was squeezing my brain. I couldn't think!" Even so, Septien rarely blamed other people—with one exception. Once after a field goal attempt went wide, he turned to his holder, quarterback Danny White, and said, "No wonder! You placed the ball upside down!"[2]

Aren't we the same way at times in excusing our own actions? Our shortcomings are very obvious to others, but we lose ourselves in our excuses. Whatever we did or did not do in our marriages is history. After we admit our mistakes and learn from them, being free means not having to make excuses for our shortcomings. We should be willing to try new approaches in solving our problems. We resolve to change our thoughts and actions. Only then will we live our lives unshackled by our past mistakes. Excuses only tempt us to avoid reality and escape responsibility.

Do you feel regret about the failure of your marriage? If so, you may be experiencing the pain that comes from comparing "what is" with "what might have been." If we have done our best to save our marriages, we cannot continue to hope for what we cannot have after the divorce is final.

In 1904, William Borden, heir to the Borden dairy estate, graduated from a Chicago high school as a millionaire. His parents gave him a trip around the world. Traveling through Asia, the Middle East, and Europe gave him a burden for the world's hurting people. It was then that Borden decided to become a missionary, writing in his Bible two words: "No Reserves."

After graduating from Yale and turning down high-paying job offers in order to pursue his goal, he added two more words in his Bible: "No Retreats." Borden completed studies at Princeton Seminary and set sail for China to work with Muslims. He stopped briefly in Egypt to further prepare for his work. There he contracted cerebral meningitis and died within a month.

His life ambition unfulfilled, we may weep over this loss and mourn the apparent waste of it all. Not so in Borden's eyes. When he died, his Bible carried another addition under "No Reserves" and "No Retreats." He had written, "No Regrets." Regret causes us to agonize over what we didn't do with our ex-spouses. But we cannot look back and live in the past. We must move on.

Nowhere in this book do we refer to ourselves as "victims," unless domestic violence is present. We do not need self-pity. Thinking of ourselves as victims only serves to reinforce that limitation. We reject the negative message that we were not good enough for our ex-spouses. Instead we accept that what we had to offer was not enough to satisfy their needs. As divorce survivors, we see ourselves as victors. We accept our personal limitations but set new priorities for the future. We can conquer our fears. We move on from a marriage where love died and continue to love others.

Breaking Free

> If you hold to my teaching, you are really my disciples.
> Then you will know the truth, and the truth will set you
> free. . . . So if the Son sets you free, you will be free indeed.
> (John 8:31–32, 36).

There is a big difference between knowing what to do, and doing what you know. We have the power to free or enslave ourselves. It depends on our approach to life. Our focus affects the finale.

It is curiously sad that a divorcing couple finds themselves going in such different directions after it is over. But all of us usually find what we are looking for—good or bad. As Steve Goodier once noted, "Both the hummingbird and the vulture fly over our nation's deserts. All vultures see is rotting meat because that is what they look for. They thrive on that diet. But hummingbirds ignore the smelly flesh of dead animals. Instead they look for the colorful blossoms of desert plants. The vultures live on what was. They live on the past. They fill themselves with what is dead and gone. But hummingbirds live on what is. They fill themselves with freshness and life. Each bird finds what it is looking for. We all do."[3]

If you really wanted to make yourself unhappy or depressed, just think of a time during your separation or divorce when you were really miserable—then dwell on it. Who would pay to go to a depressing movie a second time? Yet that's what so many of us do with unpleasant events of the past or worries of the future! We play them over many times in our minds. We begin to imprison ourselves with questions like, "Why do bad things happen to me?" or "Why don't people like me?" or "Why can't I be happy?"

Years ago, comedian Steve Martin appeared on the *Tonight Show* when Johnny Carson was the host. As Martin came on stage, he had an enormous wood vise clamped onto his head. When Johnny asked how he was feeling, Martin complained, "Okay, I guess. But you know, Johnny, lately I've been feeling like my head's in a vise." When Johnny told him his head really *was* in a vise, Martin removed it while exclaiming, "Ah, that's *much* better!" Sometimes our thoughts and actions put us into a vise after a separation or divorce. Breaking free means taking off the clamps. But how? We must rediscover the freedoms we have as children of God.

Jesus promised that holding to His teaching would make us His disciples. In doing so, we will know that His truth sets us free. When we are feeling captive within ourselves, how can we know this truth? It begins with realizing that we are not God. This may sound silly. Who would admit thinking this way? Yet at times we all think we are God, or we put someone else in God's place.

In an interview by *US* magazine, Ringo Starr reflected on life with the Beatles. "I went absolutely mad 'round about 1964. I thought I was a god, a living god. And the other three looked at me and said, 'Excuse me, I am the god.'"[4] I appreciate that honesty. It is a commentary on life.

As we become our own gods, we imprison ourselves with self-righteousness, or mire ourselves in guilt or fear through worshiping others in God's place. Those experiencing the freedom Christ promises know that only Christ is King. True freedom comes from humbly following His example in trying to please the Father (John 8:25–29, 35–36).

After we realize that we are not God, we must recognize ourselves for what we really are—sinners who have fallen short of God's glory (Rom. 3:23). This involves more than merely confessing, "Okay, yeah, I'm a sinner." It means having the humble attitude of the tax collector in the temple rather than the prideful scorn of the Pharisee (Luke 18:9–14).

We should never be confident of our own "righteousness" because it may cause us to look down on everyone else. "If we claim to be without sin, we deceive ourselves and the truth is not in us. . . . If we claim we have not sinned, we make him out to be a liar and his word has no place in our lives" (1 John 1:8, 10). The humble are exalted in freedom. An awareness of our sin unceasingly motivates us to move toward God. It prompts us to reject pridefully thinking of ourselves more highly than we ought.

Finally, freedom comes with the assurance that God loves us despite our sin. We are prodigal sons and daughters coming home to our Father. It is God's love and acceptance that helps us crucify the sin in our lives. Receiving His love and forgiveness frees us from unhealthy guilt feelings and self-condemnation.

We obey Him to abide in His love, not to earn it.

Our Constitutional Rights as Christians

As Christian survivors of separation or divorce, we have an eternal "constitution" and "bill of rights" given by God, assuring us of certain freedoms.

First, we are free to have faith in God. Our faith sustains us when the storms of life wipe us out. Faith is not only having dreams of how life could be but coping with how life is for us right now. It is having the assurance of what we hope for and being certain of what we do not see (Heb. 11:1). Faith gives meaning to our lives and circumstances. Having faith in God's promise to provide for us frees us from the prison of broken marriages.

Second, God gives us freedom to make our own decisions. This is an awesome responsibility. Gone are the excuses and scapegoats. We can respond to people and events as we choose. And we are free to count the cost in advance of the inevitable consequences of our choices.

Third, we are free to change our lives. We can accept suffering without resentment or bitterness. Through faith we understand how God is stretching and strengthening us in our trials. Knowing that all things work together for good in the lives of those who love God helps make troublesome times more bearable (Rom. 8:28). We adapt and adjust with His help.

Finally, we are free to love. After the sharp edges of separation or divorce have cut us to the bone, the experience changes our perspective on life. As we tap into God's resources for survival during a crisis, we receive a greater appreciation for life. Suddenly we become more aware and empathetic of the suffering of other wounded souls. We are brothers and sisters who know what pain really is. The sacrifice Jesus made on the cross for us has far greater power than it ever did before.

How to Exercise Our Freedom as Formerly Married Individuals

Exercising our freedom responsibly is our goal in leaving broken marriages behind. Here's how:

Enjoy freedom as a single person. Married couples must consistently coordinate time schedules, goals, and priorities with each other. A joint commitment like this can bring great joy. But we can find joy as single persons, as well. Isn't it nice to ask yourself, "What do *I* want to do today?" Divorce does release us from the responsibilities of a shared household.

Enjoy this new independence. You have different choices from those made with your mate. You are thinking on your own. You can go wherever you want. You can eat dinner when and where you want it. Stay up late. It's okay. Accept these good feelings. Enjoy the release they provide.

Freedom empowers us to remove negative self-restraints. We can express our true feelings to others rather than suppressing them. If we take a special night out to a nice restaurant, we can enjoy it. We do not always have to condemn ourselves with how expensive or fattening it is.

But our new freedom also brings new responsibilities. What is the greatest challenge single persons face? It is not coping with loneliness, rejection by others, or sexual temptation. It is not fear of commitment to others. It is the alluring voice of a sophisticated self-centeredness. Yes, we are free to decide how to live our lives, but God warns us not to use our freedom to indulge our sinful nature (Gal. 5:13). In 1 Corinthians 7, Paul reminds Christians that being single provides excellent opportunities to use time and resources to serve God. How will we respond to this encouragement? As we enjoy our freedom and feel better about ourselves, let's avoid the trap of a selfish lifestyle.

Develop reasonable expectations. There were many times during your separation or divorce when mental fantasies helped you cope with your situation, right? They kept you going and inspired hope. Beginning life again as a formerly married, single person is also fruitful ground for fantasies and unobtainable goals. We may want unlimited excitement, romance, and adventure. We may expect a Prince Charming or a lovely princess to be waiting patiently for us on the courthouse steps after the divorce is final. We dream of that perfect person standing by, ready to whisk us away into the life we've yearned for. But it may not happen.

Be patient and content to grow slowly in your recovery. Do not expect wounds to heal overnight. Be grateful that you are free from the stress and anxiety of quarreling and sharing a house with one who no longer loves you.

Unreasonable expectations lead to frustration and anger. Continually redefine what is obtainable now. Think about what realistically can happen in the future and adjust accordingly. You may have a fulfilling and productive single life, or you could find companionship that gives you a fresh start in a new relationship. But be open to whatever comes.

Find new relationships. Look for new friends of the same sex. Sometimes marriage moves a couple away from good same-sex friendships as they devote time to each other. Becoming a single person once again provides new freedom to rediscover many of those pre-marriage joys. Sometimes it is good to take a vacation from the opposite sex for a while, if only to gain greater perspective on romantic relationships. It also removes the pressures of dating while post-divorce healing is taking place.

Also be ready for some rejection. Many people have a silent fear of singleness or falsely view singleness as a curse that could be contagious. Some married people may fear that their spouses will abandon the marriage and leave them for someone else. If this is a problem, it is best to seek relationships with other single persons. Befriend married couples as they feel secure with you and actively invite your friendship.

We also must prepare *ourselves* for these new relationships. Are we ready for others to come into our lives? Are we intolerant of others who do not live up to our expectations? Are we able to trust others and be sincere and compassionate? Are we good friends, able to give of ourselves unselfishly without always expecting something in return? Above all, find loving people you can freely talk to about your life.

Use reasoned judgment when making new commitments. Newly divorced men and women often feel the need to start acting like singles too soon. We are tempted to show the world, "I am having the time of my life. I'm happier being single." But racing into a new life can bring uncertain, sometimes disastrous results. Buying new cars, taking expensive vacations, and living a fast life can be hazardous to our health and well-being. We can lose control by talking too much, being overanxious in making new relationships, and spending too much on our desires. Trying to make too many decisions too fast can exhaust us and result in fatalistic thinking.

Luke 8:14 warns us that "life's worries, riches and pleasures" can choke out God's Word in our lives. Poor choices and distorted values strangle our lives in Christ. Why allow this to happen? Take it slow. Buy only what you need for a while rather than what you want. Live within your means. Make it your ambition to lead a quiet life, minding your own business, so others will respect you, and so you will not be dependent upon anybody (1 Thess. 4:11–12). Watch for the Lord's gentle direction.

Date others in moderation. Dating causes fantasies and unreasonable expectations to run wild at times—especially when we are vulnerable and lonely after a divorce. We begin our quest to find the "ideal mate." We search for someone to join us in a trouble-free relationship, a new love who will fulfill us like our spouses never did. We may keep a mental checklist of features and qualities to see who comes closest to our romantic ideal. But are our standards so high that they invite disappointment?

Let's be realistic about our situations and what we have to offer others. We need to relax and enjoy the single life—at least for a while. Every date need not be part of this quest for romance. Allow people to be themselves. Cherish their good qualities. Enjoy their unique gifts. Dating friends with whom you have no romantic interest is especially fun and very relaxing while trying the dating process once again.

Above all, avoid comparisons between your ex-spouse and dates. Brace yourself for some rejections, but be confident that some will find you interesting and attractive.

Don't remarry right away. Why? Because divorce shakes anyone up enough that one's identity is a little uncertain for a while. We need time to adjust from being "Michelle's husband" or "Jack's wife" to being just us. After divorce, changing these labels is uncomfortable and difficult. We are no longer "married" but "single" and "divorced." This can frighten people. So they rush back into a marriage as quickly as possible to keep the familiar labels, though a different person is in the "spouse" slot.

Samuel Johnson once described a second marriage as "the triumph of hope over experience." The U.S. Census Bureau found that almost half the marriages in the USA during 1990 were remarriages for at least one of the partners. It reported that 64 percent of divorced women remarry. Divorced white women waited an average of 26.5 months to remarry, while Hispanic women waited 29.9 months, and black women typically remarried after 38.3 months. Sadly, approximately 60 percent of all remarriages end in divorce, with 39 percent dissolving within ten years. (See Appendix "F" for more facts and statistics about divorce and remarriage.) This tells us that we should not remarry in haste.

Remarriage can be an exhilarating experience, but it is a major life commitment. It requires counting the cost. If you are scripturally free to remarry and wish to do so, explore different options. But be cautious. Remarriages can be deceivingly challenging and alluring. More questions are necessary.

If you find someone interesting, ask yourself: Do I enjoy talking to this person? Are our conversations stimulating? Can we communicate openly and honestly? Do I genuinely like this person? Can I care for his or her needs? Do I like this person's appearance? Do I really want to look across the breakfast table at her or him for the rest of my life? Where is this person spiritually? Do we share a common love for Christ? Can we discuss matters calmly and work out a mutually acceptable solution whenever we disagree? Does this person have the character I wish to see reproduced in my children? Do I respect this person?

Unless a potential mate is spiritually, intellectually, emotionally, and sexually attractive, we must question whether that person is right for us.

Single parents have additional considerations. A stepparent is threatening to children in a number of ways. Will they lose the personal love and attention of their remaining natural parent to this stranger? Will they ever be able to accept the stepparent as a substitute for their missing biological parent? How will they respond to discipline from this new person in their family? Will they become territorial when a "new" brother or sister shares their room? How will elder children or the baby of the family feel about giving up rank to other children more senior or junior to them? What happens if the noncustodial parent causes problems? Adults in love with each other frequently rush into remarriage and overlook the suspicious, sometimes hostile reactions of the children involved. Children that come with a remarriage can wedge between the remarried couple, too. No one can force "togetherness." Remarriage is a *family* decision.

Remarriage requires a lot of "give and take" and adjustments item-by-item. There are too many factors arising in a remarriage to cover in this book. It involves respecting the privacy and needs of everyone involved—not just in the immediate household but also with in-laws and grandparents. Having the necessary patience, tolerance, and respect for everyone concerned is no small task. But if those in remarriages can rise to the challenge, their families can enjoy a dynamic, loving home.

(For more information on remarriage and blending family issues, please refer to the companion volume to this book, *Making a NEW Vow: A Christian Guide to Remarriage and Blending Families*, by Joseph Warren Kniskern.)

We'll Know We're Free When . . .

We come to the end of our rope before we come to the end of our lives. We realize that we cannot make it in life without God's help. Our failures and weaknesses wake us up to this truth. Only then can we depend upon God and take hold of that which is truly life (1 Tim. 6:19).

Anne Alexander once said, "The circumstances of life, the events of life, and the people around me in life, do not make me what I am, but reveal what I am." That's what trials are for—to show us what we're made of. And God makes tough people! When we embrace this truth and can thank God for it all through our intense pain, we can experience a miraculous release and freedom filled with hope and optimism.

Believe it—your divorce is going to reveal the real you. Receive the revelation with gratitude.

We are not shackled by the opinions of others. There is an old fable about an elderly man traveling with a boy and a donkey. When the man led the donkey through one village with the boy close behind, the villagers called the old man a fool for walking instead of riding. To please them, he climbed on the animal's back. But the people in the next town criticized him severely for making the child walk while he enjoyed the ride. So, to please *them*, the man got off, set the boy on the animal's back, and continued on his way.

In the next town, the people accused the child of laziness for making the old man walk. They suggested that both ride the donkey. The old man climbed on and they set off again. In the last village, the people were incensed and indignant at the cruelty to the donkey because he had to carry two people. The frustrated man was last seen carrying the donkey down the road.

We cannot please everyone. If we try to do so, we could end up with a burden greater than that of the old man carrying the donkey. It is always a challenge to risk displeasing our critics. One of my all-time favorite quotes about critics is from Teddy Roosevelt, who said this about living life to the fullest, regardless of failures and criticism:

> It is not the critic who counts, not the man who points out how the strong man stumbled or where the doer of deeds could have done them better. The credit belongs to the man who is actually in the arena; whose face is marred by dust and sweat and blood; who strives valiantly; who errs and comes up short again and again, because there is no effort without error and shortcoming; who does actually try to do the deed; who knows the great enthusiasms, the great devotions, and spends himself in a worthy cause; who at the best knows in the end the triumph of high achievement; and who at the worse, if he fails, at least fails while daring greatly; so that his place shall never be

with those cold and timid souls who know neither defeat nor victory.[5]

Why worry about what others may think of us? The old joke is that at the age of twenty, we don't care what the world thinks of us; at thirty, we *worry* about what it thinks of us; and at forty, we discover that the world was not thinking of us at all. Trying to please people to win their respect can be fruitless, and it restricts our freedom in Christ.

Too often others will not have our best interest in mind. Susan Matice once shared a story about taking her two dogs to a dog training workshop. The instructor carefully explained that if an owner falls down and pretends to be hurt, a dog with a bad temper will tend to bite his master, while a good dog will show concern by licking the fallen owner's face. After arriving home, Matice decided to put her two pets to the test. While eating pizza in her living room, she stood up, clutched her heart, screamed, and fell to the floor. Both dogs looked at her, then looked at each other, and raced to the coffee table for her pizza!

Many times our "friends" can be like man's best friend. To paraphrase former Los Angeles Dodgers manager Tommy Lasorda, it's not good to talk about our troubles to everyone. A majority of the people who hear us don't care, and the rest may be glad we're having trouble!

Advice and encouragement of others is helpful to a point, but we must remain on guard not to become enslaved by baseless opinions of others. I am *not* saying that we should avoid the counsel of others; we have stressed the importance of receiving advice from competent and godly advisors. As Christians, we must be shrewd as snakes but as innocent as doves (Matt. 10:16). We must seek the counsel of those who will tell us what we *need* to hear. "The kisses of an enemy may be profuse, but faithful are the wounds of a friend" (Prov. 27:6). But when we feel overloaded to the point of frustration and confusion, we also must feel secure and free to decide what is best for us by relying upon our own wisdom from God's Word.

We no longer fear independence. For a while after a divorce, it is only natural that we automatically think of our ex-spouses whenever something goes wrong, illness comes, or a crisis arises. Who do you call when you awaken to strange noises in the dark? Who will be there to rush you to the emergency room if you have an accident? But slowly, over time, this dependence upon our missing mates will change into a natural and comfortable independence that helps us care for ourselves.

337

Independence does not come naturally for us. It is easier to depend on others. Deep down, we still yearn for someone to take care of us. We may want others to make decisions for us to avoid personal responsibility. But unreasonable dependence upon others is a trap that keeps us from reaching our full potential.

Independence does not mean isolation; isolationists become detached and out of touch. We do not seek independence only to become dependent on television and surfing the Internet or content to live in our home or apartment cocoons. Shutting ourselves off from the world forfeits our freedom to experience new relationships. Instead we launch out into the world, mindful of who we are and what we want to accomplish in life. We move out of personal comfort zones so we gradually overcome shyness and fear. Being an independent thinker is not the same as being different out of rebellion. Avoiding conformity is no less a trap than being dependent and conformist. Refuse to join what Thomas Jefferson called the "herd of independents."

In exercising independence, we must learn to cope and adjust. We will find new ways to take care of ourselves. In doing so, we experience more confidence in ourselves. That freedom will help us mature as individuals and better equip us to deal with life. Feeling secure in our independence prepares us to enjoy interdependent, healthy relationships. We can build relationships with others as whole, complete individuals rather than as needy persons with low self-esteem.

We use our strengths to overcome our weaknesses. What are your strengths right now? How about your weaknesses? Write them down and consider each one. How can you use them in your life?

Freedom means being sharp and alert, ready to use the talents God has given us by making the most of every opportunity (Eph. 5:16). Remember the old story of two men who cut wood all day? One man worked straight through the day without stopping to rest. He stacked an impressive pile of logs. But the other man chopped for fifty minutes, took a ten-minute break, then repeated this routine through the day. When he finished, he had a much larger pile.

"How did you chop more?" asked the man who had worked without stopping. His friend replied, "When I stopped for rest, I sharpened my ax." That is using one's resources wisely.

Leading from our strengths means being wise in looking for direction in life. An outstanding architect once built a cluster of office buildings with a central green tree area. When the landscapers asked him where they should lay out the sidewalks, the architect's reply was, "Just plant grass between the buildings." Puzzled about this, they did as he instructed. By late summer, pathways of trodden grass laced the new lawn as people, over time, walked between points of easiest connection. Each path turned in easy curves rather than at right angles, sized according to traffic flow. When fall came, the architect simply paved in the pathways.

Many times we don't receive full satisfaction of our needs. Why? Because we try to blaze our own trails instead of watching for the road the Lord marks out for us. "This is what the Lord says: 'Stand at the crossroads and look; ask for the ancient paths, ask where the good way is, and walk in it, and you will find rest for your souls'" (Jer. 6:16). True freedom flows from our ultimate source of strength and wisdom—the living God!

Do you sometimes feel like you are trying to pound a round peg into a square hole? Have you considered your options in developing your God-given talents and abilities in new ways? If you are not happy with what you are doing, perhaps you're not working from your strengths. You may be forcing your way along in weakness. Identify what you do best. Look for ways to put your strengths into action!

We fully reconnect with daily life. After a separation or divorce, a great opportunity arises to remake our lives in positive and encouraging ways. Daily routines give us comfort and enjoyment. But we also can discover new ways of living. We can reject those routines that no longer work for us.

How can we reconnect with life? Why not write a love letter to God, thanking Him for your mind, body, and skills. Buy ten cards and send them to others who need reassurance. Open your home to others with warmth and hospitality. Join a community organization and bring a Christian presence there. Go to church early and greet folks as they arrive. Be the first to tell others "hello." Find something to compliment in everyone you meet. Pray for someone you do not particularly like. Start a neighborhood Bible study/prayer group or have a block party. Stop and buy something from kids selling from roadside stands. Quietly do one act of kindness for others each week without seeking any recognition or reward. Encourage them to pass it on. Really *listen* and become more aware of what is going on around you. Take time to dream about the future. Think about what life without Christ would be like and the difference He makes each day in your outlook.

Involve yourself in groups and activities with people having interests similar to your own. Church is an obvious choice. But there are many others, including interesting singles groups.[6] Use your freedom to enjoy daily joys. Life is too short to let it pass by unexplored.

Intimacy returns to our relationships. We are understandably on guard against others for a while after a separation or divorce. Losing intimacy, one of the first and greatest casualties in a failing marriage, can leave us shell-shocked for a time. But as emotional beings, we still deeply desire intimacy with someone. We can restore it, beginning with our personal relationship with God. New, close relationships with others grow from that spiritual bond we feel with the Lord.

Intimacy does not come without personal risks, however. It begins with self-disclosure. If we do not open up to others, healthy bonding in new relationships is rare. But treasuring our freedom and slowly feeling more secure about ourselves gives us the confidence to be open and vulnerable to others. Sure, there will be disappointments as we take these risks. First encounters with potential friends can raise our hopes. Sometimes we see that nothing clicks. But then a match will come. And it will feel so good and refreshing to have that special someone take an interest in us.

You'll know when you feel intimacy in a relationship. As Merle Shain has said, "Intimacy is a haven where your vulnerabilities don't humiliate you . . . and all your funny lines are understood. It's knowing someone so well . . . [that it is like] the cartoon in which one old person says to another, 'Which one of us doesn't like broccoli?' It's an eye that catches yours across the room; it's pet names and making plans. . . . . It's a hug when you need it, and even when you don't."[7] If God sustains us, we can risk laying aside our defenses to allow others to know us as we are.

With God's help, we accept full responsibility for our own growth and happiness. God gives us power to change our lives and reach our full potential as His children. We are the agents for making positive change possible in our lives by seeking godly counsel and making wise decisions. We have the personal responsibility to seek everything available that will challenge us to grow and improve.

Being personally responsible for ourselves also means respecting where God has drawn the lines. Awhile after divorce, seeking company of the opposite sex can be a stumbling block with emotional and sexual temptation. Many will tell you that sexual relations outside of marriage are okay, but you know they are not. Though we live in a society and a "formerly married" subculture that's increasingly tolerant of extramarital sex, it makes no difference. Paul tells us:

> It is God's will that you should be holy; that you should avoid sexual immorality; that each of you should learn to control his own body in a way that is holy and honorable, not in passionate lust like the heathen, who do not know God; and that in this matter no one should wrong his brother or take advantage of him. The Lord will punish men for all such sins, as we have already told you and warned you. For God did not call us to be impure, but to live a holy life (1 Thess. 4:3–7).

Dealing with reality means serious problem-solving—not mere appearance management. If we deceive ourselves into pretending to be who we are not, we will never be free. We end up spending time and energy making sure that piling lie upon lie will not backfire and reveal us for who we are. When we can see our faults, confess them to others, and take steps toward correcting them, we walk down the road to freedom.

We can be equally happy and complete either as singles or as remarried persons. What would you receive out of marriage that you wouldn't receive by being single? Psalm 23:1 assures us, "The Lord is my shepherd, I shall lack nothing." Paul tells that in Christ, "I have learned to be content whatever the circumstances" (Phil. 4:11). The danger, of course, is in feeling incomplete as a single person, falsely believing that we will only be happy and free if we remarry. Seeking remarriage out of fear of independence or loneliness is a recipe for disaster. If we remarry because of a negative self-image or a need to have sexual relations, we are sowing seeds of destruction in the new relationship before we begin. If we see positive benefits in remaining single, and we desire to remarry *after* putting our hearts at rest and surrendering to God's will in either event, then considering remarriage is appropriate. We remarry with the sincere desire to share with someone else the abundance of what we have in our own lives, not out of deficit neediness for another person to fulfill us.

Remarriage becomes an option if we desire intimate companionship with another person out of a sacrificial love for him or her, with a goal of working together to fulfill each other's needs in a godly way. It is timely to remarry if we are scripturally free to do so and we believe it is God's will that we marry the person we love after receiving prayer and counsel. In the meantime, as formerly married persons, let us allow God to work in our lives. Allow Him to strengthen our ability to change and adapt to the situations we are in, developing empathy for others. Then we can grow in emotional stability and have good communication with those around us.

We are willing to be vulnerable in our love and risk feeling pain. I recall a story about a man who had to cross a wide river on the ice. Fearing that it might be too thin, he began to crawl on his hands and knees in great terror that he might fall through at any moment. As he neared the opposite shore in sheer exhaustion, however, a neighbor glided past him nonchalantly sitting on a sled loaded with pig iron!

Sometimes we are overcautious, too guarded. What happens when we fear taking risks or become tentative when times are good? The temptation often is to ignore God and rely upon ourselves. As a result, we miss out on some joys in life and opportunities to grow and enjoy our freedom.

Consider this gem of wisdom from an unknown author:

RISK IS FREEDOM
To laugh is to run the risk of looking foolish;
To cry is to take the risk of being sentimental;
Getting close to another person is to risk being compromised;
To show emotion is to risk being known;
To present to people your ideas and dreams is to put them at risk;
To love is to risk not being reciprocated;
To live is to risk dying.

If you allow yourself hope, you run the risk of becoming desperate.
In any attempt to perform, there is the risk of failing.
But risks have to be taken,
Because the greatest danger in life is not to risk anything.

He who never takes risks, does nothing, has nothing, and is nothing.

Maybe he can save himself suffering and pain, but he can't learn,
Or feel, or change, or grow, or love or live.
Chained by certainty, he will be a slave; he will sacrifice being free.
Only by taking risks do you consecrate freedom.

The essence of the Christian of life is to "live by faith, not by sight" (2 Cor. 5:7). This simply means that when God asks for our obedience, we trustingly rely on Him, whether or not we can fully understand the reasons. We become willing to take risks by putting our faith into action during times of uncertainty. It is our *faith* that gives us our footing for action, not what we see.

What can increase our faith? Relying on God in a crisis. What kills our faith? Not putting the faith we have into action. As James tells us, "Faith without deeds is dead" (James 2:26). As Will Rogers once said, "Even if you're on the right road, you'll get run over if you just sit there."

We do not take ourselves too seriously. Do you have a sense of humor about your situation? A divorcee once wrote a poem closing with this verse, "It's so unfair that they took my money. Now I don't even have my honey. She took my house, my cars, my furs. What's left is what I'm wearin', and it looks like hers!" Another person wrote, "When I think of single bliss, which is doomed to be my lot, I make a list of all the men whose wives I'm glad I'm not!" Others say divorce proves one thing: whose mother was right in the beginning! Hurting people can still laugh through the tears!

Look for harmless ways to find some humor in your situation if you can—ways that do not hurt your ex-spouse or others around you. People are drawn to those who are cheerful and optimistic. A person enjoying freedom is someone who laughs frequently and can take good-natured kidding from others. Proverbs 17:22 tells us, "A cheerful heart is good medicine, but a crushed spirit dries up the bones." Allow God and others in your life to help you have a cheerful heart. It is an excellent pain killer.

We are experiencing God's love more deeply day-by-day. We know God feeds and watches over the sparrow. But after divorce, we may feel like the one who fell to earth. God watches over us—twenty-four hours a day for the rest of our lives. Do we truly believe this? It is easier to focus on life if we know that God is backing us up. He is our safety valve in times of trouble.

Asaph certainly knew sorrow and pain in his life. But see where he sought his strength:

> When my heart was grieved and my spirit embittered,
> I was senseless and ignorant; I was a brute beast before
> you. Yet I am always with you; you hold me by my right
> hand. You guide me with your counsel, and afterward you

> will take me into glory. Whom have I in heaven but you?
> And being with you, I desire nothing on earth. My flesh
> and my heart may fail, but God is the strength of my heart
> and my portion forever (Ps. 73:21–26).

If we struggle with experiencing God's love and assurance, it's hard not to worry about the many pitfalls in this life. This is why we need to return continually to reading the Bible. We need reminders of those great and precious promises God gives us to participate in the divine nature and escape the corruption in the world caused by evil desires (2 Pet. 1:4).

We need to communicate with God more through prayer. Prayer is the language of this most intimate, spiritual relationship. It is having daily communion with Someone who genuinely cares about us. When we talk with God, we heal where we are hurting the most. We begin to understand ourselves better. It is a peaceful time for release, relief, joy, and renewal.[8]

As Christians, we are free—and can truly experience what that means. But let us also be aware of the ongoing struggle we face. The cycle many experience is to break out of bondage with spiritual faith and to experience freedom. But as freedom provides us with whatever we need, we may become selfish because we fear losing what we've gained. This selfishness leads to complacency and apathy. If unchecked, we can eventually fall into a dependency or addiction to alcohol, drugs, or sex. We feel like we need something that numbs the pain while giving us a temporary thrill to relieve the boredom. Those dependencies and addictions return us to bondage. This worldly rhythm plays itself many times over if we are not careful.

Therefore, our task is to continually test everything with God's help. We must remain alert to where we are in life so that we can hold onto what is pure and good (1 Cor. 15:2; 1 Thess. 5:21).

Do you see the common themes in recovery from separation or divorce and the freedom to live a fulfilling life in Christ? There is an optimism in being glad to be alive. There is a commitment to and daily involvement with God and other people. Life calls us to be active and engaged in new challenges. When we lose a relationship, we cultivate an ability to adapt by making new relationships. Our faith in God increases as we face our pain and depend upon Him more. We keep our sense of humor and avoid being easily angered. We ease into a peace that surpasses all understanding. These measures make our lives a springboard toward a joyful existence!

A Sincere Plea
To Those Who Have Not Decided

The late Bart Giamatti was speaking about baseball when he said this, but he could have been talking about an unhappy marriage that ends in divorce: "It is designed to break your heart. The game begins in the spring when everything else begins again. It blossoms in the summer, filling the afternoons and evenings. Then, as soon as the chill rains come, it stops and leaves you to face the fall alone." Divorce never fails to leave a trail of tears. The Chinese proverb is true that states: "In the broken nest there are no whole eggs."

To those still thinking about divorce, consider the fruit of your decision. By the mid-1980s, the annual divorce rate was over 1,160,000, or nearly half the weddings. That means over two divorces every minute of every day! A century ago in the U.S., there was only one divorce for every eighteen weddings. This rate increased only gradually (except for a brief surge after World War II) until the 1960s. But now, we have experienced a divorce explosion where the rate of divorce has more than tripled. In 1998, approximately 10 percent of all adults (19.4 million) were "currently divorced," according to the U.S. Census Bureau.

In her book *The Case Against Divorce*, Diane Medved found that divorce left men and women emotionally distraught for an average of seven years, some even for decades. The following letter from a divorced man to the late advice columnist Ann Landers some years ago gives us some clues as to why:

> Dear Ann Landers: Ten years ago I left my wife and four teenagers to marry my secretary with whom I'd been having an affair. I felt I couldn't live without her. When my wife found out about us, she went to pieces.
>
> We were divorced. My wife went to work and did a good job educating the boys. I gave her the house and part of my retirement fund.
>
> I am fairly happy in my second marriage, but I'm beginning to see things in a different light. It hit me when I was a guest at our eldest son's wedding. That's all I was—a guest. I am no longer considered part of the family. My

first wife knew everyone present, and they showered her with affection.

She remarried, and her husband has been taken inside the circle that was once ours. They gave the rehearsal dinner and sat next to my sons and their sweethearts.

I was proud to have a pretty young wife at my side. But it didn't make up for the pain when I realized that my children no longer love me. They treated me with courtesy, but there was no affection or real caring.

I miss my sons, especially around holiday time. I am going to try to build some bridges, but the prospects don't look very promising after being out of their lives for 10 years. It is going to be difficult re-entering now that they have a stepdad they like.

I'm writing in the hope that others will consider the ramifications before they jump. Just sign me—Second Thoughts in PA

Dear Second Thoughts: I could use the rest of this column to reflect on "sowing and reaping," but it would serve no useful purpose. I'm sure you also know that a father can't disappear for 10 years and expect his sons to welcome him back with open arms. Sorry, mister. Your wife has earned their respect and devotion, and what's left over is going to the man who is now making their mother happy.

Others have discovered firsthand that the grass is not greener on the other side of the fence:

Dear Ann Landers: It's time someone told the world what it's like for a woman to be widowed or divorced. I hope your female readers will find this letter useful. I'm 45. People say I'm very attractive and that I look 35. I am financially secure, have a good job, own my home and have two children, ages 20 and 22. I became a widow three years ago. Here's the true picture:

Eligible men between 40 and 55 are virtually nonexistent. Your pool of "prospects" will be in singles bars, parent groups and singles organizations. The ratio of women to men is about 20-1. So, if you are contemplating divorce and are 40 or older, take another look. Is there any possibility that your marriage can be salvaged? The quality of available men will shock you. If your spouse is an ordinary, run-of-the-mill guy, he will be snatched up immediately. YOU will not be so fortunate.

Available women are a dime a dozen. If you're not aggressive or gorgeous, you'll spend a lot of time alone. I invested $2,000 in a vacation, and all I got out of it was the knowledge that I'd better learn how to be single again.

When you become [single] . . . everyone wants to be your friend—for about three months—then you're on your own. It's not that people stop caring, they just need to get on with their own lives.

My experiences with singles groups have been disastrous. . . . The divorced ones are bitter and angry and talk of nothing but their ex-husbands, how difficult it is to get child support and how badly they were treated.

The prognosis is dismal. Once you've been married, it's lousy to be alone. Sign me—Not Bitter, Just Realistic.[9]

Are you absolutely sure that you can accept a divorce? Is it what you and your spouse want? Have you counted the cost? Are you willing to pay the price? Doris Mae Goldberg sadly expresses the painful aftermath and loneliness of surviving a divorce this way:

I have lost my husband, but I am not supposed to mourn.
I have lost my children; they don't know to whom they belong.
I have lost my relatives; they do not approve.
I have lost his relatives; they blame me.
I have lost my friends; they don't know how to act.
I feel I have lost my church; do they think I have sinned too much?
I am afraid of the future, I am ashamed of the past,
I am confused about the present.

347

I am so alone,
I feel so lost.
God, please stay by me,
You are all I have left.[10]

Divorce is causing our society to disintegrate. In his 1947 book *Family and Civilization*, sociologist and historian Carle Zimmerman compared the cultural and corresponding family disintegration in several societies. He identified eight patterns of behavior contributing to the breakdown:

- Marriage loses its sacredness and is frequently broken by divorce.
- The traditional marriage ceremony loses its meaning.
- Feminist movements abound.
- Public disrespect for parents and authority in general increases.
- An acceleration of juvenile delinquency, promiscuity, and rebellion occurs.
- More people with traditional marriages refuse to accept family responsibilities.
- There is a growing desire for and acceptance of adultery.
- There is an increasing interest in and spread of sexual perversions, and sex-related crimes exist.[11]

See any parallels to our society today? If Zimmerman's observations are correct, our private crisis in the breakdown of our families is a picture of the challenge America is facing today.

What about the children? Erik Ericson once observed, "The most deadly of all sins is the mutilation of a child's spirit." How will divorce scar our children? How will they cope? Pat Conroy, who wrote about his own divorce in *Death of a Marriage*, sadly noted, "Divorces without children are minor-league divorces. To look into the eyes of your children and to tell them that you are mutilating their family and changing all their tomorrows is an act of desperate courage that I never want to repeat. . . . It felt as though I had doused my entire family with gasoline and struck a match."

In her classic book, *Second Chances*, clinical psychologist Judith Wallerstein concluded her ten-year study of children of divorce with this disturbing message: they don't easily get over it. More than a third of the children suffered clinical depression and functioned poorly five years after a divorce. After ten years, 35 percent had poor relationships with both parents. After a decade, 75 percent still felt rejected by their fathers. Time did not take away the fear of trusting people. It adversely affected their own family relationships. In a *Reader's Digest* article, Wallerstein was quoted as warning: "Divorce is deceptive. Legally it is a single event, but psychologically it is a chain of events strung through time that forever changes the lives of the people involved."[12]

In commenting on Wallerstein's findings, writer David Neff has noted that "painless divorce" is a myth and a contradiction in terms. For example, when we call our children our "flesh and blood" but divorce their parent, we are cutting ourselves off from a family member that can be like the amputation of a limb. Neff astutely points out that one with a severed limb can feel phantom pain in the missing member for years. Likewise, severed family relationships will continue to ache.

Divorce not only kills a marriage, it can also steal away your longevity in life. In a study of 7,651 people across America conducted by the University of California-San Francisco, researchers believe that divorce causes unmarried middle-age men and women to face twice the risk of dying within ten years as those still living with their spouses.

The study found that 23 percent of all men between forty-five and fifty-four who lived alone or with another single person died within a decade. In contrast, only 11 percent of married men died during that same period. Of unmarried women in the same age group, 7.7 percent died compared to only 4 percent of married women. "Both men who live alone and those who live with someone other than a spouse are equally disadvantaged for survival," remarked Maradee Davis, an associate professor of epidemiology and biostatistics. "The critical factor seems to be the presence of a spouse."

Divorce leads to other breakdowns in society as well. The faltering American economy and the federal deficit are problems which will be with us for many decades to come. Skyrocketing consumer bankruptcies fuel these fires. Bankruptcies rose from 289,979 in 1980 to more than 640,000 in 1990, and the number is still rising. From 1980 to 2004, personal bankruptcy filings increased 443.45 percent. More than 2 million Americans—an all-time high—petitioned for bankruptcy in 2005, with 619,588 filings in October alone, according to the American Bankruptcy Institute. What is causing the increase? One reason may be that bankruptcy filings roughly approximate the rise in the American divorce rate. As Americans divorce, financial obligations of the marriage often fall disproportionately on one party who is unwilling to pay the debt. One spouse sues the other. When the debt is overwhelming, either or both spouses file for bankruptcy. As this trend continues, businesses and credit providers suffer. Soon we all feel the pinch and pay the price.

Fear of divorce influences many people to forego marriage. Are people becoming more cynical about marriage? Data from the Census Bureau confirms that the number of marriages has been declining. The proportion of Americans who married in 1991 was lower than any year since 1965. Men in the thirty-five to thirty-nine age group who had never married increased to 17.6 percent in 1991, up from 7.8 percent in 1980. The percentage of never-married women in the same age group increased from 6.2 percent in 1980 to 11.7 percent in 1991. These trends have escalated in the twenty-first century.

Every action we take has a ripple effect on others, perhaps our entire country. Each of us has a personal responsibility to become part of the solution to this tragedy rather than passively become another statistic and part of the problem.

What has become of our marriage vows? Newlyweds in the Netherlands have a custom as they enter their house for the first time as husband and wife. They enter through a special door and lock it off from use again until one spouse dies. Only then is the body removed through that same door. God's design for marriage is a lot like that house. Two enter the house through a narrow door to become "one flesh" for life. Vows made in a loving commitment before God between a husband and wife are the lock on that special door. The door to the world is not meant to be opened again until death takes one mate from the other.

Where is the commitment spouses make to one another? In his book *Courtship After Marriage*, Zig Ziglar tells the story of Sir Edmund Hillary, the first man in history to reach the summit of Mount Everest. All the way, Hillary was accompanied by Tenzing Norgay, his trusted native guide. As they were coming back down the mountain tied to each other, Sir Edmund lost his footing and began to slide. But Tenzing kept the line taut and saved both of them from falling to their deaths by digging his ax into the ice. That is what we need in more marriages when lovers start to slip. Where are the heroes who dig in their ax to save the couple from divorce?

Marlo Thomas once said, "A successful marriage means taking a vow that only one of you will go crazy at a time." You may feel that your spouse is causing you to break that vow, but do not give up!

If you or your spouse have not fully decided to accept divorce as a final solution, my best advice to you is this: Do not do it. Stick it out. Make your marriage work if you are not the victim of domestic violence. Sometimes the better comes after the worst in a marriage. But the best commitment in marriage is not to marry for better or for worse, but for good!

If you are the unwilling participant in a divorce, the thoughts and suggestions in this book are given to help you have the mind of Christ (1 Cor. 2:16; Phil. 4:7). It will cost you something to handle your situation responsibly, reasonably, and lovingly. You can always find ways to come out on top financially in a divorce. You can beat your spouse at the divorce game. But is it right? Is it best? How much destruction must be suffered to win? Finally, will it please God?

In his novel *Cannery Row*, John Steinbeck poignantly noted: "The things we admire in men, kindness and generosity, openness, honesty, understanding and feeling, are the concomitants of failure in our system. And those traits we detest, sharpness, greed, acquisitiveness, meanness, egotism and self-interest, are the traits of success. And while men admire the quality of the first, they love the produce of the second."

Are we, as Steinbeck says, agreeing with qualities of mercy and forgiveness but falling prey to expediency and self-protection at the expense of others? Will we go for the jugular vein in our divorce situations whenever the going gets tough or it becomes easy to do so?

If you have any control over the divorce process, think it over—carefully.

And in the End

While writing this book, my friends remarked, "Writing out your thoughts must help you work through your feelings." My consistent response has been, "Well, I could have had more of a catharsis watching a Florida Gators football game. Writing a book is hard work!" Frankly, what kept me going was the thought of presenting this book to readers like you. You are the one I had in mind when I didn't feel like writing. Your prayer for help from someone who understands helped me persevere. This book is my love letter to you as you cope with your own marriage situation.

I have two goals in sharing this book: if you are *seeking* a divorce, to make sure it is what you really want, that you have counted the cost and can face the consequences; and if you are *proceeding* with a divorce as an unwilling participant, to provide you with ways to minimize the damage.

Your marriage situation is unique. It may not be best to try to shoe-horn all the solutions suggested in this book into your particular situation. Every problem you face may have circumstances and dimensions that no author could foresee.[13] Perhaps you have already made regrettable decisions that cannot be undone. We all use our best creative resources to peer dimly into the future and prepare for a storm as best we can. Even so, as we shelter ourselves against the hurricane of divorce, it may still tear our lives apart in unexpected ways. Therefore, always remember to be flexible. Adjusting to changes and continually revising courses of action are crucial.

In the end, you must decide how you will use the this book. Remember the analogy in the introduction about the Sea of Galilee, the Jordan River, and the Dead Sea? How will you receive what you have learned? Will you consider solutions to your problems but fail to act? Will the fear of failure paralyze you? Will you isolate yourself, hoping your situation will miraculously improve? Do not limit your thinking or seal yourself off from creative solutions of your own. Share your problems with your professional counselor, legal advisor, and friends competent to counsel you. Since they will see different viewpoints, their input will help make your decisions sound. Make every effort to help your marriage last. As much as it depends upon you, strive to live at peace with your spouse (Rom. 12:18). If your marriage must fail, let it down gently. Be faithful and gracious in defeat. As Paul encourages us:

> Therefore, I urge you, brothers, in view of God's mercy, to offer your bodies as living sacrifices, holy and pleasing to God—which is your spiritual worship. Do not conform any longer to the pattern of this world, but be transformed by the renewing of your mind. Then you will be able to test and approve what God's will is—his good, pleasing and perfect will (Rom. 12:1–2).

Much of the Bible is written to those who already believe in Jesus, the Son of God (1 John 5:13). Much of this book is written to the same group. As Jesus says in Matthew 13:16, "Blessed are your eyes because they see, and your ears because they hear." If anything in these pages has helped you to see and hear His voice, thank Him.

We know that surviving a separation or divorce takes its toll on us—

physically, spiritually, financially, and emotionally. If divorce truly was unavoidable in your situation, after it is over and you feel a closure to your own situation, celebrate in a manner that is healthy and meaningful to you. Reflect on what you have learned. Thank those who helped you make it through. Feel a sense of fulfillment that you have survived one of the most severe personal crises that any human faces in a lifetime.

The Indians have a wonderful saying: "When you were born, you cried, and the world rejoiced. Live your life in such a manner that when you die, the world cries, and you rejoice." The challenge is ours. We have a wonderful opportunity, born out of pain, to comfort and serve others. With the Lord's help, we can make the world a better place. But *nothing* in this life is more important than our personal relationship with God. Allow yourself to become a trophy of God's grace and power so that at the end of your life, we can rejoice together in the presence of the King of kings. Yearn to hear Him say, "Well done, good and faithful servant!"

May God bless you as you seek Him as a single and formerly married person. As an unknown observer has written before,

May you have enough happiness to keep you sweet;
trials to keep you strong;
sorrow to keep you human;
hope to keep you happy;
failure to keep you humble;
success to keep you eager;
friends to give you comfort;
wealth to meet your needs;
enthusiasm to make you look forward to tomorrow;
determination to make each day better than the day before.

God loves you. He *always* will.

To him who loves us and has freed us from our sins by his blood, and has made us to be a kingdom and priests to serve his God and Father—to him be glory and power forever and ever! Amen (Rev. 1:5–6).

Appendix A

Form of "Tough Love" Letter

The following sample letter is an example of how you can write your own "tough love" letter to your spouse, as we discussed in chapter 9. Do not make the mistake of copying this letter to send to your spouse. However, feel free to use any of the ideas and concepts in telling your mate how you feel in your own words.

This letter to your spouse needs to be firm but fair. You are setting boundaries and helping your spouse feel the consequences of leaving the marriage. It is critical that he or she knows that you disagree with the divorce decision being made, but that you can only go so far in trying to stop it.

Dear [Husband/Wife],

This is a letter that is probably long past due.

I've been through some very tough times since you decided to leave me, as you know. At first, I didn't want to face the possibility of life without you. To a person like me who expected to marry only once and to remain committed for life, it is an enormous and emotionally severe shock to see our relationship come unraveled.

So many people have advised me to "Let go!" of you that it's finally sinking in. It's curious how a person loses perspective by being so close to a problem. It becomes difficult to see issues clearly. But in the last few weeks, I've been able to pull back a little bit from our difficulties and see things in a new light. God has called us to peace. If someone wants to go, *let them go!*

After much soul-searching and prayer, I want you to know that you are free from me, and I am free from you. This will be my declaration of independence in as firm but as loving a manner as I can say it.

Do you remember that night you told me you wanted a divorce? Well, that was a night I will never forget. You told me that you felt trapped in our marriage and you just had to be free. Do you remember the next day when we talked about things? I asked you about various options. Could we work things out? Could we go to a counselor? Was a trial separation possible? You said no to everything. You wanted *out!*

Against the advice of virtually everyone, however, I became passive and tried to appease you because I loved you so much. I offered to do many things to help you during our separation because I worried about you. But now I think I made a big mistake in doing all this. You made a decision to be free of me, and here I was, still invading your life. I didn't honor your decision as I should, and I have paid the price for it.

As I look back over these past months, I can see how I have reacted with panic and desperation. I have begged. I have pleaded. I have tried to hold onto you, which controlled your freedom. But now I see how much of a doormat I have made of myself in trying to pursue you.

Now I am beginning to understand how trapped you must feel. Only now am I realizing that our marriage is on the line. As you started to pull away from me, I felt panic and pursued you. But it was too late. You said you felt smothered by me. I can see why. The more you struggled to get your freedom (or even a

355

little breathing room), the more I, in my panic, clung to you. I can see now that my actions were possessive and demanding—not really loving on my part. Please forgive me for this.

Early on in our relationship, when we were dating, you said that you were in awe of me and held me in deep respect. Remember? You married me of your own free choice. I did not force you to do it. It was a decision you made to respect and honor me as your mate without pressure from me. That's what made it so special to me. But now there is no mutual respect and admiration. There is no *mutual acceptance*. There was a time that I could do no wrong in your eyes. Now it appears that I can do nothing right. There's absolutely nothing I can do about this. But I don't want you to feel like you are being held in our marriage against your will.

I have to let you go. I cannot force you to stay now any more than I could have forced you to marry me many years ago. And now, with your feelings for me being what they are, I can see how I have been losing my own self-respect and compromising my own self-esteem in pursuing you. While my real crime over the past months is probably in loving you too much after you walked out on me, the punishment that this has wrought on my psyche is not healthy for me as a person. Well, I am tired of expending enormous emotional and physical energy and sending it on a one-way trip in your direction. It's depleting me, and it's smothering you.

As everything comes into clearer focus for me, here are the things I need to share with you to break out of the unhealthy patterns both of us are in right now:

Freedom. That's a precious thing. While we are married to each other, I don't own you and you don't own me. I cannot, and I will not, deprive you of your freedom any more unless you voluntarily surrender it to me, as I have surrendered mine to you up until now. But now, you are free from me, and I am free from you. I am withdrawing my freedom from you. If you ever want to allow me to share your space again, then I will let you share mine, but not until then. I will no longer try to stop you from leaving.

Divorce. If you want it, you can have it. This is not what I want. It never has been an option for me. But if it is what you want, then so be it. I accept it. I'm not giving up on you. I'm just honoring your decision.

I'm going to start today by being totally honest with close friends and relatives who ask about you. If they ask how you are, I will tell them that I do not know because we are separated. If they ask whether we are getting divorced, I will say that I think so, but that the final decision is up to you. They will know that this is not what I want, but I am not going to fight it.

If divorce is inevitable, then I hope we can go through it and settle our business affairs peacefully between ourselves without a lawyer coming between us. My hope is that we can leave the lawyers to advise us of things we may not have considered and to get the court work done—nothing more. If we cannot do this, then I'll deal with it in due course.

I have asked you to tell me what you feel you need to settle our affairs. If it is reasonable, I will do whatever it takes to settle up with you quickly. If it is not, then we'll let the judge decide.

As for any friendship between us after the divorce, I'm sorry, but there's just no way. I cannot handle that. When the door closes on our marriage, as it is doing now, it's over. Pure and simple. When the divorce is finalized, I'm going to do my best to forget you were ever in my life. I have to. It's just too painful otherwise.

You asked me if I would remarry after our divorce. Until now, I never thought of remarriage to anyone else. But I'm thinking about it now. I have to consider my options. So when you leave me, as you are doing now, I intend to seek other relationships after our divorce is final without regret. I like being married. I enjoy being a parent. If you don't want a married life with me, I have faith that the Lord will work in my life and show me what's best. If you do not want me, then I believe others will.

Boundaries. We've talked about them a lot, but we've never honored them. From my perspective, I feel like I have made my life an open book to you and put all my cards on the table. I have spoken my heart to you and told you exactly how I feel. I feel you have been somewhat open about certain things, but for the most part you've held your cards close to your chest. I feel you have been evasive, mysterious, and deceptive. I don't know what you're doing with your life. I have no idea whether you're going to church, who you spend your time with, or whether you even read your Bible. But you know all those things about me. I have tolerated this double standard for too long. I guess I just loved you so much that I was willing to do anything you demanded, just to keep you from leaving me.

I have heard your complaints about how the laundromat was tearing up your clothes and how you missed using the washer and dryer at the house. I did feel sorry for you—too much for my own good. But you are on your own now. You have put me out of your life. You should do the responsible thing now and take care of yourself without relying on me. Your clothes may tear up, but that's the way you'll have to live your life. If it's any consolation, my feeling is that my life and emotions have been torn up a whole lot worse than your clothes.

We absolutely must set boundaries and get our lives untwined from each other. Therefore, please do not call me anymore, except to the extent you need to give me a message or discuss winding up our business affairs. Don't visit me anymore. Don't do anything for me. I won't contact you either unless it's about something you need to know. I will give you all your keys, and I will expect mine from you. I will leave your mail outside the front door of the house so that you can pick it up on your way to work if you want. But you will not see me, and I will not see you.

I am going to take all the pictures of you and me together at home, the office, and anywhere else and put them in a safe place. The things you left behind at the house are going into storage. Until we are divorced, the only thing tangible reminding me of our marriage will be the ring around my finger. When we get divorced, that comes off too. There will be no more "love gifts" or help from me. We are going to live totally separate lives if we are not going to be married.

Counseling. I have never regretted getting counseling. We both were long overdue. But from the very beginning, you made it very clear that you were attending solely for "divorce counseling" and nothing else. Nothing ever changed that. I, on the other hand, came for marriage counseling and for reconciliation if possible. While I have learned a lot with the help of our counselor, I feel the time has come for me to stop. If you change your mind and want to get marriage counseling, then let me know. If you don't, I'm gone.

Trust. When you told me that someone else had come between us, I lost all trust in you. Up until that time, I trusted you 100 percent. I never checked up on you. I took you at your word. I wasn't perfect, but I never violated your trust by getting involved with anyone else since I pledged myself to you. I feel that you have violated my trust and broken faith with me in our marriage. Nothing that

I have done to offend you—nothing—could ever justify this action. It became a whole new situation when this happened.

If I'm no longer special to you, then I'm just one of the crowd. Actually, I'm a little less than others in the crowd because you know me, and all the others are always going to appear more mysterious and exciting. Well, I cannot live with that. If you really think you can go and find a person who loves God and loves you more, then go. That is between you and the Lord.

This letter is no power play on my part. I'm not playing games. This is no bluff. I am being honest so that I can live with myself and have a good night's sleep once again. There are limits to what I can tolerate, and I'm way over my limit already in this matter. I have been pushed, prodded, tested, abused, and had my self-esteem assaulted enough. I'm through with trying to chase after you. You're going to be history very quick if that is what you want.

I'm not perfect, but neither are you. The fact is, I have always accepted you, but you are rejecting me. Of course, that's your choice in exercising your freedom and independence. The bottom line is that if we cannot accept each other as Christ does each of us, then it is best for you to go. I am absolutely, positively through preaching at you, pulling after you, pining away for you, being passive, and appeasing you.

This entire experience has been painful beyond belief—a real nightmare! But I'm going to make it. I'm going to sleep deeply through the night once again without worrying about you. The Lord has been with me thus far, and He'll go with me in the future.

You and I had some wonderful times together. But those times are gone. I will continue to pray for you. I trust that God will guide you in the years ahead. But I am making no more promises beyond what I have already made. Now I'm going to do everything possible to remove you from my life and stop punishing myself for what's happened. It's not going to be easy. You were my special love—my only love. You were the only one I ever really wanted. But that was then, and this is now. God bless you. I will miss you.

Appendix B

Financial Disclosure Letter

The following sample financial disclosure letter is an example to help you explore property settlement possibilities with your spouse, as we discussed in chapter 12. Do not copy this letter. Instead, use it as a guide in preparing your own letter. This letter should be delivered with copies of the documents described in the letter at a face-to-face meeting with your spouse, if reasonably possible.

IMPORTANT NOTE: SINCE A LETTER LIKE THE FOLLOWING SAMPLE COULD SIGNIFICANTLY AFFECT YOUR LEGAL RIGHTS, DO NOT SEND ANY SUCH COMMUNICATION TO YOUR SPOUSE WITHOUT FIRST REVIEWING THE FULL CONTENT IN ADVANCE WITH YOUR LEGAL ADVISOR.

Dear [Husband/Wife],

Please forgive the "businesslike" tone of this letter, but I am assuming that you will show this letter and all of the papers I am giving to you to your attorney. Accordingly, I must try in this letter to walk both of us through some matters that will be important from a legal standpoint if you remain decided that you want to divorce me.

Please be very careful to keep all the information in this letter and in the attached folder strictly confidential between you and your attorney while we are trying to work out an acceptable settlement.

In the folder with this letter are copies of documents of our financial matters as I have itemized them below. Also, on the various copies of the property that either of us owns, I have noted those which in my opinion are marital assets and those which are not. If you disagree with anything I've marked down, let's talk about it. Here's what the folder contains:

1. All our income and expense reports for the past three years. (These reports include all of my income and expenses, but do not include yours for the time we have been separated since I do not know what those are.)

2. Copies of federal and state tax returns for the past three years.

3. A copy of statements from all of the checking and other accounts that I have in my name. (I do not have yours, but assume that you will advise me of this soon.)

4. Statements as to all stock that we own.

5. A brief summary of information as to any pension plans or retirement plans that you or I have.

6. Copies of various appraisals and invoices of all of the personal property we acquired during our marriage that I could find.

7. Copies of our automobile titles.

8. A list of all real property owned by either of us, and copies of all appraisals that have been completed over the years as to the value.

9. A listing of all life, health, disability, automobile, and homeowner's insurance policies that we currently have in force (to the best of my knowledge).

10._____ *(add anything else that applies to your situation)*

For the purpose of our attorneys preparing a settlement agreement for us, it would be helpful to them if we can both agree on certain facts relating to our marriage. As best as I can recall, here are some of those facts (which you may feel free to correct if there is anything that is in error or inadvertently omitted). I have stated them using "You" to refer to yourself, "I" or "Me" for myself, and "We" or "Us" for both of us, to make matters clearer.

1. You and I are presently husband and wife. We were married on _____ at the church in _____.

2. On the date of the marriage, I had already completed _____ of my education and paid for the same by _____. During the marriage, I completed _____ of my education and paid for the same by _____.

3. On the date of the marriage, You had already completed _____ of your education and paid for the same by _____. During the marriage, You completed _____ of your education and paid for the same by _____.

4. Prior to the date of the marriage, I had already worked as a _____, earning _____. During the marriage, I worked as a _____, earning _____.

5. Prior to the date of the marriage, You had already worked as a _____, earning _____. During the marriage, You worked as a _____, earning _____.

6. On the date of the marriage, I owned the following property: _____, and You owned: _____. During the marriage, we purchased and still own: _____.

7. During the marriage, You and I handled our finances and purchases of household and personal needs in this manner: _____.

8. The following children were born during our marriage: _____. No child is presently conceived, and no further children are presently contemplated by Us.

9. The decision to divorce was made by _____ for the following reason(s): _____.

10. On _____, We separated and lived in different locations as follows: _____. During this separation We have, at all times, maintained independent households, and We have independently conducted our personal lives as We believed to be in our best interest.

11. On _____, We voluntarily entered into marital counseling with _____ and met jointly and separately from time to time in a good faith effort to try and reconcile our marriage. All such efforts at reconciliation have not been successful to date.

12. Both of Us desire to amicably settle our personal and property claims and demands with each other. The provisions of this letter are not in any way intended to facilitate or promote the procurement of a divorce. However, You presently believe that You can no longer live together with Me because our marital difficulties are so deep and so substantial that no reasonable effort could eradicate the same so as to enable Us to live together in a normal marital relationship. Therefore, You no longer want to continue with the marriage relationship at the present time.

13. At the present time, the mental competency of neither of Us is in question or dispute for the purpose of reaching an amicable settlement. Both of Us have resided in the State of _____ for a period of _____ prior to the date of this letter.

14. At all times during our settlement discussions, each of Us has had the benefit of independent legal counsel to the extent desired. You have been represented by _____, and I have been represented by _____.

I hope this will help both of us in working out a fair and reasonable settlement, as I hope and pray we will in short order. Look everything over, think it through, and I will meet with you again at _____ to answer any questions you have or to provide you with any additional information you need.

Once again, please excuse the "businesslike" tone of this letter. This is not how I enjoy writing to you. I hope you understand that discussing this matter is a necessary part of the very unpleasant divorce process. Always remember that this is not what I want for us. I am honoring your decision as to what you feel you want to do with your life.

[See chapter 12 for a sample settlement letter.]

Appendix C

Attorney-Client Legal Representation
Agreement Letter

In chapter 13 we reviewed many matters involved in selecting and hiring an attorney. The following letters together form a sample legal representation agreement between a lawyer and client. These letters are more detailed than most typical legal representation agreements. This is done to help you understand the issues and know what to expect when you hire your own attorney. The first letter is sent from the lawyer to the client addressing what the attorney believes to be important in undertaking the representation:

Sample Letter from Attorney to Client

Dear Mr. Client:

This will confirm our office conference of _____, 20___ at which time you requested our Firm to represent you in the dissolution of your marriage currently pending in _____ Court (Case No._____).

_____ _____, Esquire, one of our Family Law partners, will be overseeing this matter with the assistance of her Associate, _____, if you have no objection. We trust that you will feel free to establish regular communication with each other as this matter proceeds.

Our fees shall be charged on an hourly basis during this representation. Our present (20___) range of rates for partners is $_____ to $_____ per hour for our most senior partners. Ms. _____'s present hourly rate, which shall apply through the end of calendar year 20___ , will be $_____ . Naturally, the hourly rates for our associates who may work on this case, such as Mr. _____ whose hourly rate is $ _____, will be lower. We will make every effort to use associates and other support staff in our office to do some of the legal work involved at lower hourly rates as the opportunity arises in order to limit your expense in this regard.

In general, our Firm will provide legal services to you in accordance with provisions set forth in our Standard Terms and Conditions, attached hereto and made a part of this letter agreement. If this matter should continue beyond December 31, 20___, our rates are subject to adjustment on a semi-annual basis in keeping with existing Firm policy to take into consideration increases in operating costs, but you will be notified in writing if there is any increase.

The file shall be billed, together with out-of-pocket disbursements made on your behalf, on a monthly basis (although we may elect to bill this matter on a less frequent basis as a courtesy to you). Our statements cover both fees and our usual and customary disbursements advanced on your behalf. If our statements for professional services are outstanding for over 30 days after issuance, in compliance with Firm policy we must reserve the right to withdraw from this representation. However, we are confident that this situation will not arise in this representation.

Above all, we want to reassure you that, as usual, we will provide you with the best legal representation available in this matter. If at any time you have any ques-

362

tions or comment regarding our work or any statements received from us, please do not hesitate to contact Ms. _____ or the undersigned at your earliest opportunity. (For your records, the undersigned's direct telephone number is noted in the letterhead above, while Ms. _____'s direct telephone number is _____) We have 24-hour voicemail available to take any message you wish to leave for us if we are temporarily unavailable. Above all, we will make every effort to please and accommodate you and strive for fairness in all endeavors.

Trusting that the above is acceptable to you, we are pleased to proceed on this basis. Toward that end, kindly sign the enclosed copy of this letter at the place indicated below and return the same to us in the stamped, self-addressed envelope also enclosed for your convenience. If any of the above is not in accord with your prior agreement and understanding, kindly notify us immediately.

Very truly yours,
HONEST ABE LAW FIRM
Joseph Friendly
Managing Partner

RECEIPT of this letter agreement is hereby acknowledged and the terms and conditions hereof agreed to as of the _____ day of 20___ .

_____
William Client

Standard Terms and Conditions of Engagement

1. Fees: We take into account many factors in billing for services rendered. The principal factor is generally our schedule of hourly rates. Most statements for services are the product of the hours worked multiplied by the hourly rates for the attorneys and legal assistants who did the work.

If the firm plays a material role in obtaining a result with benefits to the client which are disproportionate to the time expended, we may propose a fee which exceeds our base hourly charges in order to more fairly reflect the value of our services. If the matter is one which requires our services over a long period of time, our monthly billings would ordinarily be on an hourly basis, reserving until the conclusion of the matter any additional fee based upon such factors as the difficulty of the assignment, novelty of the issues or the solution, time pressures associated with performance, uniqueness of the services rendered by the firm, significance of the result obtained, and benefits to the client.

Our schedule of hourly rates for attorneys and other members of the professional staff is based on years of experience, specialization in training and practice, and level of professional attainment. Currently our hourly rates are reconsidered semiannually.

2. Costs: It is often necessary for us to incur expenses for items such as travel, lodging, meals, toll telephone calls, witness fees, experts, investigators, printing costs and deposition transcripts. Similarly, some matters require substantial amounts of costly ancillary services such as photocopying and computerized legal research. In order to allocate these expenses fairly and keep billable rates as low as possible for those matters which do not involve such expenditures, these items are separately itemized on our statements as "costs advanced" or "disbursements."

Some "costs advanced" represent out-of-pocket costs, some represent an allocation of overhead costs associated with the items, and others represent a combination of both factors. From time to time we may ask you to pay some more significant costs directly to the vendors who provide the materials or services we have used on your behalf.

3. Billings: Our statements generally are prepared and mailed during the month following the month in which services are rendered and costs advanced. We expect payment promptly following the statement date. In litigation matters in which a money judgment is rendered in the client's favor, we shall have a lien on the process thereof to the extent of any unpaid fees or costs.

4. Late payments: We are confident that our clients make every effort to pay us promptly. Occasionally, however, a client has difficulty in making timely payment. To avoid burdening those clients who pay their statements promptly with higher fees reflecting the added costs we incur as a result of clients who are delinquent, we reserve the right to impose a service charge of 1 percent per month for late payments. In no event will the service charge be greater than permitted by applicable law. In the unlikely event that we are required to institute legal proceedings to collect fees and costs owed by the client, the prevailing party would be entitled to reasonable attorneys' fees and other costs of collection. Naturally, we do not expect that any of the provisions of this paragraph will have to be applied to any particular client, and look forward to a wholly amicable relationship. Our clients shall also agree that we shall have all general, possessory, and retaining liens, and all special or charging liens, provided by law, and a lien on your files and records to the extent necessary to ensure the satisfaction of all of your obligations under this retainer agreement.

5. Advance for disbursements: Occasionally it is necessary for us to require payment of anticipated out-of-pocket expenses before we render services. This could happen when we are about to start a trial or similarly large undertaking. In addition, when we foresee that "costs advanced" on a matter may amount to a substantial sum, we may ask the client to pay them directly or to fund them in advance.

6. Termination: The client has the right to terminate our representation at any time. We have the same right, subject to an obligation to give the client reasonable notice to arrange alternative representation.

7. Applicable law: The laws of the State of _____ will govern the interpretation of this agreement.

Some Revisions to the Attorney's Agreement to Consider

The following is a sample response letter from the client to this attorney. It will give you some ideas on how to protect yourself from a number of potential misunderstandings regarding your lawyer's representation, as well as explore ways to limit your legal expense. You might consider sending a letter of this type back as a cover letter to your signed copy of your own attorney's Legal Representation Agreement. You should expect that many reasonable attorneys will not agree to all of the points in the following letter, but it will open the way for you to discuss some of the more important issues and win some concessions.

Dear Mr. Friendly:

I am pleased that your Firm will be representing me and am confident that your work will reflect favorably upon me. I am also aware that the attorney-client relationship must be founded on confidentiality, good communication, and my trust in you that you will do the best work possible on my behalf. However, please understand my concern that, together, we must find a mutually satisfactory way to control my legal costs in a way that will compensate your law firm fairly for your work.

As part of my representation, I would therefore propose that we adopt procedures for my case that will supplement and, in instances of any conflict, supersede the terms and conditions outlined in your legal representation letter to me of _____, 20___. This will assure that we both use your Firm's time wisely and knowledgeably. This can only be accomplished by good and repeated communication between us, which I greatly desire and will do my best to foster. Toward that end, I want to communicate to you my expectations of how my case will be handled in advance in order to encourage continual communication between us about the scope of your work and the status of the matter you are handling for me. I am confident that if we can both agree to follow these procedures, it will ensure that the attorney-client relationship is rewarding for both of us.

My Role as Client: My objective is to be assured that I will receive high quality, cost-efficient representation. This means: (i) written work which is easily understood by me, as a layman, and reflects a thorough treatment of options and risks that you see in my case; (ii) advice which is responsive to our goal of settling the case or completing the lawsuit as quickly as possible; and (iii) fees which are competitive with those charged by other firms for similar services and bear a reasonable relationship to the matters involved in my case. The procedures outlined in this letter are designed to help us work together to achieve this objective without any misunderstandings.

My personal involvement in the case will vary according to the task involved and what you require of me to do your work. I would like to be involved at the outset in setting up a legal strategy and budget for handling my case along the following lines:

• define the objectives to be achieved by you;

• outline the role and specific work expected of you, including required research, written work product, etc.;

• develop a strategy and budget;

• clarify the role to be played by me; and

• identify the attorney at your Firm who is to be my primary contact ("Client Contact") if I have questions or encounter a problem with how things are going.

After these issues are discussed between us, (and some are already addressed in your letter), I will work with you to make sure that our understanding will be reduced to writing and each of us will have a copy.

Developing a Strategy and Budget: Although I am not a lawyer, I recognize that many matters entail variables which are difficult to control, such as whether my spouse and the opposing attorney will settle, fight discovery, or use delay tactics. Nonetheless, in this rather unpredictable setting, I believe that developing and updating a strategy and budget will prove mutually beneficial. This gives both of us a clear understanding of the work to be done, and allows us to make informed judgments about the appropriate level of legal work.

At the outset, I expect that the lawyer handling my case will prepare a brief, general strategy and put the same in writing for me to consider and understand. This strategy should include an outline of the proposed course of litigation, including pre-trial motions, the scope of discovery, and trial strategy. It would also be helpful to break down the strategy (and anticipated budget of my legal expense) into phases. At the end of each phase, the budget and strategy should be reviewed by both of us.

It will be your responsibility to monitor your fees and expenses on my case to make sure that I am being billed in a fair and reasonable manner in accordance with our representation agreement. If you discover a likelihood that the budget for my legal expenses in any particular phase will be exceeded, I expect that your Client Contact will advise me of the same promptly, so that both of us can determine whether to revise our budget or modify the strategy. The budget for legal services on each matter for which you are engaged represents the amount of work you have been authorized to perform for me. If you are not authorized in advance to perform work that will generate fees in excess of the budget, please do not undertake any such work without checking with me first.

Billable Items: I expect that your hourly billable rates will include your Firm's overhead. Unless otherwise agreed upon in advance and in writing between us, however, I do not want to pay for overhead or Firm costs in addition to the billing rates, such as:

• administrative or clerical services, including secretarial, docket, word processing, accounting, library, or other clerical staff time;

• secretarial overtime, unless necessitated by the urgency of my specific case and not the general press of business;

• "opening file" administrative charges; time charges for preparation of bills; mark-ups for "Lexis/Westlaw" computerized legal research; copying costs in excess of _____ cents a page;

• charges for sending or receiving telecopies or facsimile transmissions (except long distance phone calls);

• meal costs, except for a reasonable cost if a matter related to your representation of me must be addressed with an outside party during the meal; or

• automobile mileage in excess of _____ cents per mile.

I expect you to be sensitive to the costs of multiple representation at meetings and hearings, high staffing levels, rotating persons onto matters with which they are unfamiliar, training young lawyers on my case, and polishing work. If you are concerned about my expectations with respect to specific items of this nature, please discuss them with me now.

Travel: Since the majority of my case can easily be handled in the local area of your Firm's office, the need for overnight travel is probably not going to be a factor. However, if out-of-town travel is necessary, please comply with these requests: (i) travel should not be made by more than one attorney; (ii) expenses for lodging, restaurants, or transportation should be fair and not extravagant; and (iii) charges for airfare should be at the coach rate only.

Format of Billing Statements: I understand that you will submit an invoice for services and disbursements monthly. Each statement for services and expenses should be submitted in a format that includes, at a minimum, the following information:

- my file number with your Firm;
- the name and telephone number of your Client Contact for my case;
- itemized hourly descriptions of services with detail sufficient to communicate to the reader what was done;
- the name and hourly billing rate of each person who rendered services, with a monthly summary of the hours and charges for services of each;
- an itemized description of all costs and disbursements for the billing period, including rates at which services such as copying are charged; and
- major individual disbursements (which must be approved by both of us before the expense is incurred) such as retention of appraisers, experts, consultants, or similar service organizations.

Unless both of us have approved a different billing format, statements which vary from this format will be returned for revision without payment. The following is the billing format I would like to receive:

SAMPLE BILL
HONEST ABE LAW FIRM

January 31, 20___

Client: _____
Matter: _____
File: Mr. Client—Dissolution of Marriage
Client Contact: _____, Esquire
Direct Telephone: _____

LEGAL SERVICES:

Date	Professional Services Rendered	Atty	Hours	Amount
01/17/20__	Telephone call from Mr. Frank Smith regarding resolution of case	JF	0.20	$30.00
	Telephone conference with Mr. Attorney for Client's wife; letter to Mr. Attorney re same	SA	0.40	46.00
01/26/20__	Telephone call from Client	SA	0.30	34.50
				$110.50
	Disbursements			
	Photocopying (40 @ .10)			$4.00
	Total Disbursements			$4.00
	Current Charges Due			$114.50

ATTORNEY SUMMARY:

Attorney	Hours	Rate	Total
Joseph Friendly (JF)	.20	$150	$30.00
Suzanne Associate (SA)	.70	$115	$80.50

There may be instances where, in your legal judgment, I would be better served by not disclosing the precise nature of actions taken in detail, agreements reached, or discussions held in my billing statements. In these instances please ensure that the Client Contact is aware of the circumstance and reason for the omission of detail so that the same can be discussed with me.

Fee Disagreements: In the unlikely event that we have disagreements about fees or reimbursable expenses, I will do my best to discuss the same with the Client Contact without delay. I am confident that if both of us are reasonable, any disagreement that may arise will be disposed of promptly. However, if we cannot agree on a fair settlement, then we both agree that you will secure court approval to withdraw so I can secure alternate counsel without jeopardizing my case. I will, of course, be responsible for reasonable fees and costs to the date of substitution of my legal counsel. If we cannot agree on a fair and reasonable settlement, we agree that our dispute shall be submitted to arbitration or mediation for resolution before the Bar Association for the State of _____. If no such arbitration or mediation is available, then each of us can pursue our legal remedies.

Form and Research Coordination: To avoid unnecessary duplication of research efforts and to benefit from forms developed in connection with previous cases of this type, I would like you to contact me before commencing any major research or documenting my case. If I can assist by securing documentation or finding information myself, I would prefer to do that in order to lower my legal expense. Conversely, in order to keep my files up-to-date, please send me copies of any significant memoranda, pleadings, or documents prepared by you on my behalf.

Fairness: Remember that your actions as my lawyer, and the perceptions of others in the course of your representation of me, are a reflection on me, my family, my church, and close friends. Above all, I want you to be fair to others in your dealings on my behalf. If we act in a manner that demonstrates good faith and inspires trust, we will resolve my case at the earliest possible time, as is my desire.

Early Settlement of Disputes: Naturally you are encouraged in your representation of me to look for creative ways to settle my case as early as possible. I know my potential loss in litigation is not limited to the attorneys' fees and costs for which I am responsible. The time, stress, and antagonism which result from litigation are very significant factors that we must both take into account continually throughout your representation in determining whether to settle.

Communication: Since communication is the key to a mutually satisfactory relationship, I expect you to bring to my immediate attention anything I do that interferes with your ability to represent me efficiently. Similarly, I want to freely discuss with you any of my concerns. Above all, I want to be copied with all letters, pleadings, and other documents going in and out of your office relating to my case so I can be prepared to discuss matters with the Client Contact from time to time and keep my personal files current.

I appreciate your help. I know we can work together during this difficult personal struggle. Kindly sign the enclosed copy of this letter confirming your agreement and return it to me as soon as possible.

Very truly yours,
William Client
AGREED TO:

Honest Abe Law Firm
By: _____
Joseph Friendly
Managing Partner

After you have hired a qualified attorney and guarded yourself against the matters discussed above and in chapter 13, you will be in good shape to let your lawyer protect your interests. Above all, remember that if you are wise in making your decision about the attorney who will serve as your advocate in your divorce, you can be confident that a number of the smaller decisions resulting from your selection will be reasonable and prudent as well.

Appendix D

Suggested Reading List for Further Encouragement

If you are going through a separation or divorce, you may not have much time to read books on how to cope. Naturally, to the extent you have time, the most important book to read is the Bible to help you keep your spiritual focus. However, many want to read a variety of books in order to have a broad perspective on what is happening. Here are some books that might prove helpful:

American Bar Association Section of Family Law, *The Never-Ending Divorce—A Handbook for Clients: How to Step Away and Stop Fighting* (ABA, Vol. 22, No. 4, Spring 2000); *Divorce Forms—A Handbook for Clients: Gathering Information for Your Case* (ABA, Vol. 24, No. 1, Summer 2001)

These excellent booklets were prepared by the editors of the ABA's *Family Advocate* journal. Written in easy-to-understand language for the layperson, these publications address many questions people have about the legal process of divorce. Although written from a secular viewpoint, readers will find them most useful in becoming familiar with what happens in divorce litigation.

Beattie, Melody. *Codependent No More: How to Stop Controlling Others and Start Caring for Yourself (15th Anniversary Edition)*. New York, NY: Hazelden Publishing and Educational Services, 2001.

Ms. Beattie is a recovering alcoholic and former chemical dependency counselor. Her book was responsible for bringing the term "codependency" into the common vernacular. Although the book focuses on people close to alcoholics and persons with compulsive disorders, it provides penetrating insight into codependency. If you find yourself so absorbed in your spouse's problems that you ignore your own needs, this book will open your eyes.

Burkett, Larry. *How to Manage Your Money*. Chicago, IL: Moody Publishers, 2002, and *Victory over Debt: Rediscovering Financial Freedom*. Chicago, IL: Moody Press, 1992.

Prior to his death in 2003, Mr. Burkett was recognized as one of the top national commentators on sound financial management using biblical principles. He was the founder of the Christian Financial Concepts organization as well as a national Christian radio commentator and conference speaker. These very helpful books still provide sound biblical advice on how to deal with tough financial crises in a format that is very interesting and easy to understand.

Burns, Bob, and Whiteman, Tom. *The Fresh Start Recovery Workbook: A Step-by-Step Program for Those Who Are Divorced or Separated*. Nashville, TN: Nelson Books, 1998.

Written by two of the principals behind the excellent *Fresh Start* seminars for the separated or divorced. This book is one of the best resources available to help you work through your emotions and consider your options from a Christian perspective. Questions, self-tests, exercises, and practical information focus on all the key issues arising in a separation or divorce.

Campbell, Susan M. *The Couple's Journey: Intimacy as a Path to Wholeness.* San Luis Obispo, CA: Impact Publishers, 1980.

This book offers understanding and insight into the five-stage path of growth traveled by every intimate relationship: romance, power struggle, stability, commitment, and co-creation.

Carlson, David E. *Counseling and Self-Esteem (Resources for Christian Counselors Series, Vol. 13).* Nashville, TN: W Publishing Group, 1995.

This book is a volume in the series of *Resources for Christian Counseling* edited by Dr. Gary R. Collins. Although it is primarily intended for counselors, it also provides very biblical and practical advice for the layperson on how to deal with low self-esteem.

Carter, Les. *Grace and Divorce: God's Healing Gift to Those Whose Marriages Fall Short.* Hoboken, NJ: Jossey-Bass Publishers, 2004; *The Anger Workbook: A 13-Step Interactive Plan.* Nashville, TN: Thomas Nelson, Inc., 1992; and *The Prodigal Spouse: How to Survive Infidelity.* Nashville, TN: Thomas Nelson, Inc., 1990.

Although Dr. Carter heavily emphasizes God's truly amazing grace—so much so that one might feel that at times he may minimize some scriptural precedent—these books definitely offer hope to couples attempting to deal with anger and marital infidelity issues through forgiveness and grace.

Chapman, Gary. *Hope for the Separated: Wounded Marriages Can Be Healed.* Chicago, IL: Moody Publishers, 2005.

Highly regarded and popular Christian author/speaker Gary Chapman focuses on ways to reconcile separated couples to a restored, enriched, growing marriage. He offers good advice on how to handle living apart, what to do with the time, and how to approach reconciliation. He truly gives you hope when you feel there is none.

Coleman, William L. *What Children Need to Know When Parents Get Divorced (Revised Edition).* Minneapolis, MN: Bethany House, 1998.

Discusses the causes and results of divorce, with emphasis on the needs of children who must understand their parents' feelings as well as their own while adjusting to the changes that divorce brings about in their lives. It has short, 1–2 page chapters on topics that kids are concerned about when facing their parents' divorce. Great questions serve as a good discussion primer.

Crabb, Larry. *Inside Out (10th Anniversary Edition).* Colorado Springs, CO: Navpress Publishing Group, 1998.

Dr. Crabb is the founder and director of the Institute of Biblical Counseling, a ministry committed to training Christians to resolve life's problems biblically. He has been chairman of the Biblical Counseling Department at Grace Theological Seminary. This challenging book encourages readers to look inside themselves and face the inner pain rather than avoiding it, earnestly seeking God's help in their lives. You will find many answers in this book.

Curran, Dolores. *Traits of a Healthy Family.* **New York, NY: Ballantine Books, 1984.**
This book discusses the fifteen traits of a healthy family: communication, affirmation and support, respect, trust, play and humor, responsibility, ethical foundation, rituals and traditions, interaction, religious core, respect for privacy, service to others, shared table time, shared leisure time, and admitting and seeking help with problems.

Dobson, James C. *Love Must Be Tough: New Hope for Marriages in Crisis.* **Sisters, OR: Multnomah Publishers, 2004, and** *What Wives Wish Their Husbands Knew About Women.* **Wheaton, IL: Tyndale House Publishers, Inc., 1988.**
Dr. Dobson has often been called the leading Christian family counselor in America. He is the founder of Focus on the Family, a nonprofit corporation dedicated to the preservation of the home. Many of Dr. Dobson's books are excellent, but these very practical books broke new ground. *Love Must Be Tough* provides many practical ways to deal firmly with the serious and destructive causes of a family breakup through loving toughness. Dr. Dobson's books focus on dealing with separation and divorce, romantic love, in-law conflicts, self-esteem, children, finances, loneliness, sex, and many other vital topics. They are outstanding resources.

Eggerichs, Emerson. *Love and Respect.* **Brentwood, TN: Integrity Publishers, 2005.**
Scripturally examines how important it is for husbands to receive unconditional respect from their wives, and how wives need unconditional love in return. Understanding this vital "communication code" between spouses can help restore marriages in crisis. An excellent Christian marriage resource!

Friedman, James T. *The Divorce Handbook (Revised Edition).* **New York, NY: Random House, Inc., 1999.**
This is a secular book written by a family law attorney. It is written in a question and answer format, addressing well over 200 of the most common questions people have about the legal side of divorce. It is very worthwhile and a quick and handy reference.

Gardner, Dr. Richard A. *The Parents Book About Divorce (2nd Edition).* **Cresskill, NJ: Creative Therapeutics, 1999.**
Until his death in 2003, Dr. Gardner was a clinical professor of child psychiatry at Columbia University, College of Physicians and Surgeons, a nationally known child psychiatrist, and an expert on the effects of divorce on children. This book provides clear, practical guidelines (from a secular viewpoint) for parents who face divorce and want to know how their decision affects their children. The book is probably one of the best books available on this topic. It also provides good information on the psychological aspects of the legal process and child custody decisions.

Grissom, Steve, and Leonard, Kathy. *DivorceCare: Hope, Help, and Healing During and After Your Divorce.* Nashville, TN: Thomas Nelson, Inc., 2006.

Offered by the leaders of the well-known DivorceCare ministry, this excellent 365-day devotional book for those experiencing separation or divorce is exceptionally encouraging, inspiring, and thought-provoking. Some of today's most respected, well-known Christian leaders and psychologists provide daily entries.

Harley, Jr. Willard F. *His Needs, Her Needs: Building an Affair-Proof Marriage.* Grand Rapids, MI: Revell Publishers, 2001.

Nationally acclaimed clinical psychologist Willard F. Harley, Jr., PhD is the author of many books on marriage, including *Love Busters* and *The Five Steps to Romantic Love.* He also runs the very practical Marriage Builders ministry for couples in crisis. In this book, Harley identifies and compares the ten most vital needs of both husbands and wives, showing how to satisfy these uniquely different parts of our God-given makeup. This best-selling book has helped thousands of couples revitalize their marriages.

Hart, Archibald D. *Helping Children Survive Divorce (Revised Edition).* Nashville, TN: Thomas Nelson, Inc., 1997.

In this book, Dr. Hart, a highly regarded Christian psychologist (and the child of parents who divorced when he was twelve) provides specific ways to help children cope with the psychological, social, and spiritual difficulties surrounding their parents' divorce. Topics include minimizing damage to children, common mistakes made by divorced parents, how to handle guilt, essential steps to help children cope with depression and anger, ensuring a child's healthy post-divorce development, four issues that must be dealt with in the event of remarriage, and do's and don'ts for successfully building a blended family.

Heth, William A., and Wenham, Gordon J. *Jesus and Divorce.* Carlisle, England, UK: Paternoster Publishing, 1984.

This book is among the most scholarly works studying the Scriptures as to divorce and remarriage issues by examining the views on this subject by the religious world throughout history. Seven major positions are summarized and evaluated. It is challenging to read, but well worth it if you are struggling with what the Bible says.

House, H. Wayne. *Divorce and Remarriage: Four Christian Views.* Downer's Grove, IL: InterVarsity Press, 1990.

This is an excellent companion volume to Heth and Gordon's book noted above (which takes a very conservative view of Scripture on divorce and remarriage). Realizing that reasonable people can disagree on certain interpretations of Scripture, Mr. House brings together four authors of note (J. Carl Laney, William Heth, Thomas Edgar, and Larry Richards) and allows them to present their very different perspectives on all divorce and remarriage issues addressed in Scripture. Each essayist also critiques the position of the other. Case studies at the end of each essay help make theory face reality. This book is very instructive and helpful to everyone who wants to think biblically about these important concerns.

Kesler, Jay. *Is Your Marriage Really Worth Fighting For?* Elgin, IL: David C. Cook Publishing Co., 1990.

When a couple is on the eve of going to divorce court, is it too late to rescue a failing marriage? Mr. Kesler asserts that it is not. He provides comfort and help to a hurting couple who desperately needs to forgive each other, work through their pain, and rejuvenate their relationship.

Ketterman, Grace. *When You Can't Say "I Forgive You": Breaking the Bonds of Anger and Hurt.* Colorado Springs, CO: Navpress Publishing Group, 2000.

Ketterman has a deep, personal connection to her topic: she had already divorced her successful husband when he called to tell her that he had been arrested and needed her help. They worked through their problems and remarried after he was released from prison. This is an excellent guide to letting go of hurt and anger and being able to live a meaningful life.

Kniskern, Joseph Warren. *When the Vow Breaks: A Survival and Recovery Guide for Christians Facing Divorce.* Nashville, TN: B&H Publishing Group, 1993, (Updated and revised 2007); *Making a NEW Vow: A Christian Guide to Remarriage and Blending Families.* Nashville, TN: B&H Publishing Group, 2003; and *Courting Disaster: What Runaway Litigation Is Costing You and What You Can Do to Stop the Fallout.* Wake Forest, NC: Church Initiative, 1995.

From his perspective as a Christian attorney, family mediator, and Divorce-Care facilitator (and as one who has divorced and remarried), Kniskern focuses on all of the issues and dilemmas faced by most separated and divorced persons. Addressing psychological, legal, spiritual, and emotional concerns of most individuals, these practical and personal books are among the most comprehensive and best researched publications available on divorce and remarriage.

MacArthur, John. *On Divorce.* Chicago, IL: Moody Publishers, 1985.

This is actually a book adaptation of an excellent six-tape audio teaching series of lessons given by evangelist and *Grace to You* national radio speaker John MacArthur. It is a particularly well done analysis of Old and New Testament Scriptures on divorce and remarriage, with an emphasis on Matthew 19.

Medved, Diane. *The Case Against Divorce.* New York, NY: Ivy Books, 1990.

Although written from a secular perspective, Ms. Medved's conclusion is that divorce creates more problems than it solves. Research and statistics support her conclusion.

Munroe, Myles. *Single, Married, Separated, and Life after Divorce (Expanded Edition).* Shippensburg, PA: Destiny Image Publishers, 2005.

From a Christian perspective, Munroe brings greater understanding of what it means to be a successful Christian single, not controlling people to meet your needs, and being a "whole" person before entering into a relationship with someone else. He emphasizes that singleness has less to do with marital status, and more to do with attitude and inner self.

Northington, Jan. *Separated and Waiting*. Wake Forest, NC: Church Initiative, 1994.

Waiting to be reconciled or divorced can bring confusion, despair, and hopelessness. Being in limbo while a spouse decides what he or she will do is hurtful, as well as difficult to understand. This book offers the motivation and understanding you need to bring wholeness back into your life, despite the uncertainty of the future of your marriage.

Palmer, Nancy S., and Tangel-Rodriguez, Ana. *When Your Ex Won't Pay: Getting Kids the Financial Support They Deserve*. Bedford, OH: Pinion Press, 1995.

Palmer is a Christian family law attorney and former chairperson of the Florida Bar Marital and Family Law Section. She also is a highly successful mediator and lecturer (see her foreword at the front of *When the Vow Breaks*). Palmer's book provides many practical insights into options and alternatives for securing much-needed support funds for children of divorce.

Petersen, J. Allan. *The Myth of the Greener Grass (Revised Edition)*. Wheaton, IL: Tyndale House Publishers, Inc., 1992.

Petersen is a family counselor who deals frankly with the problem of marital infidelity and offers practical advice for couples. This book has become somewhat of a classic in examining the "myth" that extramarital affairs promise happiness.

Petherbridge, Laura. *When Your Marriage Dies*. Colorado Springs, CO: Life Journey, 2005.

From her Christian perspective as a divorcee and remarriage partner, as well as a featured expert on the new DivorceCare recovery video series, Petherbridge offers an honest look at the ways divorce can affect one's life perspective. It addresses many different aspects of the stages of divorce and is a very good read.

Rainey, Dennis and Barbara. *Building Your Mate's Self-Esteem*. Ventura, CA: Gospel Light Publications, 1986.

Dennis Rainey is the president and cofounder of FamilyLife, which began as the family ministry branch of Campus Crusade for Christ. Both he and his wife, Barbara, have spoken at hundreds of FamilyLife conferences across the nation. This popular book provides many practical suggestions on how to increase self-esteem using Christian principles.

Richards, Larry. *Remarriage*. Waco, TX: Word Incorporated, 1981.

This is a biblical study of remarriage for Christians after a divorce and shows how remarriage may be God's gift of healing and the start of a new life.

Richmond, Gary. *Successful Single Parenting (Expanded Edition)*. Eugene, OR: Harvest House Publishers, 1998.

Richmond is a pastor who has led a divorce support group in California for many years. Packed with advice, this complete guide covers how to set financial priorities, help children change, explain the other parent's absence, deal with discipline, handle visitation, and more. It is a useful companion to Dr. Archibald Hart's book referenced above.

Rothman, Bernard. *Loving and Leaving: Winning at the Business of Divorce.* Lexington, MA: Divorce Press, 1991.

Mr. Rothman is a family lawyer in New York. Although written exclusively from the secular viewpoint of an attorney, this book provides many "war stories" about what to expect in court. Mr. Rothman also advocates use of an interdisciplinary team approach between attorneys and mental health professionals in working together for the best interests of the family.

Slattery, Juliana. *Finding the Hero in Your Husband: Surrendering the Way God Intended.* Deerfield Beach, FL: Faith Communications, Inc., 2004.

Christian psychologist Dr. Juliana Slattery examines, from a biblical perspective, how God has given wives tremendous power in their relationships. This indispensable guide shows women how to use their strength in ways that encourage their husbands' potential instead of dominating and destroying it. An excellent resource for Christian wives who want to save their marriages.

Smoke, Jim. *Growing Through Divorce.* Eugene, OR: Harvest House Publishers, 2007.

Mr. Smoke is nationally known for his ministry to single adults through his Growing Through Divorce Seminars and his speaking at singles conferences. This book offers practical guidance based upon the author's firsthand experience in working with thousands of formerly married persons. It gives readers a lot of encouragement and hope for a new life after divorce while emphasizing the need to assume responsibility for oneself.

Sweet, Rose. *A Woman's Guide to Healing the Heartbreak of Divorce.* Peabody, MA: Hendrickson Publishers, 2001.

Sweet's book is an easy read. Notable in this very touching and personal book is inclusion of a "love letter" to you from God at the beginning of every chapter, with a comparison of fear versus faith issues at the conclusion of each chapter.

Talley, Jim A. *Reconcilable Differences: Healing for Troubled Marriages (Expanded Edition with Study Guide).* Nashville, TN: Thomas Nelson, Inc., 1991.

Is it possible for a couple whose marriage is in serious trouble, or a couple who is already divorced, to restore harmony—even love—to their relationship? Dr. Talley says, "Yes!" This book shows why reconciliation is worth the effort, and provides practical, biblical advice on how to resolve conflicts and develop a relationship based upon mutual love, respect, and trust.

Thompson, David A. *Counseling and Divorce.* Nashville, TN: W Publishing Group, 1989.

Like David Carlson's book on self-esteem mentioned above, this book also is a volume in the series of *Resources for Christian Counseling* edited by Dr. Gary R. Collins. It analyzes the causes and crisis of the divorce process using Christian principles and is very useful.

Towner, Jason. *Jason Loves Jane, But They Got a Divorce.* **Nashville, TN: Impact Books, 1978.**

For a good understanding of the feelings of failure endured by a Christian getting a divorce, this book is very helpful. Mr. Towner tells the story of his own divorce in a very personal manner that lets the reader feel the emotional impact of it.

Wallerstein, Judith, and Blakeslee, Sandra. *Second Chances: Men, Women, and Children a Decade after Divorce.* **Boston, MA: Houghton Mifflin Publishers, 2004.**

This secular study by highly regarded psychoanalyst Wallerstein tracks and rigorously researches sixty white, middle-class families through the stages and aftermath of divorce since 1971. It is the largest such research project ever undertaken, offering a unique psychological road map of the long-term aftereffects of marital collapse and the heavy toll divorce takes on children of divorcing families. This amazingly insightful book will open your eyes about the effects of divorce on both parents and children.

Wright, H. Norman. *Seasons of a Marriage.* **Ventura, CA: Regal Books, 1982, and** *Before You Remarry: A Guide to Successful Remarriage.* **Eugene, OR: Harvest House Publishers, 1999.**

Mr. Wright's first book noted above discusses the stages of a growing marriage—initial expectations, early years, midlife transitions, the empty nest, affairs and unfaithfulness, the healing process, parent-child reversal, and a time to die. The second book builds upon his findings as to how couples adjust in second marriages. It provides many useful motivational exercises for a couple to try in promoting a thorough interaction on the major issues of remarriage before it actually occurs.

Yates, Cynthia. *Living Well as a Single Mom: A Practical Guide to Managing Your Money, Your Kids, and Your Personal Life.* **Eugene, OR: Harvest House Publishers, 2006.**

Combining her own experiences as a single mom with the insight of other moms, Yates (who also authored *Living Well on One Income*) shares the practical and emotional way to live life well when a woman is raising her children alone. With empathy and biblical wisdom, she offers suggestions, guidance, and candid advice on self-care, time management, finances, choosing safe child care, discipline, peer pressure, and emergency preparedness, one day at a time, to assist mothers with kids of all ages.

Appendix E

Resource Groups and Organizations

This list of resources provides contact information about groups and organizations you can call or write to help you cope with your separation or divorce. Consult your local directory for organizations or groups in your area.[1]

Abortion

In Our Midst Ministries
1151 Eagle Drive, Suite 325
Loveland, CO 80537
(970) 669-1096
Fax (970) 669-1849
www.inourmidst.com

Restoring The Heart Ministries
P.O. Box 2772
East Setauket, NY 11733
(631) 689-6686
www.rthm.com

Alcohol and Substance Abuse

Adult Children of Alcoholics
World Service Organization
P.O. Box 3216
Torrance, CA 90510
(310) 534-1815 (messages only)
www.adultchildren.org

Al-Anon/Alateen
Family Group Headquarters
1600 Corporate Landing Parkway
Virginia Beach, VA 23454-5617
(757) 563-1600
Fax (757) 563-1655
www.al-anon.org

Al-Anon Canada
Capital Corporate Center
9 Antares Drive, Suite 245
Ottawa, ON K2E 7V5
(613) 723-8484
Fax (613) 723-0151
www.al-anon.org

Alcoholics Anonymous
World Services
P.O. Box 459

New York, NY 10163
(212) 870-3400
www.alcoholics-anonymous.org

Cocaine Anonymous World Services
3740 Overland Avenue, Suite C
Los Angeles, CA 90034
(310) 559-5833
Fax (310) 559-2554
www.ca.org

Families Anonymous
P.O. Box 3475
Culver City, CA 90231-3475
(800) 736-9805
Fax (310) 815-9682
Web: www.familiesanonymous.org
(A group of concerned relatives and friends whose lives have been adversely affected by a loved one's addiction to alcohol or drugs.)

Nar-Anon Family Group Headquarters
22527 Crenshaw Boulevard, Suite 200B
Torrance, CA 90505
(800) 477-6291 or (310) 534-8188
Fax (310) 534-8688
www.nar-anon.org

Narcotics Anonymous World Services
P.O. Box 9999
Van Nuys, CA 91409
(818) 773-9999
Fax (818) 700-0700
www.na.org

National Association
for Children of Alcoholics
11426 Rockville Pike, Suite 301
Rockville, MD 20852
(301) 468-0985
Fax (301) 468-0987
www.nacoa.org

**National Council on Alcoholism
and Drug Dependents—Hope Hotline**
(800) NCA-CALL (622-2255)

**National Drug and
Alcohol Treatment Hotline**
(800) 662-HELP (622-4357)

**National Institute on Drug Abuse /
National Institutes of Health**
6001 Executive Boulevard, Room 5213
Bethesda, MD 20892-9561
(301) 443-1124
www.nida.nih.gov

Overcomers Outreach
P.O. Box 922950
Sylmar, CA 91392-2950
(800) 310-3001
(877) 9OVERCOME (968-3726)
(818) 833-1803
Fax (818) 833-1546
www.overcomersoutreach.org
*(Christian outreach to alcoholics and adult
children of alcoholics.)*

RAPHA Christian Counseling
3021 Gateway Drive, Suite 290
Irving, TX 75063
(877) 257-0449 or (972) 257-0449
Fax (972) 258-0449
www.rapha.info
*(Largest provider of in-hospital treatment
in U.S. for psychiatric and substance abuse
from a Christian perspective. "Rapha"
comes from the Hebrew name for God,
Jehovah Rapha—"our God who heals.")*

Sierra Tucson Treatment Center
39580 South Lago del Oro Parkway
Tucson, AZ 85739
(800) 842-4487 or (800) 624-9001
www.sierratucson.com
*(Nationally recognized center for
treatment of alcoholism, drug addiction,
and eating disorders.)*

Child Support and Related Issues

**Administration for Children and Families
(U.S. Dept. of Health and Human Services) Office of Child Support Enforcement**
370 L'Enfant Promenade SW
Washington, DC 20201

www.acf.hhs.gov
*(Mission is to enhance well-being of
children through assistance in obtaining
support, including financial and medical,
by locating parents, establishing paternity,
establishing support obligations, and moni-
toring/enforcing those obligations.)*

American Association for Lost Children
539 Fred Rogers Drive
Latrobe, PA 15650
(800) 375-5683 or (724) 537-6970
www.aaflc.org
*(Unlike resource organizations, this non-
profit, international Christian organization
physically goes out and finds missing or
kidnapped children and reunites them
with their loved ones at little or no cost
to the families.)*

American Association of Retired Persons
601 E Street NW
Washington, DC 20049
(888) OUR-AARP (687-2277)
www.aarp.org
(Provides information on pension issues.)

**Association for Children
for Enforcement of Support (ACES)**
3474 Raymont Boulevard, 2nd Floor
University Heights, OH 44118
(800) 738-2237
www.childsupport-aces.org
(Provides information on collecting support.)

Child Find of America
P.O. Box 277
New Paltz, NY 12561-0277
(800) I-AM-LOST (426-5678)
www.childfindofamerica.org
*(National non-profit organization
dedicated to prevention and resolution
of child abduction)*

**Childhelp USA's
National Child Abuse Hotline**
(800) 4-A-CHILD (422-4453)
TDD (800) 222-4453
*(Provides multilingual crisis intervention
and professional counseling on child abuse,
and gives referrals to local social service
groups offering counseling on child abuse,
24 hours a day, 7 days a week.)*

Children's Defense Fund
25 E Street NW
Washington, DC 20001
(800) CDF-1200 (233-1200)
(202) 628-8787
www.childrensdefense.org

Child Welfare League of America
2345 Crystal Drive, Suite 250
Arlington, VA 22202
(703) 412-2400
Fax (703) 412-2401
www.cwla.org
(Legal and legislative advocacy to ensure safety and well-being of children, referrals.)

Confident Kids Support Groups
2422 Divide Way
Santa Maria, CA 93458
(805) 614-2824
Fax (805) 614-2844
www.confidentkids.com
(Has been helping families throughout the U.S. work through important family issues for almost 20 years. Affiliated with Christian Recovery International.)

DivorceCare For Kids (DC4K)
P.O. Box 1739
Wake Forest, NC 27588
(800) 489-7778 or (919) 562-2112
Fax (919) 562-2114
www.dc4k.org
(DC4K is a special group helping children heal from the pain caused by separation or divorce in a safe and neutral place where they can recognize and learn to share their feelings. Offers 13-week video session/support groups across the U.S.—a powerful ministry for kids 5–12 years of age.)

Families First
1105 West Peachtree Street NE
P.O. Box 7948, Station C
Atlanta, GA 30357-0948
(404) 853-2800
www.familiesfirst.org

Fathers for Equal Rights
701 Commerce Street, Suite 302
Dallas, TX 75202
(214) 953-2233
Fax (214) 749-4622
www.fathers4kids.com

(The vision of this organization is that society will recognize every child's right to have a healthy relationship with both parents. Offers membership allowing for consultation with family lawyers.)

Focus on Your Child
Colorado Springs, CO 80995
(800) A-FAMILY (232-6459)
www.focusonyourchild.com
(Membership program run by Focus on the Family organization helping parents make the most of parenting years.)

Kids Peace Hotline
(800) 543-7283
(Parents and relatives can call about problems. Children in crisis will be connected with a social worker for immediate help.)

National Center for Missing and Exploited Children
Charles B. Wang Int'l Children's Building
699 Prince Street
Alexandria, VA 22314-3175
(800) 843-5678 or (703) 274-3900
Fax (703) 274-2200
www.missingkids.com
(Information on missing or exploited children. Technical assistance and training programs.)

National Center for Missing and Exploited Children Hotline
(800) THE-LOST (843-5678)

National Center on Fathers and Families
University of Pennsylvania
3440 Market Street, Suite 450
Philadelphia, PA 19104-3325
(215) 573-5500
www.ncoff.gse.upenn.edu
(Strengthens men to be better fathers.)

National Child Abuse Hotline
(800) 25-ABUSE (252-2873)

National Child Support Enforcement Association
444 North Capitol Street, Suite 414
Washington, DC 20001-1512
(202) 624-8180
Fax (202) 624-8828
www.ncsea.org

(NCSEA is a widely recognized resource for information on every aspect of child support.)

**National Resource Center
on Child Abuse and Neglect**
63 Inverness Drive East
Englewood, CO 80112-5117
(800) 227-5242 or (303) 792-9900
Fax (303) 792-5333
(This resource center is operated by the American Humane Association, and supplies resources to improve the capability of public and private agencies to respond effectively to the problem of child abuse and neglect.)

National Runaway Switchboard
3030 North Lincoln Avenue
Chicago, IL 60657
(800) 344-2785 or (773) 880-9860
Fax (773) 929-5150
www.1800runaway.org
(Lists of shelters, counseling, food pantries, transportation. Suicide and crisis counseling. Message relay from kids to parents, or from parents to kids, 3-way calls arranged.)

National Runaway Switchboard Hotline
(800) RUNAWAY (786-2929)
(All calls are confidential and free 24 hours a day, 365 days a year. Operators talk through problems and help you find a plan of action.)

National Youth Crisis Hotline
(800) 442-HOPE (442-4673)
(Provides counseling and referrals to local drug treatment centers, shelters, and counseling services. Responds to youth dealing with pregnancy, molestation, suicide, and child abuse. Available 24 hours a day, 7 days a week.)

Older Women's League
3300 North Fairfax Drive, Suite 218
Arlington, VA 22201
(703) 812-7990
Fax (703) 812-0687
www.owl-national.org
(National grassroots membership organization focusing solely on issues to women as they age, striving to improve the status and quality of life of midlife and older women.)

Parents Without Partners
1650 South Dixie Highway, Suite 510
Boca Raton, FL 33432
(800) 637-7974 or (561) 391-8833
Fax (561) 395-8557
www.parentswithoutpartners.org
(International organization providing variety of resources to those raising children alone, contending with the emotional conflicts of divorce, never-married, separation, or widowhood.)

Vanished Children's Alliance
991 West Hedding Street, Suite 101
San Jose, CA 95126
(800) VANISHED (826-4743) *(sightings)*
(408) 296-1113
Fax (408) 296-1117
www.vca.org
(Oldest and second-largest missing children's organization in the U.S., providing prevention, location, recovery, and reunification of missing and abducted children since 1980.)

Counseling and Psychotherapy

**American Association
of Christian Counselors**
P.O. Box 739
Forest, VA 24551
(800) 526-8673 or (434) 525-9470
Fax (434) 525-9480
www.aacc.net
(Provides telephone numbers of 50,000 local professionals whose counseling is based on Christian principles.)

**American Association
for Marriage and Family Therapy**
112 South Alfred Street
Alexandria, VA 22314
(703) 838-9808
Fax (703) 838-9805
www.aamft.org

American Psychiatric Association
1000 Wilson Boulevard, Suite 1825
Arlington, VA 22209-3901
(703) 907-7300
www.psych.org
(Your local APA society can refer you to psychiatrists in your area.)

American Psychological Association
750 First Street NE
Washington, DC 20002-4242
(800) 374-2721
Fax (202) 336-5500
www.apa.org
(Resource organization. For referrals, call 800-964-2000.)

**Christian Counseling
and Educational Foundation**
1803 East Willow Grove Avenue
Glenside, PA 19038
(800) 318-2186 or (215) 884-7676
Fax (215) 884-9435
www.ccef.org

Institute for Biblical Counseling
655 West Eleventh Avenue
Escondido, CA 92025
(760) 747-9252
Fax (760) 747-9347
www.ibcd.org
(Offers on-site and distance training opportunities, books, and audio and video-tapes supporting God's Word as sufficient to meet the challenges of a chaotic and materialistic world.)

Life Counseling Services
1440 Russell Road
Paoli, PA 19301
(800) 882-2799
www.lifecounseling.org
(Affiliated with Fresh Start divorce ministries.)

The Minirth Clinic P.A.
1200 East Collins Boulevard, Suite 300
Richardson, TX 75081
(888) MINIRTH (646-4784)
(972) 669-1403
Fax (972) 669-1403
(Provides Christian counseling services.)

**National Christian
Counselors Association**
5260 Paylor Lane
Sarasota, FL 34240
(941) 388-6868
(Association of ministers, professional Christian counselors, testing specialists, medical doctors, and teachers who believe

that counseling is self-centered and useless unless it is founded upon and directed by the Word of God.)

Credit and Financial Matters

Major National Credit Bureaus
Under the FACT Act amendments to the Fair Credit Reporting Act, you are entitled to one free credit file disclosure in a 12-month period. Contact the Central Source online at www.annualcreditreport.com, or by calling toll-free (877) FACT-ACT (322-8228).

Equifax Credit Information Services
P. O. Box 740241
Atlanta, GA 30374
(800) 685-1111 (24 hours a day)
www.equifax.com

Experian
475 Anton Boulevard
Costa Mesa, CA 92626
(888) 397-3742 (24 hours a day)
www.experian.com

TransUnion LLC
120 South Riverside Plaza, Suite 19
Chicago, IL 60606
(877) 322-8228 (24 hours a day)
www.transunion.com

(Most people have credit files at one or more of the foregoing three major credit bureaus. A copy of your file can be obtained by contacting them.)

[NOTE: For a nominal fee, any of these organizations can also provide you with a combined, easy-to-read report from all three of these major credit bureaus, but you must contact the bureaus directly to correct errors.]

Other Credit and Financial Matters

Bankcard Holders of America
524 Branch Drive
Salem, VA 24153
(701) 389-5445
(Provides a list of credit card issuers with low interest rates and no annual fees for a nominal charge.)

Crown Financial Ministries
P.O. Box 100
Gainesville, GA 30503-0100
(800) 772-1976
www.crown.org
(Formerly Christian Financial Concepts, this organization was founded by the late Larry Burkett, one of the most highly regarded financial counselors in the country using Christian principles. Also provides these award-winning daily radio programs: "Money Matters" and "How To Manage Your Money.")

Debtors Anonymous
P.O. Box 920888
Needham, MA 02492-0009
(781) 453-2743
Fax (781) 453-2745
www.debtorsanonymous.org
(Helps people recover from unmanageable credit card debt and overspending. Local support groups across the U.S.)

Fair Credit Reporting Act
Consumer Response Center
Federal Trade Commission
Washington, DC 20580
(877) FTC-HELP (382-4357)
www.ftc.gov
(Although the FTC cannot act as your lawyer in private disputes, you may file a complaint to prevent fraudulent, deceptive, and unfair business practices under the Fair Credit Reporting Act.)

Internal Revenue Service Hotline
(877) 777-4778

National Foundation
for Credit Counseling
801 Roeder Road, Suite 900
Silver Spring, MD 20910
(800) 388-2227 or (301) 589-5600
Fax (301) 495-5623
www.nfcc.org
www.debtadvice.org
(More than 900 local offices throughout the U.S., many NFCC members are known as the Consumer Credit Counseling Service (CCCS), providing financial counseling to more than 1 million people annually. Debt-Advice.org is a service of NFCC, helping consumers understand the wise use of credit

and locate a certified counselor for personal assistance. Ask for the "Do-It-Yourself Credit Repair and Improvement Guide.")

Social Security Administration—
Dept. of Health and Human Services
Office of Public Inquiries
Windsor Park Building
Baltimore, MD 21235
(800) 772-1213
TTY (800) 325-0778
(Ask for booklets "Understanding Social Security" and "Survivors.")

Crisis Intervention and Suicide

[NOTE: All suicide threats or implied threats should be taken very seriously, with immediate action!]

Boys Town Suicide and Crisis Hotline
(800) 448-3000
TDD (800) 448-1833
(Provides short-term crisis intervention and counseling, with local referrals. Operates 24 hours a day, 7 days a week.)

Covenant House "NineLine" Hotline
(800) 999-9999
(Crisis line for youth, teens, and families, with local referrals. Operates 24 hours a day, 7 days a week.)

National Suicide Hotline
(800) SUICIDE (784-2433)

SAFE (Self-Abuse Finally Ends) Hotline
(800) DONT-CUT (366-8288)

Divorce Support and Recovery

Association of Marriage
and Family Ministries
8283 North Hayden Road, Suite 258
Scottsdale, AZ 85258
(480) 585-0109
Fax (480) 585-7662
www.amfmonline.com

DivorceCare
(Church Initiative Ministries)
P.O. Box 1739
Wake Forest, NC 27588
(800) 489-7778 or (919) 562-2112

Fax (919) 562-2114
www.divorcecare.com
(See the DivorceCare page in this book! Provides outstanding 13-week Christian video series for adults, in conjunction with thousands of support groups meeting throughout the U.S., Canada, and nearly 20 other countries. Website has easy locator of available groups in your area.)

DivorceCare For Kids (DC4K)
P.O. Box 1739
Wake Forest, NC 27588
(800) 489-7778 or (919) 562-2112
Fax (919) 562-2114
www.dc4k.org
(DC4K is a special group helping children heal from the pain caused by separation or divorce in a safe and neutral place where they can recognize and learn to share their feelings. Offers 13-week video session/support groups across the U.S.—a powerful ministry for kids 5–12 years of age.)

Divorce Source
P.O. Box 1580
Allentown, PA 18105-1580
(610) 820-8120
Fax (610) 770-9342
www.divorcesource.com
(People in the divorce process need practical information. This organization offers an effective way to locate information and communicate with professionals and individuals sharing similar thoughts and experiences.)

Family Dynamics
P.O. Box 682549
Franklin, TN 37068-2549
(800) 650-9995 or (615) 627-0751
www.familydynamics.net
(Founded by noted relationship expert Joe Beam. Christian ministry helps churches and organizations take proactive steps to prevent marriages from reaching state of distress and to revive those already in distress. Claims 75% success rate for marriages in crisis.)

Fresh Start Seminars
1440 Russell Road
Paoli, PA 19301
(888) 373-7478
Fax (610) 644-4066
www.freshstartseminars.org

(The excellent seminars offered by this Christian ministry are designed to provide hope and new direction for broken lives. It ministers to adults and children through seminars, support groups, books, and tapes.)

Marriage Builders
12538 Ethan Avenue North
White Bear Lake, MN 55110
(651) 762-8570
www.marriagebuilders.com
(Organization founded and run by noted relationship expert Dr. Willard F. Harley. Provides practical ways to overcome marital conflicts and quickly restore love. Outreach has saved thousands of marriages from the pain of unresolved conflict and the disaster of divorce.)

Marriage Restored
(877) 844-2262
www.marriagerestored.com
(Outreach of Assemblies of God Marriage Encounter. Weekend of hope for couples in crisis who have experienced adultery, addiction, pornography, separation or other marriage-threatening circumstances.)

**North American Association
of Separated and Divorced Catholics**
P.O. Box 10
Hancock, MI 49930-0010
(906) 482-0494
Fax (906) 482-7470
www.nacsdc.org

<u>Domestic Violence and
Emotional/Physical Abuse</u>

**AMEND
(Abusive Men Exploring New Directions)**
2727 Bryant Street, Suite 350
Denver, CO 80211
(303) 83-AMEND (832-6363)
Fax (303) 480-9661
www.amendinc.org

Batterers Anonymous
1040 S. Mount Vernon Ave., Suite G-306
Colton, CA 92324
(951) 312-1041
(Self-help for men who want to control their anger and stop abusive behavior toward women.)

Domestic Violence Hotline
(800) 829-1122

Emotions Anonymous International
P. O. Box 4245
St. Paul, MN 55104-0245
(651) 647-9712
Fax (651) 647-1593
www.emotionsanonymous.org
(A 12-step organization similar to Alcoholics Anonymous. As of 2007, over 1,000 chapters in 35 countries, including the U.S.)

FaithTrust Institute
2400 North 45th Street, Suite 10
Seattle, WA 98103
(206) 634-1903
Fax (206) 634-0115
www.faithtrustinstitute.org
(International, multifaith organization working to end sexual and domestic violence.)

**Friends of Battered Women
and Their Children Hotline**
(800) 603-HELP (603-4357)

**National Coalition
Against Domestic Violence**
1120 Lincoln Street, Suite 1603
Denver, CO 80203
(303) 839-1852
TTY (303) 839-1681
Fax (303) 831-9251
www.ncadv.org
(Organization to influence public policy against domestic violence.)

**National Council on
Child Abuse and Family Violence**
1025 Connecticut Avenue NW, Suite 1000
Washington, DC 20036
(202) 429-6695
Fax (202) 521-3479
www.nccafv.org
(Founded in 1984, this organization provides intergenerational violence prevention services through community interaction to prevent domestic violence, child abuse, and elder abuse.)

**National Domestic Violence /
Child Abuse / Sexual Abuse Hotline**
(800) 799-SAFE (799-7233)

TDD (800) 787-3224
Spanish (800) 942-6908
(24-hour a day hotline provides crisis intervention and referrals to local services and shelters for victims of spouse abuse. Staff has extensive database of domestic violence treatment providers in all U.S. states and territories.)

Parents Anonymous
675 West Foothill Boulevard, Suite 220
Claremont, CA 91711-3475
(909) 621-6184
Fax (909) 625-6304
www.parentsanonymous.org
(For parents who are or may become abusive when disciplining their children.)

**Survivors of Incest Anonymous
World Service Office**
P.O. Box 190
Benson, MD 21018-9998
(410) 893-3322
www.siawso.org
(Provides local directory of meetings available for victims.)

Gambling Addictions

Chance to Change (Church Initiative)
P.O. Box 1739
Wake Forest, NC 27588
(800) 395-5755 or (919) 562-2112
Fax (919) 562-2114
www.chancetochange.org
(Offers video/support group curriculum featuring 40 Christian counselors and experts who specialize in helping people overcome gambling addictions.)

**Gamblers Anonymous
International Service Office**
P.O. Box 17173
Los Angeles, CA 90017
(213) 386-8789
Fax (213) 386-0030
www.gamblersanonymous.org

Gam-Anon International Service Office
P.O. Box 157
Whitestone, NY 11357
(718) 352-1671
Fax (718) 746-2571
www.gam-anon.org

National Council on
Problem Gambling Hotline
(800) 522-4700

Homosexuality

Cross Ministry
P.O. Box 1122
Wake Forest, NC 27588
(919) 569-0375
www.crossministry.org
(Non-denominational Christian organiza-
tion focusing on the reality of change for the
homosexual through Jesus Christ.)

Exodus International
P.O. Box 540119
Orlando, FL 32854
(888) 264-0877 or (407) 599-6872
www.exodus.to
(The largest information and referral min-
istry in the world addressing homosexual
issues.)

Legal Resources

American Bar Association
Family Law Section
321 North Clark Street
Chicago, IL 60610
(312) 988-5145
Fax (312) 988-6800
www.abanet.org
(Lawyer referrals may be obtained from
local referral services, or you may contact
FindLegalHelp.org from the ABA Division
of Legal Services, or call the ABA Service
Center at (800) 285-2221.)

American Academy
of Matrimonial Lawyers
150 North Michigan, Suite 2040
Chicago, IL 60601
(312) 263-6477
Fax:(312) 263-7682
www.aaml.org

Assnociation of Family
and Conciliation Courts
6525 Grand Teton Plaza
Madison, WI 53719
(608) 664-3750
Fax (608) 664-3751
www.afccnet.org

(An interdisciplinary association of judges,
lawyers, mediators, and mental health pro-
fessionals dedicated to family law services
as a complement to the judicial process.
Provides newsletter on family law issues
and other resources.)

Christian Legal Fellowship
1673 Richmond Street, Suite 140
London, ON, Canada N6G 2N3
(519) 641-8850
Fax (519) 641-8866
www.christianlegalfellowship.org
(This is a Canadian organization fulfilling
the same sort of function as the Christian
Legal Society.)

Christian Legal Society
8001 Braddock Road, Suite 300
Springfield, VA 22151
(703) 642-1070
Fax (703) 642-1075
www.clsnet.org
(This is a professional society of over 3,400
Christian lawyers, judges, law professors,
and law students in over 1,100 cities across
America and in 10 foreign countries, who
exercise their Christian faith in the practice
of law in association with pastors and con-
cerned laypeople.)

Lawyers for Children America
151 Farmington Avenue, RW4A
Hartford, CT 06510
(860) 273-0441
Fax (860) 273-8340
www.lawyersforchildrenamerica.org
(Lead child advocacy organization protect-
ing the rights of children who are victims
of abuse, abandonment, and neglect by
providing pro bono legal representation.)

National Women's Law Center
11 Dupont Circle NW, Suite 800
Washington, DC 20036
(202) 588-5180
Fax (202) 588-5185
www.nwlc.org
(Provides newsletter, analysis of legislation
and policy, monitoring of agency compli-
ance with the law.)

Marriage and Family

American Family Foundation
P. O. Drawer 2440
Tupelo, Mississippi 38803
(662) 844-5036
Fax (662) 842-7798
www.afa.net

**Association of Couples for
Marriage Enrichment (Better Marriages)**
P.O. Box 21374
Winston-Salem, NC 27120
(800) 634-8325 or (336) 724-1526
Fax (336) 721-4746
www.bettermarriages.org

**Family Service America
(FAST—Families and Schools Together)**
11700 W. Lake Park Drive
Milwaukee, WI 53224-3099
(800) 221-3726 or (414) 359-1040
Fax (414) 359-1074
www.wcer.wisc.edu/fast

Focus on the Family
Colorado Springs, CO 80995
(800) A-FAMILY (232-6459)
(719) 531-5181
www.family.org
*(This long-standing and highly regarded
non-profit Christian family organization
was founded by noted author and psychologist Dr. James C. Dobson and dedicated to
strengthening the home. It produces several
national radio programs and magazines as
well as family-oriented books, films, videos,
and more from a Christian perspective.)*

Insight for Living
P.O. Box 269000
Plano, TX 75026-9000
(800) 772-8888
www.insight.org

Insight for Living Canada
P.O. Box 2510
Vancouver, BC, Canada V6B 3W7
(800) 663-7639 or (604) 272-5811
www.insightforliving.ca
*(This ministry, started by author/evange-
list Chuck Swindoll, provides tapes, study
guides, and other materials for biblical
guidance and instruction.)*

InStep Ministries
3957 East Speedway Drive, Suite 208
Tucson, AZ 85712
(520) 721-0800
Fax (520) 721-9069
www.instepministries.com
*(This Christian organization is committed
to equipping singles and stepfamilies for life,
with numerous biblical resources.)*

Stepfamily Association of America
650 J Street, Suite 205
Lincoln, NE 68508
(800) 735-0329
Fax (402) 477-8317
www.saafamilies.org
*(Provides educational information and re-
sources for anyone interested in stepfamilies.)*

Stepfamily Foundation
333 West End Avenue
New York, NY 10023
(800) SKY-STEP (759-7837)
(212) 877-3244
Fax (212) 362-7030
www.stepfamily.org
(Counseling for stepfamilies in crisis.)

Successful Stepfamilies
7905 London Court
Amarillo, TX 79119
(806) 356-7701
www.successfulstepfamilies.com
*(Ministry founded by author, therapist, and
stepfamily educational specialist Ron L.
Deal, this organization empowers stepfamilies toward healthy living with a wide
variety of excellent resources.)*

Mediation

Academy of Family Mediators
P.O. Box 51090
Eugene, OR 97405
(541) 345-1629
www.mediate.com
*(AFM is the largest family mediation
organization in existence.)*

American Arbitration Association
1633 Broadway, 10th Floor
New York, NY 10019
(800) 778-7879
www.adr.org

Association for Conflict Resolution
1015 18th Street NW, Suite 1150
Washington, DC 20036
(202) 464-9700
Fax (202) 464-9720
www.acrnet.org

**Association of Family
and Conciliation Courts**
6525 Grand Teton Plaza
Madison, WI 53719
(608) 664-3750
Fax (608) 664-3751
www.afccnet.org
*(An interdisciplinary association of judges,
lawyers, mediators, and mental health professionals dedicated to family law services
as a complement to the judicial process.
Provides newsletter on family law issues
and other resources.)*

Peacemaker Ministries
2590 Holman Avenue, Suite A
Billings, MT 59102
(406) 256-1583
Fax (406) 256-0001
www.peacemaker.net
*(Mission of this ministry is to equip and
assist Christians to respond to conflict biblically. Provides conflict coaching, mediation,
and arbitration services to resolve church
and ministry disputes, lawsuits, family
divisions, and business conflicts. Former Association of Christian Conciliation Services
(ACCS) merged with this organization in
1993.)*

Pornography Addictions

Faithful and True Ministries
15798 Venture Lane
Eden Prairie, MN 55344
(952) 746-3882
www.faithfulandtrueministries.com
*(Christian recovery ministry under the
oversight of Dr. Mark Laaser for individuals
and couples who struggle because of sexual
addiction.)*

Man On The Road Ministry
P.O. Box 211
Madison, TN 37116
www.manontheroad.org

*(Ministry under oversight of Tom Buford.
Focuses primarily on men who spend the
majority of their time away from their
families, but reaches out to all pornography
addicts and the people who love them.)*

Pure Life Ministries
14 School Street
Dry Ridge, KY 40135-7422
(888) 740-8828
www.purelifeministries.org
*(Christian ministry serves individuals deal-
ing with sexual sin throughout the world by
providing biblically based counseling and
teaching materials.)*

Singles Groups and Resources

Single Adult Ministry
P.O. Box 681982
Franklin, TN 37068
(615) 794-4920
www.singleadultministry.com
*(Encourages Christian single adults—
including divorced singles—to discover
God's purpose for their lives as whole
individuals through their personal
relationship with Jesus Christ.)*

Single Booklovers
P.O. Box 1658
1237 State Road
Andalusia, PA 19020
www.singlebooklovers.com

The Single Life
P.O. Box 8222
Lowell, MA 01853-8222
(978) 441-2765
Web: www.thesinglelife.org
*(A support organization of divorced,
separated, widowed, and never-married
men and women.)*

Appendix F

Facts and Statistics about Family Relationships

"Anyone who conducts an argument by appealing to authority [and statistics] is not using his intelligence; he is just using his memory."—Leonardo da Vinci

"There are two kinds of statistics, the kind you look up, and the kind you make up."—Author Rex Stout

[NOTE: Beginning with the 2000 Census, the U.S. Census Bureau no longer included a box for citizens to indicate whether they're married, single, divorced, or widowed on forms received by most Americans. Also, the National Center for Health Statistics cut back their work in gathering complete national divorce statistics in the 1990s.]

General Trends

• The overall U.S. divorce rate had a brief spurt after World War II, followed by a decline in the 1950s. The divorce rate rose again in the 1960s, and even more quickly in the 1970s, before leveling off in the 1980s and declining slightly.

• Measuring the "divorce rate" today is difficult—perhaps impossible to determine—especially since statistical data is limited.

• In a report released in June 1999 and produced by the National Marriage Project at Rutgers University, the overview stated: "Key social indicators suggest a substantial weakening of the institution of marriage. Americans have become less likely to marry. When they do marry, their marriages are less happy. And married couples face a high likelihood of divorce. Over the past four decades, marriage has declined as the first living together experience for couples and as a status of parenthood. Unmarried cohabitation and unwed births have grown enormously, and so has the percentage of children who grow up in fragile families. . . . As an adult stage in life course, marriage is shrinking. Americans are living longer, marrying later, exiting marriage more quickly, and choosing to live together before marriage, after marriage, in between marriages, and as an alternative to marriage. A small but growing percentage of American adults will never marry. As a consequence, marriage is surrounded by longer periods of partnered or unpartnered singlehood over the course of a lifetime."[1]

Marriage and Family—General

• Married couples with children represent only 26% of households in 2000.[2]

• According to the National Center for Health Statistics, the percentage of Americans getting married is at an all-time low. Meanwhile, the number of divorces has increased almost 200% between 1960 and 1990. In 1960, there were 73.5 marriages for every 1,000 unmarried women, and 9.2 divorces for every 1,000 married women. By 1987, there were only 55.7 marriages, but the number of divorces had risen to 21 per 1,000 married women.[3]

Divorce—General

• The often quoted statistic that 50% of all U.S. marriages end in divorce is inaccurate. This statistic arose when someone at the Census Bureau noticed there had been 2.4 million marriages and 1.2 million divorces in 1990. Comparing these two figures without taking into account the 54 million marriages already in existence gave birth to this quotable, but highly inaccurate, statistic.[4]
• Approximately 45% of new marriages will end in divorce.[5]
• Approximately 40% of all married adults in the 1990s have already been divorced.[6]
• Approximately 43% of first marriages end in either divorce or separation within 15 years. One in three first marriages dissolve within 10 years. One in five first marriages terminate within 5 years.[7]
• Divorce rates rose in 44 of 50 states after adoption of no-fault divorce legislation.[8]
• In 1998, approximately 10% of adults (19.4 million) were "currently divorced," according to the U.S. Census Bureau.
• According to Barna Research Online in August, 2001, "born-again Christians" are just as likely to get divorced as are adults who are not born-again.

Children of Divorced Parents

• The number of children whose parents divorced grew by 700% from 1900 to 1972.[9]
• About 25% of Americans aged 18 to 44 are the adult children of divorced parents. Approximately 67% of children grow up with divorces and remarriages of one or both parents. Only a fraction bonded with all members of the blended families. More than 1 million children a year have experienced parental divorce since 1970.[10]

Widowed Persons

• Approximately 45% of women 65 years and older were widowed. Of the elderly widows, 7 in 10 lived alone.[11]

Single Parenting

• The number of children living with both parents declined from 85% in 1970 to 68% in 1996. Between 1970 and 1996, the proportion of children under 18 years of age living with one parent grew from 12% to 28% (20 million), according to a 1998 U.S. Census Bureau Report.
• According to the U.S. Census Bureau, during the 10 year period ending in 2000, households headed by single mothers increased by more than 25%, while those led by single fathers grew by almost 62%.

• According to the U.S. Census Bureau, the percentage of children in single-parent families has risen from 9% in 1960 to 28% in 1998.

• Based upon current trends through 2001, it is predicted that half of the children living today will spend at least part of their childhood in single-parent homes.[12]

Remarriage—General

• In 1993, approximately 80% of all divorced persons remarried. About 83% of all divorced men and 75% of all divorced women remarried. Approximately 50% of those whose first marriages ended in divorce remarried within three years. Approximately 80% of divorced men, and 70% of divorced women, remarried within five years.[13]

• In 1998, the median age for remarriage of widowed men was 63.1 years, and 54 for widowed women.[14]

• Approximately 46 of every 100 marriages in 1998 were remarriages for one or both partners. Of those, 24 were remarriages for both persons.[15]

• According to noted researcher Judith Wallerstein, in 2000 approximately 60% of remarriages ended in divorce.[16]

• According to the National Center for Health Statistics in 1995, remarriages ending in divorce lasted an average of 7.4 years for men, and 7.1 years for women. The average age of men divorcing from their second marriage was 42 years; for women it was age 39. For those divorced three or more times, the average age of men was 46.5; for women it was 42 years.

• One-half of all women who experienced divorce in first marriages and re-married did so within two and one-half years after their divorce.[17]

• Approximately 39% of all remarriages dissolve within 10 years. But age makes a difference. If a woman remarries under 25, the likelihood of separation or divorce is 47%. If she is 25 or older, the likelihood falls to 34%.[18]

• According to Barna Research Online, 35% of born-again Christians have experienced divorce. Most of these people remarry (75%) and many have experienced divorce a second time (23%).

Stepfamilies—General

• According to the U.S. Census Bureau, the number of stepfamilies increased 36% from 1980 to 1990, to 5.3 million. About 21% of all married couples with dependent children now include at least one stepparent. In 1990, 7.3 million children were in stepfamilies.[19]

• In 1990, 20.8% of all two-parent families had stepchildren, up from 16.1% in 1980.[20]

• In 1990, one of three Americans is either a stepparent, stepchild, step-sibling or other stepfamily member. Approximately 1,300 new stepfamilies were formed every day in the 1990s.[21]

Chapter Notes

Chapter 1

[1] C. S. Lewis, *Mere Christianity* (New York: The Macmillan Company, 1958).

[2] Zig Ziglar, as quoted in *Sermons Illustrated*, April, 1993.

[3] Wayne Thompson, Mark James, Johnny Christopher, "Always On My Mind," Warner Bros. Music Co., 1971.

Chapter 2

[1] George Scriven and C. C. Converse, "What a Friend We Have in Jesus." *Songs of the Church*, edited by Alton H. Howard (West Monroe, LA: Howard Publishers 1977), song 623.

[2] The apostle Peter's speech to the crowds in Jerusalem who had crucified Christ in Acts 2:14–41 is an excellent example of how God helped the Israelites feel objective guilt that motivated them to repentance and salvation.

[3] According to information on file with the National Depressive & Manic-Depressive Association in Chicago, Illinois, some of the warning signals of depression are these: extreme loneliness and "heaviness;" feeling detached or "outside" one's self; inability to feel any human warmth; nightmares or restlessness with long periods of sleeplessness or waking up throughout the night or too early (3 or 4 a.m.) or, to the other extreme, sleeping excessively (12 to 15 hours a day); withdrawal from others and making excuses to avoid contact; neglect of appearance (not shaving or putting on makeup); compulsive overeating with rapid weight gains of 30 to 40 pounds, or drastic diets and weight loss by tens of pounds; frequent or unexplainable crying spells, or wanting to cry but not being able to do so; complaints of feeling hopeless, depressed, and hurting all over inside and believing, "I'll never get over this;" loss of interest in a job, family, friends, and hobbies that once brought joy; getting little or no pleasure out of anything in life; overreacting with excessive irritability over trivial matters; overly aggressive behavior, or anxiety and agitation by being unusually restless or fidgety, or not reacting at all; loss of energy with difficulty in thinking and concentration, loss of memory and inability to make decisions; low self-esteem and self-blame for everything that goes wrong; tension headaches, stomach disorders and ulcers, cardiovascular disease, constipation or, to the other extreme, experiencing ambiguous physical pains that defy diagnosis; and, if the depression becomes especially severe, recurrent thoughts of death or suicide. If you are experiencing some or many of the symptoms of depression, you should seek competent professional counseling without delay.

[4] William Shakespeare, *Much Ado About Nothing*, Act III.

Chapter 3

[1] Throughout this excerpt I have substituted the term "my wife" for her name to protect her anonymity.

[2] Why is this? Because restitution is *not* built-in repentance. Restitution is a legal transaction. One returns or replaces what was taken or destroyed. But repentance is a change of will brought about by godly sorrow, which leads to reformation of life. Restitution comes from the pocketbook, but scriptural repentance comes from the heart. We are called to repent and turn to God and prove our repentance by our deeds (Acts 26:20). But if one's heart is right before God, restitution flows willingly. Zachaeus provides a beautiful example of this for us in Luke 19:1–10. The key point is that God looks on our *hearts* and searches out those in the world who are fully devoted to Him (2 Chron. 16:9; Luke 16:15). Restitution fulfills the requirements of the law, but restitution alone does not make our hearts right—that begins with repentance.

[3] This story is found in *Homemade*, Vol. 17, No. 1, January, 1993.

[4] Certainly, repentance must be present. Also, in some marriage relationships conditions are not only appropriate but absolutely necessary. For example, it is one matter for an

alcoholic spouse to return home saying, "I repent of drinking. Will you forgive me?" But if the same spouse comes home saying those words while drunk and holding a bottle of liquor in front of the children, who would say it is wrong to throw the person out the door unless and until he returns sober? We will talk about how tough love and unconditional love *work* together in later chapters.

Chapter 4

[1] A "sacrament" is an outward or visible sign, ordained by God or Christ, bringing forth an inward or spiritual blessing. The Lord's Supper is an example of this.

[2] Augustine contended that marriage was a sacrament based upon use of the Latin word *sacramentum* for the Greek root word *musteerion* (*mystery* in verse 32, literally meaning "a mystic or hidden sense that is not obvious to understanding") in his interpretation of Ephesians 5:21–33. From this premise, he then formed the standard for the Western church that marriage was indissoluble, even in cases of adultery. But is this premise correct? Further review of this passage in Ephesians 5 shows that the marriage union is used instead as an *analogy* for our understanding of the union between Christ and His church. Paul uses the unity and fidelity of a marriage as an *example* in the flesh of Christ's marvelous spiritual union with the church. During the Middle Ages, to protect this sacramental view of marriage, the church immersed itself in marriage laws. Ceremonies with ministers began in the tenth century. Support for Augustine's position grew as Thomas Aquinas concurred with his views in the thirteenth century. But the Protestant reformers rejected this sacramental view and absolute indissolubility of marriage. They vowed to return to what they perceived as the more biblical view—that marriage is holy and to be honored, but that certain acts (e.g., adultery) can break a marriage. Nevertheless, the Catholic church first memorialized a sacramental view of marriage and its absolute indissolubility at the Council of Trent in 1545–63, largely as a reaction to what was perceived as Protestant leniency. With the Reformation, however, the consensus of religious opinion seemed to reject the sacramental view of marriage, instead considering it a matter of private intent and agreement between a couple and God.

[3] The husband gave his wife a *get* (coming from the Hebrew word for "document"). Only men could issue this document. No similar right existed for women under Jewish law, although a wife could ask a Jewish court to compel her husband to give her a "get" under certain circumstances (e.g., if the husband was impotent or had a loathsome disease). A get is a 12-line document written by a scribe in Hebrew and Aramaic describing a written release from marriage. To be valid, the certificate of divorce must meet all the expressed or implied requirements of Jewish law, be properly signed by the husband, and be dated and witnessed. It must specifically recite that the woman is now free to marry any man. Another man who married the divorced woman with a valid certificate of divorce did not have to worry about the first husband claiming any rights under the first marriage. The executed certificate was effective with delivery to the woman by putting it in her hand. An invalid certificate brought harsh penalties to the divorced woman, including: (1) possible forfeiture of her lump sum divorce settlement previously agreed to with her former husband (*ketubah*), although this would be forfeited anyway if the woman was divorced for violating the law of Moses; (2) possible loss of any increase in any property she owned personally but used by her former husband prior to the divorce (*melog*); (3) possible risk that her children by a second husband following an invalid divorce would be considered bastards (*mamzerim*) by being born from an adulterous relationship. Even today, Orthodox and Conservative Jews struggle with issues surrounding the husbands giving their wives a get. Some husbands refuse to make delivery to their wives unless they receive money, child custody, or liberal visitation privileges. In fact, abuse of this sort compelled some Jewish women in New York to form an advocacy movement called G.E.T. (Getting Equitable Treatment) to help spouses who have been denied a get, even after a Jewish court (called a Beth Din) has ordered that they be given one. Without a get, a Jewish woman becomes

an *agunah*—literally, a woman chained to a man. All of this is described in Jewish law and traditions, not in the Bible.

⁴ Hebrew, *tame*, or "to become unclean." Leviticus 18:20 and Numbers 5:13–14 use the same term to refer to adultery. In context, this defilement may exist only in the wife in relation to her first husband, but not with other men.

⁵ The answer to this question may not hinge as much on any overlap between the law of Moses and the New Testament, but on *how God views* the conduct being addressed. If conduct is detestable to God in the Old Testament, it is hard to imagine the same conduct being acceptable under the new covenant. For example, did the conduct described as detestable to God in Proverbs 6:16–19 become acceptable after the death of Jesus on the cross? This is highly unlikely.

⁶ For example, in Numbers 25:6–15, an Israelite man brought a Gentile woman into his family. Aaron's grandson, Phinehas, drove a spear through both man and woman for this violation, and God commended him for it.

⁷ But, as we discuss in chapter 6, if an unbeliever abandons a marriage, the believer is "not bound" to preserve it (1 Cor. 7:15).

⁸ Genesis 9:6; Leviticus 20:10. Where adultery was suspected but could not be proven by witnesses, the matter could be established by the ordeal of bitter waters, as described in Numbers 5:11–31.

⁹ Because of examples like this, some try to strike a deal with God: they like to sin, and God likes to forgive. But this is an attitude of one with a serious spiritual heart problem. Galatians 5 warns us in the strongest terms to forsake any license to sin. Seeking independence from God, disobeying His commands, or selfishly indulging the desires of the flesh can have severe consequences. The grace of God and the love of Christ compel us to say no to ungodliness and worldly passions and to live self-controlled, upright, and godly lives (2 Cor. 5:14–15; Titus 2:11–14). Our attitude should always include a desire to please God *more* than ourselves.

¹⁰ Interestingly, the Jews knew from Deuteronomy 24:1–4 that a husband was not permitted to take back his divorced wife after she had been married to another man. Even so, they expected God to take back the nation of Judah despite committing spiritual adultery with many other lovers (Jer. 3:1b–5). And God was faithful. He graciously invited Israel to return, upon the condition that she confess her wrongdoing (Jer. 3:11–14). Eventually He took Israel and Judah back and made a new marriage-like covenant with them by forgiving whatever happened in the past (Jer. 31:31–34).

Chapter 5

¹ Some passages are very challenging. Reasonable men and women can disagree about what Jesus is saying. In those instances we must draw our own conclusions as God leads us. But an interpretation is not false simply because we have not heard of it before or because we cannot accept it. Neither is it true simply because we cannot disprove it or most people believe it to be true.

² Tough situations as well as exceptionally abused or denied people in life move our emotions and tempt us to cry out, "Enough! I don't care what the Bible says about it. This cannot continue!" But situational ethics that ignore God bring questionable results.

³ As a young Christian lawyer, I could understand rules and principles in Scripture. Bible studies were neat and tidy; rule meshed into rule, and law into law. In our Bible study groups we would liken Scripture to the natural law of gravity, allowing our Bibles to fall to the floor to prove that His laws (like the natural law of gravity) transcend human existence. You do not break God's laws as much as you break yourself against them. Rules and principles provide a convenient yardstick to measure growth. Biblical standards help define who's "in" and who's "out" of favor with God. But if we become too comfortable with rules and regulations, sometimes it is difficult to grasp the fullness of God's grace and mercy. Many times grace can bridge gaps of disobedience under any law in a single bound

without progressive planks of logic. It speaks of second chances to try again when the law says, "Strike one, you're out!"

[4] Rubel Shelly, "The Eternal Tension: Law & Grace," *Image* magazine, May, 1990, p. 10.

[5] For example, if someone rushes to the hospital to save a dying relative or deliver a child, the judge takes this into account. Speed laws may be broken, but the judge has discretion in applying the penalty. Result? Similar crimes can result in different sentences. This is not neat and tidy justice. Unlike God's law where He is Judge, however, truly unjust inconsistencies and inequities arise under civil law forged by imperfect judges and juries. But if a judge under civil law can consider "mitigating circumstances" (factors that may justify otherwise illegal conduct) in determining a proper penalty, why is it so hard to accept God doing the same? Consider the mitigating circumstances that Jesus referred to as He healed the paralytic on the Sabbath in Matthew 12:1–14, for instance.

[6] Over the years, God has helped me to deal with my legalistic righteousness. I have learned to appreciate how God has always been merciful and compassionate. Oh, yes, intellectually I was aware of Deuteronomy 4:31, Hosea 6:6, and so many other Old Testament passages that spoke of our God being merciful. But in my heart, I failed to see how much God's grace and mercy were the foundation of everything He shared with His people in the law of Moses, through Jesus Christ and His apostles—everything.

[7] Since the law usually required two or three witnesses to convict and stone an adulterer (Deut. 17:6–7; 19:15), some informants to the Pharisees may have spied out this transgression and reported it to them.

[8] She is the picture of all humankind—guilty and deserving of condemnation and death at the hands of her accusers. Given his bargaining with God over Job (Job 1:6–12; 2:1–7) or his temptation of Jesus in the wilderness (Luke 4:1–13), no doubt Satan, the Prince of Darkness, was pleased with darkness in the hearts of these people who were now confronting Jesus, the Light of the world (John 8:12).

[9] Perhaps He thought the Pharisees were correct about the law. Adultery is so serious that the law commands death by stoning (Lev. 20:10; Deut. 22:13–24). But where was the compassion of those bringing this woman forward? The Pharisees publicly exposed her without mercy solely for a round of religious gamesmanship with Jesus. This was vindictive behavior at its worst. The woman knew her sin, but the Pharisees deceived themselves into hypocritical self-righteousness by using the law to condemn her while harboring murderous intent toward Jesus. Too often those with the greatest sin are the most merciless in attacking others!

[10] Paul also used this distinction when describing himself in Romans 7:17–25. Separating the person from the sin allows for consideration of a repentant heart despite past mistakes.

[11] What if the woman had said, "Thanks, Lord! You really got me out of a jam!" What would have happened if she had run back to her lover? To the contrary, a repentant attitude made forgiveness and the pardon from punishment a reality in her life. Who can doubt that her love and appreciation for Jesus grew intense after this episode? After all, isn't this the type of faith—one moving us to the Savior—that's really what the law of Moses is all about?

[12] Matthew 5:32; 19:3–12; Mark 10:2–12; Luke 16:18, discussed in detail later in this chapter. However, adultery also can occur outside of remarriage, as when a married person has sexual relations with someone other than his or her mate. Dictionaries define *adultery* as the sexual infidelity of a married person, or voluntary sexual intercourse between a married person and someone other than his or her spouse. (Ezek. 16:32 metaphorically defines an adulterous wife as one who receives strangers instead of her husband.) Since Jesus defines marriage as a "one flesh" relationship between one man and one woman in Matthew 19:5–6, it follows that adultery occurs through any sexual infidelity that violates that relationship.

[13] Perhaps this is why the law of Moses required verification of sins like this by at least two witnesses (Deut.17:6–7; 19:15; Matt. 18:16. But see Num. 5:11–31 for situations where there were no witnesses to a wife's unfaithfulness).

[14] Remember that Moses had acknowledged that a man may divorce his wife "because he finds something indecent about her, and he writes her a certificate of divorce, gives it to her and sends her from his house." Two distinct rabbinic schools of thought on divorce received the most credibility. Rabbi Shammai held to the conservative view that "something indecent" required adultery. A wife could be mean and extremely difficult to live with, but no divorce could occur unless she committed adultery. Rabbi Hillel, however, held the liberal view that a man could divorce his wife for anything not pleasing to him. This Hillel-Shammai divorce controversy intrigued the Pharisees. They decided to put Jesus to a test by tying Him up in public debate on this issue.

[15] The Greek root word is *suzugnuo*, used only in Matthew 19:6 and in Mark 10:9. It means to "fasten to one yoke, or to yoke together" as two oxen are yoked together to pull a plow. How does God "join" husband and wife together in marriage today? It springs from His creation of the marriage relationship and the pronouncement that the couple is "one flesh." God does not have to perform individual wedding ceremonies before "joining" a couple together. The details of how, where, and when this happens are left to the couple to decide as they agree to be married. On a related point, some believe God does not join together in marriage those who are out of a covenant relationship with Him (such as, today, non-Christians). But if true, this would mean: most couples in the world today are in a sinful relationship, having illegitimate children; and Christians who attempt to marry non-Christians are not married and also have illegitimate children (contrary to Paul's statement in 1 Cor. 7:14). But God's plan for marriage arises from the creation of humankind and applies universally to everyone as a blessing from God—just as many other blessings are.

[16] The root word for "not separate" (Greek, *chorizo*, meaning "to separate, divide, part, or to put asunder") also appears in Romans 8:35 and 39—nothing can *separate* us from the love of God in Christ Jesus. In 1 Corinthians 7:10, 11, and 15, Paul uses this term to instruct Christians not to separate from their mates. It clearly expresses that breaking a marriage bond is not pleasing to God. Husbands and wives can physically sever their relationship with each other (unscripturally, if no marital unfaithfulness [*porneia*] occurs) and change their marital status to "unmarried" by leaving a marriage with no intention to return. This is considered a divorce. However, they are not free to remarry as long as no *porneia* exists and both mates remain alive (Matt. 19:9; 1 Cor. 7:10–11).

[17] However, there may be circumstances where it is *necessary* to separate, as when there is unreasonable duress through verbal, physical, or mental abuse that endangers the lives of a spouse and children. (We discuss domestic violence situations in more detail in chapter 7 and in part 3 of this book.)

[18] Greek, *skleerokardia*, meaning "a characteristic of one whose heart is hard, harsh, stiff" similar to how Israel refused to listen to God in Ezekiel 3:7. The term is used in only two other instances in the New Testament—Mark 10:5, in a parallel passage on divorce, and in Mark 16:14 where Jesus rebuked His disciples for their stubborn refusal to believe those who had seen Him after He had risen.

[19] We may ask, "Aren't the hearts of men and women still hard today? Why doesn't Jesus permit divorce like Moses did?" Perhaps it is because we can have a personal relationship with a risen Savior during our lifetimes. God has given us the power to live the Christian life in a way not available during Moses' time. Before Christ fulfilled the law of Moses (Gal. 3:15–29), God graciously made concessions to those under the law due to humankind's failure to live a righteous life. His people desperately needed grace and forgiveness because of missing the mark and falling short of God's standard. Jesus paid our penalty on the cross. Jesus confirms that divorce under Moses was an abnormal, stopgap measure. The real issue today is whether Christians will open wide their hearts to God (2 Cor. 6:11–13).

[20] Note that Jesus addresses slightly different divorce situations in Mark 10:11–12.

[21] Greek, *apoluo*, or "to loose from, sever by loosening, undo, repudiate, dismiss from your house." This term is used 69 times in the New Testament, including Mark 1:19 where Joseph considered putting away Mary due to her pregnancy. It should be said that, just as the Bible specifies no ceremony for marriage (discussed in chapter 4), it is true that no divorce procedures are prescribed either. It is a matter of private decision between husband and wife. Even so, a couple' s decision to divorce, or compliance with a human civil court procedure for divorce, are irrelevant to God if His requirements are not met. As we shall see, unless marital unfaithfulness (*porneia*) occurs in a marriage, a civil divorce does not end the relationship even if a court says it does.

[22] Greek, *gameo*, meaning "to lead in marriage; to take a wife; to get married." We find this word throughout the New Testament, including in Mark 6:17 and 1 Corinthians 7:9, 10, 28, 33, 34, 36, and 39 discussed in chapter 6.

[23] For example, assuming that verse 9 has universal application to all humankind, different people interpret verse 9 as: (1) not permitting divorce at all (Mark 10:11–12); (2) permitting divorce only after marital unfaithfulness has occurred, but not remarriage under any circumstance as long as both spouses live; (3) permitting divorce for "something indecent" and remarriage as Hillel interpreted Deuteronomy 24:1 (meaning divorce for almost any reason and freedom to marry others); (4) permitting divorce for both spouses, but with remarriage to another partner *only* available to the spouse not guilty of marital unfaithfulness; or (5) permitting divorce and remarriage for *both* spouses after either or both spouses commit marital unfaithfulness (which can occur before or after divorce, or when one spouse marries another person).

[24] As we shall see in chapter 6, however, Jesus is directly speaking in verse 9 of divorce in general. The unique problems of marriages between Christians and non-Christians arising after His resurrection may not be directly addressed here by Jesus. In 1 Corinthians 7, Paul may provide a special exception permitting divorce for *Christians* in such mixed marriages.

[25] Some argue that marriage is a covenant, and divorce breaks a covenant to remain married and faithful for life. Support for this view focuses on Israel's turning away from God in spiritual adultery (such as idolatry, Jer. 3:1–14). But as we shall see, *porneia* goes beyond non-sexual covenant-breaking or even figurative adultery. The term includes all forms of *sexual infidelity*. (The NIV translation of "marital unfaithfulness" is somewhat misleading.) In addition, it is possible to *violate* a covenantal relationship while not *dissolving* it. (For example, Saul violated the covenant of Israel with the Gibeonites by putting some to death in Samuel 21:1–9, but he did not revoke the covenant, which continued for many more centuries.) In a marriage, a husband may violate a covenant to love his wife as himself (Eph. 5:28) in many ways not involving any sexual infidelity, but breaking this covenant does not authorize dissolution of the marriage itself. By making this exception in verse 9, Jesus implies that *sexual infidelity* is what breaks the "one flesh" relationship and can destroy the marriage relationship through divorce—not mere "covenant-breaking."

[26] Thayer, Arndt, and Gingrich to name a few.

[27] Many may wonder about the whole concept of infidelity and how it really begins. Is it exchanging secrets with someone else about matters that your spouse does not even know? Is it having lunch with someone you are attracted to without your mate knowing about it? In terms of sexual infidelity, does this mean intercourse or some other sexual activity short of it? Isn't an emotional involvement with a stranger just as devastating to a marriage as a sexual situation? This in turn tempts people to wonder, "How far can I go and still be considered faithful to my spouse?" Even the logistics of infidelity require hiding and secrecy that focuses more on pragmatic solutions than what is happening in one's heart. How can one see a lover, and where will the meeting be held? How will one contact the other? What excuses can be given to one's spouse and children? I believe, however, that if these thoughts are running through one's mind, the *desire* to commit *porneia* may be growing. It will not be long before some *opportunity* arises to commit *porneia* as Jesus describes in Matthew 19:9. Also, it highlights the idea that one's *heart* is not right before God.

[28] God endured Israel's spiritual adultery for hundreds of years before divorcing her. (He also took her back after divorce.)

[29] Matthew 18:15–17, discussed in the next chapter, may not apply here. The "two or three witnesses" in that passage are present to verify the *response* of one being challenged for past sin—not witnesses of the sin itself.

[30] *Leonard v. Leonard*, 259 So.2d 529, 530 (Fla. 3d DCA 1972).

[31] God's graciousness should cover any errors in that belief. In any event, if the errant spouse has already divorced his or her mate unscripturally and remarried, adultery has occurred. But remember, the key is not to focus on justification for divorce. Instead, we must always turn our hearts toward forgiveness and reconciliation to preserve a marriage as God has willed. Even if sexual infidelity has occurred, it is reasonable to believe that God would still approve of reconciliation between spouses (in the same spirit that God reconciled with Israel—even after divorce, and in the same graciousness that Hosea took back Gomer). If that fails, it is time to move on.

[32] It is a sin to murder someone else. But once the murder has occurred and the victim is dead, the murder does not continue. One does not keep on murdering a dead person. Some argue the same thing occurs with *porneia* in breaking a marriage bond.

[33] This assumes that the spouse committing adultery by remarriage to another person is, in doing so, terminating the first marriage, thereby rendering the remarriage no longer adulterous. But there are some serious problems with this view. For example, if God is seen to approve of a man and woman in an initially adulterous (but immediately thereafter legitimate) remarriage, is He somehow participating in their adulterous act? Does this view also allow an adulterer to legitimize an unscriptural divorce from a faithful spouse by remarriage to a lover? Does this view actually *encourage* people to commit adultery while pursuing remarriage?

[34] Mark 6:18; 1 Corinthians 5:1–5. This would be equally true of any such remarriage among Christians, and of those in such relationships as non-Christians who later become Christians. However, if *porneia* occurs through consummation of the adulterous remarriage, does this not make the formerly unscriptural divorce in the first marriage (one without *porneia*) now effectively a *scriptural* divorce? If so, how can adultery continue if the first marriage is now terminated scripturally?

[35] This brings us back to the question of whether a person can return to a spouse from a prior marriage if this remains an abomination to God as described in Deuteronomy 24:1–4.

[36] The word "causes" in Greek is *poyeo*, meaning "to be the author of; to cause; to make ready; to prepare."

[37] This is similar to Jesus' teaching on another occasion in Luke 16:18b.

[38] This is in accord with Romans 7:2–3 and 1 Corinthians 7:10–11, which we will review in chapter 6.

[39] He also implicitly reaffirmed the need for reconciliation until it becomes impossible through scriptural divorce or death.

Chapter 6

[1] See 1 Corinthians 7:8. It is possible that Paul married at one time, however, as a voting member of the Sanhedrin, the Jewish Supreme Court and the highest religious tribunal in Jerusalem (see Acts 26:10—members of the Sanhedrin were married.) If so, we do not know what happened to his wife.

[2] The term "Corinthian girl" was a euphemism for prostitute. If a Corinthian character appeared in a Greek play, the role was frequently as an alcoholic.

[3] Also see 2 Corinthians 1:1. The Spirit inspired Paul to write 1 and 2 Corinthians, a series of letters to the church in Corinth, while Paul was away on missionary journeys. Note also that although Paul writes directly to the Christians in Corinth, the message of his letters applies to "all those *everywhere* who call on the name of our Lord Jesus Christ." The letters have universal application.

⁴ In verse 1, the words, "has his father's wife" in Greek means "to have or use a woman (unlawfully) as a wife." John the Baptist used similar terms to challenge Herod that it was unlawful to have his brother Philip's wife (Matt. 14:4; Mark 6:18). The woman referred to was probably the Christian's stepmother, or Paul would have referred to her as the man's "mother." She was also not a Christian, or Paul would have spoken against her as well as the Christian man.

⁵ Compare Paul's reaction with that of Jesus with the adulterous woman in John 8 (discussed in the previous chapter). Was Paul unloving in calling for disfellowship of the man? Did grace not apply in this case? But there is a major difference between this man and the adulterous woman Jesus met. The latter was not a believer when she first met Jesus, nor did she pretend to be. She had a change of heart when faced with her sin. But this Christian man in Corinth believed that nothing was wrong about the liaison with his stepmother! The prideful complacency of this man made his deed all the more grievous. God would never accept this relationship. His gracious nature required strong action to motivate repentance.

⁶ In 1 Corinthians 5:4–5, Paul challenged the Corinthians to use church discipline to rebuke this man for everyone's good if he did not repent. In commanding, "Expel the wicked man from among you," Paul exhorted the Christians to use urgency in separating themselves from this sinful influence. This is the same type of urgency commanded under the law of Moses in Deuteronomy 17:7; 19:19, 22:21, 24; and 24:7 in order to purge evil from among the people of God. It is a *very* strong statement indeed! The law of Moses formerly commanded physical death for such sinners. God spared this man's life under the new covenant. We may think it harsh to disfellowship anyone, but God is graciously exercising personal discipline in this way to encourage repentance. He disciplines those He loves (Heb. 12:1–13).

⁷ We discuss this concept in more detail in chapter 9.

⁸ Paul undoubtedly desired to restore the man's heart to God. To do this, he allowed the man to suffer the consequences of his actions. By putting the man out of the life and fellowship within the Lord's church and into the world controlled by Satan (Col. 1:13; 1 Tim. 1:20; 1 John 5:19), Paul hoped he would come to his senses. Like the prodigal son, perhaps he would see his need and return once again to his brothers and sisters in Christ.

⁹ It is important to note a critical problem with this relationship. If God considered it a valid marriage, the parties to it faced a dilemma. By continuing the relationship, they sinned due to its incestuous nature. If they divorced and remarried others, they might commit adultery. But if this relationship was an *invalid* marriage in God's sight, as appears to be the case, the relationship could have dissolved without the additional concerns inherent in separating a husband and wife. The point is this: determining one's true *marital status* before God is a critical factor before applying Scripture on divorce and remarriage to one's circumstances.

¹⁰ Greek, *pornos*, meaning "a fornicator; a man who indulges in unlawful sexual intercourse; a man who prostitutes his body to another's lust for hire." It is a root word for "pornography." It is the same word used repeatedly in 1 Corinthians 5:9–11. (It is also found in a similar warning in Eph. 5:5.)

¹¹ A reference to those who practice *moikaomai*, discussed in detail in the previous chapter in connection with the term "marital unfaithfulness" (*porneia*) in Matthew 19:9.

¹² This raises another question. Does Paul imply that becoming "one flesh" with a prostitute means one becomes "married" to him or her? Obviously not, since there was no leaving and cleaving involved in this temporary relationship. It is also hard to imagine that God would ever see this circumstance as a marriage. More likely, Paul is giving another reason why illicit sex is wrong. The partners unite in such an intimate way reserved only for a marriage relationship that it affects one's spiritual relationship with Christ. It is the ultimate defilement of our bodies as a sacred dwelling place for God, who dwells in our hearts by faith in Christ.

[13] It was probably more than persecution—that is always a problem for Christians (2 Tim. 3:12; 1 Pet. 4:12). Also unlikely is a reference to Christ's return. Paul makes a separate reference to His coming just three verses later (v. 29) as a future event. Some believe it was a severe famine in Corinth. According to archaeological evidence, there was a severe famine affecting the whole region of Achaia in the early part of the decade following A.D. 50. Perhaps inevitable starvation and illness were the "present crisis." But no one knows for sure.

[14] Greek, *agamos*, meaning "an unmarried person," used in 1 Corinthians 7:8, 11, 32 and 34.

[15] Greek, *parthenos*, meaning "a virgin; a marriageable maiden; one who has never had sexual intercourse," used in 1 Corinthians 7:25, 28, 34, 36 and 37. It is the same term used to refer to Mary, the mother of Jesus, in Matthew 1:23 and Luke 1:27.

[16] Greek, *loipos*, meaning "the rest, who are not of the specified class or number" also used in Matthew 27:49, Luke 8:10, and Acts 2:37. Some believe "the rest" refers to the remainder of the Corinthians' *questions* to Paul on marriage. In context, however, this is debatable since Paul continues to answer many questions throughout the remainder of 1 Corinthians.

[17] But by making this statement in context with verses 10 and 11, the unmarried (formerly married) Christians referred to here by Paul must include only those *scripturally eligible* to marry.

[18] Greek, *chorizo*, meaning "to separate, divide, put asunder; depart; go away." This is the same word used by Jesus in Matthew 19:6, and by Paul in 1 Cor. 7:15 in referring to unbelievers. Husbands and wives can physically sever their relationship with each other and become "unmarried" by leaving a marriage with no intention to return. In contrast to a couple living together as husband and wife, they have terminated normal marital relations. This is a divorce. But it does *not* necessarily break the marriage bond. Since God instituted marriage by joining man and woman in marriage, He tells us in Scripture when it is *scripturally broken.* (see also Matt. 19:9; 1 Cor. 7:15.) A *scriptural* divorce changes one's *marital status*, with freedom to remarry thereafter.

[19] Proof that divorce is referred to here is Paul's description of the separated wife as "unmarried" in 1 Corinthians 7:11, meaning no longer married (as we discussed in our prelude to 1 Cor. 7). The warning not to separate is strong, employing the same word used to assure us that nothing can separate us from the love of Christ (Rom. 8:35, 39).

[20] See also 1 Corinthians 7:39; Romans 7:3. Although Paul does not mention the "marital unfaithfulness" exception of Jesus, this does not nullify its validity. He is most likely addressing Christian spouses who have divorced for reasons *other than* marital unfaithfulness (*porneia*). In any event, verses 10–11 are consistent with Matthew 19:9. Unless the marriage is scripturally broken, forgiveness, and *reconciliation* are God's will if the spouses do not live separate lives (Eph. 4:32).

[21] What does it mean to be "yoked together with unbelievers"? Imagine two oxen tied together with a wooden crosspiece to pull a plow. Oxen yoked like this are chosen by similar size, strength, and temperament. They carefully train to respond to the same commands. A mismatch in any important way would leave the plowed field a mess! They must be a team working in tandem. What farmer would team up two animals that stubbornly refused to go in the same direction? What if one followed the farmer's instructions but the other did not? There would be no teamwork; the work would never be done. Without like-minded dedication, chaos reigns.

[22] But Christians are not to *initiate* separation or divorce if an unbeliever desires to stay in the marriage.

[23] Greek, *douloo*, meaning "to make a slave of; reduce to bondage," as one becomes a slave of God (Rom. 6:18, 22).

[24] A key question to ask is whether one is married or not married in *God's* view. This becomes an important factor in comparing the teachings of Jesus and Paul. By referring to "anyone who divorces . . ." in Matthew 19:9, Jesus is by implication referring to a couple who is validly married before God. He tells us that one or both validly married spouses who

401

divorce may not remarry without committing adultery as long as both spouses live and no *porneia* occurs because the couple is still married to each other in God's sight. As Paul echoes in 1 Corinthians 7:10–11, the couple must remain separate or reconcile. By contrast, in 1 Corinthians 7:15, Paul addresses a *believer* who has been separated from (divorced by) an unbeliever. Paul says the believer is "not bound" to the unbeliever in marriage. By implication, Paul's inspired judgment is that the believer's marital status before God is no longer "married," but "unmarried" and free of the marriage bond. Consequently, since Paul did not give the believer the same command in verse 15 that he did to another believer in verse 11, it is possible that the believer is no longer "bound" to the marriage or "married" before God. Therefore, they may be free to remarry without committing adultery. Remember, adultery arises when a validly *married* spouse remarries.

[25] This may be why David could keep Bathsheba as his wife after Uriah's death. It also brings us back to a question discussed in the previous chapter. Could these verses suggest that *spiritual* death (besides *physical* death) of a spouse may have some relevance? Remember that the law of Moses decreed *physical* death by stoning for adulterers. With the adulterer's death, the surviving spouse was then free to remarry, as noted in Romans 7:2–3. Does this apply to the "marital unfaithfulness" exception Jesus gives us in Matthew 19:9? If God is gracious toward adulterers today in not commanding *physical* death for their sins, does a *spiritual* death occur so as to free the faithful spouse to remarry? This may be why Jesus acknowledges the "marital unfaithfulness" exception in his teachings on divorce and remarriage.

Chapter 7

[1] Our review of Deuteronomy 24:4 in chapter 4 tells us this: God abhors sexual promiscuity, as when a woman moves from man to man, even if the legal technicalities are complied with. Adultery in a relationship is so repugnant to Him that one could easily conclude that He does not desire reunion—especially of a couple after *porneia* occurs. But then there is the example of Hosea taking back Gomer at God's command. God also took back His spiritually adulterous bride, Israel. The New Testament does not forbid a spouse from taking back an adulterous mate. When viewed with forgiveness, grace, and mercy under the new covenant, we have a precedent from God that seems to promote reconciliation whenever reasonably possible. Nevertheless, God also tells us that we will not be faulted for divorcing an adulterous mate *without* first exploring reconciliation.

[2] We get confused by the civil process of divorce. If a state court tells us we are divorced, we may believe that this somehow legitimizes and validates a divorce. But not so with God. The only divorce God recognizes is one that is *scripturally* permitted. If no such divorce occurs, the marriage continues—even if separation between spouses or a civil divorce has occurred. The couple's status remains "married." And if the marriage relationship is not terminated, a relationship with another person can result in adultery.

[3] This freedom does not arise from the innocence or guilt of the spouses involved but by virtue of their *unmarried status*. Some have analogized it this way: Imagine a husband and wife bound together in handcuffs. If the handcuff is removed from one spouse, the other is no longer bound either. Each is free to move in a different direction. But this creates a serious moral issue for many. If remarriage is available to *both* spouses after one spouse commits *porneia* to break up their marriage, what are the consequences of this sin? The "guilty party" should repent of sin and seek forgiveness from God (and the former spouse). But by being free to remarry simply by virtue of no longer being married, is this moral and just? Should the "guilty party" have any right to remarry? But how does denying any remarriage to a guilty spouse under any circumstances allow for God's grace to work in the situation? Should the guilty party forfeit remarriage forever? Can this person ever receive forgiveness and grace to have a second chance at marriage? See the next note for further consideration of this issue.

[4] May a spouse guilty of *porneia* and breakup of a marriage remarry? Some of the arguments *against* allowing remarriage are: (1) it gives the guilty spouse an incentive to

commit *porneia* in order to get out of an unwanted marriage; (2) the guilty spouse receives the same freedom to remarry as the innocent spouse, without punishment for the sin of breaking the marriage; (3) it allows a guilty spouse to maintain an adulterous remarriage; and (4) the guilty spouse is allowed to remarry when other parties to an *unscriptural* divorce (without *porneia*) may *not* remarry (e.g., the "innocent spouse" in Matt. 5:32b, and a Christian couple referred to in 1 Cor. 7:10–11). On the other hand, *porneia* breaks the marriage bond. The guilty spouse's marital status before God is that he or she is no longer a "married" person. Can any adultery continue if the marriage is broken? Furthermore, if the guilty spouse has remarried, does repentance (and restitution) require breaking up the remarriage? Won't this cause more problems—especially if children have been born of that remarriage? Even so, there will always be consequences for *porneia*, as there are for any sin. (See the story of David and Bathsheba.) Without a repentant heart, a guilty spouse faces eternal judgment.

[5] The Jewish historian Josephus, in his work *Antiquities of the Jews*, records that Herodias divorced Philip before she married Herod. [book 18, chapter 5:4] If so, the customs and laws of that time may have legitimized the marriage to Herod. But not so with God. Although she had divorced Philip and remarried Herod, Herodias is still referred to as "Philip's wife."

[6] Remember that 1 Corinthians 7:15 speaks of a Christian not resisting a *divorce by an unbeliever*. It does not appear to authorize a Christian to *initiate* a divorce against an unbeliever who wants to stay in the marriage.

[7] A related question is how does one repent of an unscriptural *divorce?* If the spouses *continue* in a divorced state, is this pardoned by God? Some argue that divorce is like murder—it has happened, but no one can bring the victim back to life. Furthermore, 1 Corinthians 7:11 says that an unscripturally divorced spouse has a choice—to remain unmarried or to reconcile. Therefore, God recognizes a state of separation or divorce (without remarriage) to another person. Others would say, however, that repentance from causing a divorce is shown in a *willingness* for reconciliation between husband and wife.

[8] God's law applies to all creation—the entire world. If anyone violates God's law, that person will be subject to whatever God provides though he or she may not yet be a citizen in God's kingdom. The gospel of Christ is for *all* people. There is only *one* road to salvation. The Word of Christ will judge the entire world—Christians and unbelievers (John 12:48). God clearly wants all people to come to repentance (2 Pet. 3:9). He commands *all* men and women everywhere to repent (Acts 17:30–31). Therefore, God's Word applies to all people—Christians and unbelievers alike—as much as the natural law of gravity (Mark 16:15–16; 1 Cor. 6:9–11; Gal. 5:19–21).

[9] In 1 Corinthians 7:20, Paul tells Christians to remain in the situations they were in at conversion. But this refers to *cultural*, not sinful situations. Paul surely did not counsel new converts to remain in sinful situations or he would not have, for example, commanded the church in Corinth to expel the man referred to in 1 Corinthians 5.

[10] Abusive spouses focus their rage and anger toward those who must put up with it. Since no one tolerates this conduct at work, it naturally comes out in the home against his or her mate and family. The more compliant and forgiving the victim spouse is in bearing up under the abuse, the more it negatively reinforces the abuser's continued violence. Submission in this context does not stop violence—it feeds it! The abuser does not suffer the consequences of his or her behavior. No one confronts an abusing husband with his manipulation or forces him to examine his own emotions *regardless* of whether his wife has irritated him. Instead, some hold the abused wife responsible for the abuser's violence. The counsel? *She* must change so as not to incite the husband to abuse. Nothing could be more destructive to the wife!

[11] Four million women are severely assaulted by their current or former partner each year. Abuse of this sort is the leading source of injury for women between the ages of 15 and 44 (*Time*, June 29, 1992, p. 57). In 1996, among all female murder victims in the U.S., 30 percent were slain by their husbands or boyfriends. (Federal Bureau of Investigation, U.S.

Department of Justice, Uniform Crime Reports of the U.S., 1996). In 2001, intimate partner violence made up 20 percent of all nonfatal crime experienced by women (*Domestic Violence Ten Years Later*, Edward S. Snyder and Laura W. Morgan, American Bar Association, GP/Solo Law Trends and News, Vol. 1. No. 4, August 2005).

[12] Also cited is 1 Corinthians 7:2 where Paul acknowledges the prevalence of immorality and calls for each man to have his own wife, and vice versa. But, in context, 1 Corinthians 7:9 must be read in conjunction with 1 Corinthians 7:11 and Matthew 19:9 or Paul contradicts himself in the span of just two verses. First, 1 Corinthians 7:9 must address unmarried (formerly married) persons who are *scripturally free* to remarry—those to whom verse 11 that follows is not applicable. Also, in the Greek, 1 Corinthians 7:2 is addressing *married* persons. It literally says that each spouse should have sexual relations with his or her spouse *who already belongs to him or her*. It is addressing the problem of married persons withholding conjugal rights from each other—not a natural right to have a mate.

[13] The late Dr. Thomas B. Warren, former professor at the Tennessee Graduate School of Christian Doctrine and Apologetics, stated the logical syllogism this way: *If* marriage is governed by God, not merely the desires of men and women (Mark 16:15; Matt. 5:31–32; 19:9); *and* the Bible teaches that there are some who voluntarily abstain from sexual relations in their devotion to God (Matt. 19:10–12); *and* Christians who are separated from their Christian mates must remain unmarried or else be reconciled with their spouses (1 Cor. 7:10–11; also Matt. 19:9); *and* Jesus taught that some who divorce may not remarry (Matt. 5:31–32, 19:9); *and* one can act in such a way as to forfeit certain rights (Heb. 12:14–17; Num. 12–14), *then* the theory that celibacy is unnatural is false.

[14] I desire and need to remain open to reason and correction. You may have an insight from the Lord that I do not possess. I would welcome an opportunity for you to share that with me if you wish. Lord Halifax once said, "Nothing has an uglier look to us than reason, when it is not on our side." But the Bible encourages us to reason correctly (1 Thess. 5:21; Acts 17:11; 1 Pet. 3:15). Understanding God's truth in a deeper way is something I desire with all my heart.

[15] Second Corinthians 6:14–17 commands that Christians not be "unequally yoked" (KJV) to unbelievers. Relationships entrapping Christians, as described in this passage, must end. But does this Scripture preclude all marriages between Christians and unbelievers? Obviously not, because it would directly conflict with the command in 1 Corinthians 7:12–15 that Christians *remain* in marriages with unbeliever spouses (as long as the unbelievers stay in the marriage). Therefore, this passage must be warning Christians to avoid any relationships (work, social, marriage, etc.) that cause us to compromise our faith. If Christians must choose between relationships with unbelievers and a personal relationship with God, our commitment to God must prevail. But if a Christian can have a relationship, even a marriage, with an unbeliever and *not* compromise his or her faith, this Scripture does not appear to absolutely prohibit it. Nevertheless, it is *highly* preferable that Christians only marry other Christians, as we discussed in chapter 6. This gives a couple common ground on a very important commitment in life. It also puts us in the best position to avoid compromising our faith.

[16] I am persuaded that if anything is abhorrent to God at one time in history, then our unchanging God probably feels the same way today. Since the New Testament does not specifically address remarriage of spouses after an intervening marriage, we have no scriptural basis to conclude that God looks at this situation differently today. However, we leave open the possibility that God, in exercising grace and mercy, may accept those spouses who do reconcile in this manner with the gracious spirit of Hosea.

Part Three Introduction

[1] William Cowper and Guillaume Franc, "God Moves in a Mysterious Way," *Songs of the Church*, edited by Alton H. Howard (West Monroe, LA: Howard Publishers 1977), song 135.

Chapter 8

[1] Between 3:00-6:00 a.m.

[2] Larry Crabb, *Inside Out* (Colorado Springs, Colo: Navpress, 1988), 32.

[3] Dr. David J. Davis, former pastor of the Plymouth Congregational Church in Coconut Grove, Florida.

[4] Winston Churchill, radio address to Britain, June 18, 1940.

Chapter 9

[1] I strongly recommend that you read *Love Must Be Tough: New Hope for Marriages in Crisis* by Dr. James C. Dobson (Sisters, Ore.: Multnomah, 2004). You will find his pioneering work on this subject most encouraging and very practical in dealing with a separation or divorce.

[2] For example, Jesus loved the adulterous woman in John 8 and the rich young ruler in Mark 10, but He did not accept their conduct.

[3] As quoted by William Raspberry of the *Washington Post* Writer's Group, in editorial, "Tough Love: The Best Prescription for Troubled Young," appearing in the *Miami Herald*, March 29, 1991, 21A

[4] Dobson, 65.

[5] Ibid., 206.

[6] Guy N. Woods, "Love, the Supreme Attribute" *Gospel Advocate*, March 7 1985, 2.

[7] C. S. Lewis, *The Four Loves* (New York, N.Y.: Harcourt, Brace & World, Inc., 1960), 169.

[8] Naturally, if the divorce involves minor children, some congenial relationship with the former spouse is necessary to avoid unnecessarily disturbing custody and visitation rights. But expressing a desire not to have a post-divorce friendship between a childless couple may be timely and appropriate in a tough love letter. The spouse should know that divorce truly is the end of the relationship so he or she will not proceed under false hopes.

[9] To help you in writing your own "tough love" letter to your spouse, a *sample* letter appears in Appendix A that follows the same illustrations used in this chapter. Remember, it is important for your letter to be personal and specific to your own circumstances. Avoid relying on this sample too much.

Chapter 10

[1] Unfortunately, licensed marriage and family therapists seldom can collect from health insurance unless they have a license in other individual therapy as well.

[2] For example, as a personal ministry during my own separation and divorce, I organized a private group to meet in my home once a week. I hired a Christian counselor to lead the group without cost to the members. Many financially disadvantaged individuals attended and had access to the counselor for no cost. Also, as the counselor developed relationships with the group, he arranged private counseling sessions under special fee arrangements for those with urgent needs.

[3] I prefer using a computer with hard copies of entries printed out and filed in a loose-leaf notebook.

Chapter 11

[1] If we had children, I might have moved out temporarily to keep peace in the home.

[2] Some might see this as being contrary to tough love. Each person should bear the *full* consequences of their decisions. This might mean *no* support. But in this case, she was legally entitled to support. Also, after considering all factors involved, I believed it best to give her a full opportunity to think through the larger matter of divorce without the distraction of fighting for support.

[3] Even if her budget had been unreasonable, in my heart I committed to meeting it. I did not want her to feel cheated in fulfilling my support promise. But her budget was very reasonable. As we reviewed it together, I learned she had not estimated enough for some

expenses and had overlooked some other costs. Together we adjusted her budget upward to cover these items.

[4] One of the requirements for spouse support payments like this to be deductible for income tax purposes is that divorced or legally separated parties must not live in the same household at the time of payment. §71(b)(1)(C) of the Internal Revenue Code. This does not apply to temporary support court orders, however.

[5] I paid these expenses only after she agreed to go with me to a marriage counselor, at least for the six-month support period.

[6] Her health was important to me for three reasons: I loved *her* unconditionally and did not want her to be destroyed by a calamity; I did not want her at risk without mercy; and her good health affected future spouse support by law.

[7] This was not a vindictive move but a tough love consideration. It was important for her to move on her own without help from me, and even struggle some in doing so, as part of facing up to the consequences of her own decision to leave the marriage.

[8] If a physical separation in different locations cannot occur, try to find separate living quarters in the same house. Separation of any sort gives each spouse time to think and reconsider issues. If tempers flare, always go to that personal spot and "cool down." If arguments arise, focus any anger toward constructive action. But the best solution for emotional stability is for one spouse to move out. The courts should take this decision into account in reviewing who wants a divorce and why.

[9] We discuss many of the issues and concerns of children in chapter 15.

[10] The person who said, "What you don't know can't hurt you" never checked his or her credit report. Negative credit postings from a former spouse can haunt you in adversely affecting loan applications for a long time. For less than $20 or even no cost at all, you can receive your credit report from one of the three national credit reporting bureaus. (If you have been denied credit or employment because of credit problems in the past six months, the report is free.) What you will receive is a "consumer report" or an "in-file report." See Appendix E for information on the major credit bureaus.

[11] Mediation is discussed in chapter 12.

[12] Unfortunately, many husbands ignore women entitled to receive spouse or child support. Sometimes this is a form of blackmail if the husband wants leverage in settlement negotiations or revenge. But many husbands resent paying support to wives who have left marriages or become romantically involved with others. They believe that if a spouse stops honoring marriage vows, the marriage is broken. Therefore, why should support obligations penalize the one wanting to continue the marriage? But consider this: "If anyone does not provide for his relatives, and especially for his immediate family, he has denied the faith and is worse than an unbeliever" (1 Tim. 5:8). Denying support may be selfish and wrong while the marriage exists, regardless of the circumstances. By balancing tough love with legal considerations, a good approach might be to pay only the minimum amount of support that a court would allow. But do not withhold payments altogether.

[13] The family's standard of living is a major consideration. Courts review each spouse's gross income and take-home pay, as well as employment history, supplemental income and bonuses, overtime, tips, deferred benefits such as pension or profit-sharing plans and deferred compensation, and employment benefits ("percs") such as insurance plans, expense accounts, and travel reimbursements.

[14] Support can become a tremendous burden for either spouse. What if the spouse paying support cannot pay utility bills or other unavoidable expenses? It is difficult to ignore those debts. Why become homeless to pay support? What about the supported spouse? He or she must pay equally important living expenses. This is when negotiation, compromise, and prudent financial management by both spouses is essential. By sacrificially and creatively working out these problems, everyone survives and chances for reconciliation increase.

[15] If you are an abused spouse, be alert for how you are dealing with the situation. If you find yourself in a constant state of high anxiety and restlessness directly related to your

abuse and become withdrawn or isolated, seek counseling right away. You may be experiencing behavior called "battered women's syndrome," similar to stresses that war veterans experience. If untreated, you may want to return the violence against your spouse to stop the abuse—a double tragedy.

[16] We discuss hiring an attorney in chapter 13. If you cannot afford an attorney and your spouse is financially able to pay for it, you may be able to ask the court for temporary support to cover this expense. But if you are the party being asked to pay for your spouse's lawyer, be on guard. You may provide him or her with a legal war chest to make your life miserable. We address some of these issues in chapter 14 on what to expect from the courts.

[17] The first action most attorneys will take is to shield clients from their spouses. Lawyers know that spouses going through separation or divorce are emotional, sometimes irrational, and desperate for good advice. They try to shut down communication between spouses because they do not want to risk having more problems arise that make legal issues more difficult. But each spouse may have a sincere desire to be compassionate; they may want to negotiate. This alarms some attorneys because as advocates, they want power to take charge of the case and champion the cause of their clients. This is why it is critical for clients to use their own discretion and govern his or her use of an attorney wisely.

[18] Provided that certain requirements are met, spouse support payments are, under §71 of the Internal Revenue Code, included in the gross income of the spouse receiving payments and, under §215, allowed as a deduction from the gross income of the spouse making payments. It may not be necessary that all such spouse support payments be made directly to the spouse. Direct payments of a spouse's personal financial obligations (such as mortgage payments, utilities, real estate taxes, auto loans, uninsured medical bills) may under some circumstances be deductible. §71(b)(1)(A) Child support payments are not tax-deductible. For more information, see Publication 504, Divorced or Separated Individuals, Tax Topics 406, Alimony Received, and 452, Alimony Paid. Publications and forms may be downloaded from www.irs.gov or ordered by calling toll-free, (800) TAX-FORM (800-829-3676).

[19] Many times the property is not the issue at all. It is wanting control and not "giving in" on anything. It is better by far to lose property in a gracious spirit than to further alienate a spouse.

[20] It takes approximately one to two weeks to process a change of address notice after filling out postal form No. 3575. Thereafter, first-class mail is forwarded for one year; second class mail is forwarded for sixty days; and bulk mail is dumped.

[21] Filing a joint return was better for most all taxpayers under the tax laws prior to 1970. But with the enactment of individual rate tables under the Tax Reform Act of 1969, married taxpayers filing joint returns and earning about the same income no longer had an advantage over unmarried individuals. Many referred to this as the "marriage penalty." (It spawned sham divorces to avoid it.) This penalty has been reduced by adjustments in the tax rates since 1986, especially with the Jobs and Growth Tax Relief Reconciliation Act of 2003. Check with your tax advisor as to current tax planning measures. Filing separately as unmarried, divorced individuals may be more advantageous than filing as marrieds.

[22] Rules for allocating child dependency exemptions between separated or divorced parents appear in §152(e) of the code. Generally, the custodial parent is entitled to the exemption, but he or she can release it to the noncustodial parent by executing Form 8332 or a similar document. §152(e)(2) The tax savings depends upon the amount of the exemption and the tax bracket of the person claiming it. Since 1990, this amount is adjusted for inflation. This exemption can be a significant bargaining chip in settlement negotiations. For example, since wealthier spouses may be barred from using some or all of this exemption due to phase-out of personal exemptions as adjusted gross income increases under §151(d)(3), releasing the exemption to the poorer spouse helps that person without losing much in return. *However*, be aware that Form 8332 has two parts to it. Part 1 releases the exemption to another person for the *current tax year only*, while Part 2 releases it for future

years. Many attorneys instruct their clients to execute only Part 1. This allows the parties to re-evaluate the exemption each tax year in the event child support payments become a problem.

[23] Whether spouses can file jointly or as unmarried individuals depends upon their marital status at the end of the tax year. Individuals legally separated by divorce or separate maintenance agreements according to local state law are considered as not married for tax purposes. §7703(a)(2) This allows you to reap the gains of having unmarried status without divorce for tax purposes if you qualify.

[24] Property received as part of a divorce settlement carries the same tax basis the original owner had under §1014(b) of the code just as though it were a gift. The one making the transfer has no gain or loss, and the spouse receiving property takes it without paying tax. But a low tax basis in the property could result in a large tax when it is sold in the future. Be sure to account for a low tax basis in agreeing to any property values for settlement purposes. Also, since the couple's principal residence is their most valuable property, be sure your tax advisor advises you of ways to avoid tax by qualifying for certain exemptions under §1034 of the code.

[25] Although the IRS is subject to the Freedom of Information Act requiring disclosure of all government information unless prohibited by law, Congress enacted stringent anti-disclosure laws to protect IRS information. The code allows disclosure of tax-return information to the taxpayer; an authorized representative (attorneys, CPAs and others qualified to practice before the IRS to whom the taxpayer has given a power of attorney—Form 2848); or an authorized disclosure recipient (anyone authorized by the taxpayer to receive copies of returns—Form 8821). Each spouse is entitled to receive a copy of any joint tax return.

[26] One spouse may be protected from liability in limited cases arising from misreporting of tax by the other spouse if he or she qualifies as an "innocent spouse" under §6015 of the code, which is now easier to do since enactment of the IRS Restructuring and Reform Act of 1998 than was true under prior IRS code requirements. Indemnity provisions give one spouse a right to seek reimbursement from the other, but these agreements do not stop the IRS proceeding against either or both spouses for the *entire* tax liability (assuming that one does not qualify as an "innocent spouse")—and usually against the spouse having the most money. This problem can create a real hardship, particularly for women who are forced to pay their ex-spouses' taxes many years after a final divorce. Therefore, since indemnities may be worthless after divorce, filing separate tax returns during a separation or divorce may be the best option to avoid this potential problem.

[27] In some states, any such relations could adversely affect legal grounds for granting a divorce.

[28] Some states consider adultery in limiting spouse support.

[29] Title III of the Omnibus Crime Control and Safe Streets Act of 1968 (18 U.S.C. §§2510–2522) is a comprehensive federal law making it unlawful for any person to intercept any wire, oral, or electronic communication except as specifically permitted by law. Under §2511(2)(d) of the act, it is not unlawful to intercept a communication if you are party to the communication or where one of the other parties has given prior consent, but do not even risk trying to qualify for this very limited exception. Courts are not in agreement on how far any exception goes. [See, for example, the discussion in *Glazner v. Glazner*, 347 F.3d 1212 (11th Cir. 2003), and *Dommer v. Dommer*, Indiana Court of Appeals, Case No. 64A03-0409-CV-410 (2005).] Remember, exceptions like these can conflict with reasonable expectations of privacy of the parties involved, of which courts are becoming increasingly protective. (Also, state laws may not ever allow for this exemption.) Congress enacted this law after extensive legislative hearings of widespread abuse of electronic surveillance—primarily in the area of divorce disputes. The majority of courts deal with violations by divorcing spouses *very* severely. A related matter is the use of computer spyware (software installed on a computer without the target user's knowledge and meant to monitor the user's conduct—especially email traffic, chat room conversations, etc.). As of

June 2005, no federal law regulated such spyware, but this probably will change. Meanwhile, various states have enacted varied forms of anti-spyware laws, computer privacy laws, and computer trespass laws that could make any surveillance efforts illegal as well.

[30] For nearly three months prior to their divorce in 1987, Tom Heggy of Oklahoma recorded his wife's conversations with others on an extension phone in his barn without her consent. When his wife discovered this, she sued Heggy for violation of federal wiretapping laws, resulting in a jury verdict against her ex-husband of $75,000 in compensatory damages and $140,000 in punitive damages. *Heggy v. Heggy*, 944 F.2d 1537 (10th Cir. 1991), *cert. denied U.S.*, 112 S.Ct. 1514, 117 L.Ed.2d 651 (1992).

Chapter 12

[1] When I married, I owned some real property titled in my own name, including the house my wife and I lived in during our marriage. Estate planning and personal liability concerns might have prompted me to change these titles later in our marriage, but I did nothing right away. My reasons? My wife and I enjoyed the full benefit of these properties while married, regardless of who owned the title. If I were to die, these properties would probably go to my wife (assuming we were married) by my will or even by law. But if I had changed the titles before my divorce, the court could assume I gave away all or part of my property interest to my wife. I prefer to give—or to retain—whatever I owned as my wife and I decided. I did not want any court to make any foregone conclusions about this matter.

[2] Just before I married, my law partners urged me to have a premarital agreement; I declined. Legally, however, such agreements are a good idea for dispute resolution. Premarital agreements (also known as antenuptial agreements) are subject to state regulation. The Uniform Premarital Agreement Act (UPAA—9B Uniform Laws Annotated [Master Edition] 369 [1987], with full text available on the Internet at http://www.law.upenn.edu/bll/ulc/fnact99/1980s/upaa83.htm), adopted (or some variation of it) by a majority of states as of 2007, provides that almost any matter may be contracted for in a premarital agreement as long as it is "not in violation of public policy," excluding child support and custody matters.

[3] The manner in which courts divide property under American law is heavily influenced by English common law. In England, the national church had exclusive jurisdiction over the regulation of marriage. The common law viewed women as legal dependents of their husbands, restricted in their ability to own property. Women received alimony in ecclesiastical courts as compensation for the inability to hold separate property. Almost all common law states distributed property by title, beginning in the nineteenth century. Therefore, since women were restricted in owning property, and property was distributed by title in divorce, women understandably came up short. More recent equitable distribution provisions of the no-fault laws changed this, however. These allow property to be redistributed notwithstanding who owns the title (although title ownership is still a factor to be considered).

[4] The laws of each state can vary considerably. This is especially true if you and your spouse are domiciled in a "community property" state (Arizona, California, Idaho, Louisiana, Nevada, New Mexico, Texas, Washington, or Wisconsin). In community property states, for example, each spouse acquires an automatic one-half interest in all property and income of the marriage. By contrast, in non-community property states each spouse has an interest in the marital property, but when considering this interest for equitable distribution, it may not automatically equate to a one-half interest.

[5] Courts usually divide marital assets between the spouses while separately awarding non-marital assets to one spouse or the other.

[6] For example, if one spouse is in more financial need than the other, the court may award more property toward the support of the needy spouse. Child custody issues also can affect property distributions, such as awarding the homestead to the parent having primary

custody. If one spouse has clearly worked harder in making a marital asset more valuable, that also affects the distribution percentages.

[7] To help you get started, a sample settlement invitation letter appears in Appendix B. Resist the urge to copy this letter, however. This must be *your* personal letter, with facts appropriate to your case.

[8] This will show that you have nothing to hide. It also recognizes the role your spouse's lawyer serves and confirms that you are not skirting him or her.

[9] Relevant facts are: the date of your marriage; the college education of each spouse and manner of payment; names of all children and whether the wife is now pregnant; term of any marriage counseling; time period and conditions of any separation; which spouse believes the marriage is irretrievably broken; present state of residence of each spouse, and relevant dates; all sources and amounts of income for each spouse; and the names, addresses, and telephone numbers of each spouse's attorney.

[10] There are significant legal and tax consequences to consider. If each party does not have independent legal advice, a court could be skeptical about your agreements and set them aside if anyone has any "second thoughts." Breaking agreements is more difficult if each spouse receives legal advice before anything is finalized.

[11] If this is not done, either intentionally or by oversight, the court could set aside your agreements.

[12] In my own private settlement conference, I decided to honor (within reason) whatever requests my wife made—even if they were somewhat unfair to me. My hope was for her to review everything in my letter and papers, think and pray about everything, talk to her attorney, then tell me what she wanted. My desire was to meet her requests with little or no changes if there was any reasonable way possible to do so. Naturally this is risky and expensive! However, in my case, my wife's welfare was more important to me than what I would lose.

[13] Since this step in the settlement process is a biblical step of faith, do not be surprised if attorneys or others not familiar with the Bible react negatively to this suggestion. When I quoted 1 Corinthians 6 in a letter to my wife's attorney and suggested that we try church mediation, he wrote back flatly refusing to be involved in any such procedure. He described the entire suggestion as "bizarre and outrageous." But this is to be expected from those who are not familiar with matters that are spiritually discerned (1 Cor. 2:6–16).

[14] Matthew 18:15–17 outlines an important four-step process for dispute resolution that should be followed in strict order: Step 1—meet privately with the person, one-on-one to protect reputations from any false accusations; Step 2—if no reconciliation comes from this private meeting, bring one or two others along to help mediate the dispute and serve as witnesses to the facts and help determine what is fair and just; Step 3—if the meeting with witnesses fails to bring reconciliation, then bring the matter to the church for a decision; Step 4—if even the church's decision does not bring reconciliation, the person who refuses to abide by the church's decision should be treated as an unbelieving outsider. The clear goal of each step is not to "win" an argument but to promote reconciliation of the parties.

[15] There is one female friend of both spouses from their church. From the wife's perspective, having a personal female friend involved should provide some comfort. The other two panel members are men in leadership from another congregation. Neither of them knows either spouse very well; however, both men are knowledgeable about biblical principles. One member is a minister, while the other is an elder. The elder in this panel happens to be a family law attorney. He should be helpful in considering legal and biblical matters.

[16] Also consider the resources of the Christian Legal Society and, more particularly, Peacemaker Ministries, which is affiliated with that organization. The Christian Legal Society is a nationwide network of Christian attorneys who believe the Bible to be the inspired Word of God. Many of these attorneys volunteer hours of free time to help disadvantaged Christians resolve disputes pursuant to 1 Corinthians 6 and Matthew 18. There are contacts for Peacemaker Ministries in every state. For further information, see the listing in Appendix E.

[17] The reasoning for this is based upon the biblical principle that God originally made one man and one woman. In so doing, He expressed an intent that man and woman be joined as one. Marriage is a partnership (Mal. 2:14). In the beginning, God made man and woman equal. But sin in the garden of Eden moved God to start a system of authority that placed the man at the head. That, however, did not destroy the partnership, oneness, and equality of marriage.

[18] This is especially true if one spouse had more assets than the other prior to marriage.

[19] In reality, sharing equally rises above judging that spouse. Instead it leaves the judgment to God. We must examine our motives to see if giving that spouse less would be our taking vengeance (Rom. 12:17–19).

[20] This letter assumes a 50/50 split of all marital and non-marital assets. Naturally, your settlement offer may be totally different.

[21] These deadlines are important to promote quick settlements and to stop any games your spouse's attorney may play. For example, my wife's attorney consistently waited until the day *after* any deadline to ask for an extension. Twice I agreed to requested extensions. But when he tried a third time, despite warnings that it would jeopardize his client's acceptance of my settlement offer, he was too late. I warned him that I would withdraw my offer, and I kept my promise. My wife had no one to blame for this conduct but her own attorney. She must bear the responsibility for her agent if she chose not to accept the settlement offer directly.

[22] In 2007, fees for mediators generally vary between $80 to $175 an hour. Some mediators charge a flat fee for the first two hours of mediation—even if the dispute is resolved in a matter of minutes—with a reduced hourly rate for the remainder of the mediation time. The charges usually are split between the parties to the mediation. While these fees are not inexpensive, considering that lawyers for each spouse can charge $100 to $300 an hour and accountants at $100 to $200 an hour, mediation is much less expensive in the long run.

[23] For example, in Step 3 you may have offered a settlement with a 50/50 split of all marital and non-marital assets. The law of your state may only require equitable distribution of marital assets, with each party holding non-marital assets as separately owned property. Therefore, your mediation offer would propose a fair split of the marital assets only in a manner that the courts might rule. Therefore, your spouse has nothing more to gain by spending time and money in going to trial.

Chapter 13

[1] Finding a lawyer matching your temperament is extremely important. Some lawyers are reluctant to share power with clients. They want almost exclusive control and expect clients to follow their directions with a minimum of questioning. Other lawyers patiently listen to clients and answer endless questions, try to fulfill their stated desires for the case, share decision-making responsibilities, and encourage client participation in preparing the case. Find out what type of lawyer your candidate is *before* you commit to any representation.

[2] You can determine whether an attorney has the minimum level of competence by receiving knowledgeable referrals; checking out references; calling the State Bar Association to find out if the lawyer is a member in good standing, whether there have been any disciplinary complaints made in the last five years, and whether he or she is certified to practice in family law; and by researching the attorney's background and ratings in the Martindale-Hubbell Law Directory—discussed later in this chapter.

[3] A partner in a now defunct national law firm once said, "Praise your adversary; he is your friend. Curse your client; he is your enemy." This person is selfishly thinking more about generating legal work for his firm than professionally serving the needs of the client. Florida lawyer M. Craig Massey expressed the regrets of many good lawyers by observing, "We have allowed the law and the use of the courts to become a game. It is not a means to the end of justice for everyone or for the parties in any singular case. It has become one

of gamesmanship to see who can reach the best bottom line, notwithstanding the effect on one's client, much less the opponent's client. . . . This bottom line is money. The legal business, formerly a profession, has become one of seeking the best dollar return for the attorney, notwithstanding, again, its impact on whoever may be involved." *The Florida Bar News*, November 1, 1992, p. 2. Find an attorney who puts his or her profession and service to clients *first*.

[4] Abraham Lincoln echoed these thoughts by once advising his fellow lawyers: "Resolve to be honest at all events; and if, in your own judgment, you cannot be an honest lawyer, resolve to be honest without being a lawyer. Choose some other occupation, rather than one in the choosing of which you do, in advance, consent to be a knave."

[5] Bradley P. Jacob, executive director of the Christian Legal Society, eloquently noted the advantage of hiring a Christian lawyer this way: "Christianity is not a Sunday-morning religion that leaves our daily professional lives unchanged. Accepting Christ as Savior and Lord means serving Him in all aspects of our lives. For lawyers, this means that questions of ethics, priorities, lifestyle, interpersonal relationships, money management, career choices, and even substantive legal issues are analyzed from a different perspective than that of non-Christian attorneys." Christian Legal Society *Quarterly*, Fall 1991, 15.

[6] The Rules of Professional Conduct governing the legal profession in most states requires a lawyer to be an adviser, an advocate, a negotiator, an intermediary, and an evaluator. Quite often, there is a right way—and a wrong way—to achieve these goals.

[7] One of my law firm partners is going through a divorce. I asked him how he was going to choose his lawyer. His reply? "Well, first I'm going to wait until my wife chooses her attorney. If she chooses a jerk, then I know a mean lawyer to hire. If she chooses a lawyer who's going to be reasonable, then I know a reasonable attorney to hire." This "eye for an eye" approach is tempting when one is upset and bitter. But pitting two hardnosed lawyers against each other is like putting two cats in a bag—you'll have a fight that just won't quit!

[8] *The Florida Bar News*, March 15, 1993, 17.

[9] Before meeting with your lawyer-candidate, you might prepare a typewritten autobiography and a list of priorities regarding your divorce by outlining your: educational background; history of employment; property owned before and during the marriage, including down payments made and approximate values of each; contributions to help your spouse with education, business assistance, living expenses or purchase of assets; income over the years, and that of your spouse as well; contributions to child-rearing; your view of the cause for the marriage breakup; and list of results desired in any divorce, among other matters.

[10] Some crafty people interview the most outstanding divorce lawyer in town without delay, with no intention of hiring the attorney, solely to disqualify him or her from representing a spouse on grounds of confidentiality.

[11] Be aware, however, that many lawyers have reciprocal referral understandings or joint publishing or seminar projects with their references that could affect your receiving an unbiased appraisal.

[12] The American Bar Association Model Rule of Professional Conduct 1.5 requires that a lawyer's fee be reasonable and that a lawyer clearly communicate to a client at the beginning of the representation the basis on which the client will be charged.

[13] Unfortunately, in recent years monetary goals and quotas for billable hours are becoming daily pressures for attorneys in many firms in order to survive financially. Sometimes this attention to the bottom line causes attorneys in large firms to feel equal or greater accountability to a billing committee than to the client.

[14] This has really been the norm since World War II. According to a national survey of 400 law firms of all sizes in 1991 by the Price Waterhouse accounting firm, hourly rates peaked in 1989 and began to drop in 1990. In 1991, average partner hourly rates were $210 to $212, while associate rates averaged $128 to $130. A 1992 survey by Altman Weil Pensa, a Philadelphia-based management firm, found that rates varied substantially geographically, with average partner rates in California being $221, while the east/central U.S. average was $153 and $192 in the northeast. As of December 1991, hourly rates for

firms nationwide with fewer than nine lawyers averaged $138; $152 for firms with nine to twenty lawyers; $153 for firms with twenty-one to forty lawyers; $157 for firms with forty-one to seventy-four lawyers; and $203 for firms with more than seventy-five lawyers. *Corporate Legal Times*, (December 1992), 1, 10–11. Obviously, over the years these rates have been creeping upward. For example, the Florida Bar's Research, Planning, and Evaluation Department found that in 2006, the average or standard hourly rates for Florida's private practice attorneys were as follows: 14 percent charged $300/hour or more, 15 percent charged $250–$299, 23 percent charged $200–$249, with the majority (29 percent) charging $150–$199 (*Florida Bar News*, July 1, 2006, 2). *However*, a 1992 Louis Harris poll showed that 68 percent of the lawyers surveyed want to be paid based on the value and quality of their work rather than billable hours. *The Florida Bar News*, October 1, 1992, 17. Therefore, the twenty-first century may be a time of innovation and change to alternative billing arrangements for many lawyers.

[15] Sample legal representation agreements covering the matters discussed in this chapter are attached in Appendix C.

[16] *Every* time you receive a statement, ask yourself whether you have received reasonably fair value for what you are being asked to pay. If not, talk it over with your lawyer directly rather than meekly pay the bill and become bitter or resentful.

[17] Object to any "clumping" or "grouping" in bills of work completed on a single day. Have the time spent for *each task* on a single day itemized separately.

[18] Have your lawyer prepare a brief, written case strategy in plain English for you to approve in advance. It should include an outline of the issues, the proposed course of litigation—including pre-trial motions, the scope of discovery, trial strategy, what your options are, what responses you can expect from the other side, and estimated fees and costs through the end of the case. It also is helpful to break down the strategy (and budgeted legal expense) into phases. At the end of each phase, review the budget and strategy with your attorney.

[19] For example, if you call your attorney two times in one day for ten minutes each, or make a call for ten minutes one day and ten minutes the next day, are the charges the same? Negotiate to limit time billing increments to no more than six minutes each.

[20] If your lawyer goes to the courthouse for hearings on several cases, or performs research useful to several clients, are you billed a fair allocation?

[21] Office overhead includes secretarial time and overtime, word processing time, charges for after-hour and weekend air-conditioning and other utilities, the cost of meals and transportation provided to attorneys and staff who work late or on weekends, accounting, library, or other clerical staff time.

[22] These services include computerized research, photocopies made by outside vendors, postage, overnight deliveries, outside messenger services, long distance telephone charges, air and auto transportation and parking (other than at the office and courthouse), hotels, working meals, filing and service of process fees, court reporter and witness fees, and similar charges. "Actual cost" means the amount paid to a third-party provider of goods or services without adding a profit surcharge, handling fee, or other administrative charge. The attorney should retain receipts and other documentation for all expenditures over $50 and make the same available to you upon request. In a 1991 study of 357 law firms in twelve major cities conducted by the National Survey Center, a private market research company in Washington, D.C., 95 percent of these firms charged no mark-up on third-party charges. *ABA Law Journal*, April 1992, 24. Although the costs of practicing law certainly increase year-to-year, there really is no justification for markups of this type.

[23] You should not pay for time spent addressing, stamping, and stuffing envelopes, filing, photocopying, or "supervising" any of these activities by anyone.

[24] In its 1991 study, the National Survey Center found that the vast majority of law firms surveyed charged their clients twenty cents per page or less. Since the date of that study, costs have increased to approximately twenty-five to thirty-five cents per page. The actual cost should be determined by the purchase or lease cost of the copy machine and

supplies (including the space occupied by the machine), plus maintenance costs, but *not* including time spent operating the machine.

[25] Negotiate that there be no charge for the cost of working meals at restaurants or private clubs. Reimbursement for actual cost only of food catered to the lawyer's office in the course of meeting with you is acceptable, provided that the purpose is to allow the meeting to continue through a normal meal period.

[26] This applies to travel requiring one hour or more, round-trip. Anything less should not be reimbursable. The 1992 per-mile travel amount recognized by the IRS pursuant to §274(d) of the code was twenty-eight cents. This allowance increased to 40.5 cents per mile as of December 6, 2004 (Internal Revenue Bulletin 2004-49).

[27] Disciplinary committees investigate misconduct and impose sanctions on this conduct. This action may not resolve your personal dispute with your lawyer, but it will protect others from further misconduct of this attorney. However, be aware that some attorneys try to sue those reporting them to a bar association for libel and slander. Make *very sure* you have a complaint that can be fully supported by the evidence *before* filing.

Chapter 14

[1] No-fault laws promoted several ideals: if a marriage fails, no one person is usually at fault, so assigning blame is unnecessary; marriage partnerships have assets requiring liquidation similar to dissolution of any business; as equal partners in marriage, husbands and wives deserve equal treatment in divorce; and both spouses should move on with their separate lives with a minimum of restrictions (permanent alimony, for example).

[2] As of 2006, and as an additional condition for obtaining a divorce, many states also have a separation or "cooling off" period where a couple actually is living separate and apart for periods from sixty days to two years.

[3] It is probably unjust to ignore fault entirely. Why should a faithful spouse suffer loss through divorce simply because a mate decides to break the marriage vows? Shouldn't an adulterous spouse still bear some individual accountability for his or her actions? Many also believe that courts should consider fault in order to avoid, for example, rewarding the errant spouse who has attempted to murder a mate, abandoned the marriage and stolen the family savings, used physical abuse, or made life intolerable through alcohol or drug abuse. Certainly those spouses who destroy a short-term childless marriage should not be able to claim benefits equal to those that would have been provided had the marriage remained intact over a long term. For these reasons, a strong minority of states still consider fault in awarding dissolution, property division, or alimony. Even some states with strict no-fault requirements, such as Florida, retain consideration of fault in property division and alimony. §§61.075 and 61.08, Florida Statutes.

[4] In 1992, for example, Florida began organizing such family court divisions. These divisions coordinate marital legal disputes with other services like court-ordered mediation, domestic violence assistance programs, guardians for needs of children, and psychological home assessment programs. One judge monitors all divorce and related legal matters concerning one family. Divisions of this sort will eventually have separate and specialized rules different from other civil law cases.

[5] Prior to a domestic violence prevention pilot program in 1991, only 30 percent of the victims sought relief through Dade County, Florida, courts. During the program, those pressing charges in court increased to 68 percent. Reason? The courts took Florida's domestic violence laws seriously. Coordinators earnestly organized the domestic violence section of the Family Law Division and put it into action. A hot line was available twenty-four hours a day. "Safe Space" shelters offered alternate living arrangements for those needing to escape violence. A circuit court judge was available on weekends, nights, and holidays to help abuse victims obtain restraining orders for protection. Counselors, health specialists, and members of victim's advocate groups comforted victims throughout the proceedings. Drug and alcohol referrals were made. Support groups provided forums for victims to comfort each other. Spouse batterers were ordered into a twenty-six-week domestic

intervention program to stop the violence. The courts produced a triweekly cable television series called "Total Eclipse of the Heart" that profiled different aspects of domestic violence and offered tips on where victims could receive help. Spliced into each show were interviews with judges, victims, psychologists, and even batterers themselves, with taped scenes from actual courtroom cases. Due to the outstanding success of the pilot program, these measures are now a permanent part of the Family Law Division. Victims now feel safer in reporting incidents of violence with confidence that their complaints will be taken seriously and acted upon promptly.

[6] How do you know where to draw the line on private conduct? A good example of questionable information is that found in a private investigator's report about a spouse's immorality. From a scriptural standpoint and for peace of mind, we may need to know the truth about any infidelity. Legally securing such a report without violating any privacy rights promotes wise decisions. In no-fault divorce states, the court may not consider this report; it is not necessary for granting a divorce. If spouse support or child custody issues are in dispute, however, such misconduct can affect these issues at trial in many states. This requires an important decision: is our defense worth the shame it will bring upon our spouses? The answer to this question means considering the conduct and attitude of our spouses in the court case. If they try to create a charade of good conduct, lie under oath, or act unreasonably in prolonging the litigation, use of the report may be very appropriate— not for revenge but to help our spouses face the truth. Nevertheless, this important decision requires careful and prayerful consideration. It is always good to ask, "What would Jesus do?"

[7] Even as a lawyer, it would be foolish for me to handle my own case. Abraham Lincoln aptly said, "The man who represents himself has a fool for a client." This is why we devoted an entire chapter to hiring the best lawyer you can afford.

[8] The complaint will usually ask the court to grant the divorce and award legal fees and costs, custody of any children, and title and possession to various property owned by either spouse to the plaintiff spouse. You will think matters in the complaint are unreasonable or unfair. But don't let this alarm you; they are only *requests* made to the court. It does *not* mean the court will do everything asked for in the complaint. The plaintiff must prove all facts before you are bound by them. However, be sure to point out any inaccuracies to your attorney as soon as possible.

[9] In some states these documents may arrive by mail. In others, a police officer or private process server may deliver them.

[10] However, the defendant's attorney will only file this pleading if the plaintiff's complaint states proper legal grounds. If it does not, the attorney may ask the judge to dismiss the case and require the plaintiff to file a new or amended complaint before requiring any legal response.

[11] Since this document ends up in the court file, never put bank or credit card account numbers in this pleading. If the opposing attorney asks for the account numbers, have your attorney supply this information in a private letter or when producing personal income tax returns for inspection.

[12] This means that some attorneys must spend one or two hours waiting for the judge to spend five minutes on their cases. To limit this expense, ask your attorney to discount this waiting time. Also, ask your lawyer whether your state allows hearings by telephone conference with the judge and opposing attorney on a specific date and time. This saves legal fees.

[13] The judge's involvement in a pre-trial conference is an advantage that third-party mediators in court-ordered mediation do not have. The judge and lawyers for each spouse can address legal issues while the spouses try to agree on the non-legal matters.

[14] In a few states, a divorce may not be effective for three to six months. Check with your attorney about this.

[15] This misconduct could also adversely affect that spouse's consideration as a custodial parent of any children.

[16] Many states had a "tender years doctrine" which specifically held that young children needed the nurturing of their mother.

[17] To avoid surprise, use attorneys effectively to influence the judge with any information that may escape the expert.

[18] This requires deeds, assignments of lease, or land trust beneficiary transfers from one spouse to the other. Transferred automobile titles must be filed with the state. There is endorsement of stock and other securities and registration with the company for issuance of new certificates to the spouse entitled to the same. Changing of beneficiaries on life insurance policies or cancellation of policies occurs, if this does not jeopardize valuable benefits. Health and liability insurance policies change to reflect the single and independent status of each spouse without losing existing coverage. Bank accounts and certificates of deposit are transferred and the money properly accounted for to each spouse. Income tax returns, whether filed jointly (if allowed by existing tax laws) or separately, are coordinated so that each spouse properly lists the same support and other payments. Wills, trusts, and other estate planning documents are changed. Any personal property and household furnishings not divided before are delivered to the proper party. The former wife also may want to restore her maiden name through court order.

[19] If not, since creditors hold both spouses liable on any joint debts—even *after* a divorce—the spouse responsible for payment usually gives the other spouse an indemnification/hold harmless agreement. This agreement provides that, if the creditor sues the former spouse no longer responsible for payment on the debt, that spouse can sue the other spouse for any costs or damages suffered.

[20] How is a witness impeached? Obviously, if everyone was scrupulously honest about testimony, no one would have to worry about this problem. But desperate people do desperate things. Finding out if someone is lying is extremely difficult. Let's assume that you have a private investigator's report. It confirms your spouse and a lover have been spending the night together. Without revealing the existence of this report, your attorney might ask your spouse questions under oath such as, "Has any person of the opposite sex ever spent the night with you in your apartment?" or "Does anyone other than you and your apartment manager have a key to your apartment?" If the answer is evasive or negative, then he or she has lied under oath and is ripe for impeachment. This can be done in several ways. Your attorney can ask the lover the same questions under oath. If that person answers the same questions truthfully, it proves one of them is lying and hurts the credibility of both. If that person also lies or, even worse, first tells the truth and then tries to lie and cover up, then the private investigator can testify about what was seen. Impeachment of a witness is a means of arriving at the truth.

[21] Experts suggest that men under thirty might wear a white shirt, striped tie, sports jacket, and khaki pants with socks and polished loafers. Older men might consider a white shirt, dark tie and suit, socks, and polished dress shoes. Women would do best by wearing fashionable, simple clothes that are not too revealing. A white blouse and a comfortable, long full skirt that allows for shifting of position without being distracting is a good choice. Avoid bright colors. Keep jewelry to a modest minimum.

[22] This is a trick question to see if people will tell the truth. It tempts evasive people feeling guilty about their testimony to say no when everyone present knows this is not true.

[23] For example, the examining attorney may ask, "How long did your wife stay in her apartment after you ordered her out of the house?" This assumes that you "ordered" your wife out of your house, which may not be true at all.

[24] Your attorney may object to the form of the question, saying that it assumes facts not in evidence. This should alert you to the problem with the question.

[25] Other reforms being considered include requiring mandatory security deposits from those not making prompt support payments. Support payments may soon become credit card debts, with all financing charges imposed on the paying spouse. Courts will advise credit bureaus of delinquent spouses. Informal administrative hearings to enforce

support (as alternatives to court hearings) will speed up enforcement. Ask your attorney to advise you of the remedies available to you.

[26] Factors considered by the judge include: which parent is likely to be more cooperative in allowing frequent and continuing visitation by the noncustodial parent; the love, affection, and other emotional ties existing between the children and each parent; the relative ability of each parent to provide the children with food, clothing, medical care, and other material needs; the length of time the children have lived in a stable, satisfactory environment and the desirability of continuing that arrangement; the permanence, as a family unit, of the existing or proposed custodial home; the moral fitness and mental and physical health of the parents; the home, school, and community record of the children; and the reasonable preference of each child, assuming that the court considers the child to have intelligence, understanding, and experience to express a preference.

[27] Review chapters 11 and 13 on dealing with the money crunch during separation or divorce and how to hire an attorney.

Chapter 15

[1] Erma Bombeck, *Reader's Digest*, December 1977.

[2] Quoted by Judge Hugh S. Glickstein in his article, "1992: A Year to Rediscover the Best Interests of the Child," *Florida Bar Journal*, February 1992, 70.

[3] In fact, not until 1874 did abused children achieve legal status as individuals—and then only after the American Society for the Prevention of Cruelty to Animals moved in court to protect a little girl under laws barring cruel treatment of animals. But more thoughtful recognition of children's rights are changing the laws. For example, on November 20, 1989, the U.N. General Assembly adopted the Convention on the Rights of the Child containing many human rights never before protected in an international treaty—including the child's right to identity.

[4] Even so, it is probable that this case will spawn many other children's rights cases in the future. In March 1993, a twelve-year-old Brevard County, Florida, girl filed suit to leave her stepfather and mother and live with her maternal grandmother. (*The Miami Herald*, March 5, 1993, 1A, 6A). Over objections of the parents, Brevard County Circuit Court Judge Charles Holcomb ruled that the girl did have the right to maintain the court action and to intervene in custody determination issues pending between her parents. "I sit here week after week and hear divorce cases where the mother and father go at each other with tooth and claw and with every dirty and nasty thing that they can dredge up and throw at each other," Judge Holcomb remarked in making his ruling. "I see it over and over where the parties don't seem to be so much interested in their children as they are in venting their own anger and getting what they want out of the divorce. I think the child has to have an independent voice to tell the court what the child's perspective is in the whole thing." (*The Miami Herald*, March 27, 1993, 1A).

[5] The March 1991 report of the Florida Study Commission on Child Welfare concluded that each child needs protection from harm; supply of basic food, clothes and shelter; provision of necessary medical services; a basic education; and opportunities for cognitive, aesthetic, and emotional development. But more than this, a child needs to know that he or she is being heard in expressing personal concerns.

[6] Mothers remember worrying about eating the right foods during pregnancy and taking care not to miss those middle-of-the-night feedings with newborns. This maternal instinct for care and protection stays with them as children grow up.

[7] Of course, the *absence* of conflict may be just as damaging to children if it results in apathy, disdain, and boredom. The point is that if a child does not see a loving, cooperative parenting relationship within an intact and involved family unit, there will be problems even before a separation or divorce occurs.

[8] Why should you not disparage the absent spouse? Simply because the child has developed his or her self-concept from *both* parents. In running down the spouse, the child may view it as a personal attack. This will only backfire on the parent making the comments.

[9] If children are of different ages, begin with the oldest child. This allows parents to refine the message to its simplest terms when meeting with younger ones. The older children can begin processing information and help reassure the youngest.

[10] They also can go through the grieving cycles discussed in chapter 2. Briefly explain the grieving process to them so they will not feel odd, frightened, or guilty about their feelings.

[11] An adolescent feels ambivalence in living between childhood and adulthood; distancing from parents as peer groups become more important; loneliness and inner emptiness from not knowing where life is leading; sexual preoccupation and exploration with the opposite sex; and conceptualization of dreams and ideals arising from confusion over an emerging adult identity. Into this volatile mix, one can only imagine how separation or divorce impacts this young person.

[12] Some psychologists recommend keeping pictures or a videotape of a child's happy times with the noncustodial parent handy to share with the child whenever lonely times come between visits.

[13] Many young children have an egocentric view of the world. They believe the environment around them exists for their benefit. They don't understand that adverse events happen through no fault of their own.

[14] Typically the topic may not have involved the child's conduct at all, but rather personal, parental disagreements on childrearing.

[15] Emphasize that life has both happy events and sad events. Help the child work through this by reflecting on some good memories, like, "Remember the great birthday party you had last year with all of your friends?" or "Remember the Christmas when you made that funny snowman?" Then move to a sad time: "Remember how sad you felt when Granddad died? But you also remember how we all pulled together and everything became happy once again?"

[16] For example, there will be fewer arguments and less tension around the home. Instead of dwelling on the loss of a parent from the home, stress the advantages of having parents in two places. Now children can live in two houses rather than just one.

[17] Before moving, work with the child in looking over his or her current bedroom with an eye toward finding ways to improve it in the new place. Make it a game. In planning for setting up the child's new room, cut up a brown paper bag and use it as a floor plan to stick on cutouts of the bed and other furniture. Involve the child in decision-making by asking, "Where will your bed go?" "Where will you do your homework?" and "Where will your stuffed animals live?" As the child participates in the planning, positive expectations develop about the move. Take advantage of the free children's moving kits that many moving companies offer with pages to color, stories, stickers, puzzles, and games. Anticipate that some post-move adjustments may be required, but assure your child that you will discuss these matters as they come up. If possible, pack up the child's room last as part of the move and make it the first for unpacking in the new location. Keep the child's favorite toy or keepsake unpacked so it can always be kept close at hand for comfort.

[18] There are many ways to illustrate the continuity of life to children. In *Group* magazine (September 1989), Cindy Parolini and Rick Lawrence suggested buying a healthy plant such as a philodendron, then cutting off a sprig just beyond the joint. By pointing out that the sprig can still grow, even though broken off from the plant, prove it by planting the sprig in new potting soil and nursing it into a healthy plant. Helpful Scriptures to share as part of this exercise are Psalm 34:17–18; 51:16–17; and Isaiah 61:1–3.

[19] In recent years some states have moved away from use of the term *custody* in describing which parent is the "custodial parent" or "noncustodial parent." One reason for this is that the term incorrectly implies that one parent has possessory rights or may make parenting decisions to the exclusion of the other parent. Consequently, some state legislatures are using the more neutral terminology of "primary residential parent" and "secondary residential parent." However, since the term "custody" remains a more familiar term in most states, we will use this reference in this book.

[20] The shared parental responsibility doctrine is generally defined as a court-ordered relationship in which both parents retain full parental rights and responsibilities with respect to their child, and in which both parents confer with each other so that major decisions affecting the welfare of the child are determined jointly.

[21] What factors determine who is the "principal nurturing parent"? If a court reviews this matter, it will look for the parent who has primary responsibility for preparing and planning of meals; housing, bathing, grooming, and dressing; purchasing, cleaning, and care of clothes; medical care, including nursing and trips to physicians; arranging for social interaction among peers after school, such as transportation to church meetings, Cub or Girl Scouts, or houses of friends; arranging for temporary care such as day care or babysitting; bedding the child for the night and attending to illness or needs throughout the night, and waking the child in the morning; administration of discipline measures, including public courtesies and manners and toilet training; religious, social, cultural education; and teaching basic learning skills (reading, writing, and math).

[22] Florida District Court Judge Miner expressed it this way: "Frequent shifting of physical custody of children, particularly toddlers, between parents, not only serves to introduce an element of instability into the children's lives, but also heightens, rather than reduces, animosity between the parents. Thus, the long-term relationship between children and parents, who are required by law to share responsibility for their upbringing, is undermined from the start." *Sullivan v. Sullivan,* 17 FLW D1979 (1st DCA Aug. 21, 1992).

[23] The psychological concern is that this arrangement could result in more conflicts between estranged parents and children. Inevitable battles for affection or control arise. Children will question parental authority. Continuity from parent to parent is not the same and can be confusing to the child. However, this form of custody works best if both parents are equally capable in parenting skills and can cooperate with each other to foster a coparenting arrangement.

[24] For example, there was one case in Florida where the parents rented an apartment as the primary residence for the children. Each parent, who also maintained separate residences for themselves, then lived with the children for different periods of every week. Imagine the many logistical problems that this arrangement could bring!

[25] Factors courts will consider include: the willingness of the grandparent to encourage a close relationship between the child and the parents; the length and quality of the prior relationship between the child and grandparent; the preference of the child (if the child is determined to be of sufficient maturity to express a preference); mental and physical health of the child; mental and physical health of the grandparent; and any other relevant circumstances.

[26] Each parent would do well by reading 1 Kings 3:16–28 to learn how King Solomon determined who had a child's best interest at heart in a custody dispute. This vivid story from the Old Testament reminds us that pressing custody disputes too far may hurt the children we love. The truly loving parent wants what is best for the child—even if it means losing custody.

[27] In fact, Washington D.C., divorce lawyer Marna Tucker is not surprised with the rash of recent courthouse violence, much of which occurs in family law cases. She notes that people going through a divorce are reviewing several years of life in the span of a few weeks at trial and are required to make thousands of decisions that "cut to the heart." But the greatest rage that Tucker sees is not over money but over children. "People are willing to die for their kids!" *ABA Law Journal,* "Domestic Retaliation: Escalating Violence in the Family Courts" by Henry J. Reske, July, 1993, 50.

[28] Since 1973, the number of single fathers with custody of young children has changed dramatically. In a U.S. government study completed by Daniel Meyer (University of Wisconsin) and Steven Garashy (Iowa State), single-father families grew at a faster rate than any other family type—including those headed by single mothers. Even so, life can be more difficult for single fathers. While admirers praise a man for being a caring father, they will still think that he receives help with the children from his mother, his

sister, or a housekeeper. Single fathers feel more limitations in finding groups with whom they can connect. It's not easy for a single father to sit in a park chatting with mothers about kids. In addition, according to Meyer and Garashy, few single fathers receive child support awards from courts. In part, their study found, this could be due to single fathers generally being better off economically than single mothers. To assist the needs of single fathers, various loosely knit organizations have sprung up around the country such as Fathers for Equal Rights. For a reasonable annual membership fee, groups like these help fathers and children work together. Many organizations offer a staff of lawyers, social workers, and other specialists to fathers struggling with custody issues.

[29] Before relocating out of state with a child subject to a custody order, the parent wishing to relocate usually must demonstrate to the court that he or she has a compelling interest to move and that it is in the best interests of the child. The noncustodial parent may try to show that he or she is a suitable temporary custodial parent and that the child should not be uprooted. Courts will then apply a balancing test to determine if custody arrangements should be changed. Factors considered include the following: whether the move is likely to improve the quality of life for the custodial parent and child; the motives for seeking to move (and specifically whether the intent is to defeat the noncustodial parent's visitation rights); the likelihood that the custodial parent will comply with substitute visitation schedules after the relocation; and whether adequate visitation between the child and noncustodial parent can be afforded (in terms of travel and other expenses).

[30] When a sexual abuse charge was raised in the past, evaluators were impressed by any detail provided by a child. But now that significant detail of sexual matters is readily accessible to children through the media and the Internet, and one can never discount the "coaching" a child receives from a desperate parent, more sophisticated methods of detection are being used. Ironically, if such fabricated charges are found meritless by the court, the accusing parent may lose custody of the child.

[31] This occurs when a parent intentionally programs a child to poison his or her mind against the noncustodial parent rather than facilitating the relationship, often referred to as "parental alienation syndrome," discussed later on in this chapter.

[32] Fortunately, enforcement of kidnapping laws in interstate abductions is available throughout the United States under the Uniform Child Custody Jurisdiction Act which allows for transfer of witnesses, social service investigative reports, and other evidence from state to state if necessary. The Federal Parental Kidnapping Prevention Act, (28 U.S.C §1738A), which includes administration of a parent-locator service to track down kidnapping parents and enforcement by the U.S. Department of Justice, is also available. In international abductions, the Hague Convention on the Civil Aspects of International Child Abduction may apply under the International Child Abduction Remedies Act (42 U.S.C. §§11601–610). Under the Convention, the removal of a child from one country to another is wrongful when it breaches the custody rights being exercised by a person under the law of the state where the child was "habitually resident" (determined by geography and passage of time) immediately before the removal. Your lawyer should immediately contact the office of Citizens' Consular Services in the Child Custody Division of the U.S. Department of State in Washington D.C. However, the Convention has some limitations. Not every country is a participant in the Covention. Also, it is not an extradition treaty and contains no provision for imposition of criminal sanctions. If the Convention does apply, mandatory return of the child may be denied if the wrongful removal occurred more than twelve months prior to filing an action under the Convention; if the parent was not actually the custodial parent at the time of removal; if a "grave risk" to the child (if returned) is shown by clear and convincing evidence; or if the child is sixteen years or over. These limitations frustrate many parents into using self-help measures and forcible re-abductions, but extreme caution warns against acting illegally in this manner.

[33] Eighteen to twenty-one years, depending upon the state. However, this may be different if the child is mentally retarded or impaired or otherwise dependent upon the parent obligated to pay child support.

[34] After this is done, the court then has the flexibility to adjust either or both parent's share of the minimum child support award by considering factors such as: extraordinary medical, psychological, educational, or dental expenses; independent income of the child; payment of spouse support and child support to the same spouse (to account for a custodial parent using child support payments for needs otherwise covered by spouse support); seasonal variations in one or both parent's income and expenses; the age of each child, taking into account the greater needs of older children; special needs traditionally met with the family budget (such as advanced football training programs or gifted pianist lessons); the custodial arrangement, such as where the noncustodial parent spends a lot of time with the children and reduces the financial expenses of the custodial parent or, alternatively, to account for the greater expense incurred by the custodial parent where the noncustodial parent fails, neglects, or refuses to become involved in the lives of the children; the total assets available to each parent and each child; and any other factors the court believes reasonable, necessary, or fair.

[35] This is another area where compromise between the parents is vital. If support includes payment for college, courts usually limit it to four years of undergraduate studies or similar trade school training.

[36] It may be possible to apply for some benefits through the Office of Family Assistance (OFA) to help children (http://www.acf.hhs.gov/programs/ofa/). The OFA is located in the U.S. Department of Health and Human Services, Administration for Children and Families, and oversees the Temporary Assistance for Needy Families program (TANF) created by the Welfare Reform Law of 1996 (and reauthorized in February 2006 under the Deficit Reduction Act of 2005). TANF became effective July 1, 1997, and replaced what was then commonly known as welfare: Aid to Families with Dependent Children (AFDC) and the Job Opportunities and Basic Skills training program (JOBS).

[37] 42 U.S.C. §652(a)(8)(1988). This Commission adopted extensive recommendations designed to improve enforcement of interstate child support obligations. The report introduced into Congress is called "Supporting Our Children: A Blueprint for Reform (1992)."

[38] Individual states governed child support enforcement until 1975, when a federal-state child support enforcement program was created under Title IV-D of the Social Security Act. Yet even with this stronger federal role under the Act, states still operated their own programs within federal guidelines in order to receive federal funding. States are still responsible for locating absent parents (with some federal help) and establishing and enforcing support orders. Even though federal law was strengthened in 1984 and again in 1988 to require income withholding and establish additional support guidelines, the Act allowed a lot of flexibility at state and local level which resulted in lack of uniformity of state laws and procedures, inadequate enforcement remedies, insufficient resources, and often conflicting support orders. All these problems make interstate child support enforcement extremely difficult. Hopefully more states will adopt the Uniform Interstate Family Support Act to help alleviate this problem.

[39] As quoted by Margaret Graham Tebo, "When Dad Won't Pay," *ABA Journal*, September 2000, 60.

[40] Florida Eighteenth Judicial Circuit Judge O. H. Eaton, Jr., "Frustrated by a Deadbeat Parent? Try Invoking the Dog Law," *Florida Bar Journal*, March 2000, 64.

[41] *United States v. Mattice*, 186 F.3d 219 (2d Cir. 1999); *United States v. Mathes*, 151 F.3d 251 (5th Cir. 1998); *United States v. Ballek*, 170 F.3d 871 (9th Cir. 1999).

[42] *Miami Herald*, August 19, 2002, 10A.

[43] David Blankenhorn, interviewed in *Insight Magazine*, March 27, 1995. In his excellent book *Bringing Up Boys*, Dr. James Dobson, president of Focus on the Family, also makes a *powerful* case for how important it is for fathers to be proactive with their sons for their mutual best interest. I urge you to read it!

[44] *Miami Herald*, May 28, 1995, 3C.

[45] Certainly this isn't the only reason parents fail to pay support. Even writing a monthly check to an ex-spouse for whom the noncustodial parent is resentful and bitter may

cause extremely negative feelings. But automatic wage deductions can relieve noncustodial parents of this emotional task. Because the noncustodial parent doesn't see the money going out, he or she may be better able to adjust to living without it. But loss of contact with one's children is a *pervasive* problem.

[46] The U.S. Census Bureau confirms that fathers who have joint custody or regular visitation with their children pay child support about 70 percent of the time, while those with little or no visitation pay only about 35 percent of the time.

[47] *Schutz v. Schutz*, 581 So.2d 1290 (Fla. 1991)

[48] Be careful—children also can exploit this situation for personal advantage. It is best to use discretion in addressing those conflicts of opinion between parents that are most confusing for the child, temporarily letting the rest go.

[49] Once again, this is also fruitful ground for the child to use manipulation in holding out for greater privileges. Kids will test the boundaries of parents to see what they can get away with. Each parent needs to respect reasonable limits for the child to provide synergy among everyone concerned during visitation.

[50] Fortunately, God created children as surprisingly hardy souls who are resilient to change. Children receive the best push in life when parents feel good about themselves rather than having to atone for the trauma of separation and divorce. As parents work through the grieving process and take care of themselves, new ways open up for a mutually fulfilling relationship with each child.

Part Four Introduction

[1] Quoted in *Sermons Illustrated*, April, 1989.

Chapter 16

[1] Is there any way to end a marriage formally? Mountain View, California, therapist Jean Hollands believes that, if *both* spouses are willing, a final meeting of about ten minutes in the presence of a minister, family counselor, or psychologist to say goodbyes and to give the relationship a natural death is helpful. Vows at such ceremonies include promises to "release" each other, reflections on the good things from the marriage, and the giving of reassurances to the children. Others find this to be too much of an emotional challenge. Some partners want reconciliation, but their mates may want to get away from the marriage as soon as possible.

[2] If divorce is difficult for you (and who among us is exempt?), I urge you to look into participating in a 13-week DivorceCare group in your area. (See the information page for this excellent ministry at the end of this book.) Also, attend a Fresh Start Seminar if you can (http://www.freshstartseminars.org). Regrettably, DivorceCare wasn't available when I was going through my own separation and divorce in 1989–1991. But I have been actively involved in supporting this ministry over the past twelve years and can assure you that it is the absolute best divorce recovery program available to Christians (as well as nonbelievers) today. Fresh Start Seminars, another divorce recovery organization with a biblical emphasis operating out of Paoli, Pennsylvania, offers an outstanding special weekend retreat to those separated or divorced. This group includes professional counselors who travel all over the U.S. giving seminars in local churches and other places. The seminars emphasize personal interaction with attendees who have gone through a separation or divorce in a comfortable and non-confrontational setting that is most soothing. Seminar leaders give very practical talks on the stages of divorce and recovery, the separation and reconciliation struggle, re-entry into single life, and many other vital topics. From personal experience, I can tell you that the entire seminar provides excellent help. Sharing your experience with others going through separation and divorce is a personal catharsis. It recharges your emotional batteries. It helps you move toward a healthy acceptance of your own situation. But don't stop there. With the encouragement I received from the group, I was able to develop friendships with other seminar participants. Together we formed a small support group of our own, meeting every week in my home. We discussed positive and practical ways to recover from

divorce. We pooled our resources and hired a professional Christian marriage counselor to help guide our discussions. Those regularly attending this group showed marked improvement in their adjustments to separation and divorce and their positive attitudes about life. Frequently some would remark, "Meeting with this group is the high point of my week—I really look forward to it!" Consider starting your own group for caring, encouraging, and sharing with fellow divorcees.

[3] Quoted by Dr. David E. Carlson, *Resources for Christian Counseling: Counseling and Self-Esteem*, (Dallas: Word, Inc.,1988), 84. Used with permission.

[4] Quoted in *Sermons Illustrated*, August, 1991

[5] Remember our definition of biblical forgiveness from chapter 3? It is to: *release bitterness and resentment* that is self-destructive; *focus our anger* toward motivating repentance in those who have wronged us for their benefit; and *offer to restore and reconcile* broken relationships whenever possible, even if others will not repent and accept it. If the person we forgive repents and wants to accept our offer of reconciliation, *then* we should try to restore the relationship promptly if *reasonably* possible (Luke 17:3b–4). Biblical forgiveness encourages repentance from sin by offering the best incentives to restore fractured relationships.

[6] After my divorce, I wrote a letter to my in-laws expressing sincere regret that my marriage to their daughter (and sister) had ended. I thanked them for sharing my private pain in trying to save the marriage, even as they quietly bore their own sorrow over the situation. I expressed gratitude for the many ways they did not take sides between my wife and me. In their eyes, we were both family. They courageously grieved for both of us and our situation as impartially as they could. I praised them for how they gave to both of us, under the most trying of circumstances, until they could give no more. But after sharing those personal thoughts, I also acknowledged what we all knew was true. As the marriage ended, we could not pretend that the family ties were not broken as well. The divorce altered each of our lives. It was time to recognize, sadly, that a broken marriage needed closure of family ties as well. It was not what any of us wanted, but it was reality. I expressed to them how much this hurt me. I was not only losing my wife but her family as well. Seeing or hearing from each other would only be a reminder of the painful divorce process all of us had endured. Continuing relationships with in-laws also could create suspicion and distrust between my ex-wife and themselves. In my case, it had to end.

[7] Some move furniture around to make the home look different. Others sell the marriage bed or put it in another room.

[8] At a time when life is a bit discouraging, there are few exercises that will lift one's spirits more than being a part of God's life cycle in nature. Getting in touch with living things reaffirms hope. It reminds us that life is a continual process of renewal and change. Plant your own garden. Water your flowers. Watch them grow up into something beautiful, and see what it does for you.

[9] If getaway vacations are not possible, use the weekends to de-stress life. Take a drive into the country for an afternoon or overnight stay. Go for a long walk. Enjoy the seasons of life. (Think about it. If you live to be 100 years old, you will only see fall come 100 times. Don't miss it!) Smell the roses. Pet an animal. Listen to your favorite music. Invite a friend on a picnic or hike.

[10] Some of the material in this section is adapted and extracted from Josh McDowell's excellent book, *His Image, My Image* (San Berardino, CA: Here's Life Publishers, 1984).

[11] Ibid. "For by the grace given me I say to every one of you: Do not think of yourself more highly than you ought, but rather think of yourself with sober judgment, in accordance with the measure of faith God has given you" (Rom. 12:3). We make a realistic appraisal of ourselves as God sees us *now*, using reasoned judgment based upon the evidence.

[12] After my divorce was completed, I decided that I wanted to get in touch with who I was as a child. I revisited the houses where I lived growing up. I saw the grade schools I attended. I looked up old neighbors and friends to thank them for their positive influences

in my life. We laughed and cried about old friends and funny times of years past. It was also an opportunity to tell them how much I enjoyed being a Christian. Traveling back in time for a short while made me feel rich in good feelings and emotions. I found myself thanking God for how far He had brought me since my childhood. The trials and troubles of the moment fell into perspective. I was glad to be who I was—and where I was—in my life.

[13] This does not mean that God accepts our disobedience or rejection of Him, but He will *always* love us unconditionally.

[14] Dr. David E. Carlson, *Resources for Christian Counseling: Counseling and Self-Esteem*, (Dallas: Word, Inc., 1988), 241–242. Used with permission.

[15] H. G. Spafford and P. P. Buss, "It Is Well with My Soul," *Songs of the Church*, edited by Alton H. Howard (West Monroe, LA: Howard Publishers, 1977), song 280

[16] *The Miami Herald*, August 28, 1992, 5A

[17] *The Miami Herald*, August 31, 1992, 14A

[18] Jim Smoke, *Growing Through Divorce*, (Eugene, Ore: Harvest House Publishers, 1986), 103. Used with permission.

Chapter 17

[1] Quoted in *Sermons Illustrated*, May 1989.

[2] Quote from "The Sports Hall of Shame," *Sermons Illustrated*, May 1991.

[3] Quoted in *Sermons Illustrated*, March 1993.

[4] Quoted in *The Miami Herald*, July 26, 1992, 2A

[5] Theodore Roosevelt speech before the Hamilton Club, Chicago, Ill, (April 10, 1899).

[6] Since I enjoy reading and writing, I decided to join a national "Single Booklovers" club (http://www.singlebooklovers.com) started in 1970 by Bob Leach, a widower with three children. Bob later married Ruth, a divorced mother of four. Together from their home in Gradyville, Pennsylvania, they managed an enormous network of single booklovers who enjoy meeting one another through letters. (Bob and Ruth have since turned over this work of love to Katherine and Gene Borish, who now run this organization.) Each member completes a personal profile describing interests and hobbies. The summaries circulate through the membership. Any member having an interest in contacting you simply writes the organization and asks for your profile that provides them with a way to reach you. Quite often love grows. Over the years, hundreds of members married others met in the club. For $54 a year, and although a secular organization, this is just one of many good opportunities to meet people from all over the world.

[7] Quoted in *Sermons Illustrated*, February 1993.

[8] Our prayer life is a barometer of our faith. As we consider Nehemiah's enormous task in rebuilding the destroyed walls of Jerusalem, repeatedly we see how much he was a man of faith and prayer. He began with a worshipful and humble prayer for success in the face of distress (Neh. 1:4–11). Throughout the rebuilding effort, Nehemiah went back to God in prayer time after time. He prayed for God to strengthen his resolve. He asked God to remove all hindrances to his work. What an example of faith and prayer he is for us! We need to have the faith and daily commitment to prayer that Nehemiah had as we rely upon God's power day-to-day.

[9] Permission for use of these letters was graciously granted by Ann Landers and Creators Syndicate.

[10] Quoted in *Sermons Illustrated*, July 1987.

[11] Quoted in *Sermons Illustrated*, March 1988.

[12] Barbara Dafoe Whitehead, "Divorce and Kids: The Evidence Is In," *Reader's Digest*, July 1993, 120.

[13] My purpose in this book has been to provide you with facts to arrive at your own solutions for your particular problems—not to overwhelm you with information that leaves you hopelessly confused. I sought to use breakthrough thinking filtered through the faithful use of biblical principles. You have received advice that has been both analytical (guidelines

by which to evaluate your own situation) and intuitive (providing solutions to comfort you that are consistent with the big picture of surviving separation and divorce). But in offering some solutions to the problems arising in separation and divorce, you must realize that no one solution can work all the time or for all situations. Always be sure to consult your legal and spiritual advisors before taking any action suggested in this book.

Appendix E

[1] This list does not include every organization that deals with the various aspects of divorce. Inclusion on this list does not constitute endorsement by the author or publisher of this book. Neither the author nor the publisher exercises any control over the work performed or materials provided by any group or organization on this list or any fees that may be charged.

Appendix F

[1] David Popenoe and Barbara Defoe Whitehead, "The State of Our Unions: The Social Health of Marriage in America," The National Marriage Project, Rutgers University, 1999, 2. To access this report via the Internet, please see http://marriage.rutgers.edu.

[2] Karen S. Peterson, quoting Judith Wallerstein, author of *The Unexpected Legacy of Divorce: A 25 Year Landmark Study*, in "Happily Ever After: Children of Divorce Grow into Bleak Legacy," *USA Today*, September 5, 2000.

[3] *Current Thoughts and Trends*, November 1994, 13.

[4] *Leadership*, Summer 1996, 69.

[5] *Supra*, at Note 2.

[6] *Supra*, at Note 2.

[7] Karen S. Peterson (quoting Center for Disease Control and Prevention, based upon a 1995 federal study of 10,847 women aged 15-44), "43% of 1st Marriages End In 15 Years—Study Finds Age Linked To Success," *USA Today*, May 25, 2001.

[8] Karen S. Peterson (quoting University of Oklahoma researcher Joe Rodgers), "Saying No to the Notion of No-Fault Divorce," *USA Today*, January 25, 1996.

[9] Kingsley Davis, "The American Family in Relation to Demographic Change," in *Demographic and Social Aspects of Population Growth*, Vol. 1, Charles R. Westoff and Robert Parke, eds., Commission on Population Growth and the American Future. Gov't Printing Office 1972.

[10] *Supra*, at Note 2.

[11] U.S. Census Bureau Report "Marital Status and Living Arrangements: March 1998."

[12] "Breakdown on Family Breakdown," *The Washington Times*, March 25, 2001, B2.

[13] James B. Meyer, "Beyond A Reasonable Doubt: Positive Psychology in Marital Agreements," *The Florida Bar Journal*, February 1994, 71.

[14] Dick Randall, "Remarrying Can Bolster Self-Esteem," *Miami Herald*, June 1, 1999, 3C, citing National Center for Health Statistics information.

[15] Carl Brecheen, "Helping Stepfamilies," *Christian Chronicle*, February 1999, 12 (and sources cited therein).

[16] *Supra*, at Note 2. See also, National Center for Health Statistics "National Vital Statistics Report: Births, Marriages, Divorces and Deaths, Provisional Data for 1998," Vol. 47, No. 21.4, pages PHS 99–1120.

[17] Margaret L. Usdansky (quoting from Census Bureau Report, "Marriage, Divorce and Remarriage in the 1990s), "1990s' Wedding Bell Blues—New Report Echoes Trend of the '70s," *USA Today*, December 9, 1992.

[18] *Supra*, at Note 7.

[19] Karen S. Peterson, "Out of Step—Some Worse Off When Parent Marries Again," *USA Today*, January 14, 1996.

[20] *Supra*, at Note 20.

[21] *Supra*, at Note 15.

Index

Epilogue

Each divorce story is tragic. Mine is no different. In early July, 1984, when I was thirty-three years old, I married a beautiful young Christian woman. We weathered the ups and downs experienced by any married couple, but my partnership in a Miami law firm required too much of my time. This often left my young wife alone at home.

Highly capable and eager to be sociable, my wife chose to rejuvenate a successful career in the theater. She avoided loneliness at home and blossomed in the adulation of her excellent performances before a live audience. At the same time, her affections for me waned. In the early morning hours one day in late July 1989, she returned home to announce, "Warren, I love someone else more than you. I want an immediate divorce. You draw up the papers, and I'll sign."

Needless to say, I felt absolutely shocked! Although we agreed to seek counseling, my wife did not want to meet with a Christian counselor. Our secular counselor's advice to my wife? "Follow your heart." (Of course, Scripture clearly warns—in Jeremiah 17:9—that the heart is deceitful above all things and beyond anyone's understanding.) My wife would not be dissuaded from filing for divorce. So in July, 1991, it was finalized. (Interestingly, my ex-wife and I had spent part of our honeymoon cruising through the Greek Islands on the ship *Oceanos*. In a fitting event of utmost irony, this great ship capsized and sank off the coast of South Africa a few weeks after completion of our divorce.)

Life-changing lessons inundated me during that extremely difficult and challenging time following our divorce. As I pondered them, the Lord touched my heart. I felt a compelled desire to help others work through the crisis of divorce. Early one morning in August, 1991, the outline for a book on how to survive and recover from divorce from a Christian perspective flooded my consciousness. Although I had never written a book before, the ideas flowed together like tributaries into a great river. Words rushed faster than I could write them down.

This personal awakening led to publication of the book you are now reading. As you may have noticed, I dedicated this book of love and reconciliation to my first wife, trusting the Lord would guide it into the hands of hurting individuals who needed it most. It sent a message of grace and forgiveness to many unknown readers.

How amazing to watch God prosper this work and move it across North America over the years with very little assistance from me! That's as it should be. My work is done as a mere scrivener on His behalf. I can rejoice and step back from this work of love to give Him the glory.

As I have moved on in my life, I have continued to reflect upon many of the principles in this book. More and more I am drawn to the beautiful story of Hosea and Gomer, treasuring in my heart how God first divorced Israel after hundreds of years of spiritual adulteries (Jer. 3:6–8) yet lovingly took her back.

What would God desire for me even several years after my spouse divorced me?

In late February 1994, my ex-wife left Miami for good. Even though I accepted my unwanted divorce and let her go, the day after was a sad time for me. But through it all, and even after being separated for four and a half years, I wanted with all my heart to be faithful to God in doing the right thing. So while this certainly was a controversial move on my part, I wrote her a letter.

This is what I said:

"Please excuse me typing this letter, but I can type much faster than I can write and I am having a rush of thoughts right now. In every way, I would like you to receive this letter in the loving and personal way in which it is being written.

It's now been over four and a half years since you wanted out of our marriage. As you leave Miami, I would like to share a few thoughts and feelings with you from my heart one last time.

Please forgive me for whatever I did, or did not do, that led you to your decision. I hope that someday, you will help me reach a full understanding of why you felt so strongly that our marriage was not worth saving. But whatever happened between us that is my fault, I am sincerely sorry and ask for your forgiveness. I have always loved you. Whatever my failings have been, I would never intentionally hurt you in any way.

I do know that I did not give you the attention you needed and deserved during some critical times in our marriage. I cannot change the past. As you know, there were significant struggles going on at work and at church that sapped my energies and, unfortunately, took its toll on both of us. Though you were by far the most important person in my life, you were neglected during these storms. Also, I did not know of the personal struggles you were undergoing at that time. I'm so sorry for not being there for you when and where I should have been as your Christian husband. The Lord knows that I did the best I could, but it was not enough to meet your needs. Forgive my naïveté in taking you for granted.

To the extent you have done anything against me or our marriage, I forgive you unconditionally and without reservation.

As I shared with you on Saturday afternoon, all my dreams are coming true—except for the most important one of being able to share my life with you. I have finally been able to ditch the rat-race of a high-powered law firm for a private practice. I am now fulfilling my lifelong desire to become an author. My Christian ministry in helping others less fortunate is now a part of my daily work. But it is not the same without you by my side. I miss so much of the laughter we had together—you really could make me smile! The irony is that I now have the time to devote to you that I did not have a few years ago. But you are gone. And my life will always be incomplete without you.

You said on Saturday that our marriage might have worked at another time and in another place. But I am in another time. My life and work situation are much different now than they were before. But everywhere I am, you are still far away from me. And I miss you there. I always will.

You may never know how much I really loved you, and needed you, and yearned for you for so long, until we stand before God. Then I hope you will understand my heart. Then I hope you will know that no one could have meant more to me than you do. I will never regret asking you to marry me in 1983.

And so, until either of us fully commits to loving another person enough to remarry, I want you to know that the door to my heart and our home will remain open to you should you ever want to return. I know that reconciliation is what God desires. In faith, it is what I want to share with you.

No matter what has happened or will ever happen in our lives, I believe that love can always build a bridge between your heart and mine. If no one else will love you as much as you deserve, I will always love you. If no one else will be faithful to you in a way that fosters absolute trust, I will be faithful. Wherever you are, and wherever you go, I will be right here waiting for you.

So as you move on to a new life in Atlanta with the confidence of *carpe diem*, remember that I am here in Miami living my life as if you will never return, but hoping against hope that someday you will. With all my faults and shortcomings, I will always be the knight of your life if you will allow it to happen.

I love you with all my heart."

So as you can see, when I encourage you to muster all the faith and forgiveness you can in remaining open to reconciliation with your spouse, I'm not talking about something I haven't experienced. With God's help, I did it. I kept this ideal alive for as long as any hope survived. Even so, my first wife left our marriage and never looked back. There was nothing more I could say or do to change things. She was gone for good, and eventually remarried a man with a background in Scientology.

But all was not lost. There is more to my story—some wonderful news of how God works in the lives of those who remain faithful to Him!

Out of the Blue

If my first wife had not divorced me, I suppose we would have had a child or two together by now. The greatest tragedy for me was losing this opportunity for parenthood. While I resigned myself to contentment as a divorced single Christian man in the aftermath of publication of *When The Vow Breaks*, I had no idea that a divorced single Christian woman in Akron, Ohio, had begun searching every book in her church library about recovering from divorce. She was single-parenting the most beautiful, sweet, little three-year-old blond boy you've ever seen! Did she select *When The Vow Breaks* from the shelf by chance? Only the Lord knows for sure. But reading this book prompted her to call in early 1996 and invite me to lunch on her next business trip to my area. (She had never written an author before.)

As a rule, I willingly meet and correspond with readers of *When The Vow Breaks*, since this outreach provides additional opportunities to serve and encourage others who are experiencing personal crises. I thought that meeting this nice woman from Ohio would be just another ministerial visit.

But Cheryl and I had a wonderful first lunch together, laughing and sharing our life experiences for hours while finding that we had many things in common. Unbelievably, Cheryl had worked closely with two separate neighbors of mine who lived only doors away from my home in Miami!

Over a two-year courtship with Cheryl, I relinquished my initial prejudice against a remarriage to a divorced spouse with children—especially if those children had also experienced the heartbreak of divorce. Seeing the pain that divorce wreaked on children overwhelmed me. But Cheryl had raised her young son well in the nurture and admonition of the Lord. I could not deny her successful parenting of Chase. One of the most endearing moments in getting to know him was hearing this sweet, little boy reciting Psalm 23 from memory. The Lord's lesson for me? Don't close doors on remarriage options that are acceptable and pleasing to Him!

After seeking much advice and counsel from our pastors, families, and friends, Cheryl and I married in a small South Florida wedding ceremony on May 2, 1998. In fact, our decision to marry included all three of us. Chase participated and also received his own special gold "family ring." This little ring reminds him that he is a vital part of our relationship with each other. What a blessing from the Lord! I have received a small taste of what Job experienced when God restored his lost fortunes. Now I have a loving Christian wife and a son who is about the same age as the child I had desired almost thirteen years before!

A Final Word, and a Hug

There are so many issues to address in such a short time in a book of this sort. "How should Christians deal with divorce? What's the bottom line?"

I've been asked those questions many times on radio shows and television broadcasts from coast-to-coast over the years since *When The Vow Breaks* was first released in November, 1993. Many times I have explained the importance of focusing on Jesus rather than ourselves, asking, "What would Jesus do in my situation?" I've outlined the worst mistakes folks often make when first faced with a divorce decision—like, impulsively running to attorneys and fighting it out, kidnapping the kids, wasting marital assets, or putting property on a higher priority than relationships.

On other occasions I have suggested that listeners consider a trial separation to save the marriage. I've recommended ways to make the best use of counseling resources, to consider mediation rather than litigation, and to be sure to minister to the "little people" who are the only true victims of divorce—our children. Almost always I have pointed people to what the Bible tells us about separation and divorce.

I have reviewed how each spouse has a role in dealing a deathblow to a marriage, and how each has a responsibility to save the relationship in the face of self-defeating litigation.

I have often recounted the story of seeing frustrated litigants standing on the Downtown Miami Courthouse steps with Day-Glo signs reading: "Divorce Lawyers—Family Butchers!" I've explained how this offends me as a Christian—and as a lawyer—to be unfairly generalized in this way. But as a divorcee, I can understand how these hurt people feel.

I will always have compassion for the separated and divorced. I grieve over the ways their lives and families have been blown apart at the hands of strangers to their marriages. I know they are bewildered by an expensive court process that often defies logic and their sense of fairness.

The plea I have carried to the public in my appearances has repeatedly been that *mediation* is the answer. It fosters healing and restoration of the marriage if reconciliation is possible, and damage control if it is not. It promotes constructive communication among spouses with the help of neutral facilitators at a critical time of separation. It allows control over one's life, children, and property in a way that cannot occur in court. For Christians, it is biblically mandated (I Corinthians 6:1–11).

There is a role for everyone in mediation. Spouses need to exercise restraint in putting aside the bitterness, resentment, and urge for revenge that pushes lawyers into action. I urge them to peacefully participate in a mediation forum and quietly separate when their marriages cannot be saved. I entreated counselors and mediators to use great care in keeping all consultations strictly confidential while serving husbands and wives in distress. They should remain neutral, impartial communicators who are strongly empathetic (rather than sympathetic) while applying the proper balance and tension between affirmation and confrontation.

Lawyers should seek to be healers in serving, not exploiting couples in crisis by providing constructive legal advice rather than continual advocacy. We must help spouses move on with their lives. We must be scrupulously honest, use sensitive and perceptive communication, and rely upon good judgment and common sense tempered by a disciplined toughness when necessary. But above all, we must be creative in helping parting spouses find constructive solutions to the many problems divorce brings their way, allowing them time to deal with the flood of emotions they are experiencing in a divorce crisis.

I have urged listeners to use a responsible forgiveness in dealing with their spouses. This means releasing the bitterness and resentment that are so self-destructive. It involves focusing one's anger in a self-controlled way to motivate repentance by using "tough love" in establishing boundaries against unreasonable conduct and helping others face the logical consequences of their own decisions. It means leaving a door open for reconciliation of the marriage partners in the spirit of the parable of the prodigal son, if it is reasonably possible to do so.

Letting go of a marriage partner who will not reconcile is a frequent topic. Completing the grieving process and arriving at a point of accepting a terminal marriage situation allows one to bend, not break. Listeners need someone to remind them only to hang on to what they have, and to let go of what is lost so they can move on in life.

Good, sound, biblical, and practical advice. Yet it's just so difficult to put into practice at times as we face the realities of our own unique circumstances!

But there is one short incident that I have seldom shared in print or on the air until now. To me, it sums up the essence of how the divorced can be ministered to in the most meaningful way at one of the lowest points in their lives.

I asked my good friend and fellow Miami lawyer, Tony Martinez, this question: "In your divorce, is there any one event that helped you cope with your situation more than anything else?"

His reply was quick and poignant: "Warren, when I felt like my world was crashing in on me, one of my best friends called me into his office and closed the door. With tears welling up in his eyes, he leaned forward to hug me and said only this: 'I love you, Tony.' Nothing more than that. That hug made all the difference to me."

What is the bottom line for helping separated or divorced Christians cope? Sometimes a hug can minister more powerfully than a thousand words of advice. I hope this book has given you a hug and given you hope. May God richly bless you as you move through your own life, seeking Him every step of the way!

Joseph Warren Kniskern
October 2007

How a divorce support group can help you.

In a DivorceCare group you will find comfort and friendship in a safe place where you can talk about your pain and know the other people truly understand. You will meet others who are facing the same confusing emotions and tough decisions as you.

You don't have to go through this alone.

We encourage you to find a DivorceCare group near you and get involved. A DivorceCare group will be a tremendous help to you during this time as you seek to stabilize your life.

Through the teaching of top divorce recovery experts on video, and through group discussion, Bible study and journaling, DivorceCare will help you have a clear perspective about your life. DivorceCare provides a healthy environment where you can sort through your feelings of anger, depression and loneliness. You will discuss concerns pertaining to finances, new relationships and sexual desires. You will learn about forgiveness and reconciliation. You will begin the healing process and grow closer to God.

You can find a group by visiting **www.divorcecare.org**, selecting "Find a Group" and inserting your zip code, area code, city or country in the "Find a Group" search engine. A list of DivorceCare groups in your area will be displayed. If you have any trouble finding a group, please call 800-489-7778 or email info@divorcecare.org.

At DivorceCare you will find help, discover hope and experience healing.

Have children?

If you have children ages five through twelve, DivorceCare for Kids is the place for them. We encourage you to seek help and healing for your whole family. Visit **www. dc4k.org** for details and to find a DC4K group in your area.

www.divorcecare.org
800-489-7778